SIXTH EDITION

Daytrips
LONDON

D1316697

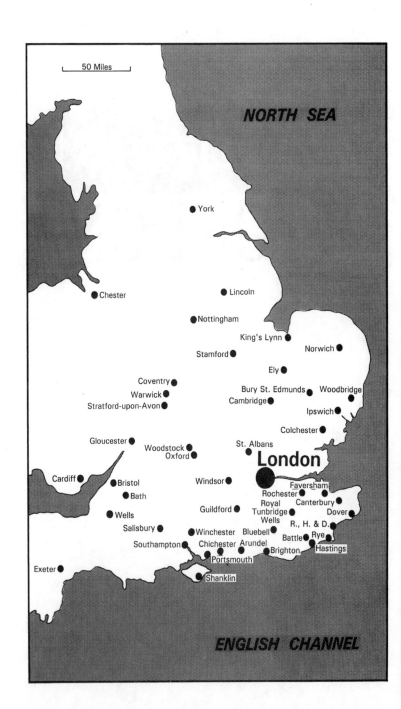

SIXTH EDITION

Daytrips
LONDON

55 *one day adventures by rail or car, in and around London and southern England*

EARL STEINBICKER

HASTINGS HOUSE
Book Publishers
Norwalk, Connecticut

While every effort has been made to insure accuracy, neither the author nor the publisher assume legal responsibility for any consequences arising from the use of this book or the information it contains.

ISBN: 0-8038-9443-0

Printed in the United States of America

10 9 8 7 6 5 4 3 2

Comments? Ideas?

We'd love to hear from you. Ideas from our readers have resulted in many improvements in the past, and will continue to do so. And, if your suggestions are used, we'll gladly send you a complimentary copy of any book in the series. Please send your thoughts to Hastings House, Book Publishers, 9 Mott St., Norwalk CT 06850, or fax us at (203) 838-4084, or e-mail to HHouseBks@aol.com. Web Site: DaytripsBooks.com

Contents

	INTRODUCTION	7
SECTION I	**DAYTRIP STRATEGIES**	9
	Getting There	10
	London as Your Base	12
	Food and Drink	13
	Practicalities	15
	Suggested Tours	17
	Tourist Information	18
SECTION II	**DAYTRIPS IN LONDON**	19
	Getting Around London	20
	The City	25
	Westminster	38
	Chelsea, Kensington, Knightbridge and Belgravia	49
	The West End	57
	Southwark and Lambeth	66
	Docklands	74
	Greenwich	79
	Hampstead	85
	Richmond	90
	Hampton Court	96
SECTION III	**DAYTRIPS FROM LONDON**	101
	Getting Around Southern England	102
	Rochester	108
	Faversham	113
	Canterbury	117
	Dover	123
	Romney, Hythe & Dymchurch	128
	Rye	131
	Royal Tunbridge Wells	136

6   CONTENTS

Battle   140
Hastings   144
Bluebell   149
Brighton   153
Arundel   158
Chichester and Bosham   162
Guildford   169
Portsmouth   174
Shanklin, Isle of Wight   179
Winchester   184
Southampton   189
Salisbury and Stonehenge   194
Windsor and Eton   200
Bath   205
Wells   212
Bristol   216
Cardiff, Wales   222
Exeter   229
Gloucester   234
Oxford   239
Woodstock   247
Warwick   251
Stratford-upon-Avon   255
Coventry   261
Chester   266
St. Albans   272
Nottingham   277
Stamford   282
Lincoln   286
York   292
Cambridge   299
Ely   306
King's Lynn   310
Bury St. Edmunds   315
Colchester   319
Ipswich   323
Woodbridge   327
Norwich   331
SECTION IV   HISTORICAL PERSPECTIVES   337
            INDEX   341

Introduction

I f ever a place was made for daytripping, it is England. Basing yourself in London puts you within easy striking distance of many of Europe's most desirable attractions, where language is no problem and getting around on your own as simple as it is back home. This book takes a fresh look at 55 of the most intriguing destinations, including ten within Greater London itself, describing in step-by-step detail a pleasurable way of exploring them on self-guided walking tours.

Walking is by far the best way to probe most places. Not only is it undeniably healthy, but it also allows you to see the sights from a natural, human perspective, spending just as much or as little time on each as you please. The carefully tested walking tours take you past all of the attractions worth seeing without wasting time, effort, or money. Which of these you actually stop at is up to you, but you won't have any trouble finding them with the large, clear maps provided. There is never a need to rush as you'll have plenty of time for each walk, even taking rest stops along the way.

The destinations should appeal to a wide variety of interests. Besides the usual cathedrals, castles, art galleries, and stately homes there are such attractions as country walks, colorful London neighborhoods, maritime museums, canals, Roman ruins, places where history happened, places of literary association, quaint fishing villages, great seaports, resorts, elegant spas, and even some ever-so-British railfan trips. Not only do these reflect a delightful sense of the past, but several of the daytrips also expose you to the excitement of a changing Britain as it finds its new role within Europe.

Dining (and drinking) well is a vital element in any travel experience. For this reason, a selection of particularly enjoyable restaurants and pubs along the walking routes are included for every daytrip. These are price-keyed, with an emphasis on the medium-to-low range, and have concise location descriptions making them easy to find.

Every trip can be made by rail, and those outside London itself by car as well. Specific transportation information is given in the "Getting There" section of each daytrip, and general information in the "Getting Around London" and "Getting Around England" chapters.

Time and weather considerations are important, so they're included in the "Practicalities" section of each trip. These let you know, among other things, on which days the sights are closed, when the colorful outdoor farmers' markets are held, and which places should be avoided in bad weather. The location, telephone number, and Internet site of the local Tourist Information Centre is also given in case you have questions.

Most of the attractions have an entrance fee, as indicated in the text. These are, of course, subject to change slightly, but the listings will at least provide a guide to anticipated expenses. Cathedrals and churches depend on small donations in the collection box to help pay their maintenance costs, so it is only fair to leave some change when making a visit.

In addition to entrance fees, most of the attraction listings also include opening times, a telephone number, and—when applicable—an Internet site and a general guide to handicapped accessibility.

Be aware that places have a way of changing without warning, and errors do creep into print. If your heart is absolutely set on a particular sight, just check first to make sure that it isn't closed for renovations, or that the opening times are still valid. The local tourist centres are always the best source of such up-to-the-minute information.

One last thought—it isn't really necessary to see everything at any given destination. Be selective. Your one-day adventures in London and around England should be fun, not an endurance test. If it starts becoming that, just stroll over to the nearest café, tea shop, or pub and enjoy yourself. There will always be another day.

Happy Daytripping!

Section I

DAYTRIP STRATEGIES

The word "Daytrip" may not have made it into dictionaries yet, but for experienced independent travelers it represents the easiest, most natural, and often the least expensive approach to exploring a European country. This strategy, in which you base yourself in a central city and probe the surrounding country on a series of one-day excursions, is especially effective in London and much of England.

ADVANTAGES:

While not the answer to every travel situation, daytrips offer significant advantages over point-to-point touring following a set plan. Here are a dozen good reasons for considering the daytrip approach:

1. Freedom from the constraints of a fixed itinerary. You can go wherever you feel like going whenever the mood strikes you.
2. Freedom from the burden of luggage. Your bags remain in your hotel while you run around with only a guidebook and camera.
3. Freedom from the anxiety of reservation foul-ups. You don't have to worry each day about whether that night's lodging will actually materialize.
4. The flexibility of making last-minute changes to allow for unexpected weather, serendipitous discoveries, changing interests, new-found passions, and so on.
5. The flexibility to take breaks from sightseeing whenever you feel tired or bored, without upsetting a planned itinerary. Why not sleep late in your base city for a change?
6. The opportunity to sample different travel experiences without committing more than a day to them.
7. The opportunity to become a "temporary resident" of your base city. By staying there for a week or so you can get to know it in depth, becoming familiar with the local restaurants, shops, theaters, night life, and other attractions—enjoying them as a native would.
8. The convenience of not having to hunt for a hotel each day, along

with the security of knowing that a familiar room is waiting back in your base city.

9. The convenience of not having to pack and unpack your bags each day. Your clothes can hang in a closet where they belong, or even be sent out for cleaning.

10. The convenience (and security!) of having a fixed address in your base city, where friends, relatives, and business associates can reach you in an emergency. It is difficult to contact anyone who changes hotels daily.

11. The economy of staying at one hotel on a discounted longer-term basis, especially with airline package plans. You can make reservations for your base city without sacrificing any flexibility at all.

The economy of getting the most value out of a railpass. Daytripping is ideally suited to rail travel since the best train service operates out of base-city hubs. This is especially true in London.

Above all, daytrips ease the transition from tourist to accomplished traveler. Even if this is your first trip abroad, you can probably handle an uncomplicated one-day excursion such as the one to Canterbury or Bath on your own. The confidence gained will help immensely when you tackle more complex destinations, freeing you from the limitations of guided tours and putting you in complete control of your own trip.

DISADVANTAGES:

For all of its attractions, the daytrip concept does have certain restrictions. There are always a few areas where geography and the available transportation have conspired to make one-day excursions impractical, or at least awkward. In Britain, these include the Cotswolds, the West Country, the Lake District, Wales, and the Highlands of Scotland. Fortunately, only the first of these is anywhere near London.

Another disadvantage is that you will have to forego the pleasures of staying at country inns. Should this deter you from making daytrips, you can still get the most from this guidebook by traveling directly between destinations while completely avoiding London. You might also consider using daytrips part of the time and touring the rest.

GETTING THERE

BY AIR:

Plenty of airlines fly to London, offering fares, schedules, and package deals that constantly change to meet the competition. As seasoned travelers know, there are certain advantages to flying one of the major airlines of the country you're visiting. For one thing, they are more familiar with your destination and can supply reliable advice and information about it. For another, despite a certain sameness of all aircraft, native lines do provide a touch of inflight ambiance that eases the passage from one culture to another. They also tend to get the most favorable landing slots and airport facilities at their home bases.

Heathrow, to the west, is London's major airport and ranks as one of the largest and busiest in the world. Its four (soon to be five) terminals are exeptionally well organized, if rather impersonal. As to transportation to and from central London, there are four options other than driving yourself: The **Heathrow Express** is a mainline rail service running every 15 minutes from around 5 a.m. to about 11 p.m., speeding passengers to and from Paddington Station in 20 minutes flat. The BritRail Pass is valid on this. Another convenient choice is the **Airbus**, which operates two routes into central London. Although slower than the train, it is cheaper and has the advantage of making downtown stops at locations convenient for travelers. If you don't have much luggage and want to save some money, the **London Underground** (subway) has a stop at terminals 1, 2, and 3; another for Terminal 4. With the right connections, it can take you directly to most destinations in London. Finally, if price is no object, you can always take a taxi (about £40). Airport information ☎ (020) 8759-4321.

Gatwick Airport, to the south, is less hectic than Heathrow, but it is some distance from central London and therefore more expensive to reach. Your transportation options are: The **Gatwick Express**, a non-stop train running to Victoria Station in 30 minutes flat. A cheaper train, running on the same route but making stops, is operated by **Connex SouthCentral**. **Thameslink** offers similar services to London's King's Cross Station. BritRail Passes are valid on all three. There are also **buses** to Victoria Station, and of course **taxis** if you don't mind the fare (about £50). Airport information ☎ (01293) 535-353.

Stansted Airport, northeast of London, is being used by more and more international flights, and is connected to central London by the **Stansted SkyTrain** to Liverpool Street Station in about 45 minutes. There are also **buses** to Victoria Station. **Taxi** fare to London is about £60. Airport information ☎ (01279) 690-500.

Two other airports are: **Luton**, to the north, used mostly by charters and connected to London by a bus/train combination; and **London City**, just east of central London and connected via bus to the Docklands Light Railway, feeding into the Underground. The latter airport is used mostly by business travelers to the Continent, Ireland, and Scotland.

BY EUROSTAR TRAIN:

Travelers coming from the Continent may very well prefer the **Channel Tunnel Eurostar** train, a thoroughly modern, high-speed service that connects London with either Paris or Brussels in about three hours, or even less when the new tracks in southeast England are completed. Railpasses are not accepted, but they will get you a substantial discount. A whole variety of fares are offered, ranging from quite reasonable to very expensive depending on class of travel (First Premium, First, and Standard/Second), age, and restrictions. Advance reservations are required, and check-in is at least 20 minutes before departure. The trains arrive at London's **Waterloo International Terminal** at Waterloo Station, with Underground connections to all of London. For information ☎ (0990) 300-003; in USA contact BritRail, ☎ (888) BRITRAIL, Internet: www.raileu rope.com.

LONDON AS YOUR BASE

Since your London accommodations will be "home" for a while, you'll want to be especially careful in choosing a place that is pleasant, priced right, and conveniently located for your daytrip plans, both within and beyond London. This dosen't mean that they must be near a train station if you're traveling by rail, but should be close to an Underground (subway) stop that connects easily to the various stations.

Advance reservations for regular **hotels** should be made through your travel agent, who has access to more hotel information than any guide-book could possibly include. Be sure to ask about the economical **package plans** offered by several airlines along with their flights. To take maximum advantage of this, it is important that you consult your travel agent as far in advance as possible and study the brochures carefully.

You can save even more money by staying at a "**Bed-and-Breakfast**" establishment. These places often call themselves hotels but in fact are more like rooming houses. Private baths are not the norm, and usually the only meal offered is breakfast, but the bedrooms are almost always clean and pleasant enough. If you're willing to use the bath and toilet "down the hall," you'll find that bed-and-breakfast places are not only a good value but, being mostly family-operated, they provide a far more personal touch than you'll ever get in a hotel. Indeed, many travelers *prefer* "B&Bs" over hotels and return to the same ones year after year.

Another good way to cut costs and feel more like a native is to rent a **furnished apartment**. Ranging from barely adequate to downright luxuri-ous, these "flats" are available for stays as short as one week, and in sizes from single studios to multiple-room suites. They usually include limited cleaning service, linens, kitchen utensils, and the like. Since cooking facil-ities are part of the deal, you can save even more by preparing some of your own meals. Shopping at local supermarkets and grocery stores is an experience that alone transforms tourists into temporary Londoners. Apartment rentals should be arranged well in advance by letter, e-mail, or phone call, then secured with a deposit. Overseas offices of the British Tourist Authority (see page 18) can furnish you with current information.

Should you arrive in London without reservations, you'll find several organizations ready and willing to secure immediate lodging for you. Among these are the offices of the **London Tourist Board** in the

Underground Station Concourse between terminals 1, 2, and 3 at Heathrow Airport, at Terminal 3 Arrivals Concourse at Heathrow, at the Liverpool Street Underground Station, at the Waterloo International Terminal, and in the forecourt of Victoria Station. Another is the **Britain Vistor Centre** at 1 Regent Street, two blocks south of Piccadilly Circus. More information about London's tourist offices will be found on page 23. **Commercial hotel booking agencies** have convenient service counters at the airports, and at Victoria, King's Cross, and Liverpool Street stations. They tend to favor mid-to-upper-price hotels and sometimes charge exorbitant booking fees. Be sure to ask about the terms first.

If you decide to stay overnight in other towns in England, perhaps using a "touring" rather than a daytrip approach, you should be aware of the **Book-A-Bed-Ahead** (BABA) service offered by most Tourist Information Centres throughout Britain. With this, you can reserve accommodations for the next day or two in another town anywhere in the country, and be secure in the knowledge that a decent night's sleep awaits you. The service charge is minimal, and a deposit on the room is required—which is deducted from the bill when you check out.

GETTING AROUND LONDON:

Transportation within London is outlined in the short chapter beginning on page 19. Details about rail and road travel throughout the rest of southern England, including railpass plans, are discussed on pages 101 through 107.

FOOD AND DRINK

Several choice restaurants and pubs are listed for each destination in this book. Many of these are longtime favorites of experienced travelers and serve typically English food unless otherwise noted. Their approximate price range, based on the least expensive complete meal offered, appears as:

£ — Inexpensive, but may have fancier dishes available.

££ — Reasonable. These establishments may also feature daily specials.

£££ — Luxurious and expensive.

X: — Days or periods closed.

The quality of restaurant food in England has been getting better, although there is still room for improvement in the middle price range. If you're really serious about dining, you should consult an up-to-date guide such as the red-cover *Michelin Great Britain and Ireland* or any of the *Egon Ronay* guides. It is always wise to check the posted menus before entering, paying particular attention to any daily set-price specials. Some restaurants add a service charge to the bill, in which case there is no need to tip unless the service was extraordinary. Where no service charge is added, the waiter expects a gratuity of 10–15%.

Besides restaurants specializing in traditional English fare, you will find many featuring foreign cuisines, most notably French, Italian, Indian, and Chinese. American favorites such as hamburgers, chili, pizza, and the like are extremely popular.

For many, the traditional **English Breakfast** is the great treat of the day. Usually consisting (more or less) of fruit juice, cereal, eggs, bacon or sausages, grilled tomatoes or baked beans (!), toast with butter and marmalade, and tea or coffee, it is served by numerous hotels, especially in the "Bed-and-Breakfast" category. Be sure to ask about this before booking so you don't get stuck with the anemic "Continental" breakfast.

Having lunch at a pub will save you time and money, and is often a very pleasant experience. Not all pubs serve meals, and of those that do, not all serve especially good food. A reliable way to judge quality before eating is to size up the other customers and note whether the pub makes a special point of preparing meals. Many pubs, especially in the city, do not serve evening meals. Most pubs are self-service in that you buy drinks at the bar, usually order food at a separate counter, and take both to a table. Tipping in this case is neither expected nor encouraged. Some pubs have full-service restaurants attached to them as well. Pubs in London are usually open on Mondays through Saturdays at 11 a.m. to 11 p.m., and on Sundays from noon to 3 p.m. and 7–10:30 p.m.

Beer, happily, remains the national beverage of Britain. It comes in a bewildering variety of tastes and local specialties. The most common types, at least on tap, are *lager*, which is similar to American and Continental beers and should be served cool; and *bitter*, the richly flavored traditional British brew, always served at cellar temperature. The latter is an acquired taste, but once you get used to it you'll probably be back for more. The best of these come from small local breweries, and are virtually never exported. "Real Ale," a term sponsored by the CAMRA organization, denotes cask-conditioned beer made the old-fashioned way without chemical additives. It is worth seeking out. A "free house" is a pub not associated with a particular brewery—it is free to sell various brands. Asking the bartender for his—or her—advice will not only get you some interesting brews, it will often open the way to spirited conversations as well.

PRACTICALITIES

WHEN TO GO:

England is at its best between mid-spring and early fall. The extra hours of sunlight in these months will greatly enhance your daytrips, as will the mild weather. While periods of rain are frequent, the showers are also brief and usually blow over quickly. Always carrying a folding umbrella is good insurance against getting wet. A light jacket or sweater will also be welcome, sometimes even in the middle of July. England's fast-changing weather is utterly unpredictable but rarely given to extremes.

HOLIDAYS:

Legal holidays in England and Wales are:
New Year's Day (January 1)
Good Friday
Easter Monday
May Bank Holiday (first Monday in May)
Spring Bank Holiday (last Monday in May)
Summer Bank Holiday (last Monday in August)
Christmas Day
Boxing Day (December 26)
Additional Bank Holiday (December 31)

THEATER:

One of the major advantages of daytripping is that it allows you to return from your excursions in time to enjoy London's renowned theatrical offerings. From hit musicals to Shakespearean drama, opera, ballet, concerts, "fringe" productions, and anything in between, you can easily find out what's playing by checking such popular publications as the London *Evening Standard, Time Out,* or *What's On In London.* You'll find these at newstands everywhere. The British Tourist Authority publishes a free monthly listing called London Planner, available at BTA offices worldwide, at at Tourist Information Centres in London.

Many of London's leading theaters are located near Leicester Square *(see page 58)* in the West End, although others are scattered all over town. Three popular venues are the **South Bank Arts Centre** *(see page 72),* **Shakespeare's Globe Theatre** *(see page 72),* and the **Barbican Arts Centre** *(see page 37).*

Tickets may be purchased in advance by phoning the box offices directly, or through ticket agents who charge an extra fee for their services. This can sometimes be quite substantial, so be sure to ask first. The good folks at the **Britain Vistor Centre** *(see page 23)* near Piccadilly Circus can steer you to reputable agents. Bargain-price tickets for same-day performances are available (to personal callers only) at the **Half Price Ticket Booth** in Leicester Square, but the choice of shows is limited.

MONEY MATTERS:

Traveler's checks are the safest way to protect your money while abroad. They often, however, entail service charges both when you buy them and again when you convert them into pounds in Britain. Depending on how exchange rates are flucuating, you might be better off purchasing the checks in pounds sterling rather than dollars; ask your friendly banker about this. Whatever you do, try to avoid dealing with the ubiquitous storefront bureaux de change (money changers) that thrive wherever tourists gather. Changing relatively large sums at one time will take some of the sting out of service charges.

Automated Teller Machines (ATMs) offer the best exchange rates to be found anywhere, and allow you to take money directly out of your home bank account as you need it. They are usually open 24 hours a day, are conveniently located throughout London and most English towns, and yield cash in pounds sterling. Check with your issuing bank before leaving home to make sure that your PIN code will work in England.

Credit cards are widely accepted at the more expensive establishments throughout England, but rarely by budget hotels and restaurants.

A WORD ABOUT PRICES:

Prices (and opening times) quoted in this book were believed to be current at the time of research, but are of course subject to change. They rarely go down—expect in many cases to pay a bit more. Still, the quoted prices serve as a guide to the relative costs of different attractions.

TELEPHONES:

Two types of **public telephones** are used in England, often paired together so you have a choice. The first uses coins of 10, 20, or 50 pence, or £1, and do not make change although unused coins are returned to you. Much more convenient are those that operate on a **Phonecard**, a prepaid magnetic debit card from which the cost of each call is subtracted until its face value is all used up. These cards are available at post offices, newsstands, travel centres, and any shop displaying the Phonecard sign. They come in denominations of £2, £5, £10, and £20. Having one in your wallet will make phoning ahead for information or reservations much easier.

Some pay phones are operated by companies other than British Telecom (BT) and require their own distinctive phonecards.

England is divided into **area codes**, which are dialed only when calling from outside that area. All phone numbers in this book indicate the area code in parentheses.

INTERNET:

Web site URLs were current at the time of writing, but are subject to change at the whim of their hosts. If you can't find the one you're looking for, use a search engine such as Alta Vista or Yahoo. It's out there. Also, if possible, check the revision dates as some sites unfortunately tend to be less than current.

SUGGESTED TOURS

The do-it-yourself **walking tours** in this book are relatively short and easy to follow. They always begin at the local train station, Underground, or bus stop since most readers will be using public transportation. Those going by car can make a simple adjustment. Suggested routes are shown by heavy broken lines on the maps, while the circled numbers refer to major attractions or points of reference along the way, with corresponding numbers in the text. Remember that the tour routes are only suggestions—you may prefer to wander off on your own using the maps as a guide.

You can estimate the amount of time that any segment of a walking tour will take by looking at the scaled map and figuring that the average person covers about 100 yards in one minute.

Trying to see everything in any given town could easily become an exhausting marathon. You will certainly enjoy yourself more by being selective and passing up anything that doesn't catch your fancy in favor of a friendly pub. Not all museums will interest you, and forgiveness will be granted if you don't visit every church.

Practical information, such as the opening times of various attractions, prices, telephone numbers, and handicapped accessibility is as accurate as was possible at the time of writing, but everything is subject to change. You should always check with the local Tourist Information Centre, or call the attraction itself, if seeing a particular sight is crucially important.

*OUTSTANDING ATTRACTIONS:

An * asterisk before any attractions, be it an entire daytrip or just one exhibit in a museum, denotes a special treat that in the author's opinion should not be missed.

TOURIST INFORMATION

Local sources of tourist information within London are discussed on page 23. Each daytrip destination outside London has its own **Tourist Information Centre**, the location, phone number, and—where applicable—Internet site of which are listed in the "Practicalities" section for that trip, and the location marked on the appropriate map. These local offices are often closed on Sundays, and sometimes on Saturdays as well.

ADVANCE PLANNING INFORMATION:

The **British Tourist Authority** has branches throughout the world to help plan your trip. Some of these are located at:

551 Fifth Avenue, New York, NY 10176-0799, **USA,** ☎ (800) 462-2748 or (212) 986-2200, fax (212) 986-1188.

625 North Michigan Avenue, Chicago, IL 60611-1977, **USA,** ☎ (800) 462-2748.

5915 Airport Road, Suite 120, Mississauga, Ont. L4V 1TI, **Canada,** ☎ (888) VISIT UK or (905) 405-1840.

Level 16, Gateway, 1 Macquarie Place, Sydney, NSW 2000, **Australia,** ☎ (02) 9377-4400.

3rd Floor, Dilworth Building, Queen and Customs St., Auckland 1, **New Zealand,** ☎ (09) 303-1446.

Lancaster Gate, Hyde Park Lane, Hyde Park, Sandton 2196, **South Africa,** ☎ (011) 325-0343.

And on the **Internet** at: www.visitbritain.com.

Section II

10 Miles

21
15
23
22 33 30
25 17 3 7 5 24
20 2 12 29 14
26 6 8 9 11 10 4 16
31 13
28
27 32 19 18

Greater London

INNER BOROUGHS:
1. City of London
2. City of Westminster
3. Camden
4. Greenwich
5. Hackney
6. Hammersmith & Fulham
7. Islington
8. Kensington & Chelsea
9. Lambeth
10. Lewisham
11. Southwark
12. Tower Hamlets
13. Wandsworth

OUTER BOROUGHS:
14. Barking & Dagenham
15. Barnet
16. Bexley
17. Brent
18. Bromley
19. Croydon
20. Ealing
21. Enfield
22. Haringey
23. Harrow
24. Havering
25. Hillingdon
26. Hounslow
27. Kingston-upon-Thames
28. Merton
29. Newham
30. Redbridge
31. Richmond-upon-Thames
32. Sutton
33. Waltham Forest

DAYTRIPS IN
LONDON

Not only is London surrounded by dozens of tantalizing daytrip destinations, but in itself it is also the most varied, and arguably the most interesting, city on Earth. Once the heart of a far-flung Empire Upon Which the Sun Never Set, London is today the dynamic, vital, and rapidly changing metropolis of a newly unified Europe. Although many of its tourist attractions have their roots in timeless tradition, you will quickly discover that there is infinitely more to London than just the preserved past.

The key to understanding Greater London (as the whole is called) is to realize that this is not just one homogeneous city, but a mosaic of often unrelated villages and towns, each with its own distinct character. It spreads over some 620 square miles stretching about 35 miles from end to end. An incredibly large amount of it exists as green parks and even forests. Within its boundaries can be found anything from high-rise office complexes to quaint rural hamlets, from elegant residential areas to colorful working-class neighborhoods. Greater London divides into 12 Inner Boroughs and 20 Outer Boroughs, besides the tiny City of London—an ancient self-governing enclave of only one square mile in the very center of things. The population is about as cosmopolitan as you'll find, with people from all over the globe filling the air with the sounds of nearly every imaginable language.

Not content to be the world's best base for daytripping, London also offers within its borders some of the most enjoyable opportunities for one-day excursions to be found anywhere. Each of the ten walking tours described in this section covers a different aspect of London's seductive personality, and all take you to the most famous attractions as well as to many little-known discoveries. Individual tours can be comfortably walked in under two hours, leaving plenty of time for sightseeing, shopping, or just relaxing at a pub. Walking is by far the best way to explore the nooks and crannies of this most likable of cities and, besides, it will help undo the consequences of a full English breakfast.

The start and finish points of all of the walking tours are easily reached by public transportation, and there are plenty of places to rest along the way if you get tired.

GETTING AROUND LONDON

Although all of the tours are designed for walking, you will still need to use some form of transportation to get to their starting points, and later back to your hotel. Here are the options:

THE UNDERGROUND:

The **Underground**, also known as the **Tube**, is one of the best and most comprehensive subway systems in the world. Quite crowded during rush hours, it is otherwise a comfortable way to travel. Most of the lines are deeply underground and are reached by long escalators or elevators (lifts), except for the Circle, District, and Metropolitan lines, which operate nearer the surface. Each of the 11 separate **lines** has a name, is color coded, and connects with other lines at frequent interchange stations. Ask for a free **pocket-size map** with a station index, which makes everything perfectly clear. The system runs from around 5:30 a.m. until about midnight (7:30 a.m. to 11:30 p.m. on Sundays and Bank Holidays). For further information ☎ (020) 7222-1234.

Fares are calculated on a zone basis, and **tickets** sold at both booths in the stations or from vending machines. To use these, just push a button for your destination and insert the required amount in coins or bills. Most of them make change. On some machines you must first check the posted station list to determine the fare. The tickets operate turnstiles and are then returned to you. Hang onto yours as it is needed to go through the exit turnstile, after which it will be returned only if it is still valid for further travel. Economical **passes** are described below.

Be aware that at some stations the same platforms are used for several different final destinations. An illuminated sign indicates the routing for the next two or three trains, along with the number of minutes until their arrival.

The Piccadilly Line of the Underground extends all the way to **Heathrow Airport**, stopping first at the outlying Terminal 4 and then at the junction of terminals 1, 2, and 3. Trains run frequently, but make sure that the one you're boarding is going all the way. The journey from central London takes about 45 minutes. Those with heavy or bulky luggage will find the "Airbus" service to be more manageable.

BUSES:

London's famous **buses**, mostly red double-deckers, offer a view along with the ride. **Bus stops** are indicated by red-and-white signs; at those marked "Request" you must hail the bus by raising your hand. Be careful to note the route number and be sure that you're going in the right direction. Free **route maps** are available at Underground stations and tourist information centres, or you can get further information by phoning (020) 7222-1234. Buses are particularly useful in those parts of London, such as Chelsea or Greenwich, that are not really served by the Underground. **Fares** are determined by distance, and tickets sold by the driver or sometimes by a conductor. Keep yours until the end of the journey. Economical **passes** are described below.

DOCKLANDS LIGHT RAILWAY:

Opened in 1987 and offering spectacular views from its elevated tracks, this is London's newest form of public transportation. The high-tech automated system at present operates from the Bank station in the heart of the City, where it connects with the Underground, or from Tower Gateway near the Tower of London, and heads east through the revitalized Docklands area to within walking distance of Greenwich. This is being expanded under the Thames, through Greenwich, and on to Lewisham. Other extensions now in operation head north to Stratford and east to Beckton. London Underground tickets and passes are valid as long as they cover the appropriate zones.

RAIL:

Regular commuter trains may seem like an odd way to get around London, but in some cases they are very practical, especially for those with a BritRail Pass or a Travelcard covering the appropriate zones. The starting and finishing points of the walking tours in Greenwich, Hampstead Heath, Richmond, and Hampton Court are easily reached by frequent trains. A careful study of the Rail Passenger Network Map or the Network SouthEast Map will reveal many interesting possibilities, including the **Thameslink** line between stations south of the river, the City, King's Cross Thameslink, and the northern suburbs. Other useful lines include the **North London Link** and the recently-modernized **Waterloo & City**. Travelcards covering the appropriate zones are valid for travel on the commuter trains within London.

There are an enormous number of stations within London itself, most of which are for local commuter trains only. Some of these double as Underground stations. Rail services for the daytrips beyond London (see Section III) depart from the mainline stations, which are shown on the map on page 105. These are all connected to the Underground system.

PASSES:

Passes for unlimited travel on London's Underground, buses, the Docklands Light Railway, and local commuter trains, are a good way to save time and money if you intend to take more than three trips a day. They include the **London Visitor Travelcard**, which can be purchased in North America and other overseas locations from travel agents or BritRail, 226 Westchester Ave., White Plains, NY 10604, ☎ (888) BRITRAIL, Internet: www.raileurope.com. This comes with a set of discount vouchers for selected tourist attractions (a nice little bonus), and is also valid for transfers to and from Heathrow Airport by Underground. A cheaper version, the **Visitor Travelcard Central Zone**, covers most tourist attractions but without airport connections. Both are available for 3, 4, or 7 consecutive days of travel. These cards are not sold in Britain.

A standard **Travelcard** for specific zones (or all zones) can be purchased at all Underground stations from vending machines or ticket windows, London Transport information centres, railway ticket offices in London, or London Tourist Board offices. They are valid for either one day, a weekend, a week, or a month. The weekend card is considerably cheaper than two one-day cards. The weekly or monthly cards require a passport-size photo available from photomat machines in nearly all stations. The standard one-day Travelcard is not valid until after 9:30 a.m. on working days, but the more expensive LT Card can be used from midnight on. For additional information contact London Transport at ☎ (020) 7222-1234, Internet: www.londontransport.co.uk.

BOATS:

Floating on the Thames is a slow but highly enjoyable way to get to your destination while seeing the sights. Boats can be used on the Southwark and Lambeth, Docklands, Greenwich, Richmond, and Hampton Court daytrips in this book. Excursion **River Boats** operate from

Westminster (near Parliament), Charing Cross, Tower, and some other piers to Greenwich, Richmond, and Hampton Court, with refreshments available along the way. For information on the various services contact **London Tourist Board Riverboat Information**, ☎ (0839) 123-432 (toll call).

TAXIS:

Taxis are a favorite way of getting around town, and not too expensive if two or more travel together. You can hail cabs in the street when their "For Hire" sign is lit, go to a taxi rank, or phone for one. Fares are metered and supplemented by charges for waiting, luggage, and additional passengers. A tip of 15% is expected.

AIRPORT TRANSPORTATION:

For information concerning getting to and from London's airports, see page 11.

BY CAR:

In a word, don't. Only a native can possibly unscramble the maze of one-way streets or magically find a legitimate parking place. Illegally parked cars either get their wheels clamped by the police or are spirited away by an amazing truck that plucks it out of its space and dumps it onto a trailer. If you insist on facing this torture, remember that you have been warned. Save the car for out-of-town trips.

LONDON TOURIST INFORMATION:

London abounds in tourist offices. For general information concerning all of Britain you should visit the **Britain Visitor Centre** at 1 Regent Street, two blocks south of Piccadilly Circus, ☎ (020) 8846-9000, Internet: www.visit britain.com. Open from 9 a.m. until 6:30 p.m. on Mondays through Fridays and 10–4 on weekends, the centre includes branch offices of the British Tourist Authority, Globaltickets, Thomas Cook Travel, a bookshop, and a money changer. Ask about the **London White Card**, a pre-paid admission card to some 15 major London museums and galleries that could save culture-hungry visitors a nice amount of change.

More specific information about London is available from the **London Tourist Board**, with offices located in the forecourt of **Victoria Station**, in the **Liverpool Street Underground Station**, and in the Underground Station Concourse of terminals 1, 2, and 3 at **Heathrow Airport**. For phone inquiries ☎ (0839) 123-456 (toll call), Internet: www.londontown.com. For accommodations only ☎ (020) 7932-2020. All three offices make hotel bookings.

Some districts of London have their own tourist information centres, as noted in the "Practicalities" section of the appropriate walking tours.

*The City

Visitors often (and quite understandably) confuse the City of London with London itself. Actually, the City (with a capital "C") refers to the semi-autonomous square mile extending from Temple Bar east to the Tower of London, and from the Thames north to the Barbican. This is the ancient core of London, the site of a prehistoric Celtic settlement and the walled Roman city of *Londinium*. It is today the commercial heart of Britain, and one of the most important financial centers on Earth.

With its own Lord Mayor and a separate police force, the City occupies a unique position in Britain's political structure. Its own local government, headquartered at the Guildhall, is elected by commercial interests, not by residents—of whom there are precious few. Even the sovereign of England cannot enter the City without symbolic permission from its Lord Mayor. You, however, can.

Over the centuries, the City has been continually destroyed and rebuilt, suffering especially from the Great Fire of 1666, the bombs of World War II and, more recently, from the hands of overzealous developers. Yet it remains an exceptionally interesting place, with many first-rate attractions such as St. Paul's Cathedral and the Tower of London scattered between the gleaming modern skyscrapers.

GETTING THERE:

The **Underground** station closest to the start of this walking tour is at Temple, on the Circle and District lines. Note that this station is closed on Sundays and holidays, when the Embankment or Charing Cross stations should be used. A great many **bus** routes also serve this area. By **taxi**, ask the driver for The Temple. The nearest **British Rail** stations are Blackfriars, City Thameslink, and Charing Cross.

PRACTICALITIES:

The City is best seen on a working day, when the streets are alive with the sound of commerce. Some minor sights are closed on Sundays and/or holidays. Oddly, even some of the churches are locked on Sundays, as are many pubs. The **City of London Information Centre**, ☎ (020) 7332-1456, is located on St. Paul's Churchyard, opposite the south side of the cathedral.

FOOD AND DRINK:

Restaurants and pubs in the City cater primarily to businesspeople and are often closed on weekends, holidays, and in the evenings. Some choices are:

Simpsons Tavern (Ball Court, 38 Cornhill, just south of the Bank of England) This old, traditional British chophouse has been around for centuries. ☎ (020) 7626-9985. X: evenings, weekends. £££

All Bar One (44 Ludgate Hill, just west of St. Paul's; also at 34 Threadneedle St., near the Bank of England) Contemporary British dishes in a pleasant setting. ☎ (020) 7248-1356 and (020) 7256-8999. ££

Poons in the City (Minster Court, Mincing Lane, 2 blocks west of Fenchurch Street Station) Chinese cuisine in a striking, modern setting with separate sections for full and light meals. ☎ (020) 7626-0126. X: Sat., Sun., holidays. ££

Barcelona Tapas Bar (15 St. Botolph St., 4 blocks northeast of Fenchurch Street Station) Spanish food and wine, with a genuine atmosphere. ☎ (020) 7377-5222. ££

Ye Olde Cheshire Cheese (145 Fleet St.) an historic pub and restaurant, last rebuilt in 1667. It seems that everyone born since then has been there at least once for a beer or the traditional English fare. ☎ (020) 7353-6170. Pub £, restaurant ££

Coffee Republic (147 Fleet St., not far from St. Bride's Church) A popular spot for light lunches. ☎ (020) 7353-0900. £

Black Friar (174 Queen Victoria St., opposite Blackfriars Station) Have lunch in an old pub with a stunning Art Nouveau interior and plenty of atmosphere. ☎ (020) 7236-5650. X: Sat., Sun., holidays. £

The Place Below (in the crypt of St. Mary-le-Bow Church at Cheapside and Bow Lane, 3 blocks east of St. Paul's Cathedral) Vegetarian dishes with ambiance. ☎ (020) 7329-0789. X: weekends. £

SUGGESTED TOUR:

Numbers in parentheses correspond to numbers on the map.

Begin your walk at the **Church of St. Clement Danes** (1), close to both the Temple and Aldwych Underground stations and a bit over a half-mile northeast of Trafalgar Square. Strangely situated in the middle of the Strand, an ancient thoroughfare linking the City with Westminster, it was built by Sir Christopher Wren in 1682 on the site of earlier churches dating as far back as the 9th century. Practically destroyed during a 1941 air raid, the church was beautifully restored in 1958 and is now the central church of the Royal Air Force. It is perhaps best known for its carillon, heard on weekdays at 9 a.m., noon, and at 3 and 6 p.m., playing the tune of the nursery rhyme, "Oranges and lemons, say the bells of St. Clement's." Outside the rear of the church, facing Fleet Street, is a statue

of Samuel Johnson, who was a member of the congregation. *Open daily,*
8–5. ☎ *(020) 7242-8282.*

Continue up the Strand to the site of the **Temple Bar** (2), the western
boundary of the City of London ever since the Middle Ages. By tradition,
this is the spot where the sovereign of England must halt and receive permission to enter the City. The gate itself—a traffic bottleneck—was
removed in 1878 and replaced by the present monument in the center of
the road, which at this point changes its name to Fleet Street.

Turn right and pass through a small gateway into Middle Temple Lane,
leading to the quiet enclave of two of London's four Inns of Court, these
two known collectively as **The Temple**. The name derives from the Order of
the Knights Templars, a religious and para-military organization that established its seat in England here in 1185. After the order was suppressed in
the 14th century, the complex of monastic buildings fell into the hands of
a group of lawyers who, as lawyers are wont to do, have occupied the
premises ever since. Most of the present structures date from Elizabethan
times and later, but a few are medieval. On the west side of the lane is the
Middle Temple (3), whose Fountain Court is an oasis of calm in the midst of
the bustling City. The adjoining Middle Temple Hall was built between the
14th and 16th centuries and restored after suffering terrible bomb damage
in World War II. Tradition has it that Shakespeare performed in his own
Twelfth Night here in 1602. The fine interior, sometimes open, is well
worth seeing if you get the chance.

Now pass through the Pump Court cloisters and into the grounds of
the **Inner Temple** (4). The **Temple Church**, built in the 12th century by the
Knights Templars, is among the most interesting medieval buildings in
London. Its highly unusual round nave is based on the Church of the Holy
Sepulchre in Jerusalem, and is perhaps the finest of the five surviving circular churches in England. An oblong chancel, in the Gothic style, was
added in 1240. *Open Wed.–Sat. 10–4, Sun. 12:45–4.* ☎ *(020) 7353-1736.*

Leave The Temple by way of Inner Temple Lane and turn right, going
through an attractive 17th-century gateway. Above this is **Prince Henry's**
Room (5), one of the few interiors to survive the Great Fire of 1666. Fully
restored, it is now owned by the Corporation of London, the governing
authority of the City. Although its connection with Prince Henry, brother
of Charles I, is tenuous at best, it does contain a splendid exhibition of
items related to the diarist Samuel Pepys, who was born nearby in 1633.

You are now on **Fleet Street**. Until a few years ago this was the center
of England's newspaper business, but the publishers have since moved
east into the Docklands and other areas. The fictional Sweeney Todd, the
"Demon Barber of Fleet Street," was supposed to have had his shop next
to **St. Dunstan's Church**. A left turn on Fetter Lane and a right at Trinity
Church Passage brings you through some narrow alleyways to **Dr.**
Johnson's House (6) on Gough Square. The first definitive dictionary of the
English language was compiled here by Dr. Samuel Johnson, the literary
giant of the 18th century, who lived in this typical late-17th-century town

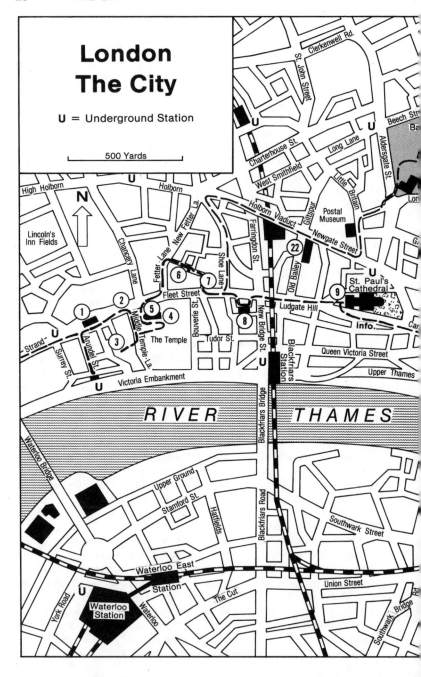

London
The City

U = Underground Station

500 Yards

house from 1749 to 1759. His spirit is still to be felt throughout the neighborhood. You can step inside to see various memorabilia, as well as a first edition of the famed *Dictionary*. *Open May–Sept., Mon.–Sat. 11–5:30; Oct.–April, Mon.–Sat. 11–5. Adults £3, seniors and students £2, children £1.* ☎ *(020) 7353-3745.*

Now follow the map to another place associated with Johnson, **Ye Olde Cheshire Cheese** pub (7), which was rebuilt in 1667. Dickens downed the occasional ale here, too, but the pub was most famous for its foul (fowl?)-mouthed parrot whose vocabulary of four-letter words astonished patrons for many years until 1926, when the bird finally expired. The attached restaurant is popular with tourists, but perhaps you'd like to step into the highly atmospheric bar for some real ale. Its entrance is on Wine Office Court, just off Fleet Street.

Continue down Fleet Street and turn right to **St. Bride's Church** (8), traditionally the house of worship for journalists. Although churches have stood on this site since Saxon times, the present structure was designed in 1675 by Wren, who rebuilt so many of the churches in the City after the disastrous Great Fire of 1666. St. Bride's is famous for its incredibly ornate steeple, at 226 feet the tallest of Wren's spires. The interior was badly damaged in World War II, and during reconstruction in the 1950s several interesting Roman and Saxon remains were discovered under the floor. These can be seen by visiting the **Crypt**, which also has an exhibition on the development of printing in Fleet Street. *Open Mon.–Fri. 8–4:45, Sat. 9–4:45, Sun. 9–12:30 and 5:50–7:30 p.m.* ☎ *(020) 7353-1301.*

Return to Fleet Street and turn right, continuing under the railway viaduct and up Ludgate Hill to one of London's stellar attractions:

*ST. PAUL'S CATHEDRAL (9), ☎ (020) 7246-8348. Internet: http://stpauls.london.anglican.org. *Open Mon.–Sat. 8:30–4. Adults £4, seniors £3.50, children £2. Additional charge for Galleries (Dome): Adults £3.50, seniors £3, children £1.50. Guided tours. Audio tours. Crypt Café. Gift shop. Partial* ♿.

St. Paul's Cathedral has long been a monument to Britain's fortitude, a testimony to its stiff upper lip. Time and again the church was destroyed by fire, decay, and bombs; yet it has always come back to remind Britons of their heritage. The first house of worship on this site appeared in the 7th century but soon succumbed to flames, as did its successors. During the 12th century an immense cathedral was begun, one whose steeple eventually reached the amazing height of 489 feet before being demolished by lightning in 1561. In 1666 the Great Fire finished off the rest of the building, which was already in a state of sad neglect following the Civil War and the Great Plague.

The magnificent Renaissance structure you see today is the supreme masterpiece of **Sir Christopher Wren**, perhaps the greatest English architect of all time. His plan for rebuilding the entire burned-out City was never adopted, but St. Paul's and many other Wren churches and secular buildings throughout London and elsewhere are evidence of a unique genius.

Begun in 1675, the new cathedral was completed by 1708. Although hit by several bombs during World War II, it survived the conflict thanks to the continual presence of a fire brigade determined to save this symbol of British perseverance. A postwar renovation has once again restored all of its former splendor.

The most outstanding feature of St. Paul's is its famous **Dome**, visible from all over London. Patterned after the great domes of St. Peter's in Rome and the Cathedral of Florence, it was the first of its type in Britain. Like those Renaissance domes of Italy, it is partly an illusion—a dome within a dome, supported by a hidden superstructure and crowned with a stone lantern. You can climb up through it for both a better understanding of its remarkable construction and for a marvelous view of the City.

Enter the cathedral through the elaborately decorated **West Front**, flanked by two Baroque towers. Wren originally designed the interior in the form of a Greek cross, but the Latin cross arrangement that was finally used was forced on him by the authorities, who may have been anticipating a possible return to Catholicism under James II. The accession to power in 1689 of William III, a staunch Protestant, insured that this would not happen.

If Wren had first conceived of the interior as being one of uncluttered elegance, it has since been filled with all kinds of monuments to national heroes, some of which are quite splendid. Don't miss Holman Hunt's piously Victorian painting, *The Light of the World*, in the south aisle of the nave. At the crossing you can look up into the interior dome, suspended beneath the hidden brick cone that supports the stone lantern and the lead-covered wooden outer dome. The early-18th-century monochromatic **frescoes** of the interior dome depict scenes from the life of St. Paul.

Stroll into the **Chancel** with its delightful **choir stalls** and organ case carved by Grinling Gibbons, the most famous English sculptor of the 17th century. The baldachin over the **High Altar** is a postwar addition, more or less following Wren's original drawings. Behind it, in the apse, is the **American Chapel** commemorating the names of 28,000 Americans based in Britain who fell in World War II. Along the south choir aisle is the only monument to have survived intact from the medieval cathedral, a macabre figure of the poet John Donne clad in a shroud. It still shows traces of the Great Fire.

The enormous ***Crypt**, believed to be the largest in Europe, is entered from the south transept. Fittingly, it contains the tomb of Sir Christopher Wren under the famous Latin inscription *Si monumentum requiris, circumspice*—"If you seek his monument, look around you." Wren died in 1723 at the ripe old age of 91. At the east end of the crypt is the Chapel of the Order of the British Empire, and nearby are the grandiose tombs of the **Duke of Wellington** and **Lord Nelson**. The **Treasury**, beneath the north transept, displays ecclesiastical vestments, illuminated manuscripts, and religious objects. Be sure to examine Wren's **Great Model**, an earlier design for the cathedral that was rejected. It is now on view beneath the nave, near the **Lecture Room** with its interesting audio-visual show. As you stroll around the crypt you will come across literally hundreds of memorials to famous English men and women.

Returning from the depths of the crypt, you may want to climb up into the *****Dome**, for which there is an entrance fee. The stairs for this are at the corner of the nave and the south transept. An easy climb brings you to the **South Triforium Gallery**, after which you continue upwards to the renowned **Whispering Gallery** with its peculiar acoustics. The slightest sound made near its wall travels completely around the dome without being heard elsewhere. A steeper climb now leads to the **Stone Gallery** for a fine view of London. Those endowed with excessive energy will, of course, want to continue all the way to the top, where the panorama from the **Golden Gallery** is unmatched.

The route now leads past the City Information Centre on St. Paul's Churchyard. Turn right on King William Street and amble out onto **London Bridge** (10) for a good view of activities on the River Thames. The first bridge on this approximate site was a wooden structure erected after AD 43 by the Romans and rebuilt many times after frequently falling down, as recalled in the famous nursery rhyme. In the 12th century it was replaced by a stone bridge whose piers blocked the flow of water to such an extent that the Thames often froze over in winter. This span carried on it a number of houses and shops, a chapel, and two gatehouses decorated with the severed heads of traitors. Until 1729 it remained the only bridge across the river. Finally, it became inadequate for the traffic and a new bridge was built in the early 19th century, which in turn proved to be too small. Carefully dismantled in 1970, its numbered stones were sold for some one million pounds to the developers of Lake Havasu City, Arizona, where it was re-erected over a small lake. The present London Bridge was opened in 1973. Tourists often confuse the name with the much more spectacular Tower Bridge, located a half-mile downstream.

Now retrace your steps and turn right to the **Monument** (11), a 202-foot-tall Doric column designed by Wren and erected to commemorate the Great Fire of 1666. According to tradition, the conflagration began exactly 202 feet from its base, in Pudding Lane. An inscription, removed in 1831, once unjustly attributed the tragedy to a Catholic plot. Yes, you can climb all 311 steps to the platform near its top, but the view is somewhat obstructed by modern office buildings. *Open for ascents daily 10–6, last admission at 5:40. Adults £1.50, children 50p.* ☎ *(020) 7626-2717.*

Fish Street leads to the busy Lower Thames Street, across which stands the **Church of St. Magnus the Martyr** (12). Rebuilt by Wren in 1676, it is noted for its formidable 185-foot steeple as well as for its splendid interior. The rector of the pre-fire church on the site, who published the first complete English Bible in 1535, is buried within. Take special note of the church's porch, through which passed the approach to the medieval Old London Bridge.

The route now takes you down Great Tower Street to the **Church of All Hallows-by-the-Tower** (13), which (surprise!) is not by Wren. In fact, its major attraction has little to do with religion, the **Undercroft** being an *in situ* **museum of Roman London**. Among the ruins of a Roman house are ashes from Boadicea's sack of *Londinium* in AD 61, bits of a Saxon church from the 7th century, an altar from the Crusades, and a model of Roman London. The aboveground part of the church, except for its 17th-century **Tower** from which Samuel Pepys witnessed the Great Fire, was almost totally destroyed during a 1940 air raid and rebuilt in the 1950s. It has historical connections with the United States, being the church where William Penn was baptized in 1644 and President John Quincy Adams was married in 1797. Although the church proper is new, it contains several treasures including a magnificent wooden font cover attributed to Grinling Gibbons, superb ship models, and a fine collection of brasses— some of which may be rubbed to make your own souvenirs.

And now on to one of England's most important tourist sights, the:

*TOWER OF LONDON (14), ☎ (020) 7709-0765, Internet: www.hrp.org.uk. *Open March–Oct., Mon.–Sat. 9–6, Sun. 10–6; Nov.–Feb., Tues.–Sat. 9–5, Sun.–Mon. 10–5. Last admission one hour before closing. Adults £10.50, seniors and students £7.90, children 5-15 £6.90. Guided tours. Gift shops. Partial &.*

Actually located just east of the City limits, this massive fortress was begun by William the Conqueror in 1067, shortly after the Battle of Hastings had established Norman rule in England. Its initial purpose was to protect the conquerors from the vanquished Anglo-Saxons, but throughout most of its bloody history it has been used more as a prison and place of execution. It also served as a sometimes royal residence until the reign of James I, although the palatial buildings have long since disappeared along with the royal menagerie. Among the other functions it once had were those of a mint, an observatory, a treasury, an arsenal, and a military garrison.

The Tower of London is an extremely popular place, attracting huge crowds during the height of the tourist season. Depending on the length of the waiting lines and the number of sights you plan to see, a visit here can easily take several hours. You may prefer to return on another day, preferably early in the morning and hopefully not on a Sunday. Those returning at another time can easily reach the Tower by taking the Underground (Circle and District lines) to Tower Hill.

Purchase your ticket and enter via the **Middle Tower**. Guided tours led by Yeoman Warders (Beefeaters) in historic costume are available here at no extra charge and make an excellent way to start your visit, after which you can poke about on your own. A causeway leads across the former moat that was drained in 1843 and is now a grassy ditch. Pass through it and continue to the **Traitors' Gate**, the medieval entrance from the Thames, where boats bearing prisoners once docked.

A left turn brings you past the **Wakefield Tower**, where the saintly Henry VI was murdered in 1471. The **Bloody Tower**, under which you pass, was the scene of the murder of the Little Princes—the deposed child-king Edward V and his younger brother, the Duke of York, in 1485, supposedly on orders from Richard III. This was also the place where Sir Walter Raleigh wrote his *History of the World* while imprisoned from 1603 until 1615. Released to undertake an expedition to the New World, he was later executed in 1618 after returning empty-handed.

You have now entered **Tower Green**, a large open space where the scaffold was located, its site marked by a brass plate. To the left stands the **Queen's House**, now the residence of the Governor; the **Yeoman Gaoler's House**, where the captured Nazi leader Rudolf Hess was incarcerated in 1941; the 13th-century **Beauchamp Tower**, long a prison; and the **Chapel Royal of St. Peter ad Vincula**, rebuilt in 1307 and used as the burial place for such beheaded victims as Anne Boleyn and Catherine Howard—both wives of Henry VIII—and many other illustrious names. Be on the lookout for some of the six **ravens** who officially inhabit the Tower's precincts; legend has it that if they leave the Tower will fall. To forestall this possibility, they are fed a generous allowance of meat.

The east side of Tower Green is totally dominated by the massive ***White Tower**, the oldest remaining part of the fortress complex. Begun in 1078 by William the Conqueror to replace his wooden structure of 1067, it was covered with whitewash in 1241, hence the name. Sir Christopher Wren enlarged the windows during the late 17th century, and a few other modifications were made, but basically the tower is the same today as it was in Norman times. The immensely strong walls are between 12 and 15 feet thick and rise to a height of 90 feet.

Enter by way of the staircase on the south side and climb to the **Chapel of St. John** on the second floor. The oldest existing church in London, this is where medieval kings spent the night before their coronations. The third floor is devoted to armor from Tudor and later times. Be sure to examine the various suits made for Henry VIII, which became larger and larger as the king grew fatter and fatter. Now descend to the ground floor for a look at weapons from the 16th through the 19th centuries.

Leave the White Tower and stroll over to the Jewel House, where you can join the inevitable queue for a hurried look at the ***Crown Jewels**, the most popular attraction at the Tower of London. Nearly all of the treasures date from after the Restoration of 1660, most of the earlier regalia having been plundered by Cromwell. The displays begin with a collection of banqueting plate, swords, maces, coronation robes, and other accoutrements of royalty. From here you move into a well-guarded vault protecting the

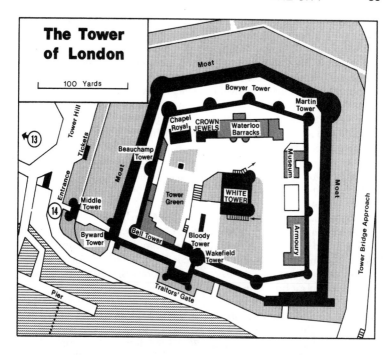

**The Tower
of London**

100 Yards

Moat

Bowyer Tower

Martin Tower

Tower Hill

Tickets

Chapel Royal

CROWN JEWELS

Waterloo Barracks

Beauchamp Tower

Museum

Moat

13

Entrance

Moat

WHITE TOWER

14

Middle Tower

Tower Green

Byward Tower

Bell Tower

Bloody Tower

Armoury

Wakefield Tower

Tower Bridge Approach

Pier

Traitors' Gate

Crown Jewels themselves. The **Royal Sceptre** contains the 530-carat Star of Africa, the largest diamond ever cut; while the Queen Mother's Crown of 1937 is fitted with the fabulous **Koh-i-Noor** diamond. All around these glitter other priceless objects, but you'll have little time to examine them as the line is kept moving right along.

There are several other attractions at the Tower of London that might interest you. The **Wall Walks** atop the south and east stretches of the Inner Ward curtain wall provide exceptionally nice views of both the precincts and the Thames, and allow visits to several restored medieval interiors. Just east of the White Tower is the **Royal Fusiliers Museum**, which traces the history of the famous City of London Regiment, and the **New Armoury** with its collection of small arms.

Every evening at 9:40 the Tower is officially locked up for the night with the colorful **Ceremony of the Keys**, an event that can be attended upon advance written application only. Ask the tourist office for current details.

Leave the Tower precincts and follow the map north to the **Tower Hill Underground Station**, near which is a section of the ancient **Roman Wall**. You have now passed the halfway point of this walking tour. The attractions that lie ahead will take considerably less time then those already covered, but if you're tired, this is a good place to stop.

The route now leads into the heart of the financial district, passing the attractive old **Church of St. Olave** (15) to which the diarist Samuel Pepys belonged in the 17th century. Its churchyard was immortalized as "St. Ghastly Grim" in Dickens' novel *The Uncommercial Traveller*, and is appropriately decorated with skulls. Just north of this is the nicely-restored **Fenchurch Street Station** of 1840, the first rail terminal to be built in the City. Continue past it and turn right on Fenchurch Street, then left onto Leadenhall Street.

At the intersection of Lime Street stands the stunning Lloyd's of London Building, built in 1986 of glass and shining steel, and behind it the colorful 19th-century **Leadenhall Market** (16), where fancy edibles are still purveyed amid all the financial dealings.

Now head north on St. Mary Axe to the **Church of St. Helen Bishopgate** (17). Begun in the 13th century, it is one of the most appealing in the City, and is noted for its intact medieval interior, monuments (note especially the one to the 16th-century financier Sir Thomas Gresham who first postulated that "bad money drives out good"), brasses, wood carvings, and a remarkable poor box of 1620.

From across Bishopgate you get a good view of the 600-foot **National Westminster Tower**, opened in 1981 as the tallest office building in Britain. Alas, its height has already been bested by the Canary Wharf tower in London's Docklands (see page 76). Turn left and continue down Threadneedle Street to the stately **Bank of England** (18), the renowned "Old Lady of Threadneedle Street," founded in 1694 to finance England's wars with France. Nationalized in 1946, it is the central bank, manages the national debt, and issues notes for England and Wales. Its arcane workings are explained at the bank's rather luxurious **Museum**, whose entrance is around the corner on Bartholomew Lane. *Open Mon.–Fri. 10–5. Free.* ☎ *(020) 7601-5545.*

From here the route leads to the **Guildhall** (19), seat of government for the Corporation of the City of London ever since the Middle Ages. The present structure dates in part from 1411, but has been substantially altered over the years, especially after the Great Fire of 1666 and the bombs of World War II. You can usually enter its magnificent 15th-century **Great Hall**, used for meetings and state banquets. Be sure to inspect the two giant wooden statues of Gog and Magog mounted on the Musicians' Gallery at the west end. Depicting legendary characters from pre-Roman Britain, these are actually post-war replicas of a pair destroyed in the Blitz. The large **Crypt**, with its columns of Purbeck marble, has survived intact since the 15th century. It is not normally open to visitors, but the officer in charge might let you go down if you ask. *Guildhall usually open daily 10–5, closed on Sun. in winter. Free.* ☎ *(020) 7606-3030.*

The **Guildhall Library**, in an adjacent building to the west, was first founded in 1425 and has a wonderful collection of old books, maps, drawings and the like. Next to it is the **Guildhall Clock Museum**, where hundreds of ancient timepieces from the 15th century to the present are on display.

Now carefully follow the map around the rear of the Guildhall, up steps and across two overpasses to the **Barbican** (20). Occupying a 60-acre site that was totally devastated by World War II bombs, this monumental construction project incorporates apartment buildings of up to 40 stories, an artificial lake, gardens, covered walkways on several levels, and the Museum of London. It is virtually the only residential area within the City. Depending on your view of 1960s modern architecture, it can seem to either represent a bold new utopia or appear to be a bleak and even brutal mass of windswept concrete. Fortunately, its coldness has been relieved by the opening in 1982 of the lively **Barbican Arts Centre** at the northern end. Home to the London Symphony Orchestra and the Royal Shakespeare Company, this complex contains a concert hall, several theaters, a library, an art gallery, exhibition halls, restaurants, and shops.

Thread your way through the maze of walkways to the:

MUSEUM OF LONDON (21), ☎ (020) 7600-3699, Internet: www.museum-london.org.uk. *Open Mon.–Sat. 10–5:50, Sun. noon–5:50. Last admission at 5:30. Adults £5, seniors and students £3, children 16 and under free, disabled and their helpers free. Free to all after 4:30. Tickets valid for multiple visits for one year. Café.* ♿.

Housed in a stunning modern structure in the southwest corner of the Barbican, the fascinating displays here trace the history of London from prehistoric times to the present, with an emphasis on the social context. Just a few of the highlights include sculptures from the Roman Temple of Mithras, the Cheapside Hoard of 16th-century jewelry, an audio-visual representation of the Great Fire, a cell from Newgate Prison, shop interiors, a Victorian pub, and a 1920's elevator from a department store. The 18th-century **Lord Mayor's Ceremonial Coach**, still used once a year, ends the exhibition on a note of grandeur.

Cross the busy intersection on the walkway, descend to street level, and follow the map to the **Old Bailey** (22). Built on the site of the infamous Newgate Prison, outside of which public hangings were held until 1868, this early-20th-century building houses the Central Criminal Court for Greater London. Fans of the fictional barrister Horace Rumpole may want to stop in and watch the proceedings in courts one and three. *Open daily 9:30–1 and 2–4:30. Free. No admission to children under 14. Use Newgate Street entrance. No cameras allowed.* ☎ *(020) 7248-3277.*

You have now reached the end of this walking tour. The nearest Underground station, St. Paul's, is at the intersection of Newgate Street and Cheapside, just a short stroll to the east. Alternatively, you might prefer to follow the map back to Fleet Street where one of the historic pubs can provide a well-earned reward.

*Westminster

This classic walk takes you through the heart of official London and the seat of the British government, passing such famous sights as Trafalgar Square, the Houses of Parliament, Westminster Abbey, Buckingham Palace, and St. James's Park as well as world-class museums including the Tate Gallery and the National Gallery. This is also where you can best witness the ceremonial pomp for which England is renowned, and delight in the colorful trappings of an empire that has long since faded.

Westminster is the royal and political district of the much larger City of Westminster, which evolved considerably later than its rival to the east, the City of London. Both cities are among the 33 boroughs that make up Greater London. Westminster first developed around an isolated 8th-century abbey then known as the West Minster for its location in relation to the City. A royal palace was built in the early 11th century on the site of what are now the Houses of Parliament. In 1529, Henry VIII confiscated the archbishop's palace on nearby Whitehall and made it into his own residence, of which only a small part remains. Throughout most of its history, the area of Westminster has been the administrative center of England, a role it continues to play today.

Expect to encounter a great many tourists along the route of this walking tour, and don't forget to have your picture taken on the bridge, with "Big Ben" in the background.

GETTING THERE:

The **Underground** station nearest the beginning (and end) of this walk is Charing Cross, served by the Bakerloo, Northern, and Jubilee lines. Those using the Circle or District lines may prefer to get off at the nearby Embankment station. A great many **bus** routes converge on this area. By **taxi**, ask the driver for Trafalgar Square. The closest **British Rail** station is Charing Cross.

PRACTICALITIES:

Any time is a good time to explore Westminster, but note that some of the sights are closed on major holidays and/or Sunday mornings.

Westminster Abbey is closed to tourists on Sundays. The **Britain Visitor Centre** at 1 Regent Street, ☎ (020) 8846-9000, is just a few blocks northwest of Trafalgar Square. Another good source of information is the **London Tourist Board** office in the forecourt of Victoria Station.

FOOD AND DRINK:

Restaurants and pubs in this area cater mainly to government workers, businesspeople, and tourists. A few good choices are:

Tate Gallery Dining Room (in the Tate Gallery) Reservations are essential for this delightful lunch favorite, where modern British cuisine is served surrounded by art. ☎ (020) 7887-8825. X: evenings. ££

Seafresh (80 Wilton Rd., 3 blocks southeast of Victoria Station) This paradise for seafood lovers offers a few landlubber dishes, too. ☎ (020) 7828-0747. X: Sun. ££

Sherlock Holmes (10 Northumberland St., 2 blocks south of Trafalgar Square) A famous old pub and restaurant filled with Holmes memorabilia, even an upstairs re-creation of 221B Baker St. Sir Arthur Conan Doyle was a regular when it was called the Northumberland Arms. ☎ (020) 7930-2644. £ and ££

The Footstool (St. John's Concert Hall, Smith Square, 3 blocks south of Westminster Abbey) The lunchtime buffet in this former-church-crypt-turned-restaurant offers real value with atmosphere. ☎ (020) 7222-2779. £ and ££

Café Rouge (Buckingham Palace Rd., near Victoria Station) French bistro fare in a popular chain restaurant. ☎ (020) 7931-9300. £ and ££

Café in the Crypt (in the crypt of the Church of St. Martin-in-the-Fields, Trafalgar Square) Light lunches and hot meals under a cozy vaulted brick ceiling. ☎ (020) 7839-4342. £

Pizza Express (154 Victoria St., near Victoria Station) This ubiquitous British chain offers good pizzas and other Italian dishes at fair prices. ☎ (020) 7828-1477. £

SUGGESTED TOUR:

Numbers in parentheses correspond to numbers on the map.

All distances to and from London are measured from **Trafalgar Square** (1), making this the true center of the capital as well as the starting point of this walking tour. It is also a favorite gathering place for Londoners and the rallying point for political demonstrations. The square, laid out in the mid-19th century, is dominated by **Nelson's Column**, an immense 172-foot-high monument to the victor at the Battle of Trafalgar, in which British naval supremacy was firmly established in 1805.

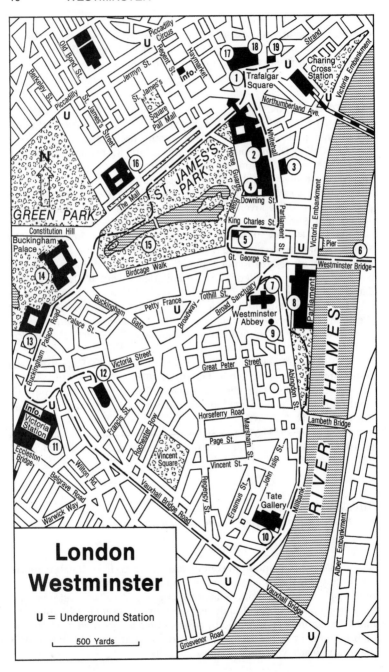

London
Westminster

U = Underground Station

500 Yards

On the north side of the square stands the **National Gallery**, the **National Portrait Gallery**, and the famous **Church of St. Martin-in-the-Fields**. Visits to these are best saved until the end of the walk, as you'll be coming back this way. At the extreme south end, on a traffic island, is the 1633 equestrian **Statue of Charles I**, with the king looking down Whitehall to the scene of his martyrdom at the hands of Cromwell. In 1655 the statue was sold for scrap by Parliament, but secretly saved and re-erected after the Restoration. It stands on the site of the 13th-century Charing Cross, which was destroyed by the Puritans. An 1865 replica of this is now in front of the nearby Charing Cross Station.

The broad thoroughfare known as **Whitehall** leads south towards Westminster Abbey and the Houses of Parliament, thus linking the government with the commercial interests of the City. Its very name has become synonymous with British administration, and the street is today lined with ministries.

Until the end of the 17th century, the great **Palace of Whitehall** complex occupied nearly all of the space on either side of the present road. Begun in the 13th century as a mansion for the Archbishop of York, it was enlarged by Cardinal Wolsey and seized in 1529 by Henry VIII, who gave it the name. Whitehall was a residence for all of the subsequent monarchs of England until William and Mary moved into Kensington Palace, after which it accidentally burned down and was never rebuilt. The only part to have survived intact is the Banqueting House, described below.

Stroll down the street, passing the handsome Old Admiralty of 1726 on the right. Just beyond this is the 18th-century **Horse Guards Building** (2), where a mounted changing-of-the-guard ceremony is held by the Household Cavalry on Mondays through Saturdays at 11 a.m., and on Sundays at 10 a.m., except in bad weather. The Horse Guards Parade, beyond the arch, is the setting for the annual Trooping of the Colour ceremony held each June.

Across the street stands the elegant Palladian-style **Banqueting House** (3), the only structure remaining from the former Palace of Whitehall. Built in 1625 for James I by the noted architect Inigo Jones, it features a fabulous **painted ceiling** by Rubens celebrating in allegorical terms the merits of the Stuart dynasty. This was commissioned by Charles I who, ironically, was led to his beheading in 1649 through a window in this very hall. The king died with great dignity on a scaffold outside, after which royalty was abolished during the 11 years of the Commonwealth. *Open Mon.–Sat. 10–5. Closed Sun., Bank Holidays, Dec. 24–Jan.1. May close at short notice for government functions. Adults £3.60, seniors and students £2.80, children under 16 £2.30.* ☎ *(020) 7930-4179.*

Continue down Whitehall to the next right turn, which is blocked off for security reasons. There, at **Number 10 Downing Street** (4), is the official residence of the Prime Minister. Its deceptively simple façade belies a large and elegant interior, which also houses the Cabinet Room. With a great deal of luck, you might be able to catch a glimpse of some dignitary coming or going. The Chancellor of the Exchequer lives next door at number 11.

Whitehall becomes Parliament Street at the Cenotaph, an austere monument to Britain's war dead. Turn right on King Charles Street and descend the steps at its far end to visit the **Cabinet War Rooms** (5), an underground command center from which Sir Winston Churchill, his cabinet, and the chiefs of staff of Britain's armed forces directed the war effort from 1939 until 1945. Time has stood still since then, and in 1981 some 19 of the cramped rooms in this fortified bunker were opened to the public under the auspices of the Imperial War Museum. Among the highlights are the Cabinet Room, the Transatlantic Telephone Room from which Churchill could hold scrambled conversations with President Roosevelt, the Map Room, and the Prime Minister's Room, which provided office space and an emergency bedroom for Churchill. *Open daily, 10–6, last admission at 5:15. Adults £4.80, seniors and students £3.50.* ☎ *(020) 7930-6961.* ♿.

Now follow the map to **Westminster Bridge** (6) and walk out on it for a splendid view of the Houses of Parliament and the world-famous Clock Tower commonly (though incorrectly) known as **Big Ben*. Actually, that names refers only to the largest bell in the clock, so-called after a rather corpulent man named Ben. There are several versions of the story, but no one really knows who Ben was. At the northwest foot of the bridge is **Westminster Pier**, from which boats depart frequently for various places along the Thames.

Retrace your steps to Parliament Square, a large open area with statues of famous statesmen including Churchill and Lincoln. South of this stands:

*WESTMINSTER ABBEY (7), ☎ (020) 7222-5152, Internet: www.westminster-abbey.org. *Open Mon.–Fri. 9–4:45 (last admission at 3:45) and Sat. 9–2:45 (last admission at 1:45). Open Wed. eve. 6–7:45, when photography and video is allowed. Closed to visitors on Sun. Adults £5, students £3, children 11-18 £2. Super Tours additional £3. Sound guides £2. Admission to services free.*

Surely the most important house of worship in Britain, Westminster Abbey is, in effect, the entire nation's church and a great repository of English history. This is where nearly all of the kings and queens since William the Conqueror have been crowned, and where a great many of them up to George II are buried along with leading statesmen and other notables. As a "Royal Peculiar" serving the Crown and the State, Westminster Abbey is independent of both the Bishop of London and the Archbishop of Canterbury.

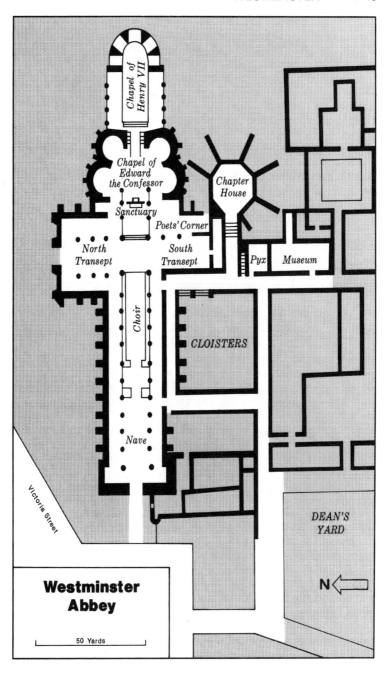

Chapel of Henry VII

Chapel of Edward the Confessor

Chapter House

Sanctuary

Poets' Corner

North Transept

South Transept

Pyx

Museum

Choir

CLOISTERS

Nave

Victoria Street

DEAN'S YARD

N

Westminster Abbey

50 Yards

The first abbey on this then-isolated site was probably built during the 8th century. This was replaced by a new church in the Norman style, started in 1050 by Edward the Confessor, who had erected his new royal palace nearby. Henry III, inspired by the magnificent French Gothic style, began in 1245 to rebuild the entire structure in the form you see today, a task that took some 250 years. The marvelous Chapel of Henry VII was added in the early 16th century, and the west towers in the 18th century. Despite these and other changes, the abbey has a remarkable sense of unity about it.

Enter through the west front and step into the lofty **nave**. Just inside the door is a simple memorial to Winston Churchill, beyond which is the **Tomb of the Unknown Warrior** of World War I. On the first pier to the right hangs the famous medieval portrait of Richard II, the earliest known painting of an English sovereign. All around you are memorials to famous people, not all of whom are actually buried here.

An admission charge is made to go beyond the choir screen, or you might prefer to take one of the excellent **Super Tours** conducted by vergers. These last about 90 minutes and are booked from a desk in the south aisle. They include visits to areas that are not otherwise accessible and are operated fairly frequently on Mondays through Fridays, and less so on Saturdays.

Continue up the north aisle to the north transept, burial place of several eminent statesmen. To the right is the Choir and the **Sanctuary**, where coronations take place. The north ambulatory has several interesting chapels, after which you step up into the utterly fantastic and profusely decorated early-16th-century *Chapel of Henry VII, with its high fan-vaulted ceiling and colorful banners. The exceptionally beautiful tomb of Henry VII is in front of the **Royal Air Force Chapel**, which commemorates the 1940 Battle of Britain. Don't miss the wonderfully carved misericords in the choir stalls. Along the north aisle is the somewhat modest tomb of **Elizabeth I**, which she shares with her sister, Mary I. In the south aisle is buried, among others, **Mary, Queen of Scots** for whom James I erected a grand tomb.

A bridge leads to the *Chapel of Edward the Confessor, raised between the two ambulatories. The shrine of this saint and king was once adorned with precious jewels, but these were looted during the Reformation. In front of it is the **Coronation Chair**, containing the fabled **Stone of Scone**. Stolen from Scotland by Edward I in 1297, this coronation stone was the mystical symbol of Scottish independence since ancient times. In 1950 it was again stolen, this time by Scottish nationalists who took it back to its native land, but was returned a few months later.

The *Poets' Corner, in the south transept, commemorates (and in some cases is the final resting place of) such renowned writers as Chaucer, Ben Jonson, Samuel Johnson, Milton, Shakespeare, Browning, Byron, Keats, Shelley, Dickens, Kipling, and just about all of the other famous names in English literature.

Exit into the medieval **Cloisters**, which date primarily from the 13th and 14th centuries. There is a good brass-rubbing center here in case you would like to make your own distinctive souvenirs.

Before leaving the abbey, you might want to take a look at the **Chapter House**, entered from the east side of the cloisters. A separate admission is charged for this, which also includes the adjacent Pyx Chamber and the Abbey Treasure Museum. The octagonal Chapter House was built about 1250 and used from the 13th to the 16th centuries as the meeting place for the House of Commons, thus making it a veritable cradle of representative government. It has been exceptionally well restored to its original appearance. Next door to it is the **Pyx Chamber**, which dates from the 11th century. Originally a chapel, it was used as a testing place for coinage after the Reformation and now houses an exhibition of church plate. The **Abbey Treasure Museum** in the 11th-century Norman Undercroft, to the south of the cloisters, traces the history of the abbey through historical artifacts and features an unforgettable collection of royal funeral effigies. A realistic likeness of Lord Nelson was added in 1806 as an early tourist attraction.

Leave the abbey through the cloisters and stroll around to the ***Houses of Parliament** (8), more properly known as the **Palace of Westminster**. A royal palace was first erected here by the saint and king Edward the Confessor, or perhaps by one of his predecessors, in the early 11th century. William the Conqueror greatly enlarged it after 1066, and successive kings made major alterations. Almost from the beginning it was the meeting place for an early form of parliament, summoned occasionally to advise the monarch.

Even after Henry VIII moved his court to nearby Whitehall in 1529, the old palace, damaged by fire in 1512, continued to be the site of a parliament that grew ever stronger as the real power of the sovereigns diminished. Then, in 1834, a disastrous fire left nearly all of the palace in utter ruin, sparing only the medieval Westminster Hall, the cloisters, and the crypt, all of which are still part of the complex. The present structure, one of the most instantly recognized buildings on Earth, is in the Gothic Revival style and was erected between 1840 and 1860. Its more than 1,000 rooms, 100 staircases, and two miles of corridors cover an area of over eight acres.

Public access to the Houses of Parliament is severely limited for security reasons. Other than being the guest of a Member of Parliament (MP), your only possibility is to attend a debate of either the House of Lords or the House of Commons. Your embassy in London might be able to help, but expect to be put on a long waiting list. A few last-minute seats are usually available at St. Stephen's Entrance, across from the rear of Westminster Abbey. The queues for these form early and the lucky ones are admitted to the House of Lords around 2:30 p.m. on Mondays through

Wednesdays, or 11 a.m. on Fridays; and to the House of Commons around 4:15 p.m. on Tuesday through Thursdays, or 10 a.m. on Fridays. That is, when the houses are in session and sitting. Check to see if a flag is flying (by day) on Victoria Tower (at the south end) or a lantern shining (at night) in the Clock Tower (at the north end). Times of visits are very variable; call ahead or check the web site. *House of Commons* ☎ *(020) 7219-4272, House of Lords* ☎ *(020) 7219-3107. Internet: www.parliament.uk.*

Just south of the abbey, opposite the south end of the Houses of Parliament, stands the 14th-century **Jewel Tower** (9). Another surviving part of the medieval Palace of Westminster, it was built by Edward III as a royal treasure house and later used as an archive, then as an assay office. Today it houses an exhibition on the history of Parliament.

Now follow the map through the riverside **Victoria Tower Gardens**, passing a cast of Rodin's statue of the *Burghers of Calais*, which celebrates an event in medieval English history. Continue on Millbank to the renowned *Tate Gallery (10), a splendid museum featuring the works of British artists from all periods along with modern foreign art. The Tate has what is surely the most comprehensive collection of British art in the world, including such illustrious names as Hogarth, Gainsborough, Reynolds, Blake, Constable, Spencer, Sutherland, Moore, and Hockney. An entire wing, the **Clore Gallery**, is devoted to an enormous collection of works by J.M.W. Turner. Modern non-British art is represented by Degas, Rodin, Matisee, Munch, Picasso, Giacometti, Pollock, Chagall, Dali, Warhol, Rauschenberg, Lichtenstein, and many, many others. *Open daily 10–6. Free. Variable charges for special exhibitions. Tours. Restaurant. Café. Gift shop.* ☎ *(020) 7887-8000.*

From here, Vauxhall Bridge Road leads to one of London's favorite — and busiest — railway terminals, **Victoria Station** (11). Actually two adjoining stations built for two rival railways, Victoria is a confused but lively place dating in part from 1860, a pleasant survivor from the earlier days of rail. It serves an unusual mix of passengers, what with commuters from the southern counties, vacationers off to Brighton, Continentals crossing the Channel by boat, and air travelers dashing for the Gatwick Express. The London Tourist Board has an excellent information office in the station's forecourt, opposite the bus stop.

Westminster Cathedral (12) is nearby, and well worth the slight detour down Victoria Street. In contrast with the ancient abbey, this Roman Catholic cathedral is relatively new, having been built between 1895 and 1903. Its highly unusual style is perhaps best described as being early Christian Byzantine. You can get a wonderful view of London from the top of its 273-foot **bell tower**, easily reached by elevator. The interior of the cathedral is still being decorated with mosaics, but the completed lower portions are quite impressive. Be sure to examine the **Stations of the Cross**, a series of low-relief sculptures on the main piers of the nave. *Open Sun.–Fri. 7–7, Sat. 8–7. Access restricted during services. Free. Bell tower lift operates April–Nov., daily 9–5; Dec.–March, Thurs.–Sun. 9–5. Lift fee: Adults*

£2, children £1. Gift shop. ☎ *(020) 7798-9055.* ♿

The route now leads up Buckingham Palace Road in the direction of the royal palace. On your left is the **Royal Mews** (13), one of the few parts of the palace complex that is open to the public. Here you can see magnificent state carriages, harness rooms, and stables. The star of the show is the **Gold State Coach**, built in 1762 for George II and still used for coronations. *Usually open Tues.–Thurs., noon–4; and from Aug.–Sept. also on Mon. 10:30–4:30. Adults £4.20, seniors £3.20, under 17 £2.* ☎ *(020) 7839-1377, Internet: www.royal.gov.uk/palaces.*

Continue straight ahead to **Buckingham Palace** (14) itself. The nucleus of this massive structure was a mansion built in 1703 for the Duke of Buckingham, which was purchased in 1762 by George III for use by Queen Charlotte. George IV got together with his favorite architect, John Nash, and in 1825 began expanding this into a real royal palace. Extravagant cost overruns delayed completion of the project until the time of Queen Victoria, when it became the official London residence of the sovereign, a status it has held ever since. The palace was greatly enlarged throughout the 19th century, acquiring its present uninspired façade only in 1913.

The only part of the palace proper that is normally open to the public is the **Queen's Gallery**, entered from Buckingham Gate along the south side. *Changing exhibitions of treasures from the Royal Collection, probably the greatest private art collection in the world, may be seen here when the gallery reopens in 2002 after renovations are complete.*

Visits to other parts of the palace are offered when the Queen is not in residence. *Usually open daily approximately Aug.–Sept. Tickets sold at the ticket office in Green Park, beginning at 9. Adults £10, seniors £7.50, under 17 £5.* ☎ *(020) 7839-1377, Internet: www.royal.gov.uk.*

The famous **Changing of the Guard** ceremony is performed in the forecourt of the palace, usually at 11:30 a.m., daily from early April through mid-August, and on alternate days the rest of the year, subject to weather and affairs of state. You may want to come back for this on another day, when you should arrive early to get a good vantage point.

Cross the vast open space in front of the palace, passing the enormous white marble **Queen Victoria Memorial** in its center. This is an excellent spot for viewing the Changing-of-the-Guard ceremony. *****St. James's Park** (15), opening to the east, is the oldest royal park in London. It was laid out over drained marshlands for Henry VIII in 1532 and opened to the public in 1662 by Charles II. Once rather formal, its attractive present-day landscaping was designed in 1828 by John Nash, who also gave the lake its natural contours. In a city full of parks, this is among the loveliest. Amble through it leisurely, then cross **The Mall**, a processional way leading from Trafalgar Square to the palace. This was originally used for playing the game of Pall Mall, an early form of croquet.

St. James's Palace (16), on the north side of The Mall, was built in 1532 by Henry VIII and became the official residence of the sovereign from 1698, when the Palace of Whitehall burned down, until Queen Victoria moved into Buckingham Palace. Although no longer used by the Royal Family, St. James's still retains ceremonial significance and ambassadors are still accredited to the Court of St. James's.

Return to The Mall or St. James's Park and stroll back to **Trafalgar Square** (1), where this walk began. There are three outstanding attractions there that you might have time for today, or perhaps see at another time:

*NATIONAL GALLERY (17), ☎ (020) 7747-2885. *Open Mon.–Sat. 10–6, Sun. noon–6, remaining open on Wed. to 9 p.m. Free; charge for special exhibitions. Restaurant. Gift shop.* ♿.

The National Gallery, dominating the north side of the square, is easily one of the greatest art museums in the world. Even though it is not particularly large by European standards, the astonishingly high quality of its collections makes a visit here an absolute must for all art lovers, and a pleasurable experience as well. Covering a vast scope of European painting from the 13th century until the beginning of the 20th, it is especially strong in works of the Italian, Dutch, Flemish, French, and Spanish schools. British art is better represented at the Tate Gallery, but the National does have some of the very best masterpieces.

The same complex also houses the **National Portrait Gallery** (18), whose entrance is around the corner on St. Martin's Place. Not an art museum in the conventional sense, this is a collection of portraits—good and bad—of just about every famous British personality who ever lived, from kings to commoners, from ancient times to the present. A veritable lesson in British history, it contains not only paintings, drawings, and sculptures, but also photos and even cartoons. All of these are arranged chronologically, starting on the top floor, which can be reached by elevator. *Open Mon.–Sat. 10–6, Sun. noon–6. Free.* ☎ *(020) 7306-0055.* ♿.

Also facing Trafalgar Square is the celebrated **Church of St. Martin-in-the-Fields** (19), an elegant Classical structure of 1726 by the noted architect James Gibbs. It is perhaps most famous for its activities in social work, theater, and music. The world-renowned Academy of St. Martin-in-the-Fields Orchestra got its start here, and there are frequent concerts by other musical groups. The crypt contains a visitors' center and a restaurant, as well as the **London Brass Rubbing Centre**, where you can make your own souvenirs. *Open Mon.–Sat. 10–6, Sun. noon–6.* ☎ *(020) 7930-0089, Internet:: www.stmartin-in-the-fields.org.*

Chelsea, Kensington, Knightsbridge and Belgravia

Put on your most comfortable walking shoes for this delightful if somewhat lengthy tour through the charming neighborhoods of Chelsea, Kensington, Knightsbridge, and Belgravia. If you should happen to get tired along the way, you can always cut the distance by using either of the two suggested shortcuts without missing too many of the sights, or sacrificing much of the area's flavor.

Among the leading attractions along the route are the 17th-century Royal Hospital, the home of Thomas Carlyle, the fashionable King's Road, a visit to Kensington Palace (where some members of the Royal Family still live), the intriguing Science Museum, the engaging Victoria and Albert Museum, and a possibly bankrupting shopping spree at Harrods.

Most of the walk is within the confines of the Royal Borough of Kensington and Chelsea, one of the entities that make up Greater London. These two dissimilar areas were politically combined in 1965, and each still retains its own distinctive character. The village-like ambiance of Chelsea, quite pronounced in its southwestern reaches, results from its long association with artists and writers, although rising prices have replaced many of the creative types with trendy young stockbrokers. Kensington is largely residential, but it boasts a major shopping street, a wonderful park, and some of the very best museums in London. The Knightsbridge area is noted for its fine shopping, while adjacent Belgravia—actually a part of Westminster—fairly reeks of old money.

GETTING THERE:

The Sloane Square **Underground** Station, served by the Circle and District lines, is right at the beginning (and end) of the suggested walk. By **bus**, just take routes 11, 19, 22, 211, or 319 to Sloane Square, or come by **taxi**. The nearest **British Rail** station is Victoria, about three-quarters of a mile to the east.

PRACTICALITIES:

Most of the attractions are closed on major holidays and Sunday mornings. Carlyle's House is open from April through October, on Wednesdays through Sundays only. Fine weather will make this largely outdoor trip much more enjoyable. The **London Tourist Board** office in the forecourt of Victoria Station, ☎ (0839) 123-456 (toll call), is your best source of local information.

FOOD AND DRINK:

This fashionable area abounds in good restaurants and pubs, just a few of which are:

Bluebird (350 King's Rd., west of Old Church St.) Imaginative, eclectic cuisine in the most stylish of contemporary surroundings. Reserve. ☎ (020) 7559-1000. ££ and £££

Oriel (50 Sloane Sq.) A trendy brasserie featuring modern European dishes; tables with a view. ☎ (020) 7730- 2804. ££

Phoenicia (11 Abington Rd., just south of Kensington High St.) This highly refined Lebanese restaurant is a real find for civilized dining. ☎ (020) 7937-0120. ££

Bistrot 190 (190 Queen's Gate, just west of the Royal Albert Hall) Eclectic European cooking with a Mediterranean twist. ☎ (020) 7581-5666. ££

Henry J. Bean's (195 King's Rd., 4 blocks northwest of the Royal Hospital) America's *haute cuisine*—burgers, chili, ribs, salads and the like. ☎ (020) 7352-9255. £ and ££

Daquise (20 Thurloe St., 2 blocks southwest of the Victoria & Albert, near the South Kensington tube station) A long-time favorite for traditional Polish food. ☎ (020) 7589-6117. £ and ££

King's Head and Eight Bells (50 Cheyne Walk, near Carlyle's House) A popular riverside pub with good light meals. ☎ (020) 7352-1820. £

Chelsea Kitchen (98 King's Rd., Sloane Sq.) A terrific bargain in tasty home cooking, always crowded. ☎ (020) 7589-1330. £

King's Road Café (Habitat, 208 King's Rd., halfway between Old Church St. and Sloane Square) Contemporary Italian dishes at modest prices, in a fashionable furnishings store) ☎ (020) 7351-6645. £

New Cultural Revolution (305 King's Rd., near Old Church St.) Chinese noodles and dumplings; bright, cheap and cheerful. ☎ (020) 7352-9281. £

Ed's Easy Diner (362 King's Rd., west of Old Church St.) Huge burgers and other American comfort food. ☎ (020) 7352-1956. £

Texas Lone Star (154 Gloucester Rd., 5 blocks southwest of the Natural History Museum) A noisy, crowded, but happy venue for Tex-Mex dishes, ribs, burgers, and the like. ☎ (020) 7370-5625. £

SUGGESTED TOUR:
Numbers in parentheses correspond to numbers on the map.

Sloane Square (1) forms the most natural entrance into Chelsea. Its tree-lined center separates the Royal Court Theatre of 1870, noted for its controversial productions, from the handsome Peter Jones department store of the 1930s. The King's Road, now a stylish shopping street leading to the west, remained a private royal path for the king's journeys to Hampton Court until 1829.

Leave the square at its south end and follow Lower Sloane Street, making a right turn on Royal Hospital Road. The **Royal Hospital** (2) was designed by Sir Christopher Wren in 1682 for Charles II as a retirement home for aged and disabled soldiers. Its inspiration, both socially and architecturally, was the Invalides in Paris, founded in 1670 by Louis XIV. Some 420 pensioners live in the Royal Hospital, where they wear traditional old-style uniforms of scarlet in summer and blue in winter. One of these veterans will be happy to show you the **Chapel**, virtually unchanged since Wren's time, and the **Great Hall**, with its large mural of Charles II on horseback and captured American flags from the War of 1812. There is also a small museum of memorabilia near the eastern end of the hospital, open from October through March. Don't miss the lovely **Ranelagh Gardens** near the southeastern corner of the property. *Open Mon.–Sat. 10–noon and 2–4. Closed for special events. Free.* ☎ *(202) 7730-0161.* &.

Continue down the street to the **National Army Museum** (3), which might be of interest to you. Its modern displays trace the history of the British Army from the 15th century up to the present, and include weapons, uniforms, models, dioramas, audio-visual presentations, and even an art gallery. Don't miss the skeleton of Napoleon's horse, Florence Nightingale's jewelry, and a large section of the Berlin Wall. *Open daily 10–5:30. Closed Good Friday, May Day Bank Holiday, Dec. 24–26, Jan. 1. Free.* ☎ *(202) 7730-0717.* &.

Many famous people have lived in the neighborhood beyond this, including the American painters J.S. Sargent and J.M. Whistler, and the writers Oscar Wilde and Mark Twain. Be on the lookout for plaques identifying former residents, especially along Tite Street, just steps north of Royal Hospital Road.

The **Chelsea Physic Garden** (4) was founded in 1673 by the Worshipful Company of Apothecaries for the purpose of growing herbs and botanicals, and was the birthplace (so to speak) of several important species including the cotton seed first used in America, the tea grown in India, and the rubber used in Malaysia. *Open mid-April to mid-Oct., Wed. 2–5 and Sun. 2–6. Adults £4, children £2.* ☎ *(020) 7352-5646.* &.

Cheyne Walk is separated from the Chelsea Embankment along the Thames by lovely gardens. Near it is the fanciful **Albert Bridge** of 1873,

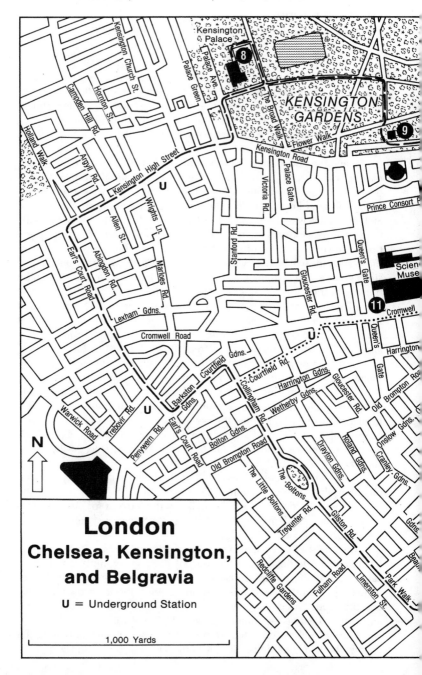

London
Chelsea, Kensington,
and Belgravia

U = Underground Station

1,000 Yards

whose strange suspension system and odd colors, along with the quaint notices requesting troops to break step, make it easily the most picturesque span on the river. Continue west to the **Chelsea Old Church** (5), which has been evolving since Norman times. It has a fine old set of chained books, the only examples of these curiosities in any London church. The 14th-century chapel was rebuilt by Sir Thomas More in 1528. More, the leader of the 16th-century Chelsea intellectuals, was Lord Chancellor of England until he opposed Henry VIII's divorce, after which he was beheaded.

Retrace your steps and turn north on Cheyne Row to **Carlyle's House** (6), where the Scottish historian and philosopher lived for 47 years until his death in 1881. It has been preserved almost exactly as he left it, with the Carlyle's own furniture, books, manuscripts, portraits, and memorabilia. One of the oldest private houses still standing in Chelsea, it also features a peaceful walled garden. *Open April–Oct., Wed.–Sun., 11–5. Adults £3.30, children 5-16 £1.65.* ☎ *(020) 7352-7087.*

Now follow the map to the **King's Road** (7), which remains nearly as fashionable as it was in the 1960s—a vital place lined with boutiques, restaurants, and especially with colorful pubs.

Beyond this, the sights get farther apart until you reach South Kensington, although the walk is quite pleasant. It is possible to take a **shortcut** there by turning right on Old Church Street and following the map to the museum complex, thus saving a few miles while missing only three attractions.

Those energetic souls going the longer distance should amble down the King's Road and turn right on Park Walk. Becoming Gilston Road, it leads past The Boltons, a wooded oval in the center of the street, lined with fine homes. Continue following the map through a prosperous area of mostly 19th-century town houses. Another **shortcut** can be made at Courtfield Road, leading past the Gloucester Road Underground Station to the museum area. Otherwise, stick to the route on the map, passing the Earl's Court Underground Station and Cromwell Road. This brings you into Kensington proper.

Kensington High Street is another main shopping district. Follow it as far as Palace Avenue and turn left to **Kensington Palace** (8), a royal residence ever since William III purchased it in 1689. Alterations and additions made by Sir Christopher Wren and Nicholas Hawksmoor have left the exterior largely as you see it today, although there were interior changes in the 18th century. In general, its unpretentious design reflects the simple tastes of Dutch-born William III, who with his wife and co-sovereign Queen Mary II moved here to escape the foul riverside air at Whitehall. Queen Victoria was born in this palace in 1819, but moved to Buckingham upon accession to the throne in 1837. Kensington Palace is still the London residence for several members of the Royal Family.

Most of the palace is private, but you can visit the **State Apartments** and the **Exhibition of Court Dress**. *Open May–Oct., daily 10–5. Adults £8.50,* *children £6.10.* ☎ *(020) 7937-9561, Internet: www.hrp.org.uk.*

Stroll through **Kensington Gardens**, once the private gardens of the palace and now a westward extension of Hyde Park. Lovely paths lead to the extravagant **Albert Memorial** (9), a neo-Gothic monstrosity that has to be seen to be believed. Epitomizing the sentimental tastes of the Victorian period, it is a monument to the memory of Queen Victoria's beloved consort, Prince Albert, who died in 1861. A careful examination of its ornate base will reveal many fascinating details.

The statue of the prince looks across the way to the huge **Royal Albert Hall** of 1871, a circular auditorium capable of holding 8,000 people. It is used for all kinds of events, and is especially noted for its concerts.

Continue down Exhibition Road and into the world-famous museum complex of South Kensington. On your right is the utterly fascinating ***Science Museum** (10), one of the best of its kind anywhere and a long-time favorite for children and adults alike. Anyone who loves steam engines, cars, airplanes, space exploration, computers, photography, or technology of any sort will go wild in this place, where you can watch myriad devices in action and push buttons to your heart's content. *Open daily 10–6. Closed Dec. 24–26. Adults £6.50, children £3.50. Free to all after 4:30.* ☎ *(020) 7938-8000, Internet: www.nmsi.ac.uk.* ♿.

Around the corner on Cromwell Road stands the immense **Natural History Museum** (11), an impressive neo-Romanesque edifice of 1880. Besides the dinosaurs, whales, birds, and examples of animal life you will find outstanding exhibitions of human biology, Man's place in evolution, and on the origin of species. Its geological section has magnificent gemstones, fossils, simulated earthquakes, and audio-visual exhibits. *Open Mon.–Sat. and Bank Holidays, 10–5:50, Sun. 11–5:50. Last admission at 5:30. Closed Dec. 23–26. Adults £6.50, seniors, disabled, students, children £3.50. Free to all after 4:30 on Mon.–Fri. and after 5 on weekends and holidays.* ☎ *(020) 7942-5000.* ♿.

Just across Exhibition Road stands the:

*VICTORIA AND ALBERT MUSEUM (12), ☎ (020) 7938-8500, Internet: www.vam.ac.uk. *Open daily 10–5:45. Closed Dec. 24–26. Adults £5, seniors £3, under 18 free. Restaurant. Gift shop. Mostly* ♿.

The Victoria and Albert Museum, known to generations of Londoners simply as the "V & A," has what is probably the world's greatest collection of the decorative and applied arts. It is also a lively and highly enjoyable place to visit, making it one of the most popular attractions in London. There is something here for everyone, regardless of their tastes and interests, whether these run to period room settings, Oriental art, medieval artifacts, tapestries, costumes, musical instruments, or whatever. The fine arts are not overlooked either, and are especially well represented by the Raphael cartoons and the ***Constable Collection**. You will most likely get lost in the four-storied labyrinth of rooms and passageways, but that's part of the fun. A full day could easily be spent just sampling the countless treasures, so you might want to plan on coming back later.

The route now leads down Brompton Road, a major shopping thoroughfare. Beauchamp Place, to the right, is noted for its exceptionally fine shops and boutiques. Just a bit beyond this is **Harrods** (13), one of the largest and most famous department stores in the world, where you can buy nearly anything your heart desires, or enjoy yourself by simply browsing around. Its **Food Hall**, lined with Art Nouveau tiling, is especially attractive, and there are several restaurants and places for afternoon tea throughout the store.

From here you can return to the start of the walk by following Sloane Street to Sloane Square (1), or use the nearby Knightsbridge Underground Station to get to wherever you're going. Those with energy to spare may want to take a short stroll through Belgravia, an elegant 19th-century residential area slightly to the east. Many of the finest homes, some now used as embassies, are on **Belgrave Square** (14). The route on the map will return you from here to Sloane Square.

The West End

You probably won't find the West End identified on any map of London, but the term usually refers to an area more or less centered on Piccadilly Circus, taking in portions of the City of Westminster along with the southeast corner of the Borough of Camden. However you define them, the neighborhoods covered by this walking tour include some of the most varied attractions in town, such as Piccadilly Circus, Covent Garden, Lincoln's Inn, the British Museum, Regent's Park, Madame Tussaud's, the Sherlock Holmes Museum, and the exquisite shops of Mayfair. Along the way, you will be treated to several of London's less famous but equally intriguing sights, including the fascinating Transport Museum, the delightful Theatre Museum, the strangely eccentric Sir John Soane's Museum, the magnificent Wallace Collection, Selfridges department store, the Burlington Arcade, and the Royal Academy of Arts.

The actual walking distance can be covered comfortably in under two hours, but be sure to allow plenty of time for museum visits, lunch, shopping, and perhaps a pub stop or two.

GETTING THERE:

The suggested walk starts and ends at the Piccadilly Circus **Underground** Station, served by the Piccadilly and Bakerloo lines. Alternatively, you can come by **bus** or by **taxi**. The nearest **British Rail** station is Charing Cross, about one-half mile to the southeast.

PRACTICALITIES:

This walk can be taken at any time in good weather, but note that the Theatre Museum is closed on Mondays, and Sir John Soane's Museum is closed on both Sundays and Mondays. Some of the other attractions are closed on a few major holidays, and also on Sunday mornings. The **Britain Visitor Centre** at 1 Regent Street, ☎ (020) 8846-9000, is just a few steps south of Piccadilly Circus. They can answer your questions on both London and the rest of Britain.

FOOD AND DRINK:

You'll pass hundreds of good restaurants and pubs along the route of this walking tour. Just a few of the better choices for lunch are:

Rules (35 Maiden Lane, Covent Garden) As traditional a British dining salon as you'll find; a favorite for nearly two centuries. Reserve, ☎ (020) 7836-5314. ££ and £££

Joe Allen's (13 Exeter St., Covent Garden) Contemporary American cuisine in a busy, fun place. Reserve, ☎ (020) 7836-0651. ££

Bertorelli's Café (44a Floral St., a block north of Covent Garden) Opera fans devour the traditional Italian cuisine in this modern basement café and wine bar, and also in the restaurant upstairs. ☎ (020) 7836-3969. X: Sun. ££

Museum St. Café (47 Museum St., a block south of the British Museum) A tiny restaurant renowned for its imaginative offerings; reservations are advised. ☎ (020) 7405-3211. X: evenings. ££

Belgo Centraal (50 Earlham St., 3 blocks northwest of Covent Garden tube station) Belgian specialties and beers (100 flavors!) served in a strange basement by waiters dressed as monks. Fun. ☎ (020) 7813-2233. £ and ££

Cranks (1 The Market, Covent Garden) A popular vegetarian chain restaurant. ☎ (020) 7379-6508. £

Food for Thought (31 Neal St., 3 blocks northwest of Covent Garden) An extremely popular vegetarian café with creative, healthy dishes. ☎ (020) 7836-9072. £

Maxwell's (8 James St., by the Royal Opera House, Covent Garden) America's favorite foods, from burgers to Cajun, right in the heart of London. ☎ (020) 7836-0303. £

The Fountain (in Fortnum & Mason's store at 181 Piccadilly) Refined light meals, sandwiches, salads, etc. in a world-renowned temple of gastronomy. ☎ (020)7 734-4938. X: Sun. £

SUGGESTED TOUR:

Numbers in parentheses correspond to numbers on the map.

Piccadilly Circus (1) isn't much to look at in the morning, so it is best to save its attractions for later in the day, when you'll be returning. Near its center stands a famous statue that is supposed to represent the Angel of Christian Charity, but is commonly known as **Eros**. Cast in aluminum in 1893 as a memorial to the Victorian philanthropist Lord Shaftesbury, its design was so severely criticized that the artist fled the country. Since then, however, the public has taken the figure to its heart, and Piccadilly Circus just wouldn't be the same without it.

A short amble down Coventry Street leads to **Leicester Square** (2), an entertainment center since the 18th century. Pronounced as *LES-ter*, this small spot of urban greenery is surrounded by theaters and restaurants. In its center is a statue of Shakespeare, and in the southwest corner is a more recent one of Charlie Chaplin. The **Half Price Ticket Booth** sells bargain tickets for same-day performances at West End theaters, but don't expect to find really big hits there. It is open on Mondays through Saturdays, from noon–2 for matinees and 2:30–6:30 for evening shows.

Now follow the map to **Covent Garden** (3), a large open Italian-style piazza developed by the famed architect Inigo Jones in the 17th century on the site of a medieval vegetable garden belonging to a convent. The area's association with food was continued by the construction in 1830 of a huge **Central Market Building**, which served as London's main wholesale fruit and vegetable market until 1974, when its function was transferred south of the river. A battle then raged between developers and preservationists, with the end result being that this historic district was saved and the market buildings converted into shops and restaurants.

St. Paul's Church, on the west side of the piazza, was built in 1633 by Inigo Jones as the "handsomest barn in Europe." Well known as an actors' church, it gained fame as the setting for the opening scene in Bernard Shaw's *Pygmalion* and the ensuing musical, *My Fair Lady.*

The 19th-century Flower Market Hall, in the southeast corner of the piazza, now houses two exceptionally interesting museums. The largest of these is the **London Transport Museum** (4), where a superb collection of old trams, buses, and Underground trains (including steam engines!) are exhibited along with displays celebrating nearly two centuries of public transportation in London. You can sit in the darkened cab of an Underground train and actually "drive" it, an unusual experience complete with simulated sights through the windows, sounds, and vibrations. A treat for children and adults alike! *Open Sat.–Thurs., 10–6, Fri. 11–6. Last admission at 5:15. Adults £4.95, seniors, students, children 5-15 £2.95, under 5 free. Café. Gift shop.* ☎ *(020) 7565-7299, Internet: www.Ltmuseum.co.uk.* &.

Adjacent to it is the **Theatre Museum**, whose collections of theatrical memorabilia are displayed amid preserved sections of old theaters. There is also a small auditorium for special events and an atmospheric cafeteria in this outpost of the Victoria and Albert Museum. *Open Tues.–Sun. 10–6, last admission at 5:30. Adults £4.50, seniors and students £2.50, under 16 free.* ☎ *(020) 7836-7891, Internet: www.vam.ac.uk.* &.

Leave the square on Russell Street, crossing Bow Street, where the famous Bow Street Runners—precursor of today's Metropolitan Police—began capturing muggers in the mid-18th century. This was once one of the worst slums in London. Just to the north stands the imposing portico of the **Royal Opera House**, which was built in 1860 and is now being extended towards the Covent Garden piazza.

Continue straight ahead past the **Theatre Royal**, Drury Lane, dating from 1812 and said to be haunted. Previous theaters have stood on this site since 1663, the first being where Charles II met his mistress, the actress Nell Gwynn. Kemble Street leads across busy, divided Kingsway, which requires a slight detour to the north. Near the southwest corner of **Lincoln's Inn Fields**, on Portsmouth Street, is the 16th-century half-timbered **Old Curiosity Shop**, possibly the oldest shop in London.

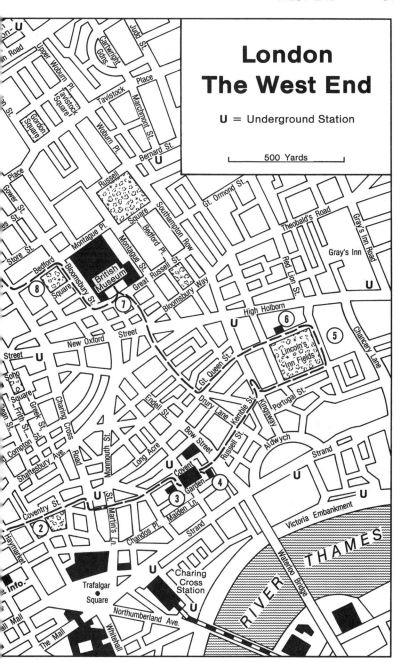

London
The West End

U = Underground Station

500 Yards

Lincoln's Inn (5) is one of the four great Inns of Court that have the right of admitting people to practice as barristers. Two of these, the Middle and Inner Temples, are described on page 27, while the other, Gray's Inn, is two blocks to the north. Lincoln's Inn, with its 15th- to 17th-century buildings, is the best preserved. Its grounds and chapel may usually be visited by asking at the porter's lodge.

On the north side of Lincoln's Inn Fields, at Number 13, is one of the most eccentric interior spaces in London. Although it is fairly well known, too many visitors completely overlook *Sir John Soane's Museum (6) and never realize what they have missed. A classical architect of great distinction, Soane arranged the interiors of these three adjoining houses as his personal residence and as a setting for his private collection of art and antiquities. When he died in 1837 he left them to the nation with the stipulation that nothing could ever be changed. Ever. The small rooms and basement are fairly crammed with fascinating treasures displayed in a unique manner, with mirrors creating the illusion of space. Be sure to see the wonderful series of *paintings by Hogarth, The Rake's Progress and The Election; as well as the alabaster **sarcophagus of Seti I**, an Egyptian pharaoh who died in 1290 BC. *Open Tues.–Sat. 10–5. Free.* ☎ *(020) 7405-2107.*

Now follow the map to the:

*BRITISH MUSEUM (7), Great Russell Street, ☎ (020) 7636-1555, Internet: www.british-museum.ac.uk. *Open Mon.–Sat., 10–5, Sun. 12–6. Free, but £2 donation requested. Possible charge for temporary exhibitions. Restaurant. Shops.* ♿.

The British Museum is arguably the greatest institution of its type on Earth and a not-to-be-missed attraction for all visitors to London. Only an empire the size and scope of Britain's could possibly have amassed such an unparalleled collection of treasures. At least an entire day is needed to merely sample them, but even the most time-pressed tourist can enjoy a cursory look at a few of the highlights in an hour or so.

Pick up a museum plan leaflet at the entrance and make your way to Room 8, where the renowned *Elgin Marbles, the 5th-century-BC sculptures rescued from the Parthenon in Athens in 1803, are displayed. While on the ground floor of the west wing, you should not miss the *Rosetta Stone in Room 25. Discovered by the French near the mouth of the Nile in 1799, this inscribed stone from the 2nd century BC bears the same message in hieroglyphs, later Egyptian characters, and Greek; thus providing the key to understanding ancient Egyptian writing.

Among the most important sights on the upper floor are the **Egyptian mummies** in rooms 60 and 61, some of which are rather macabre. Continue around to the east wing, where the **Mildenhall Treasure** of decorated Romano-British tableware from the 4th century is exhibited in Room 40. Next to this, in Room 41, is the fabulous **Sutton Hoo Treasure**, a 7th-century burial ship of an East Anglican king, whose rich contents shed new light on the "Dark Ages." You may also be interested in the antique **clocks and watches** displayed in nearby Room 44.

This quick tour has covered only a few of the greatest treasures in the museum, so you might want to come back on another day when you can devote more time to it. Happily, there is an excellent cafeteria in the west wing.

Leave the museum and follow Bloomsbury Street to the very lovely—and also very private—**Bedford Square** (8). Except for the traffic, this has hardly changed since it was first laid out in 1775. Take a look at the fine houses bordering it, once residential but now mostly the offices of architects and publishers. You are standing in the very heart of **Bloomsbury**, a neighborhood that was famous (or infamous) in the early 1900s for the many intellectuals and artists who lived there, including Virginia Woolf, Lytton Strachey, John Maynard Keynes, E.M. Forster, T.S. Eliot, Bertrand Russell, and D.H. Lawrence. Today, much of the area is occupied by the ever-growing **University of London**, and by numerous small hotels catering to tourists.

The route leads up Tottenham Court Road and turns left on Goodge Street. Follow Charlotte Street, noted for its restaurants, north past the imposing but functionally-designed **British Telecom Tower**, a major London landmark since 1964. Reaching a height of 619 feet, it was then the tallest structure in town and was designed solely for TV and telecommunications use. Fitzroy Square, just beyond this, still displays a certain elegance.

At this point, fans of Masterpiece Theatre and all those other wonderful BBC television productions might be enthralled by a visit to the nearby:

BBC EXPERIENCE (9), Broadcasting House, Portland Place, ☎ (0870) 603-0304, Internet: www.bbc.co.uk/experience. *Advance bookings strongly urged. Admission is by tickets timed to specific tours. Open Mon. 1–4:30, Tues.–Fri. 9:30–4:30, Sat.–Sun. 9:30–4:30. Last tour at 4:30 on weekdays, 3:30 on weekends. Times may vary. Adults £6.95, seniors £5.95, students and children £4.95. Café. Gift shop.* ♿.

The entire history of broadcasting—radio, television, and now the Internet—from the earliest days right up to the present, is brought to life in this combination museum and theatrical "experience." Not only are there things to see, but to do as well. Visitors can try their hand at announcing, or even editing a popular TV show.

A left turn on busy Euston Road takes you past the south entrance of **Regent's Park** (10), an excellent spot for a rest. Once a royal hunting preserve, it started to become a luxurious residential estate after 1811, but the plan was never fully developed and most of it is today a public park. **Queen Mary's Gardens**, near the southern end, is an exceptionally attractive place and well worth a visit. If you have enough time, or perhaps on another day, you might want to stroll less than a mile north on Broad Walk to the **London Zoo**.

Continue west on Marylebone Road to one of London's most popular—and crowded—commercial tourist attractions, **Madame Tussaud's** (11). This world-famous waxworks museum had its origins in pre-Revolutionary France, where Madame's uncle first opened his establishment in Paris in 1770. She learned her trade there, and during the Terror was obliged to make death marks of the guillotine's victims. Escaping to England in 1802, she traveled the country with her creations until settling down on Baker Street in 1835. In 1850, Madame died at the age of 89. Her grandsons built the present museum, which has been entertaining folks since 1884. The exhibition is continually changing to keep up with who's in the news, and also includes a section of historical personalities, all modeled in wax and set in appropriate surroundings. The popular **Chamber of Horrors** features blood-chilling scenes enlivened with realistic instruments of torture and execution, and you can take a ride through an animated history of London. *Open daily 9–5:30. Adults £10, children £6.50. A joint ticket that includes the adjacent **Planetarium** is available. Advance credit-card bookings may be made by phone, which avoids the usually long wait in line.* ☎ *(020) 7935-6861.*

Turn right on Baker Street to the engaging **Sherlock Holmes Museum** (12). Okay, so this isn't really at Number 221b despite what its sign says, and maybe Holmes never really existed, but it's still a jolly good show that his many fans will love. Faithfully re-created from Dr. Watson's descriptions, and located upstairs in an authentic period lodging house that would have made Mrs. Hudson proud, the museum celebrates the "life" of the great detective in the most meticulous detail. *Open daily except Christmas Day, 9:30–6. Adults £5, children £3.* ☎ *(020) 7935-8866, Internet: www.sherlock-holmes.co.uk.*

Stroll south on Baker Street. A left turn on Fitzhardinge Street, opposite Portman Square, leads to the somewhat secluded Manchester Square and the fabulous *****Wallace Collection** (13). Installed in the 18th-century Hertford House, this is possibly the greatest private art collection ever bequeathed to a nation. It is extraordinarily rich in French paintings of the 18th century, especially in works by Watteau, Boucher, and Fragonard. French artists from other centuries are also well represented, including Claude Lorrain, Poussin, and Delacroix. Among the Dutch and Flemish paintings are those by Rembrandt, Rubens, Frans Hals, and Van Dyck. The Italians include Titian, Guardi, and Canaletto; while there are also works by Reynolds, Gainsborough, and Velazquez. All of these are magnificently displayed in elegant surroundings filled with 18th-century French furniture and various art objects. If you love art from this era, you will love the

Wallace Collection. *Open Mon.–Sat. 10–5, Sun. 2–5. Free.* ☎ *(020) 7935-0687.*

Now follow the map to Oxford Street, one of the main shopping areas of London. A right turn brings you to **Selfridges**, a massive department store in the American style that opened in 1909. An enormously wide range of goods is offered here at prices that are generally below those of Harrods.

The route continues down Duke Street into what is practically American territory. **Grosvenor Square** (14), a pleasant park surrounded by offices of various U.S. government agencies, is totally dominated on its west side by the American Embassy, surmounted by a giant aluminum eagle. The square's association with the U.S.A. began as early as 1785, when John Adams, then ambassador and later president, moved into the house at Number 9. It was continued during World War II by General Eisenhower, whose headquarters were at Number 20. The statue of Franklin D. Roosevelt, near the center of the park, was paid for by small donations from ordinary British citizens in 1948.

Leave the square via Grosvenor Street and turn right onto **Bond Street**, here called New Bond Street. Its lower portion is known as Old Bond Street. Together, they constitute one of the most exclusive luxury shopping areas in the world. Check your bank balance before heading south past its elegant displays—you never know when temptation may strike!

The **Burlington Arcade** (15), a long covered passageway built in 1819, is lined with exquisite little shops of the highest quality. It is patrolled by uniformed beadles, who preserve a gracious atmosphere and lock it up at night and on Sundays. A stroll through this Regency gem brings you out on Piccadilly—the street, not the circus.

Just east of the arcade is the impressive façade of Burlington House, first built in the 17th century and remodeled several times since. It is home to the **Royal Academy of Arts** (16), founded in 1768 to promote British art. The painter Sir Joshua Reynolds was its first president. Changing exhibitions are on view here daily, and you might be able to see some of its interesting permanent collection as well. *Open Sun.–Thurs. 9–6, Fri.–Sat. 9 a.m.–10 p.m. Admission price varies according to current shows, usually averaging £6–8 for adults, less for children.* ☎ *(020) 7300-8000.*

Walk up Piccadilly, passing the famous, fashionable, and very luxurious **Fortnum and Mason** department store, founded in 1705. Its food department is world renowned, and this is one of the best places in London to enjoy an afternoon tea. The store's entrance is crowned by a mechanical clock on which figures of Mr. Fortnum and Mr. Mason greet each other on the hour.

In just a few more steps you will be back at **Piccadilly Circus** (1), where this walk began. One of its attractions, the **Pepsi Trocadero**, offers a variety of commercial entertainments including Segaworld and an IMAX theater. Nearby is Madame Tussaud's **Rock Circus**, telling the story of rock music with both wax and animated figures. Have fun!

**Trip 5
London**

Southwark and Lambeth

U ntil recent years there was precious little reason for tourists to venture south of the Thames. Oh, there was always Waterloo Station, the South Bank Arts Centre, and the Imperial War Museum, but these alone hardly provide the makings for a worthwhile daytrip. There was also the Dickensian atmosphere of decaying 19th-century wharfs and warehouses, noisome railway viaducts, and enough general gloom to make Jack the Ripper feel right at home.

Historically this area, once outside the jurisdiction of the City, was a neighborhood of cheap inns, bawdy taverns, theaters and other disreputable entertainments, brothels, and prisons. Today, much of its raw ambiance is being preserved as a tourist attraction, many of its industrial buildings skillfully converted to modern use, and the riverside itself opened for glorious promenades with a view.

This walking tour begins by exploring the innards of what may be London's most recognizable sight, the Tower Bridge, then crosses the Thames to wander around the restored areas of Butler's Wharf. Here you'll find the modern Design Museum along with the rather specialized Bramah Tea & Coffee Museum. Heading upriver brings you to H.M.S. *Belfast*, a retired Royal Navy cruiser that can be explored from stem to stern. In dank vaults beneath rumbling railway lines lurk the Britain at War exhibition and the gruesome London Dungeon experience. St. Thomas's Operating Theatre chills the spine even further before you find yourself in more congenial surroundings at Southwark Cathedral. The Shakespeare's Globe Exhibition brings back the days when this was London's theater district, with a reconstruction of the original Globe Theatre now a reality. From here a lovely walk along the river's edge steers you to the South Bank Arts Centre with its cultural attractions. Beyond this you pass opposite the Houses of Parliament to the Museum of Garden History before turning inland to the exciting Imperial War Museum where you can step into the virtual reality of combat.

You might want to consider making this a two-day trip, especially if you visit more than a few of the sights.

GETTING THERE:

By **Underground**, take the Circle or District line to Tower Hill, then walk around the Tower of London to Tower Bridge.

By **bus**, take routes 15 or 25 to Tower Hill, and stroll south to Tower Bridge. By **taxi**, ask for Tower Bridge.

The nearest **British Rail** station to the beginning of this trip is London Bridge. The end is fairly close to Waterloo Station.

PRACTICALITIES:

Nearly all of the attractions along this route are open daily, except around Christmas and New Year's Day. For further information contact the **London Tourist Board** at Victoria Station, ☎ (0839) 123-456 (toll call), or the **Britain Visitor Centre** at 12 Regent Street, between Trafalgar Square and Piccadilly Circus, ☎ (020) 8846-9000. You might also try the **Southwark Tourist Information Centre** on the lower level of Hay's Galleria, Tooley Street, ☎ (020) 7403-8299.

FOOD AND DRINK:

There are plenty of smart new establishments in this rapidly developing area. Among the better choices for lunch are:

Blueprint Café (in the Design Museum, top floor) Contemporary cuisine, with a view. ☎ (020) 7378-7031. X: Sun. eve. £££

OXO Tower Brasserie (OXO Tower Wharf, between Blackfriars and Waterloo bridges) Trendy dining with fabulous river views. ☎ (020) 7803-3888. £££

Le Pont de la Tour (36d Shad Thames, Butler's Wharf, just east of Tower Bridge) Light dishes at the bar, full meals in the dining room, all overlooking the Thames. ☎ (020) 7403-8403. ££ and £££

The Apprentice (31 Shad Thames, near the Design Museum) New chefs practice their skills here before moving out into the culinary world. The result: Interesting modern dishes at moderate prices. ☎ (020) 7234-0254. ££

RSJ Brasserie (13a Coin St., 2 blocks southeast of the Royal National Theatre) A good value in creative modern cuisine, served in cheerful surroundings. ☎ (020) 7928-4554. X: Sat. lunch, Sun. ££

The Fire Station (150 Waterloo Rd., near Waterloo Station) Quality dining at modest prices. ☎ (020) 7401-3267. £ and ££

Film Café (in the National Film Theatre, South Bank Arts Centre) A self-service café with interesting fare and outdoor riverside seating. ☎ (020) 7928-3535. £

SUGGESTED TOUR:

Numbers in parentheses correspond to numbers on the map.

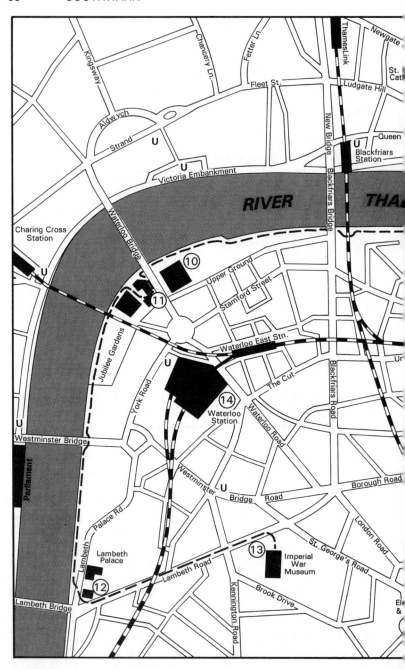

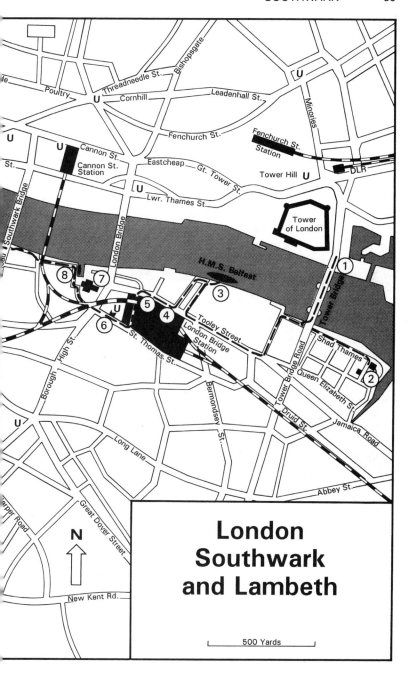

London
Southwark
and Lambeth

N

500 Yards

One of the most instantly spotted landmarks in town, *Tower Bridge (1) spans the Thames next to the Tower of London (see page 33) and forms a perfect entrance into the neighborhoods south of the river. This bascule-type drawbridge, with its tall Gothic Revival towers and elevated walkway, was built around the end of the 19th century as the most easterly crossing over the Thames. At one time it was raised quite frequently, but since large ships seldom sail this far up the river anymore, it is now operated only about five times a week.

The familiar overhead walkway, closed to the public since 1909 after it became too popular a spot for suicides and prostitutes, has now been enclosed in glass and reopened as part of the **Tower Bridge Experience**, an exhibition of the bridge and its times. The panoramic *views from it, especially of the Tower of London, are stunning. Purchase your ticket at the north tower, then ascend by lift to the walkway for a guided tour of the bridge's history, complete with animated "workers" and ghosts. As a special treat, the original Victorian steam engines that operated the bascules until 1975—when they were replaced by electric motors—have been preserved and are now part of the interesting **Engine Room** at the south end of the bridge. *Open April–Oct., daily 10–6:30; Nov.–March daily 9:30–6. Closed Dec. 24–25. Last entry 90 minutes before closing. Adults £6.15, seniors, students and children 5–15 £4.15.* ☎ *(020) 7378-1928, Internet: www.towerbridge.org.uk.*

Of course, you can just walk across the bridge free at street level, but then you'll miss the show. However you get over, descend the steps on the southwest side and cross under the south bridge approach to **Shad Thames**. This narrow alleyway tunnels its way between Victorian warehouses that are now converted to contemporary use and are still linked by overhead passages. At its end is **Butler's Wharf**, from which you'll get great views, and the white Bauhaus box of the **Design Museum** (2). Founded in 1989 by Sir Terence Conran of furniture and culinary fame, the museum celebrates good design in mass-produced items of everyday life. Not just innovative or classic design, but wonderfully-inspired kitsch as well, along with changing exhibitions of unusual concepts. *Open daily, 11:30–6. Closed Dec. 25–26. Adults £5.50, seniors, students, children 5–18 £4.* ☎ *(020) 7403-6933.* ♿.

Just steps away is the **Bramah Tea & Coffee Museum**, which tells the story of London's great trade in these marvelous beverages.

Now follow the map to *H.M.S. *Belfast* (3), a retired Royal Navy cruiser permanently moored in the Thames as an extension of the Imperial War Museum. Built in 1938, she saw action with the Arctic convoys, the D-Day landings, and in the Korean War. You can have loads of fun climbing all over her, from the depths of the engine room to the dizzying heights of the bridge, but be aware that some of the passageways and ladders are a bit cramped. Don't miss this special treat! *Open in summer, daily 10–6; in winter, daily 10–5. Last admission 45 minutes before closing. Adults £4.70, seniors and students £3.60, half-price for disabled. Café. Shop.* ☎ *(020)*

7940-6300, Internet: www.iwm.org.uk. Limited &.

Stroll through **Hay's Galleria**, a stunning shopping mall created out of 19th-century warehouses, and cross Tooley Street. Here, in the dark archways beneath London Bridge Station is the **Britain at War Museum** (4), where you can relive some of the experiences of the British homefront during World War II, including the terror of the Blitz. *This bit of re-created reality is open daily from 10–5:30, closing at 4:30 in winter.*

Prepare for a gory adventure at the next stop, the infamous **London Dungeon* (5). Secreted away in cavernous vaults beneath rumbling railway lines, a spine-chilling world of the deliciously macabre awaits its victims. Enter the milieu of Jack the Ripper! Wander through the Theatre of the Guillotine! Travel through the Traitors' Gate on a water ride to hell! Lots of gruesome fun for all but the most squeamish, and a favorite for children of all ages. You have been warned. *Open April–Sept., daily 10–6, remaining open until 9 on Mon.–Wed. in summer; Oct.–March, daily 10:30–5:30. Closed Dec. 25. Adults £9.50, students £7.95, seniors, disabled, and children 0–14 £6.50. Café. Gift shop.* ☎ *(0891) 600-0666.* &.

Joiner Street leads under the old railway station to St. Thomas Street, where you turn right. If you're up to another, more subtle, kind of horror, you might want to visit **St. Thomas's Operating Theatre** (6). Restored to its original condition of 1821, this early surgical operating room will make you even more thankful for modern medical advances. *Open Tues.–Sun. 10–4, also some Mon. Closed mid-Dec.–early Jan. Adults £2.90, seniors and students £2, children £1.50.* ☎ *(020) 7955-4791.*

Continue across the approach to London Bridge and into the grounds of **Southwark Cathedral** (7). Begun in the 13th century as a parish church, it fell on bad times after the Reformation and was not restored until the 1890s. In 1905 it became the seat of a bishop, and thus London's second Anglican cathedral. Rivaling Westminster Abbey as the finest Gothic building in London, the cathedral has an attractive interior filled with the accumulation of centuries. Of particular interest are the tombs of the 14th-century poet John Gower, a 17th-century medical quack named Lockyer, and Shakespeare's brother Edmund. The **Harvard Chapel** is dedicated to John Harvard, who was baptized here in 1607 and later emigrated to America, where he left a fortune to the famous university that bears his name. *Open daily 9–6, no tours during services. Suggested donation £2.50.* ☎ *(020) 7367-6722.* &.

Just around the corner from the cathedral, at St. Mary Overie Dock, is a berthed replica of the galleon *Golden Hinde* (8), the original of which carried Sir Francis Drake around the world in the 16th century—the first circumnavigation of the globe by an Englishman. This reconstruction has also done its round-the-world tour, taking 23 years instead of Drake's three. Today it's a tourist attraction, complete with costumed pirates. *Open daily, 10–4. Adults £2.30, seniors £1.90, children £1.50* ☎ *(020) 7403-0123.*

If the name of Clink Street conjures up thoughts of incarceration, it is because this was the location of a notorious prison called the Clink. Owned by the bishops of Winchester, the jail once held errant priests, heretics, prostitutes, and other baddies until it was destroyed by fire in 1780. Much of the atmosphere still lingers, and you can sample more at the **Clink Prison Museum** in an old warehouse on the site of the lockup. Rather commercialized, and more than a little lurid, it features a history of local prostitution along with the torture devices. *Open June–Sept., Mon.–Fri. 10–6, Sat.–Sun. 10–9; Oct.–May daily 10–6. Adults £4, seniors, students and children £3.* ☎ *(020) 7403-6515.*

Besides being London's red-light district, the neighborhood was also its entertainment quarter. In those days there was little difference, what with such spectacles as bear-baiting attracting crowds until the Puritans put an end to the fun in 1642. Shakespeare was part owner of the ***Globe Theatre** on Bankside, which has recently been re-created using the same materials, techniques, and craftsmanship as in his time. This is a nearly exact replica of the original theater, complete with thatched roof and partially open to the skies for natural light (and rain). Short of attending a performance—a must for Shakespeare fans—you can see it all by visiting ***Shakespeare's Globe Exhibition** (9), an adjacent museum that includes a tour of the Globe. *Open May–Sept. (Theatre Season), daily 9–12:15; Oct.–April daily 10–5. Closed Dec. 24–25. Advance reservations needed, especially during May–Sept. Adults £6, seniors £5, children £4.* ☎ *(020) 7902-1500, Internet: www.shakespeares- globe.org/exhibition.*

You are now directly across the Thames from St. Paul's Cathedral (see page 30). Continue along the delightful Riverside Walk, taking in glorious views and passing the amusing **OXO Tower** of 1928, an Art Deco masterpiece that has recently been reincarnated as artists' lofts, galleries, boutiques, performance spaces, restaurants, and even housing.

Continue on to the **South Bank Arts Centre** (10). This massive complex of brutal concrete was begun in 1951 and has gradually evolved in the years since, becoming more attractive as it aged. The **Royal Festival Hall**, the **National Theatre**, the **Queen Elizabeth Hall**, and the **National Film Theatre** exist, of course, for their performances; but there are some attractions here that you might want to see right now. Unfortunately, the wonderful Museum of the Moving Image is closed for reconstruction until 2003, but nearby is the **Hayward Gallery** (11), featuring temporary exhibitions of British and foreign art. If you'd rather just sit down and rest, there's an attractive cafeteria with outdoor tables overlooking the river, next to the National Theatre.

Press on past the Jubilee Gardens and Westminster Bridge, pausing for a splendid view of the Houses of Parliament across the water. Just beyond St. Thomas's Hospital, on the left, is the **Lambeth Palace**, the London residence of the Archbishop of Canterbury since the 13th century. It is seldom open to the public, but you can admire the lovely exterior. Next to this is the **Museum of Garden History** (12), beautifully housed in and around the deconsecrated 14th-century Church of St. Mary Lambeth.

Horticulturists, especially, will be attracted to its authentic 17th-century knot garden. ☎ *(020) 7261-1891.*

For many, the highlight of this walking tour will be a visit to the:

*IMPERIAL WAR MUSEUM (13), Lambeth Road, ☎ (020) 7416-5320, Internet: www.iwm.org.uk. *Open daily 10–6. Adults £5.20, seniors and students £4.20, disabled £2.60, children under 16 free. Free to all after 4:30. Gift shops.* ♿.

Ironically, the Imperial War Museum is housed in the former Bedlam Insane Asylum on Lambeth Road. More than just a collection of weaponry, this formidable institution has gone into "experiences" in a big way. Here you can climb through the trenches of World War I as "shells" burst around you, and descend into the horrors of the Blitz—led through dark, collapsing tunnels by a warden. The Secret War display covers espionage and undercover operations, while Conflicts Since 1945 spans history from the Korean Conflict right up to Bosnia. In addition to such weapons as a Battle of Britain Spitfire, a V2 rocket, a Nazi submarine, and a Polaris missile, there is a spectacular collection of war art.

The nearest Underground stations are at Lambeth North (on the Bakerloo line) and Elephant & Castle (on the Bakerloo and Northern lines). British Rail's huge **Waterloo Station** (14), terminus of the Channel Tunnel service to France, is also nearby.

Trip 6
London

Docklands

To wander through London's newest neighborhood is to experience what may well be the future of cities around the globe. At least it's a possibility. For this is one urban area that appears to be really user-friendly, with plenty of amenities and colorful links with the past scattered among its gleaming high-rise, high-tech structures.

Once among the Earth's largest and most thriving ports, Docklands suffered terrible devastation during World War II. What the Luftwaffe didn't destroy was soon done in by modern technology. Container ships, those behemoths of the sea with their deep draft and wide berth, made the old docks obsolete, and shipping moved downriver to Tilbury.

By the late 1970s the unused docks were a sea of desolation, with mile after mile of abandoned buildings. Proximity to the crowded City of London's expanding trade, however, brought hope. In 1981 the London Docklands Development Corporation was formed to direct the largest urban renewal project in Europe. A lot has been accomplished so far, but problems remain. Chronically behind schedule, much of the promise has yet to materialize, and some of the projects brought only bankruptcy. Many Londoners still consider Docklands to be out in the boondocks, situated far from the joys of the city, and littered with questionable architecture. Yet, considering the rot that was there and the economic realities of a City that had nowhere to expand, this seems a workable solution to making London into Europe's great financial center.

Along the walking route you'll enjoy marvelous views of old Greenwich, amble through an actual farm, explore a stunning world of office towers and docks, wander the back alleys of mysterious Limehouse, stroll along the Thames to the world's first underwater tunnel, then follow a watery path to the urbane pleasures of St. Katherine Docks. And perhaps stop along the way at an historic pub.

GETTING THERE:
The **Docklands Light Railway** (DLR) provides the easiest access to all areas along the way. It connects with the London Underground at Bank station (Northern, Central, and Waterloo & City lines; also via a short tunnel from Monument station on the Circle and District lines), and at Tower Gateway (a short walk from Tower Hill station on the Circle and District

lines). London Underground tickets and passes are valid as long as they cover the correct zones. Service is very frequent on these modern, completely automated trains. Take the DLR to the Island Gardens stop, where this walk begins. For information ☎ (020) 7918-4000, Internet: www.dlr.co.uk.

The Jubilee Line of the **Underground** has just been extended from Green Park via Westminster, Waterloo, and London Bridge to Canary Wharf in Docklands, and beyond.

Boats depart London's Westminster and other piers for Greenwich, where you take the pedestrian tunnel under the Thames to Island Gardens. See page 79 for details.

PRACTICALITIES:

Being a business center, Docklands is alive on Mondays through Fridays, and nearly locks up on weekends.

Although the suggested route is almost seven miles long, nearly all of it is paralleled by the Docklands Light Railway (DLR), which can be used to greatly reduce the walking distance. Since you'll probably be hopping on and off the DLR several times, and also using the Underground, you should begin the day by purchasing a Travelcard (see page 22) for the appropriate zones. This will save both time and money.

For current information, contact the **Canary Wharf Tourist Information Centre** in the Canary Wharf DLR station, ☎ (020) 7512-9800.

FOOD AND DRINK:

There are plenty of restaurants and pubs in this rapidly developing area, but few have been around long enough to acquire reputations. Fortunately, several historic riverside pubs from the old days survive, offering good food and drink with a view.

The Hothouse (78 Wapping Ln., near Tobacco Dock) Modern English and Mediterranean cuisine, in a converted warehouse. ☎ (020) 7488-4797. ££ and £££

The Grapes (76 Narrow St., on the Thames, east of Limehouse Basin) An historic Victorian pub downstairs, a good fish restaurant above, both overlooking the Thames. Real ale. ☎ (020) 7987-4396. £ and ££

Prospect of Whitby (57 Wapping Wall, on the Thames by Shadwell Basin) This very popular, historic restaurant and pub has been around since 1520. A London landmark. ☎ (020) 7481-1095. £ and ££

Dickens Inn (St. Katherine Docks) A pub and restaurant in an 18th-century warehouse, with indoor and outdoor tables overlooking the marina. Traditional English food and real ale. ☎ (020) 7488-2208. £ and ££

Seattle Coffee Company (365 Cabot Pl. East, Canary Wharf) Owned by Starbucks and soon to acquire that name, features light meals, snacks, and coffee. ☎ (020) 7363-0040. £

You might also consider taking the pedestrian tunnel (or riding the DLR) from Island Gardens to **Greenwich**, which has many places for lunch (see page 80).

SUGGESTED TOUR:

Numbers in parentheses correspond to numbers on the map. NOTE: By the time you read this, the new section of the DLR going under the Thames to Greenwich and Lewisham should be operational. Otherwise, expect the Island Gardens and Mudchute stations to be closed and replaced by bus service, as those stations are moved from elevated tracks to underground. Similarly, the Jubilee Line of the Underground should be operational to Canary Wharf, North Greenwich, and Stratford.

Begin at the **Island Gardens Station** (1) of the Docklands Light Railway, now extending south under the Thames to Greenwich and beyond, connecting with British Rail. This entire area, enclosed by a loop in the River Thames, is known as the **Isle of Dogs** after the animals that Henry VIII kept here when he lived across the river. Stroll over to the adjacent waterside park, which has gorgeous *views of the Royal Naval College in Greenwich. A curious domed structure near the water's edge is actually the entrance to the **Greenwich Foot Tunnel**, opened in 1902 and reached via lifts at either end. Since it'll only take a few minutes, you might want to amble over for a quick look at Greenwich, described in the next chapter.

Turning north, you can either walk or take the DLR to the strange and completely unexpected **Mudchute Farm** (2). A farm in London? In the very shadow of skyscrapers? Yes, indeed. This bit of rural bliss grew out of the allotment gardens of World War I, established atop the river dredgings pumped there when the Millwall Docks were first created in the 19th century. Today, visitors can wander among the sheep, cattle, pigs, and other animals, and in the adjacent public park, always enjoying great panoramic views. Just follow the path in from East Ferry Road; there's no entrance fee.

Continue north on foot or by DLR to **Crossharbour** (3). Across the street stands the gleaming **London Arena**, a sports and convention center of 1989 that's huge enough for indoor soccer matches. Stroll behind it for a good view of **Millwall Docks**, now lined with an appealing mix of the old and the new.

Docklands' most notable project to date is undoubtedly ***Canary Wharf** (4), scenically reached by following the route shown on the map, or more easily by riding the DLR. Its main building, completed in 1991 and at 800 feet the tallest in Britain, is the Tower at One Canada Square. As the jewel in the crown of England's "Wall Street-upon-Thames," this is a magnificent structure, surrounded by architecturally impressive neighbors.

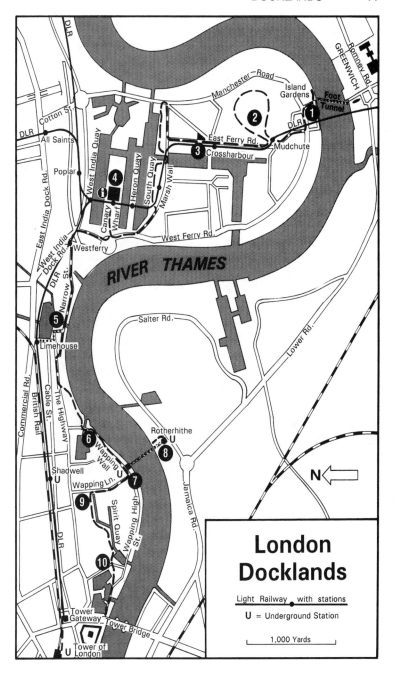

London
Docklands

Light Railway • with stations

U = Underground Station

1,000 Yards

The old West India Docks provide attractive breathing space between the buildings.

Explore the public areas of the complex adjacent to the DLR Canary Wharf station, then either make the longish trek by foot to the next attraction, or ride the DLR to its Limehouse stop. However you get there, the area around the old **Limehouse Basin** (5) is a relief after the Isle of Dogs' severe modernity. Opened in 1812 as the London terminus of the still-functioning Grand Union Canal, the basin is now used for water sports. It flows into the Thames through locks at Narrow Street, where the original 19th-century dockmaster's house is now the colorful Barley Mow pub. At one time Limehouse had a substantial Chinese population and acquired a largely fictitious reputation for vice, being sensationalized by the popular press as a land of opium dens, and worse. Those days are long gone; today's inhabitants are more likely to be young stockbrokers from Canary Wharf.

Head west along the river, making occasional inland forays to avoid inaccessible spots, to **Shadwell Basin** (6). One of the few remaining remnants of the former 27-acre London Docks of 1805, Shadwell is now surrounded by modern housing and used for water sports. Nearby, the **Prospect of Whitby** pub overlooks the river as it has since 1520—when it was known as the Devil's Tavern on account of the low-life thieves who drank there. Other customers included Samuel Pepys, Dickens, and Turner.

Continue down Wapping Wall, a narrow street lined with historic warehouses successfully converted into atmospheric residential and commercial units. Wapping High Street leads west to **Wapping Dock** (7), close to the old Execution Dock from which Captain Kidd and other pirates were hanged. From the corner of Wapping Lane you can make an easy and unusual little **side trip**. The world's first public underwater tunnel was completed here in 1843, and used by pedestrians until 1865. Since then it has carried Underground trains beneath the Thames, as it does today. Pop into the **Wapping Station** and ride the East London line to Rotherhithe, then stroll north to the river. **Brunel's Engine House** (8) originally pumped water out of the tunnel, and is now a small museum celebrating this early feat of civil engineering. It's seldom open, but the old streets around it are well worth exploring anyway.

Back at Wapping, head north on Wapping Lane to **Tobacco Dock** (9). Built in 1814 with massive vaults to store tobacco, liquor, and wine, this was once part of the now-filled-in London Docks. Surviving today as an upscale shopping center, it is beautifully situated on restored canals.

Following these waterways west brings you to the **St. Katherine Docks** (10), opened in 1825 and now heavily used by pleasure craft. This is the end of the walk; a perfect place for a well-earned rest at one of its colorful pubs. Just beyond the docks is the Tower Bridge (see page 70), the Tower of London (see page 33), and the Tower Hill Station of the Underground.

Greenwich

The lovely little Thames-side town of Greenwich is surely among the most attractive parts of London, and has long been a favorite destination for short excursions. Exceptionally rich in history, beauty, and engaging sights, it is located barely five miles east of Trafalgar Square in the ancient Borough of Greenwich, easily reached by boat, rail, bus, or car.

A great palace, once the home of royalty, stood on the green meadows by the river until the late 1600s. Henry VIII was born here, as were Mary I and Elizabeth I. For centuries, Greenwich remained the center of Britain's naval power. It is best known today, however, as the site of the Prime Meridian, that imaginary line from which all longitudinal distances on Earth are measured, and from which the world's time is reckoned using Greenwich Mean Time as the standard reference. Miraculously, Greenwich was spared the encroachment of a growing London, and it still retains much of its gracious character.

There are easily enough sights here to occupy an entire day, including the drydocked *Cutty Sark* clipper ship, the Old Royal Observatory, the National Maritime Museum, the intriguing Fan Museum, and a host of colorful pubs. Greenwich also makes a good destination for a half-day outing, or it could be combined with the Docklands trip described in the previous chapter. This is the perfect excursion for your first day in London, when jet lag makes a more demanding trip too difficult to enjoy. Depending on how you travel, just getting to Greenwich can be a large part of the fun.

GETTING THERE:

Boats depart London's Westminster Pier, just opposite Parliament, at frequent intervals for the 45-minute cruise to Greenwich. There are also departures from Embankment (Charing Cross) and Tower piers. Return boats operate until late afternoon. Refreshments are available on board, and there is often a running commentary on the sights. For further details, ☎ (020) 7930-4097 from Westminster, (020) 7987-1185 from Embankment (Charing Cross) and Tower.

The **Docklands Light Railway** provides a fast and scenic high-level trip above the revitalized Docklands area, then plunges under the Thames and continues on to Lewisham. Get off at the Cutty Sark station. Take the Underground to Bank and connect there. London Underground tickets and passes for the appropriate zones are valid on the DLR. For information ☎ (020) 7918-4000, Internet: www.dlr.co.uk.

Trains to Greenwich operated by Connex leave from Charing Cross, Waterloo East, or London Bridge stations at frequent intervals. The trip takes between 10 to 15 minutes, and return trains run until late evening.

Buses on route 188 connect central London with Greenwich town center.

By **car**, Greenwich is 5 miles east and slightly south of Trafalgar Square via local streets.

PRACTICALITIES:

The **Greenwich Tourist Information Centre**, ☎ (0870) 608-2000, Internet: www.greenwich.gov.uk, is in the Pepys Building, Old Royal Naval College, across from the Cutty Sark.

The **Greenwich Passport Ticket** combines admission to the Cutty Sark, the Old Royal Observatory, and the National Maritime Museum at a reduced price.

FOOD AND DRINK:

Greenwich is famous for its colorful pubs, and has a few restaurants, too. Some choices are:

Trafalgar Tavern (Park Row, by the Thames, just east of the Naval College) An old and celebrated combination pub and restaurant with traditional English fare. ☎ (020) 8858-2437. X: Restaurant only, Sat. lunch, Sun. eve. £ and £££

Spread Eagle (2 Stockwell St., just southeast of St. Alfege's Church) French and modified English cuisine in an old coaching inn. ☎ (020) 8853-2333. X: Bank Holiday Mon. ££

The Yacht (5 Crane St., a block northeast of the Naval College) This colorful 17th-century riverside pub offers simple bar lunches and sandwiches. ☎ (020) 8858-0175. £

Plume of Feathers (19 Park Vista, 2 blocks east of the Maritime Museum, overlooking the park) An 18th-century pub, locally popular for its bar food. ☎ (020) 8858-1661. £

Bosun's Whistle (in the west wing of the Maritime Museum) Light lunches and refreshments in a pleasant setting. ☎ (020) 8858-4422. £

SUGGESTED TOUR:

Numbers in parentheses correspond to numbers on the map.

Those coming by rail will begin at **Greenwich Station** (1). Follow the map to the **Greenwich Pier area** (2), the arrival point for boats and those coming via the Docklands Light Railway. The 19th-century clipper ship *Cutty Sark*, once the fastest ship in the world, sits in dry dock next to the

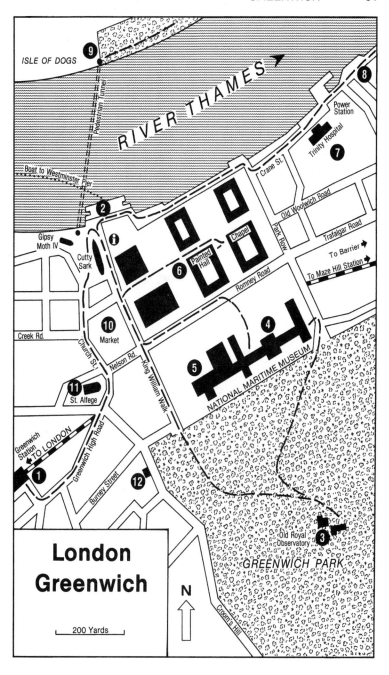

ISLE OF DOGS

RIVER THAMES

Power Station

Trinity Hospital

Crane St.

Old Woolwich Road

Park Row

Trafalgar Road

To Barrier →

To Maze Hill Station →

Boat to Westminster Pier

Pedestrian Tunnel

Gipsy Moth IV

Cutty Sark

Painted Hall

Chapel

Romney Road

NATIONAL MARITIME MUSEUM

Creek Rd.

Church St.

Market

Nelson Rd.

King William Walk

Greenwich High Road

St. Alfege

Greenwich Station

TO LONDON

Burney Street

Old Royal Observatory

GREENWICH PARK

Croom's Hill

London
Greenwich

N

200 Yards

Gipsy Moth IV, a 53-foot ketch in which Sir Francis Chichester single-handedly circumnavigated the globe in 1967. A few yards away stands the entrance to the pedestrian tunnel under the Thames, leading to Docklands (see previous chapter).

A tour aboard the **Cutty Sark** is a must for any visitor to Greenwich. Launched in 1869 for the China Sea trade, she was later used to haul wool from Australia and served as a training ship until the end of World War II. Now honorably retired, the elegant ship is a stirring sight recalling the great days of sail. In her hold is a fascinating display of nautical items including many figureheads. The *Gipsy Moth IV* may also be boarded during the same times, from Easter through September. *Open Mon.–Sat. 10–5, Sun. noon–5, remaining open until 6 in summer. Adults £3.50, seniors, students, children £2.50.* ☎ *(020) 8858-3445, Internet: www.cuttysark.org.uk. Partial* &.

From here follow King William Walk to Greenwich Park and climb uphill to the:

*OLD ROYAL OBSERVATORY (3), ☎ (020) 8312-6565, Internet: www.rog.nmm.ac.uk. *Open daily 10–5. Closed Dec. 24–26. Adults £6, seniors and students £4.80, children free. Combined admission with the National Maritime Museum, below: Adults £10.50, seniors and students £8.40, children free. Partial* &.

No longer used due to London's bright lights and pollution, the observatory buildings now house an intriguing museum of astronomical and time-keeping instruments. Light from an optic fiber marks 0° longitude, the **Prime Meridian** that separates the eastern and western hemispheres. Visitors can stand astride this, with one foot in each. Be sure to set your watch by the wonderful old clock just outside the gate, probably the most official time you'll ever get. The ornate **Flamsteed House** was built by Sir Christopher Wren in 1675 on instructions from Charles II to provide "for the Observator's habitation, and a little for Pompe." From the adjoining terrace there is a marvelous view of Greenwich, the Thames, Docklands, and the City. Note the time ball on a pole atop the roof, which drops at precisely 1 p.m. each day as a visual check for ships on the river.

A downhill stroll leads to the:

*NATIONAL MARITIME MUSEUM (4 & 5), ☎ (020) 8312-6565, Internet: www.nmm.ac.uk. *Open daily 10–5. Closed Dec. 24–26. Adults £7.50, seniors and students £6, children free. Combined admission with Old Royal Observatory, above: Adults £10.50, seniors and students £8.40, children free. Restaurant. Gift shop.* &.

Founded in 1934 and recently refurbished, the National Maritime Museum celebrates Britain's colorful seafaring heritage in a series of engrossing exhibits. The huge Neptune Hall contains entire boats, including a full-size paddle steamer. Several galleries are devoted to the careers of Captain Cook and Lord Nelson, while others cover the American and French revolutions. The Barge House is particularly intriguing with its collection of royal barges. Both a restaurant and a book shop are located in this wing.

Midway along the colonnade separating the museum's two wings stands the **Queen's House**. The first Palladian villa in England, it was begun in 1616 by the famous architect Inigo Jones as a summer palace for James I's queen, Anne of Denmark. The entrance hall is an elegant 40-foot cube, from which an outstanding spiral staircase leads to the upper floor where the reconstructed Queen's Bedroom may be visited. Closed for restoration during 1999, it will reopen for the Millennium celebrations with a major exhibition on the Story of Time. A special admission is required for this: *Adults £7.50, seniors and students £6, children £3.75. Partial &.*

Now follow Romney Road and King William Walk to the west gate of the former **Royal Naval College** (6). On this site once stood the Tudor palace of Placentia, birthplace of Henry VIII, Mary I, and Elizabeth I. Badly damaged by Cromwell's troops during the Civil War, it was torn down following the Restoration and a hospital for retired seamen erected in its place. These buildings, largely designed by Sir Christopher Wren, became the Naval College in 1873, a function they served until 1998. They are now being occupied by the University of Greenwich and the Trinity College of Music. You may visit the **Painted Hall** with its glorious ceiling, and the **Chapel**, the only parts of the college open to the public. *Open daily 2:30–4:45. Free. ☎ (020) 8858-2154. &, prior arrangement preferred.*

At this point you might want to take a delightful short walk along the riverfront to Ballast Quay. A passageway just before the pier leads to the right. Follow this past the front of the former Royal Naval College and continue on to the historic Trafalgar Tavern, a pub and luxury restaurant once frequented by cabinet ministers during the reign of Queen Victoria. From here stroll along narrow Crane Street. The Yacht Tavern is a more modest pub that recaptures some of the old nautical charm. In a short distance you will come to **Trinity Hospital** (7), an almshouse founded in 1614 and still the home of some 20 pensioners. The walk now passes a power station and leads to the Cutty Sark Tavern on the pleasant **Ballast Quay** (8), where you can relax at outdoor riverside tables before returning to the pier.

Another interesting walk is under the Thames through the old **pedestrian tunnel** of 1902, reached by an ancient elevator whose domed entrance is near the *Cutty Sark* ship. This brings you to the **Isle of Dogs** (9)(see page 76) for a classic panoramic *****view** of Greenwich.

Some other sights in Greenwich proper include the **Covered Market**

(10) of 1831, where an arts-and-crafts market operates on Saturdays and Sundays. **St. Alfege's Church** (11) was completed in 1714 by Nicholas Hawksmoor on the site of a 12th-century church, which stood on the spot where Alfege, Archbishop of Canterbury, was murdered by drunken Vikings in 1012 for quoting scriptures at them. Henry VIII was baptized in the earlier church, and the present structure has some interesting paintings and carvings.

Nearby, on Croom's Hill, is the rather unusual **Fan Museum** (12). Specializing in those elegant fashion accessories that made life bearable before the advent of air conditioning, the museum is housed in two restored Georgian townhouses and has a lovely garden. *Open Tues.–Sat. 11–4:30, Sun. noon–4:30. Remains open until 5 in summer. Adults £3.50, seniors and students £2.50, children under 7 free.* ☎ *(020) 8305-1441, Internet: www.fan- museum.org.* ⅃.

NEARBY SIGHTS:

The massive **Thames Barrier**, completed in 1982 to protect London from tidal flooding, is the world's largest movable flood barrier and may be inspected at close range from its Visitors' Centre. Working models and an audio-visual show are featured. You can get there by boat, train to Charlton, bus, or car. *Open Mon.–Fri. 10–5, weekends 10:30–5:30. Last admission one hour before closing. Adults £3.40, children £2. Cafeteria.* ☎ *(020) 8305-4188.* ⅃.

The **Millennium Dome**, the largest domed structure of its type on Earth, opens on January 1, 2000. Covering 130 acres, it has 14 themed zones celebrating the state of humanity in the 21st century. It is located at a bend in the Thames just northeast of Greenwich, at the North Greenwich station of the Jubilee Line of the Underground, which should be completed in time. Ask at the tourist office about transportation and entrance fees.

Hampstead

Although it is still in London, and only four miles from Trafalgar Square, Hampstead is a world removed with its picturesque village atmosphere, unspoiled heathland, forested hills, and secluded valleys. Famous artists and writers settled these heights shortly after it became something of a spa in the 18th century, and Hampstead is still a favorite residential area for intellectuals, architects, musicians, media folk, and other creative types. Its twisted narrow lanes and attractive old houses yield gently to the natural beauty of Hampstead Heath, crowning—at 443 feet—the highest point in London, with views to match its elevation.

Along with the scenery, this walk takes you to some first-rate attractions including the 17th-century Fenton House, the exquisite art-filled Kenwood House mansion, the romantic home of poet John Keats, and some very appealing old inns and pubs. Try to allow the better part of a day to enjoy it all at leisure, perhaps lingering over lunch and doing some shopping on the fashionable High Street.

GETTING THERE:

By **Underground**, take the Northern line to Hampstead, being careful to get on the right train as this line divides along the way.

British Rail trains on the North London Link line stop frequently at the Hampstead Heath Station. Leave Euston Station on a local train first and change at Willesden Junction, or take a local from St. Pancras Station and change at West Hampstead. Return service operates until late evening.

Bus routes 24, 46, 168, and 268 connect central London with Hampstead.

By **car**, Hampstead is a bit under 4 miles northwest of Trafalgar Square via local streets.

PRACTICALITIES:

Good weather is essential for this outdoor walking tour. Fenton House is closed from December through March, and on Mondays and Tuesdays. Kenwood House and Keats House are closed on some major holidays. Be sure to wear suitable shoes if you're walking in the woods, as the paths can be muddy in spots. For further information contact the **London Tourist Board**, ☎ (0839) 123-456 (toll call).

FOOD AND DRINK:

There are several famous old pubs in and around Hampstead, as well as a few modest restaurants. Some choices are:

Café des Arts (82 Hampstead High St.) Inventive French and Mediterranean cuisine in a relaxed atmosphere. ☎ (020) 7435-3608. ££

ZeNW3 (83 Hampstead High St.) Superb Chinese cuisine in a smart, bustling setting right on the High Street. ☎ (020) 7794-7863. ££

Holly Bush (Holly Mount, off Heath St., a block northwest of the Underground station) An early-19th-century pub with good lunches and plenty of atmosphere. ☎ (020) 8435-2892. £

Ed's Easy Diner (16 Hampstead High St., 2 blocks southeast of the Underground station) An American diner right out of the 1950s, with juicy burgers, milk shakes, and other prole delights. ☎ (020) 7431-1958. £

Pizza Express (70 Heath St., near the Underground Station) This always-reliable chain has a branch here, too. ☎ (020) 7433-1600. £

Spaniards Inn (Spaniards Lane, near the northwest end of the Heath) This 16th-century pub was once the home of the Spanish ambassador, later a favorite haunt of highwaymen, poets, and authors. Bar snacks and hot meals are offered. ☎ (020) 8455-3276. £

Kenwood House Café (in the stables of Kenwood House) A self-service restaurant with garden and indoor tables. Light lunches, pastries, and the like. £

SUGGESTED TOUR:

Numbers in parentheses correspond to numbers on the map. Those coming by British Rail to the Hampstead Heath Station should start at number 7 on the map, follow it to the end, then continue from number 1.

Begin at the **Hampstead Underground Station** (1), which has the distinction of being the deepest in London. Don't worry, an elevator will lift you up the 180 feet. Cross the High Street and follow Heath Street south to **Church Row**, a thoroughly enchanting lane lined with 18th-century terrace houses. This leads to the parish **Church of St. John** (2), whose interior contains a bust of Keats and several interesting memorials. The painter John Constable is buried in the southeast corner of its graveyard.

Now take Holly Walk north past St. Mary's Catholic Church, built in 1816 by refugees from the French Revolution. The road junction known as Mount Vernon is a bit confusing, but shelters the former lodgings of Robert Louis Stevenson and the very romantic dwelling of the 18th-century painter George Romney, both marked by plaques. Just beyond them is the delightful **Fenton House** (3) on Hampstead Grove. Built in 1693 and now owned by the National Trust, this small and simple brick mansion is set in a beautiful garden. It contains a remarkable collection of early **musical keyboard instruments**, including a harpsichord of 1612 that was once

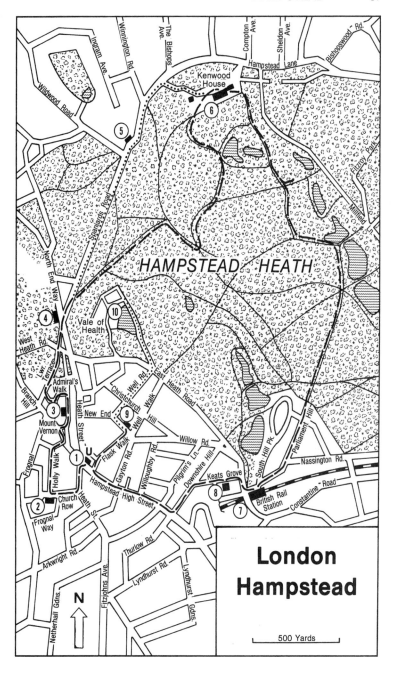

**London
Hampstead**

N

500 Yards

used by Handel. Most of these are kept tuned and may be played by music students. There is also a splendid collection of 18th-century furniture and porcelains. *Open April–Nov., Wed.–Fri. 2–5, Sat.–Sun. 11–5. Last admission at 4. Adults £4.10, children 5–16 £2.05.* ☎ *(020) 7435-3471.*

Continue north for a few steps and turn left on Admiral's Walk, passing the early-18th-century Admiral's House with its unusual superstructure. Next to it is the house where the author John Galsworthy lived from 1918 until 1933, and where he completed his monumental *Forsyte Saga.* John Constable resided near the corner of Lower Terrace, at Number 2, from 1821 to 1825. Turn north on this to **Whitestone Pond**, the highest point in London and the site of an old signal beacon that once warned of the Spanish Armada's arrival in the Channel.

Jack Straw's Castle (4), full of historical associations, is an old weatherboarded inn and pub that was rebuilt in the 1960s. From here, Spaniards Road leads into the forests of **Hampstead Heath**. You can stroll along trails through this (and probably get momentarily lost), or take the road north to the **Spaniards Inn** (5), a 16th-century tavern once favored by highwaymen and later by artists.

Whichever way you go, follow the map to the magnificent:

*KENWOOD HOUSE (6), ☎ (020) 8348-1286, Internet: www.english- heritage.org.uk. *Open April–Sept. daily 10–6:15; Oct.–March daily 10–4. Closed Dec. 24–25. Admission free, donations welcome. Cafeteria. Tours.* ♿.

This large mansion features a sweeping panoramic view of London. Remodeled in 1764 by the noted architect Robert Adam, it was bequeathed to the nation in 1928 along with its fabulous collection of art. On view in these luxurious surroundings are major works by Rembrandt, Frans Hals, Vermeer, Reynolds, Romney, Gainsborough, and many others. Be sure to see the lovely ***Library**, one of Adam's best interiors. There is an excellent cafeteria in the adjoining Coach House, whose outdoor tables makes it a perfect spot for an inexpensive lunch. Outdoor concerts are held by the small lake during the summer. Don't miss this special treat.

Now follow the map through a more open and park-like section of the immense 825-acre Hampstead Heath. Again, you'll probably get lost. Just keep heading downhill, passing several ponds along the way, and exit onto Parliament Hill. This leads to the **Hampstead Heath British Rail Station** (7), the beginning of the tour for those who came by train.

Just a few steps from here is Keats Grove, a small street lined with attractive detached cottages. One of these is **Keats House** (8), where from 1818 to 1820 the great poet John Keats spent the most productive two years of his short career, and where he wrote his inspired *Ode to a Nightingale* by the plum tree in the garden. The present tree is, of course, a replacement. You can also visit the house, filled with memorabilia of the poet's life along with original manuscripts. *Open April–Oct., Mon.–Fri. 10–1 and 2–6, Sat. 10–1 and 2–5, Sun. 2–5.; Nov.–March, Mon.–Fri. 1–5, Sat. 10–1 and 2–5, Sun. 2–5. Closed on a few major holidays. Admission free.* ☎ *(020) 7435-2062.*

Make a left turn on Downshire Hill and a right onto Hampstead High Street, one of the most attractive shopping streets in England. Some of the little alleys leading off this are interesting, particularly the **Old Brewery Mews** and **Flask Walk**. The latter leads to the early-18th-century **Burgh House** (9), now used as a museum of local history enlivened with changing exhibitions of local artists' work. *Open Wed.–Sun. noon–5, Bank Holiday Mon. 2–5. Closed some major holidays. Admission free. Café.* ☎ *(020) 7431-0144.* ᶜ.

If you still need more exercise, you might want to continue up Well Walk and into a curious enclave called the **Vale of Health** (10), whose name was probably invented by 18th-century real estate promoters anxious to sell what was then malaria-infested swamp land. Its cluster of lovely little houses has been home to various famous writers throughout the years.

Richmond

The London Borough of Richmond-upon-Thames, spread along the banks of the river, is the setting for this delightful stroll through the world-renowned Kew Gardens and on to the historic old town of Richmond. The Royal Botanical Gardens alone can keep you pleasantly engrossed for half a day, while other attractions include the intriguing Kew Bridge Steam Museum, the smallest royal palace in England, one of the loveliest urban greens anywhere, superb riverside views, and a great selection of colorful pubs. This is really a day for casual pleasure, an easy escape from the steady rounds of great monuments and cultural institutions.

GETTING THERE:

Trains operated by South West Trains depart London's Waterloo Station frequently for the 25-minute ride to Kew Bridge, where the walk begins. Return trains from Richmond Station operate until late evening.

By **Underground**, take the District Line marked for Richmond to the Kew Gardens Station, then walk north to the beginning of the tour. If you prefer to start at the Kew Royal Botanical Gardens, you can enter them more conveniently from the Victoria Gate near the Underground Station. You will be returning from the Richmond Underground Station, on the same line.

Boats operate from Westminster Pier, opposite Parliament, to Kew Gardens (1.5 hours) and Richmond (2.5 hours) several times daily from early April through September. ☎ (020) 7930-2062 for information.

PRACTICALITIES:

Good weather is necessary for this almost totally outdoor trip. The gardens at Kew are at their peak in spring and early summer, but remain enjoyable all year round. The **Richmond Tourist Information Centre**, ☎ (020) 8940-9125, is located in Richmond's Old Town Hall, near the river and the bridge.

FOOD AND DRINK:

Some good pubs and restaurants are:

Wine & Mousaka (12 Kew Green, near the entrance to the gardens) This congenial Greek restaurant features kebabs, dolmades, and the like. Outdoor tables in season. ☎ (020)8 940-5696. X: Sun. ££

Beeton's (58 Hill Rise, just east of Richmond Bridge) Real British home cooking in delightful surroundings. B.Y.O.B. ☎ (020) 8940-9561. X: Mon. ££

White Cross (Cholmondeley Walk, a block west of the Old Town Hall) An old riverside pub with good bar food and a restaurant. ☎ (020) 8940-6844. X: Sun. eve. £ and ££

Orange Tree (45 Kew Rd., opposite Richmond Station) Simple bar food upstairs, warm meals downstairs in this popular, lively pub. X: Sun. eve. ☎ (020) 8940-0944. £

Angel & Crown (5 Church Court, between Red Lion St. and George St., a block northeast of the Old Town Hall) Have lunch at a popular pub in the center of town. X: Sun. £

SUGGESTED TOUR:

Numbers in parentheses correspond to numbers on the map.

Begin at Kew Bridge, next to the **Kew Bridge British Rail Station** (1). From here it is only steps to the **Kew Bridge Steam Museum** (2), located in a former water works pumping station that supplied London with water from 1838 until 1958. Anyone fascinated by Victorian steam machinery will have fun examining the old pumping engines dating from as far back as 1820, especially so on weekends when some of them are fired up and operated. There are also workshops, displays on the history of London's water supply, and a typical waterworks railway. *Open daily 11–5. Closed Good Friday, Dec. 21–27. Weekday admission: Adults £2.80, seniors and students £1.50, children £1. Weekend Steaming admission: Adults £3.80, seniors and students £2.50, children £2. Café on weekends. Gift shop.* ☎ *(020) 8568-4757.* &.

Cross the bridge over the Thames and turn right into **Kew Green**, a lovely village setting with 18th-century houses built for members of George III's court. St. Anne's Church, on the green, was begun in 1710 under royal patronage. The painter Thomas Gainsborough is buried in its churchyard. At the west end of the green is the main gate leading into the fabulous

*ROYAL BOTANIC GARDENS, KEW (3–13), ☎ (020) 8940-1171, Internet: www.rbgkew.org.uk. *Open daily 9:30–6, closing earlier in winter. Glasshouses and exhibitions close at 4:45. Last admission 30 minutes before closing. Closed Christmas and New Year's Day. Adults £5, seniors and students £3.50, children £2.50. Special charge for Kew Palace and Queen Charlotte's Cottage, both Royal properties. Art museums.*

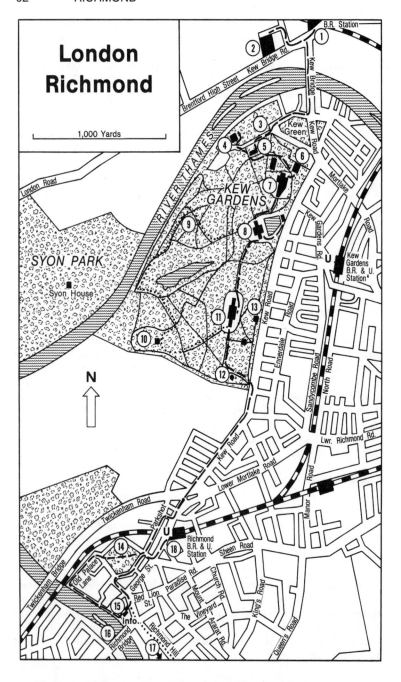

London Richmond

1,000 Yards

Restaurants, cafés. Gift shops. &.

With so much exquisite beauty spread over 300 acres of woods and gardens, it is perhaps difficult to realize that the main purpose of *Kew Gardens—as it is popularly known—is not aesthetic but scientific, for this is first and foremost a botanical research and training center. Plants from all corners of the Earth are grown here, many of them indoors under controlled climatic conditions.

The botanical gardens began in 1759 on nine acres of this former royal estate, and were soon extended by George III, who often stayed at Kew Palace. In 1841 they were given to the nation, and by 1904 enlarged to their present size.

Before ambling through the gardens proper, you might want to see **Kew Palace** (4) at their northern end. Once known as the Dutch House, this is all that remains of a royal complex that occupied the site until being demolished in 1802. Built in 1631 by a rich London merchant, the house was acquired by the Crown in 1728 for use by members of the Royal Family. From 1802 until 1818 this surviving structure served as a favorite country retreat for George III and Queen Charlotte, who died there in 1818. *Today, England's smallest royal residence is being restored and should reopen to the public in 2001.*

Begin your tour of the Royal Botanic Gardens at the **Orangery** (5), which was built in 1761 and now houses, among other things, a gift shop and restaurant. Adjacent to this is the **Filmy Fern House**. Continue on to the **Alpine House** (6), a modern glass structure where alpine and arctic plants are grown under refrigerated conditions. From here, stroll through the aquatic and grass gardens to the stunning **Princess of Wales Conservatory** (7). This huge, partially underground greenhouse re-creates tropical environments from swamps to deserts, featuring such exotica as carnivorous plants and a simulation of the Mohave Desert.

The most famous building at Kew, indeed its trademark, is the magnificent *Palm House** (8), an enormous Victorian greenhouse from 1848 that shelters a wide variety of tropical plants. Just north of this is the **Waterlily House** of 1852. The modern **Visitor Centre**, adjacent to the nearby Victoria Gate, offers introductory video shows about the gardens. Directly across the pond from the Palm House stands the newly-restored **Museum No. 1**, built in 1857 and now home to a fascinating exhibition on the impact plants have on everyday lives.

If the weather is exceptionally fine and you feel up to a long walk, you might want to make a side trip through the woods past the azalea and bamboo gardens to the **Rhododendron Dell** (9), which is just lovely in spring. This route then continues along the river, with good views of Syon House, and winds around to **Queen Charlotte's Cottage** (10), built in the 1770s as a rustic summerhouse for George III's family. *Its interior may be visited on weekends only, from April through September, 10–4.* From here, the route on the map returns you through woods and gardens to the main route near the Palm House.

Continue on to the **Temperate House** (11), a gigantic late- Victorian structure housing several thousand varieties of temperate species. Wonderful interior views can be had by climbing the spiral staircase to the upper walkway. The **Evolution House**, behind it, takes you on a journey of some 3,500 million years of plant evolution. Nearby, poking through the trees, is the **Japanese Gateway** left over from a 1910 exhibition, and the rather strange 10-story-high **Chinese Pagoda** (12) that was erected in 1761 as an ornamental folly.

The southern end of Kew Gardens has a few other points of interest, including the exquisite *Marianne North Gallery (13), a Victorian building containing hundreds of botanical and travel paintings from around the world, all by the 19th-century artist. A refreshment pavilion is nearby.

Leave the gardens via the Lion Gate and turn right on Kew Road, following the map into the historic old town of Richmond and its exceptionally attractive **Richmond Green** (14). In Tudor days this was a jousting ground whose tournaments were held next to the former Richmond Palace, of which only traces remain. The palace itself was demolished after the 17th-century Civil War, but sporting activity on the green survives to this day in the form of cricket. All around the large open square are lovely houses from the 17th and 18th centuries, many of which now serve as antique shops, boutiques, and pubs. The **Maids of Honour Row** along the southwest side is a particularly notable set of four adjoining houses built in 1724 as residences for the ladies-in-waiting to the Princess of Wales. To the right of them is an alleyway leading to the 16th-century **Gate House**, the only intact structure from the former palace. Henry VII's coat of arms still decorate its arch. Some of the houses in the courtyard beyond incorporate portions of the original brickwork from the old palace, the third on this site, where Elizabeth I died in 1603.

Continue down Old Palace Lane, passing an inviting pub called the White Swan, to the River Thames and turn left on Cholmondeley Walk. To your left is the 18th-century **Asgill House**, once a weekend retreat for the Lord Mayor of London. Beyond it, through the trees, you can see the **Trumpeters' House**, where the exiled Austrian chancellor Metternich lived in 1848–49.

The riverside path now opens into a large terraced area. At the top of this is the **Old Town Hall** (15) of 1893, home of the **Museum of Richmond**. Tracing local history from the Stone Age to the recent past, lively displays here include dioramas and a detailed model of the former palace. *Open all year on Tues.–Sat., 11–5, and also on Sun. from May–Oct., 1–4. Adults £2, seniors and students £1.* ☎ *(020) 8332-1141.* &. While you're there, check out the local tourist office in the same building. From the terrace outside you'll get an excellent view of **Richmond Bridge** (16), a handsome stone span completed in 1777 and now the oldest existing bridge over the

Thames in Greater London.

An interesting **side trip** can be made beyond the bridge by following Hill Rise and the fairly steep **Richmond Hill** (17, off the map) to its top. The splendid ***panoramic view** from here of a sharp bend in the Thames is famous, and has been painted by such artists as Turner and Reynolds. As long as you're up there, you might want to continue into **Richmond Park**, the largest and most unspoiled royal park in London. Its 2,470 acres were enclosed by Charles I in 1637 as a royal hunting ground.

Back in town, you can wander around the narrow old streets, perhaps stopping at some shops or pubs, before heading to **Richmond Station** (18), which is used by both British Rail and the Underground.

Hampton Court

Henry VIII's great royal palace on the Thames is one of London's premier attractions. First built in 1514 by the ostentatious Cardinal Wolsey, it was given to Henry in 1529 in a vain attempt to appease the king, who was angered by the thought of a commoner living better than himself. Succeeding monarchs (and Oliver Cromwell!) enjoyed its luxury right down to the death of George II in 1760. Significant alterations made by the famed architect Sir Christopher Wren during the reign of William III added Baroque elements to the original Tudor structure. No longer used by royalty, the palace and its magnificent gardens were opened to the public in 1838 by Queen Victoria.

Like Versailles outside Paris, this royal complex easily takes the better part of a day to appreciate. Besides the enormous palace, there are all sorts of gardens to explore, a slightly unnerving 18th-century maze to get lost in, and several square miles of parks to enjoy. If that isn't enough, you can also stroll along the Thames past working locks, soaking up the village atmosphere and perhaps stopping at a waterside pub.

GETTING THERE:

Trains to Hampton Court depart at half-hour intervals from London's Waterloo Station, with a journey time of about 30 minutes. Be sure to get a train to Hampton Court, not to Hampton. Return service operates until late evening.

Boats depart London's Westminster Pier, just opposite Parliament, several times in the morning for the 2.5-to-4-hour ride to Hampton Court. Return boats leave in the mid-to-late afternoon. This service operates from early April through September, ☎ (020) 7930-2062 for current details.

Buses operated by the Green Line depart from their terminal behind Victoria Station in London several times daily for the 45-minute ride to Hampton Court.

Those coming by **car** will find limited pay parking near the entrance to the palace grounds.

PRACTICALITIES:

Hampton Court Palace is open mid-March to mid-October, on Mondays from 10:15 to 6, and on Tuesdays through Sundays from 9:30 to

6, last admission at 5:15. From mid-October to mid-March it is open on Mondays from 10:15 to 4:30, and on Tuesdays through Sundays from 9:30 to 4:30, last admission at 3:45. It is closed December 24–26. Admission: Adults £10, seniors and students £7.60, children under 16 £6.60, children under 5 free. There are several places to eat there (see below) as well as gift shops. Both the palace and the grounds are generally ♿ accessible, ask a guard if you need help. Battery-powered cars for use in the gardens are available free of charge. Try to avoid the weekend or holiday crowds, and remember that good weather will greatly enhance your visit. For further information contact the palace office directly, ☎ (020) 8791-9500, or visit their Internet site at www.hrp.org.uk.

FOOD AND DRINK:

Landings Restaurant (Mitre Hotel, Hampton Court Bridge, just outside the main gate) Outdoor dining in a riverside garden. ☎ (020) 8979-9988. X: Sat. lunch. ££

Tiltyard Tea Room (near the maze in the gardens) Full meals, salad lunches, sandwiches, refreshments, and afternoon teas. £ and ££

Queen Elizabeth I's Privy Kitchen (in the palace) Light lunches, refreshments, and afternoon teas. £

SUGGESTED TOUR:

Numbers in parentheses correspond to numbers on the map.

The **Hampton Court train station** (1) is only yards from the River Thames. Stroll across the bridge to the **Trophy Gates** (2) on your right, built for William III as a grand entrance into the palace complex and later decorated by George II. Amble through them, purchase your ticket, and head straight across what's left of the moat. The **stone bridge** here was erected by Henry VIII, embellished with the "King's Beasts" stone carvings, and later buried by Charles II. Rediscovered in 1910, it once again gives proper access to the **Great Gatehouse** (3), one of the oldest parts of the palace.

Step through the doorway into the Base Court. Six different areas of the palace are open to visitors, each following a different route. Time and energy permitting, you should really see all six. **Route 1** begins between the Base and Clock courts, leading upstairs to Henry VIII's ***Tudor Royal Lodgings** (4). At the top is Henry's magnificent ***Great Hall**, originally a dining room for lesser courtiers. It is still hung with priceless 16th-century tapestries depicting the Story of Abraham. Look up at the 60-foot-high hammerbeam ceiling, every inch of which is enriched with gilded carvings, before continuing on to the **Great Watching Chamber**. The King's bodyguards once kept their watch here, surrounded by opulence. The route now enters the **Haunted Gallery**, where with luck you might encounter the ghost of Catherine Howard. Number five of Henry's six

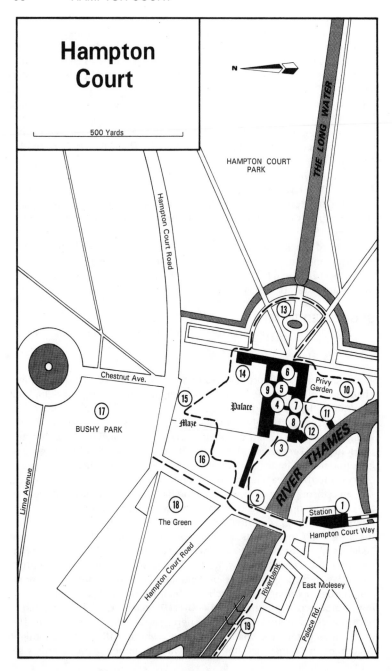

Hampton Court

500 Yards

N

THE LONG WATER

HAMPTON COURT PARK

Hampton Court Road

Chestnut Ave.

BUSHY PARK

Lime Avenue

Palace

Maze

Privy Garden

RIVER THAMES

The Green

Hampton Court Road

Station

Hampton Court Way

Riverbank

East Molesey

Palace Rd.

wives, she was beheaded for adultery in 1542, as was number two. Near the end is the elaborate **Chapel Royal**, much of which survives from the time when Henry and his wives, especially his wives, prayed there.

Route 2 begins in the Clock Court and takes you through the **Queen's State Apartments** (5). Again reached by an impressive staircase, this Baroque addition was designed for Queen Mary II by Sir Christopher Wren in the 1690s. Unfortunately, the queen died before they were finished, so the decorations are largely those of succeeding reigns. Among the highlights are the **Audience Chamber** with its canopied throne, the **Drawing Room** of Queen Anne, the **Bedchamber** with the original bed of George II's Queen Caroline, and the **Queen's Gallery** with its Brussels tapestries and lovely Delftware.

The **Georgian Rooms** (6), shown on **Route 3**, are entered from the Fountain Court. Once again reached by an elegant staircase, this group of smaller rooms sheds some insight into the lives of George I and George II, the last monarchs to reside at Hampton. In the center of the suite is the famed **Cartoon Gallery**, built by Wren for William III around 1700. Original tapestry cartoons designed by Raphael in 1515 once hung on these walls, but they are now in the Victoria and Albert Museum. In their place are copies made here in the 18th century. Continue on through the **Communication Gallery**, hung with the "Windsor Beauties" portraits of the ladies of Charles II's court. Near the end is "**Wolsey's Closet**," a survival from Tudor times that was probably decorated by Henry VIII.

Route 4, reached from the Clock Court by yet another grandiose staircase, takes you through the **King's Apartments** (7). Built for William III between 1689 and 1700, these handsome chambers were devastated by fire as recently as 1986, but have now been restored to their original condition. The allegorical paintings decorating the stairs sing thinly-veiled praises to the king, and are set off by a magnificent wrought-iron balustrade. Pass through the **Guard Chamber**, whose paneled walls are enlivened with over 3,000 arms placed there in the 17th century by the king's gunsmith. The **Presence Chamber** still has its canopied throne, bowed to by courtiers even when unoccupied. Going through the Privy Chamber and the Withdrawing Room brings you to the elaborate **Great Bedchamber**, and the adjacent Little Bedchamber where the king actually slept. Downstairs, on the ground floor, are William III's private apartments, a cozy suite beautifully restored to its original condition.

Part of the original Tudor palace of the early 16th century, the **Wolsey Rooms** (8) shown on **Route 5** feature the *Renaissance Picture Gallery of fine paintings on loan from Queen Elizabeth II. Among its treasures is a painting of Henry VIII's meeting with King François I of France in 1520, the *Massacre of the Innocents* by the elder Brueghel, and a delightful scene of *The Four Evangelists Stoning the Pope*—probably Henry's favorite work of art.

Cross the Clock Court to enter the *Tudor Kitchens** (9) on the final **Route 6**. Laid out in preparation for a great feast, this is a real treat for anyone who loves food. Two hundred people labored here feeding the 800-odd members of Henry VIII's court. A recorded audio guide describing everything may be borrowed at the entrance, making your visit all the more enjoyable. And, should you feel pangs of hunger yourself, there is a nearby Tudor-style snack bar.

Outdoors, the **Privy Garden** (10) was originally William III's private garden, but is now more a typically 19th-century Grace-and-Favor garden. Close to it is the **Pond Garden** (11) of Henry VIII, and the lavishly-decorated **Banqueting House** built in 1700 by Sir Christopher Wren as an intimate party place for William III. The **Mantegna Gallery**, housed in a former orangery, contains valuable paintings belonging to the present Queen. Planted nearby in 1768, the **Great Vine** (12) still produces grapes as it has for well over two centuries.

Behind the palace complex stretches **Hampton Court Park**, offering wonderful views of the buildings and the River Thames. It's a long walk to the end, but at least go as far as the nearby **Fountain Garden** (13) for the best perspective.

Stroll past the so-called **Tudor Tennis Courts** (14), where "real" tennis may be watched if it's open, through the **Wilderness**, and around to Queen Anne's **Maze** (15) of 1714. Deceptively simple but fiendishly conceived, this confusing route through the hedges traps most who enter. If every turn just brings you back to the same place (and it will!), you can always follow behind small children, who have an uncanny knack for finding their way out. Knights once jousted in Henry VIII's **Tiltyard** (16), but today it is home to a restaurant and cafeteria.

Northeast of the Palace Grounds is **Bushy Park** (17), designed by Wren as a grand approach to his planned north façade that never got built. Deer roam around this near-wilderness, and so can you.

Just across from the palace is **Hampton Court Green** (18), where Sir Christopher Wren lived in the Old Court House from 1706 until his death in 1723. Ambling around the green will reveal several other period houses.

Before heading back to London, you might want to wander along the south bank of the Thames to **Molesey Lock** (19) to watch pleasure boats working their way through. The river is no longer tidal at this point, and quite a bit narrower than it is downstream. There are several appealing riverside pubs in the area where you can relax before taking the train back.

Section III

DAYTRIPS FROM
LONDON

I t may be surprising to realize just how many of England's best attractions are within easy daytrip range of London. The southern part of the nation is so compact that rail travel times to its most delightful destinations range from only 25 minutes to less than two hours, with corresponding driving distances of just 20 to about 100 miles. A few additional places, lying beyond this range but still easily reached, are included because they're simply too good to miss. With so much to see this close to the capital, you can enjoy a broad variety of thoroughly English experiences without ever having to check out of your London accommodations.

The advantages of staying in one place and traveling without the burden of luggage far outweigh the additional mileage involved. By departing London around 8 or 9 a.m. you will reach your daytrip destination in midmorning, leaving nearly all of the day free for sightseeing, shopping, dining, or just relaxing before returning in time for an evening's entertainment.

A good way to add variety to your visit is to alternate between making one-day excursions and spending entire days exploring London, which also lets you sleep later on the days you choose to stay in town. Doing this is more practical with the use of "flexible" railpasses that need not be used on consecutive days.

Should you prefer following a point-to-point itinerary instead of making daytrips, you could select whichever destinations interest you and link them with direct road or rail routes, usually avoiding London completely.

The 45 daytrips described in this section cover a variety of interests and experiences. Some are to world-famous destinations, while others take you well off the beaten path to unusual adventures. Those that have most consistently pleased nearly everyone include Canterbury, Rye, Salisbury and Stonehenge, Oxford, Stratford-upon-Avon, Cambridge, and York.

GETTING AROUND
SOUTHERN ENGLAND

Getting around southern England on your own is really quite easy once you get the hang of it. This section discusses your transportation options, and then goes on to describe 45 of the most exciting daytrip possibilities within easy range of London. All of the excursions can be made by either train or car.

BY RAIL:

The British invented passenger trains and, on balance, their system is probably the best in the world. **British Rail** has the decided advantage of taking you where you want to go, when you want to go, and of doing so with a minimum of fuss. With over 2,400 destinations and some 15,000 trains a day, there are few places that cannot be reached quickly and comfortably from London. Rail stations are usually located right in the heart of towns, so close to the major tourist attractions that most of the walking tours described in this section begin right at the station. Trains have the additional advantage of neatly bypassing traffic going in and out of the metropolis, and of generally being the fastest way to cover the distances involved.

The privatization of Britain's rail system in the mid-1990s has not dramatically changed its character, although there is now a bewildering range of logos and paint jobs on the trains themselves. At last count, some 25 private operating companies now provide service on competing routes, sometimes using the same tracks and stations. The permanent infrastructure—tracks, stations, signals and so on—remain the province of Railtrack, the successor to the old government-owned British Rail, whose name and logo are still used. Equipment varies from the swift **InterCity** expresses operating at up to 140 mph to a wide variety of reliable workhorses including the **Turbos**, a new generation of self-propelled trains now in widespread use. With luck, you may still encounter some colorful old commuter trains that are mostly used south of London. All express trains and some locals carry first-class accommodations besides the ubiquitous standard-class cars, as second class is called in Britain. Most intercity runs have a buffet or dining car serving meals, snacks, and drinks.

Seasoned travelers know that riding trains is just about the best way to meet the British people on their home ground. It's not at all unusual to

Daytrips from London

50 Miles

NORTH SEA

York

Chester

Lincoln

Nottingham

King's Lynn

Norwich

Stamford

Ely

Coventry

Bury St.
Edmunds

Woodbridge

Warwick

Cambridge

Stratford-upon-Avon

Ipswich

Colchester

Gloucester

Woodstock

St. Albans

London

Cardiff

Oxford

Bristol

Windsor

Faversham

Bath

Rochester

Canterbury

Wells

Royal
Tunbridge
Wells

Dover

Guildford

R., H. & D.

Salisbury

Winchester

Bluebell

Battle

Rye

Southampton

Arundel

Hastings

Portsmouth

Chichester

Brighton

Exeter

Shanklin

ENGLISH CHANNEL

strike up engaging conversations with total strangers, making your trips even more memorable. You'll also get a view of the passing countryside from the large windows, and have time to catch up on your reading. Then too, you are spared the worries of driving, especially after making a few pub stops.

London has many **train stations**. The map opposite shows the general location of those likely to be used by tourists. All are connected to the **Underground** (subway, see page 20) and can be reached easily. Be sure you know which station you're leaving from, and allow a little extra time to orient yourself the first time you use it. All main stations have an information office where you can check the current schedules or any possible temporary variation to them. The national telephone information number for all of the various operating companies is ☎ (0345) 484-950, Internet: www.rail track.co.uk.

There is generally no need for **reservations** on British trains, especially not for the daytrips described in this section, but you might consider making them for possible long-distance trips such as London to Edinburgh. Reservations are "strongly advised" on the few departures shown on schedules with a boxed letter "**R**."

Although you really don't need it, a **Timetable Book** of the entire system is sold at major stations, or you might want to use the handy but less comprehensive **Thomas Cook European Timetable**, covering all of Europe and sold at Thomas Cook travel offices throughout Britain. It is also available at some travel bookstores in America or by mail from the Forsyth Travel Library, P.O. Box 480800, Kansas City MO 64148, ☎ (800) 367-7984, Internet: www.forsyth.com.

Train service is often reduced on Sundays and holidays, when travel may involve delays or diversions due to track maintenance work. Check for announcements at the station.

RAILPASSES are a terrific bargain if you intend to do extensive train travel, but they must be obtained before going to Britain since they cannot be purchased there. The various rail operating companies accept the following passes:

BRITRAIL CLASSIC PASS—the original railpass for Britain allows unlimited train travel throughout all of England, Wales, and Scotland for periods of 8, 15, or 22 consecutive days, or for one month; and is available in both first- and standard (economy second)-class versions for adults. A half-price pass is offered for children from 5 to 15 years of age. Senior citizens aged 60 and over enjoy substantial reductions in both classes, and youths between 16 and 25 get a price break in standard class.

BRITRAIL FLEXIPASS—This handy version of the BritRail Pass offers the same unlimited train travel on any 4 days, on any 8 days, or on any 15 days during a two-month period. Again, both first- and second-class versions are available, and there are special deals for seniors, youths, and children. Although it costs a bit more, the Flexipass allows you to take time out between your daytrips, and might in the end be the greater bargain.

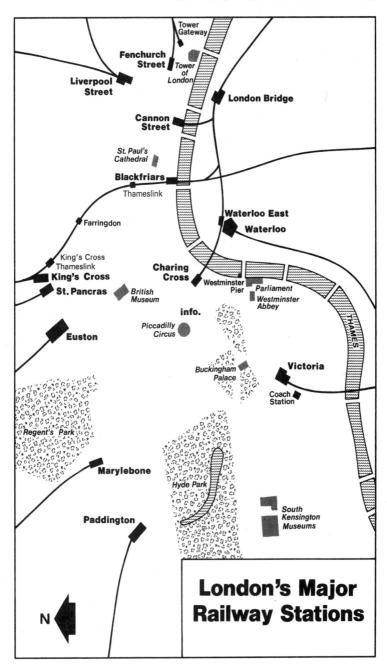

Tower Gateway

Fenchurch Street

Tower of London

Liverpool Street

London Bridge

Cannon Street

St. Paul's Cathedral

Blackfriars

Thameslink

Farringdon

Waterloo East

Waterloo

King's Cross Thameslink

King's Cross

Charing Cross

Westminster Pier

Parliament

Westminster Abbey

St. Pancras

British Museum

info.

Euston

Piccadilly Circus

THAMES

Buckingham Palace

Victoria

Coach Station

Regent's Park

Marylebone

Hyde Park

Paddington

South Kensington Museums

N

London's Major Railway Stations

BRITRAIL PASS 'N DRIVE—A package deal that combines the BritRail Flexipass with car-rental vouchers valid at Hertz locations throughout Britain, many of which are in train stations. This plan is fairly complex and involves countless permutations, but it might just be the right deal if you'd like to try driving on some of your daytrips.

BRITRAIL PASS + IRELAND—Combines unlimited rail travel in Britain, the Irish Republic, and Northern Ireland with a round-trip ferry ticket between Britain and Ireland. It is available for travel on any 5 or 10 days in one month, in first or standard class, with children 5—15 getting half off.

BRITRAIL SOUTHEAST PASS—Saving the best deal for last, this is a convenient and economical arrangement for visitors to London who are also making some of the daytrips. The low-cost option offers a 3-, 4-, or 7-day first- or standard-class flexible **railpass** valid throughout the "Network Southeast" area. This includes most—but not all by any means—of the destinations in this book.

Railpasses will probably save you a considerable amount of money if you travel extensively by train throughout Britain. Be sure to analyze the different prices and arrangements carefully in light of your plans and the amount of flexibility that you *really* need. If it fits your needs, the BritRail SouthEast Pass is definitely the least expensive option, while the BritRail + Ireland Pass is the costliest.

Even if the savings over regular fares is not great, a pass should still be considered for the convenience it offers in not having to line up for tickets, and for the freedom of just hopping aboard almost any train at whim. Possession of a pass will also encourage you to become more adventurous, to seek out distant and offbeat destinations. And, should you ever manage to get on the wrong train by mistake (or change your plans en route), your only cost will be your time—not an extra fare back!

Another consideration is that individual point-to-point purchased in Britain are valid only for travel on the specific railway operating company ticketed, not on the competition. Railpasses are valid for all of the operating companies.

Holders of validated BritRail passes are entitled to a substantial discount on the Eurostar Channel Tunnel service to the Continent.

The various railpasses **must** be obtained **before** going to Britain. Current details about prices and conditions of use, as well as the passes themselves, are available from most travel agents, from a variety of mail-order retailers, or from Rail Europe, 226 Westchester Ave., White Plains, NY 10604 ☎ (800) 438-7245, Internet: www.raileurope.com. If you live outside of the USA, contact the nearest office of the British Tourist Authority (see page 18) for information.

Railpasses must be **validated** before use. They provide transportation only and do not cover possible additional charges such as reservations, sleeping accommodations, or meals. If you have decided against a pass—or live in Britain and cannot buy one—you still have several money-saving options. Before purchasing a full-fare ticket you should always ask about special fares that might be applicable to your journey, including same-day returns, such as the Cheap Day Return ticket or the SuperSaver ticket.

BY CAR:

Making your daytrips by car is an attractive proposition *if* several people are traveling together and *if* you can cope with the hassles of London traffic. It is the preferred way to travel for a few of the trips in this book.

If you prefer to follow an itinerary instead of making daytrips, you'll find that a car is more convenient for hopping directly between destinations without returning to London. This is especially true if you stay at country inns.

It is possible to combine both car and rail travel economically, riding trains through congested areas and driving rental cars in the countryside, by using the **BritRail Pass 'n Drive** package described above. The various money-saving **Fly/Drive** deals offered by various airlines together with their transatlantic flights are another good way to cut your car-rental expenses. Ask your travel agent about both plans as far in advance as possible.

Other than getting used to driving on the left, you should have no trouble adapting to English roads, which are usually quite good. Routes prefixed with the letter "M" are Motorways (toll-free superhighways with speed limits up to 70 mph), those with an "A" are regular highways (sometimes divided), while those marked with a "B" or no letter are rural routes. Among the many excellent **road maps** of this region is the Michelin number 404 "Midlands and Southeast England." American and Canadian driver's licenses are valid, although there are usually minimum age and experience restrictions for rentals.

Trip 11

Rochester

The ancient cathedral town of Rochester is most famous for its close association with Charles Dickens, who spent much of his life nearby and used the town as a locale for many of his stories. A marvelous museum that explores his life and works in stunning audio-visual terms is reason enough for the visit, but there are other attractions as well. These include a massive Norman castle that you can climb around in, a 12th-century cathedral, remains of a Roman wall, the excellent Guildhall Museum, several buildings of historic importance, an exceptionally attractive main street, and—during the summer—cruises aboard an historic paddle steamer.

No one knows just how old Rochester is, although it probably dates from prehistoric times. The early Britons called it *Doubris*, which the Romans changed to *Durobrivae* after they built their bridge across the River Medway. The present name derives from the Anglo-Saxon *Hrofesceaster*. In AD 604 the second-oldest bishopric in England was established here, becoming the foundation for the present Norman cathedral.

GETTING THERE:

Trains to Rochester depart at about half-hour intervals from London's Victoria, Charing Cross, and Waterloo East stations, with a journey time of about 45 minutes. Return service operates until late evening.

By car, Rochester is 30 miles southeast of London via the A2 road. There are convenient parking lots along Corporation Street.

PRACTICALITIES:

The important sights in Rochester are open daily throughout the year, except around Christmas. A general outdoor market is held on Fridays, and a flea market on Saturdays. Some shops close early on Wednesdays. The local **Tourist Information Centre**, ☎ (01634) 843-666, Internet: www.medwaytowns.com, is at 95 High Street, near the Six Poor Travellers' House. A visit there includes a 12-minute introductory video, an orientation area, and an art gallery. Rochester is in the county of Kent, and has a population of about 24,000.

FOOD AND DRINK:

Some choice restaurants and pubs along High Street are:

Royal Victoria and Bull (16 High St., opposite the Guildhall) A 400-year-old inn used as a locale by Dickens. ££

King's Head (58 High St., a block south of the Guildhall) Serving traditional fare for over four centuries. ££

Castle Tea Rooms (151 High St., near Dickens Centre) Light lunches and full meals in a cozy setting. £

SUGGESTED TOUR:

Numbers in parentheses correspond to numbers on the map.

Leaving **Rochester Station** (1), turn right and follow High Street to the:

*CHARLES DICKENS CENTRE in EASTGATE HOUSE (2). High Street, ☎ (01634) 844-176, Internet: www.medwaytowns.com/eastgate.html. *Open daily, 10–5:30. Last admission at 4:45. Closed Dec. 25 & 26. Adults £3.10, seniors, students, and children £2.05.*

The 16th-century Eastgate House itself was mentioned in Dickens' novel *Pickwick Papers* as the "Westgate House," and in *The Mystery of Edwin Drood* as the "Nun's House." Inside, two floors are filled with life-size models of his characters, reconstructions of scenes from his books, mementoes of his life, and an incredible "Dream" manifestation using the latest technology to re-create the author's dreams in three dimensions. All in all, a theatrical experience that is absolutely first rate.

Upon leaving, be sure to take a look at Dickens' tiny Swiss Chalet in the garden, which was moved here from his home at nearby Gad's Hill. The gabled house on the other side of High Street is Uncle Pumblechook's house in *Great Expectations*.

Continue along High Street to the **Six Poor Travellers' House** (3), otherwise known as the Watts Charity. Founded in 1579, it provided lodging for impoverished travelers until 1947. Dickens changed its name to "The Seven Poor Travellers" in his *Christmas Tale* of 1854. *You may visit the little Elizabethan bedrooms from March through October, on Tues.–Sat., 2–5.* ☎ *(01634) 845-609. Free.*

A further stroll down High Street leads to the Corn Exchange of 1706 with its extraordinary moon-faced clock projecting over the street. This was mentioned in Dickens' novel *The Uncommercial Traveller*. Just beyond is the **Guildhall** (4), built in 1687, which now houses a town museum dealing with regional history from the Stone Age onward. The turn-of-the-century **room settings** and the splendid collection of **Victorian toys** are

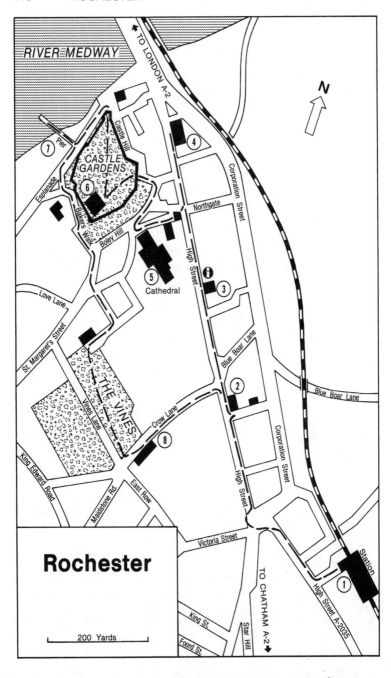

Rochester

200 Yards

especially interesting and should not be missed. Perhaps the most arresting feature here is the re-created interior of one of those infamous **prison hulks** of Napoleonic times, where convicts and prisoners-of-war were subjected to the most miserable living conditions. *Open daily except a few days at Christmas, 10–5:30. Last admission at 5. Free.* ☎ *(01634) 848-717.*

Across the street stands the Royal Victoria and Bull Hotel, which appears as "The Bull" in *Pickwick Papers* and as the "Blue Boar" in *Great Expectations.* Queen Victoria stayed there while still a princess. To the right, on High Street, is **Draper's Museum of Bygones**, a trip back in time through the past century, with period room sets, shop fronts, and nostalgic artifacts. *Open daily 10–5, closed over Christmas. Adults £2.25, seniors and students £1.75, under 16 £1.25.* ☎ *(01634) 830-647.*

Now return on High Street to Chertsey's Gate, also known as College Gate, a 15th-century structure featured in Dickens' *The Mystery of Edwin Drood.* Pass through it and look to the left. The tombstones in the graveyard of St. Nicholas' Church provided Dickens with names for some of his characters! You are now at:

ROCHESTER CATHEDRAL (5), ☎ (01634) 401-301, Internet: www.medway towns.com/cathedral.html. *Open daily 8:30–5, visits restricted during services. Suggested donation £2. Cassette tours. Light lunch and refreshments in refectory, Tues.–Sat. and summer Sun.* &.

An almost perfect example of early Norman architecture, Rochester Cathedral resembles Canterbury Cathedral and has several of the same features, including double transepts, an elevated choir, and an extensive **crypt**. The **west front**, with a magnificent doorway, is among the finest in England. Built on the site of an early-7th-century church, the cathedral was begun in 1080 and consecrated in 1130. Many additions were made through the centuries, making the mixture of styles particularly interesting.

Stroll over to:

ROCHESTER CASTLE (6), ☎ (01634) 402-276, Internet: www.medway towns.com/castle.html. *Open April–Sept., daily, 10–6; Oct.–March, daily 10–4. Closed Christmas period. Adults £3.50, seniors and students £2.50.*

The Romans had a fortress here to guard their bridge, and in later centuries Saxons fought Vikings on this hill. Of the great castle begun in 1087 by William the Conqueror, only the massive 12th-century keep remains. One of the finest examples of Norman military architecture, it is 113 feet high and has walls that are 12 feet thick. A climb to the top will reward you with a superb **panorama** of the town and the Medway estuary.

Descend through the park to the Bridge Warden's Chapel of 1387 and turn left to **Rochester Pier** (7). From here you will get a good view of activities on the river. Better still, you can enjoy a one- or two-hour **cruise** aboard the paddle steamer *Kingswear Castle,* built in 1924 to an 1880 design and now the last coal-fired boat of its type in Britain. *Operates in summer. Ask at the Tourist Office for current schedules, or ☎ (01634) 827-648, Internet: www.pskc.freeserve.co.uk.*

Follow the map past the Satis House, where Queen Elizabeth I was entertained in 1573, and the Old Hall, an early Tudor building. Continue on past Minor Canon Row, mentioned in Dickens' *Edwin Drood*; the King's School, founded in 1542 by Henry VIII; and the Archdeaconry of 1661.

Pass through The Vines, a park where monks once had their vineyard. Parts of the old Roman city wall can be seen on the north side. The **Restoration House** (8) on Crow Lane was the home of Miss Havisham in Dickens' *Great Expectations*. Its name derives from the tradition that Charles II stayed here in 1660 on his way to be crowned king following the end of the Commonwealth. A few steps down Crow Lane returns you to High Street and the end of the tour.

Faversham

L ocated at the end of a tidal creek, the ancient port of Faversham has remained a delightfully unpretentious little town for over a thousand years. Relatively few tourists venture this way, but those who do are enchanted by its simple charms. Settlements existed on this site since pre-historic times, with Faversham being mentioned in a charter in AD 811. It became a town of some importance during the Middle Ages, when many of its present structures were built. Along with Dover, Rye, and a few other towns, it was it was a member of the Cinque Ports confederation, owing allegiance only to the Crown. Despite this heritage, the town is not anoth-er preserved relic of the past but a growing community with its own thriv-ing industries. A visit to Faversham makes a refreshing change from the usual tourist circuit and can easily be combined with one to Rochester or Canterbury.

GETTING THERE:

Trains to Faversham leave London's Victoria Station at least twice an hour for the 70-minute journey. Return service operates until late evening.

By car, Faversham is 49 miles southeast of London via the A2 and M2 highways.

PRACTICALITIES:

Good weather is essential for this outdoor trip. A colorful outdoor market is held on Tuesdays, Fridays, and Saturdays. The local **Tourist Information Centre,** ☎ (01795) 534-542, Internet: www.faversham.org, is in the Fleur de Lis Heritage Centre at 13 Preston Street. **Guided tours** of the town are conducted on Saturday mornings from April to October, and there are both Open House and Secret Gardens events on a few days in summer. Ask the Tourist Centre for current details, or check it out on the Internet. Recently, commemorative plaques and viewpoint keys have been installed in the town, helping to bring history to life. Faversham is in the county of Kent and has a population of about 18,000.

FOOD AND DRINK:

Faversham is famous for its brewery, Shepherd Neame, which was founded here in 1698, is the oldest in Britain, and still makes what is called "real ale." Some choice places to eat are:

Shelleys (1 Market Place, near the Guildhall) A popular restaurant in a 16th-century building. ☎ (01795) 531-570. ££

Faversham Kebab House (64 Preston St., near the Heritage Centre) Authentic Turkish cuisine. ☎ (01795) 531-663. ££

China Village (4 Market Place, near the Guildhall) Quality Chinese cuisine in a 15th-century building. ☎ (01795) 591-000. ££

Phoenix Tavern & Restaurant (98 Abbey St.) Traditional English and Thai cuisine in an historic building. ☎ (01795) 532-757. ££

Albion Tavern (Front Brents) French and English cuisine, overlooking the Creek. ☎ (01795) 591-411. ££

The Sun Inn (West St., a block west of the Guildhall) Typical 16th-century pub and a favorite for local beer. ☎ (01795) 535-098. £

SUGGESTED TOUR:
Numbers in parentheses correspond to numbers on the map.

Leaving the **train station** (1), walk down Preston Street to the tourist office and museum. The **Fleur de Lis Heritage Centre** (2) provides an excellent introduction to Faversham's past and present. Housed in a former 15th-century inn, it has colorful displays of life in bygone days and a good audio-visual presentation of the town's history. Among the featured items are an Edwardian barber shop, a Victorian fireside, a village post office, costumes, and artifacts relating to shipbuilding, farming, and brewing. *The centre is open Mon.–Sat. 10–4, Sun. 10–1. Adults £1.50, concessions £1, children 50p.* ☎ *(01795) 534-542.*

Continue down Preston Street and turn left on Market Street. It was in the house at number 12 that King James II was held prisoner by local fishermen when he tried to flee the country in 1688. In a few yards you will come to the **Guildhall** (3), a rather elegant Georgian building set atop 16th-century pillars. An open-air **market** is held under this on Tuesdays, Fridays, and Saturdays. Established in 1086, it is the oldest market in Kent, and a wonderful place to meet the locals. Note the interesting **town pump** at the rear.

Court Street contains many fine 17th- and 18th-century houses. Follow it to Church Street and turn right to the parish church of **St. Mary of Charity** (4), which has a particularly elegant, and very rare, crown spire. It dates mostly from about 1320, though the nave is mainly 18th-century, with one Norman bay. The grotesque misericords in the choir are among the finest in England. Other features unusual for a parish church are the aisled transepts and the 14th-century frescoed pillar. This is actually the second-largest parish church in Kent, and larger than some of Britain's smaller cathedrals. Stroll around the churchyard, then follow the footpath to Abbey Place, passing the 16th-century Old Grammar School.

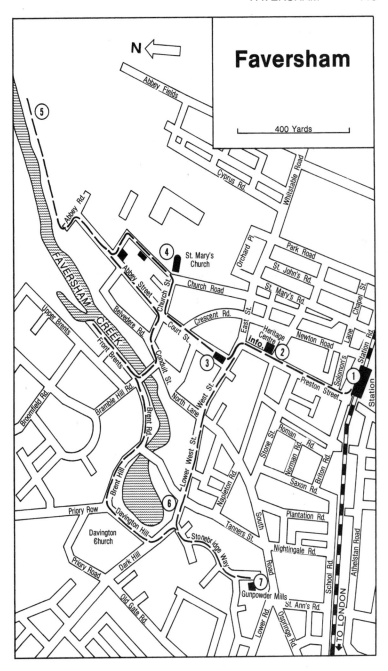

The famous 15th-century **Arden's House** on the southeast corner of Abbey Place was the scene of a notorious murder in 1551, which became the basis for the first play in English to use a contemporary event as its theme. Published in 1592, *Arden of Feversham* is still in the national repertory. Abbey Street is lined with well-preserved houses dating from the 16th and 17th centuries. Turn right on it and walk down to **Standard Quay** (5). Going past old warehouses, follow the creek until you come to a former warehouse, now beautifully converted to office use. All along here you will see old sailing barges, some of which are restored as houseboats, and which still take part in sailing barge races in the summer.

Now return to Abbey Street and make a right at Quay Lane. Cross the bridge by the brewery and walk out along Front Brents, from which you get a colorful view of the tiny waterway. Faversham's prosperity has always been closely linked with the creek, and 350 years ago it was England's main wool-exporting port, with busy trade to the Netherlands.

From here follow the map past the austere 12th-century Davington Church and down to **Stonebridge Pond** (6). Local streets opposite lead to the restored **Chart Gunpowder Mills** (7), the oldest of their kind in the world. Built in the late 18th century, they are the sole remaining link with a local industry that supplied the armed forces with gunpowder from 1560 to 1934. *The mills are open on weekends and bank holidays from Easter through October, from 2–5, but the exterior is always open.*

Return to the pond and turn right on West Street. In a short distance this becomes a charming pedestrians-only street leading back to the Guildhall.

*Canterbury

Over two thousand years of history made their mark on Canterbury, a magnet for countless pilgrimages since the 12th century. St. Augustine established the Christian Church in England here as far back as AD 597, and in 1170 the martyr Thomas à Becket was murdered in its cathedral. As a convenient place to ford the River Stour, Canterbury was a strategic settlement ever since the Iron Age. The Romans, calling the place *Durovernum*, made it an important center of trade in the 1st century AD. During Anglo-Saxon times its status increased as the name changed to *Cantwarabyrig*, and it became the capital of the Kingdom of Kent. Much of Canterbury's colorful past remains intact today, despite the ravages of Cromwell's troops and the bombs of World War II.

GETTING THERE:

Trains to Canterbury East Station, operated by Connex, depart from Victoria Station in London at least hourly, the run taking about 90 minutes. Be sure to get on the right car, as some trains split en route. Return service operates until late evening. Connex also operates similar service from London's Charing Cross and Waterloo stations, going to Canterbury West Station, near the West Gate.

By car, Canterbury is 58 miles southeast of London via the A2 and M2 highways.

PRACTICALITIES:

Any day is a good day to visit Canterbury, bearing in mind that some minor sights are closed on Sundays. The local **Tourist Information Centre**, ☎ (01227) 766-567, Internet: www.canterbury.co.uk, is at 34 St. Margaret's Street, three blocks southwest of the cathedral. You might ask there about renting a bicycle in town as this is good cycling country. Canterbury is in the county of Kent, and has a population of about 36,000.

FOOD AND DRINK:

Having attracted pilgrims and their modern counterparts since the Middle Ages, Canterbury has no shortage of restaurants and pubs in all price ranges. Some good choices for lunch are:

Cate's Brasserie (4 Church St. at St. Paul's, between the Abbey and

Burgate) Classic French brasserie food in an old half-timbered house, lunch specials or à la carte. ☎ (01227) 456-655. X: Sun. ££

Alberry's Wine Bar (38 St. Margaret's St., near the tourist office) A variety of homemade dishes, with daily specials. X: Sun. ☎ (01227) 452-378. ££

Tuo e Mio (16 The Borough, near the entrance to King's School) Italian cuisine, served by the same family for over 20 years. X: Mon., Tues. lunch. ☎ (01227) 761-471. ££

Il Vaticano (35 St. Margaret's St., near the tourist centre) Enjoy voluptuous pasta and other Italian fare in the garden or dining room. ☎ (01227) 765-333. ££

Marlowe's (59 St. Peter's St., a few blocks east of Westgate) All kinds of English and American dishes, vegetarian or otherwise. ☎ (01227) 462-194. £

Café St. Pierre (41 St. Peter's St.) Light lunches with a French touch. ☎ (01227) 456-791. £

SUGGESTED TOUR:

Numbers in parentheses correspond to numbers on the map.

Leaving **Canterbury East Station** (1), cross the footbridge over the A2 highway and turn right on the ancient city walls. *Those arriving at Canterbury West Station (17) should adjust their route accordingly.* Dating from the 13th and 14th centuries, these bastions were built atop Roman foundations. To your left is **Dane John Gardens** (2), a pleasant 18th-century park with a strange mound of unexplained but probably prehistoric origin. There's a view if you climb to the top. Continue along the walls and turn left by the bus station onto St. George's Street. The tower on the right is all that remains of St. George's Church, where Christopher Marlowe was baptized in 1564.

St. George's Street soon becomes High Street. Stroll down this and make a left onto St. Margaret's Street, leading to the Tourist Information Centre. Before exploring the town, why not brush up on your Chaucer (and have some fun!) at the:

*CANTERBURY TALES (3), ☎ (01227) 454-888. *Open daily except Christmas, 9–5:30 (4:30 in winter). Adults £5.25, seniors £4.50, children £4.* ⟨.

This popular attraction is a marvelous walk-through re-creation of the famous medieval pilgrimage. Here animated figures, light, sound, and even smells bring to life the *Knight's Tale,* the bawdy *Miller's Tale,* the fanciful *Wife of Bath's Tale,* and all those other stories you remember so well from schooldays. A great introduction to the town, and now for the real thing.

Retrace your steps and head up narrow **Mercery Lane**, the traditional pilgrim's approach to the cathedral. During medieval days this was lined

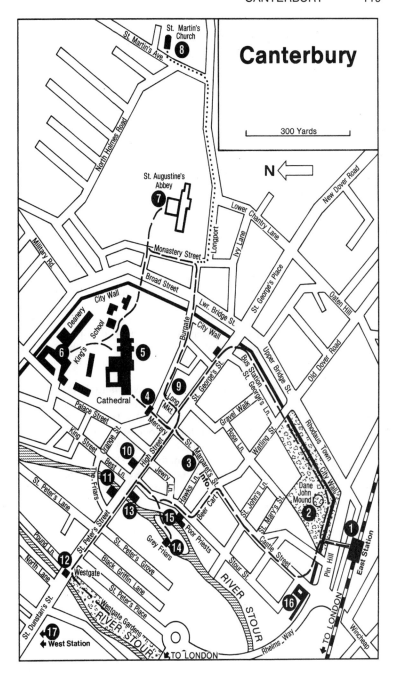

Canterbury

300 Yards

N

with stalls selling healing water from Becket's Well, medallions of St. Thomas, and other mementoes of the pilgrimage. At its far end is the Butter Market, an ancient center of trade. The magnificent **Christchurch Gate** (4), opposite, dates from the early 16th century and is the main entrance to the cathedral precinct.

Pass through the gate and enter the grounds of:

*CANTERBURY CATHEDRAL (5), ☎ (01227) 762-862. *Open Mon.–Fri. 9–5, Sat. 9–2:30, Sun. 12:30–2:30 and 4:30–5:30. Closed for 2 days in early July. Adults £3, seniors and children £2. Guided tours available.* ♿.

Canterbury Cathedral is the mother church of the Anglican faith throughout the world. For centuries it has been a center of pilgrimage and in a sense still is, although today's visitors are more likely to be tourists. Neither the largest, the tallest, nor the most beautiful of English cathedrals, it nevertheless has an attraction that is second to none.

A cathedral was built on this site by St. Augustine, the first Archbishop of Canterbury, in 602. This lasted until 1067, when it burned down. The present structure was begun in 1070 and completed in 1503, although little of the earlier work remains.

Enter the cathedral by way of the southwest porch. The lofty nave was built in the Perpendicular style during the 14th century, replacing an inadequate Norman original. Above the crossing you can see up the entire height of the magnificent **Bell Harry Tower**, whose bell is rung every evening and tolled on the death of a sovereign or an archbishop. A flight of steps to the right of the screen leads to the elevated **Choir**, one of the longest in England.

Behind the High Altar is the **Trinity Chapel**, which held Becket's tomb until Henry VIII had it demolished and the bones scattered in 1538. The tomb of the only king to be buried at Canterbury, Henry IV, and that of Edward, the Black Prince, are also in this chapel. At the extreme east end is a circular chapel known as the **Corona**, or Becket's Crown. The marble chair in its center is used for the enthronement of every archbishop.

The north aisle leads past the choir to the northwest transept, the scene of the martyrdom. It was here that Archbishop Thomas à Becket was murdered on December 29, 1170. The four knights who committed the deed thought they were carrying out the desire of their king, Henry II, although his part in it is disputed by historians. Henry certainly had reason to get rid of "this turbulent priest," his former friend and ally who had challenged the power of the State. Whatever the rationale behind the killing, it led to the canonization of Becket, the chastisement of Henry II, the role of Canterbury as a place of pilgrimage, and helped further the cause of individual freedom.

The spacious **Crypt** is the oldest part of the cathedral, dating from Norman times. Along its south aisle there is a Huguenot chapel where services in French are still held. Becket was first buried at the east end, which was also the scene of Henry II's penance.

Stroll into the early-15th-century **Cloisters** by way of the northwest transept. Adjoining it is the Chapter House and Library. Follow the passageway and turn left into the grounds of the **King's School** (6). Although it was refounded by Henry VIII, the school claims an ancestry going back to the time of St. Augustine, which would make it the oldest in England. The 12th-century Norman staircase near the northwest corner of the Green Court is superb, as are the views of the cathedral from this point.

Returning, bear left and walk around the rear of the cathedral to the Kent War Memorial Gardens. Go through the gate in the far corner and follow the map to the ruins of **St. Augustine's Abbey** (7). Originally founded in 598 and rebuilt several times since, it was destroyed by Henry VIII following the Reformation. Excavations revealed the layout of several buildings including the church, monk's dormitory, kitchen, refectory, and cloisters. A new museum of artifacts found during excavations has recently been added, and the admission price includes an interactive audio tour of the ruins. *Open April–Sept. daily 10–6; Oct. daily 10–5; Nov.–March daily 10–4. Closed Dec. 24–26. Adults £2.50, seniors £1.90, children £1.30.* ☎ *(01227) 767-345.* &.

From here you might want to make an interesting little **side trip**. Walk back around St. Augustine's and turn left on Monastery Street, then left again on Longport. Just past the jail make another left to **St. Martin's Church** (8), said to be the oldest church in England to remain in use. Parts of it date from before the time of St. Augustine and were used by Queen Bertha, Christian wife of pagan King Ethelbert. Explore the interior, noting in particular the Saxon font, then stroll through the tranquil graveyard. *Open daily 9–5, except during services. Donation welcome.* ☎ *(01227) 459-482.*

Returning to town via Longport and Church Street, walk down Burgate and turn left into Butchery Lane. The new **Roman Museum** (9) lies buried beneath a modern shopping centre, at the actual level of the Roman town. Incorporating remains of an excavated Roman villa from around AD 100, it uses modern techniques to re- create life here some 1,500 years ago. *Open Mon.–Sat. 10–5, and on Sun. in June–Oct., 1:30–5. Closed Good Friday and Christmas week. Adults £2.20, seniors £1.45, children £1.10.* ☎ *(01227) 785-575.* &.

Continuing along High Street, you will pass Queen Elizabeth's Guest Chamber, a Tudor house on the left in which the queen entertained her French suitor, the Duke of Alençon. It is now a restaurant. Farther along on the right is the **Royal Museum and Art Gallery** (10), otherwise known as the Beaney Institute. It has a fine collection of Roman and other antiquities as well as local art. *Open Mon.–Sat. 10–5. Closed Sun., Good Friday, Christmas week. Free.* ☎ *(01227) 452-747.*

The famous **Weavers' House** (11) on the edge of the River Stour was occupied by Huguenot weavers who settled in Canterbury after fleeing France in the 17th century. Now a gift shop, it is open to visitors, who may inspect the old looms and ducking stool, or even take a boat ride on the river.

Amble down St. Peter's Street to the **Westgate** (12). Built in the late 14th century, this imposing fortification once guarded the western approach to Canterbury. Its upper floor served as the city jail until 1829, and now houses a museum of arms and torture instruments. There is a superb **view** from the top., and also the opportunity to do a bit of brass rubbling. *Open Mon.–Sat. 11–12:30 and 1:30–3:30. Closed Sun., Good Friday, and Christmas week. Adults 90p, seniors 60p, children 45p.* ☎ *(01227) 452-747.*

A stroll through Westgate Gardens is very inviting. Return along St. Peter's Street to the **Eastbridge Hospital** (13), a well-preserved 12th-century hostel for poor pilgrims. Its crypt, chapel, and hall may be visited. *Open Mon.–Sat. 10–4:45. Closed Sun., Good Friday, Christmas week. Adults £1, seniors 75p, children 50p.* ☎ *(01227) 471-688.*

Turn right on Stour Street and then right again into a tiny lane marked "to Greyfriars." Follow the path onto a small island. The extremely picturesque 13th-century **Greyfriars** (14) is all that remains of the first Franciscan friary in England. From inside you can get a feeling of what monastic life in medieval Canterbury was like. *Open mid-May through late Sept., Mon.–Sat. 2–4.* ☎ *(01227) 462-395.*

Just beyond this, also on Stour Street, is the **Poor Priests' Hospital** (15). This 14th-century hostel now houses the **Canterbury Heritage Museum**, where the latest techniques are used to re-create the city's past, from Roman times to the near-present. *Open Mon.–Sat. 10:30–5, and on Sun. from June to Oct., 1:30–5. Adults £2.20, seniors £1.45, children £1.10.* ☎ *(01227) 452-747.Partial ᒼ.*

Follow the map back to the station via Castle Street. At its end, opposite the city wall, are the ruins of an 11th-century **Norman Castle** (16). Never very effective as a defensive bastion, it was later used as a jail, a coal dump, and a water tank.

Cross Castle Street and turn left at the city walls, taking the overpass to the station.

Dover

For over two thousand years the fabled White Cliffs of Dover have marked the gateway to England. Iron Age man settled these shores, and so did the Romans, who built their port of *Dubris* here in AD 43. Strategically, Dover is of paramount importance to Britain, being the closest point to the Continent and only 22 miles from France. A great fortress inevitably rose on this site, defending the island nation right down to modern times. Today, the massive 12th-century castle is a major tourist attraction, while the harbor it overlooks is the busiest passenger port in England.

GETTING THERE:

Trains to Dover's **Priory Station** leave at least hourly from either Victoria or Charing Cross stations in London, with a journey time of nearly two hours. Be sure to board the correct car as some trains split en route. Return service operates until mid-evening.

By car, Dover is 74 miles southeast of London by way of either the A2 and M2 highways, or the A20 and M20 highways.

PRACTICALITIES:

Good weather is essential for this largely outdoor trip, especially for the maritime views for which you might want to bring along binoculars. The Castle and the White Cliffs Experience are open every day except Christmas Day, Boxing Day, and New Year's, but the Roman Painted House is closed in winter and on Mondays.

The local **Tourist Information Centre**, ☎ (01304) 205-108, Internet: www.doveruk.com, is on Townwall Street, just inland from Marine Parade. **Guide Friday** offers an all-day hop-on, hop- off open-top double-deck **bus service** connecting the tourist sights, the town center, and the train station, daily from about mid-May to early October. The buses run hourly and single fares are available between stops. Full all-day fares are £6 for adults, £5 for seniors and students, and £2 for children under 12. Pay the driver. ☎ (01273) 746-205, Internet: www.guidefriday.com.

Dover is in the county of Kent, and has a population of about 34,000.

FOOD AND DRINK:

The Churchill (Marine Parade, on the seafront below the castle) In a pleasant old hotel with a good view of the port. ☎ (01304) 203-633. ££

Britannia (Townwall St., near the tourist centre) Both a downstairs pub and an upstairs restaurant. ☎ (01304) 203-248. X: Sat. lunch. £ and ££

Dino's (58 Castle St., near the Market Square) Good Italian cooking at modest prices. ☎ (01304) 204-678. X: Mon. £

Curry Garden (24 High St., near the Old Town Gaol) Indian cuisine, including tandoori. ☎ (01304) 206-357. £

Inexpensive cafeteria meals are available at both the castle and the White Cliffs Experience.

SUGGESTED TOUR:

Numbers in parentheses correspond to numbers on the map.

From **Priory Station** (1) you can either take a bus direct to the castle or follow the map into town. Here, at the **Bus Station** (2), you can get a ride up to the castle, perched dramatically atop a nearby hill. It is also possible to get there by taxi or car, or even on foot if you don't mind the stiff climb.

*****DOVER CASTLE** (3–4), ☎ (01304) 201-628. *Open Apr.–Sept., daily 10–6; Oct., daily 10–5; Nov.–March, daily 10–4. Last admission one hour before closing. Closed Dec. 24–26 and New Year's Day. Adults £6.90, concessions £5.20, children (5–15) £3.50. Partially &.*

Dover Castle is by far the finest and most fascinating military structure in England. While essentially of Norman construction, parts of it date from Saxon and even Roman times. Brutally strong, its 20-foot-thick walls have withstood sieges during its entire history. Begin your visit with the mighty **Keep** (3), surrounded by a defensive curtain wall. Built in 1180 by Henry II to replace earlier structures, the keep has been continually modified down through the centuries. You can easily spend hours exploring the many rooms and passageways, and examining the exhibitions displayed there. Be sure to get up to the roof, from which there is a fabulous *****view** extending all the way to France in clear weather. A visit to the **Underground Works** beneath the castle is well worth the effort, although it involves some steep climbs. The entry to this tunnel system is just outside the keep, and an audio guided tour is available.

The existence of a maze of secret tunnels used in World War II was declassified in 1986, and parts of the subterranean labyrinth later opened to visitors. Known as *****Hellfire Corner**, the complex is shown on tours that include control rooms and an opening in the side of the White Cliffs from which Winston Churchill watched the Battle of Britain. Even more recent history unravels at the **World of Espionage Exhibition**, where you'll uncover some of the realities behind the James Bond stories.

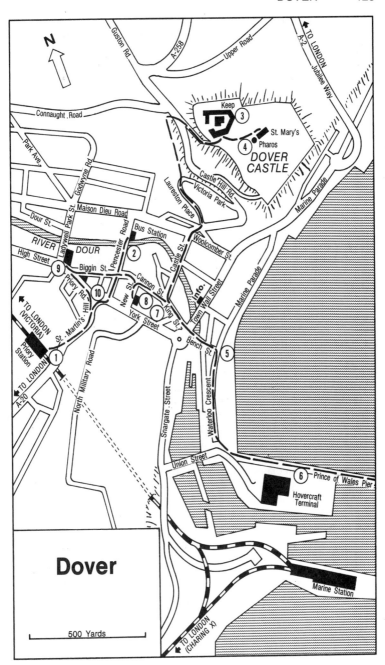

Dover

500 Yards

More of the castle's past can be seen by strolling over to the **Pharos** (4), a Roman lighthouse erected in the 2nd century AD to guide the Imperial Navy into port. This is the tallest surviving Roman structure in Britain. Directly adjacent to it stands the Saxon **Church of St. Mary de Castro**, which was heavily restored during the 19th century. Although its exact age is unknown, parts of it may date from as far back as the 7th century. From here you might want to amble around the outer ramparts before leaving the precincts. Don't miss **Queen Elizabeth's Pocket Pistol**, a 24-foot-long cannon presented to Henry VIII.

Return to the town by bus or, since it is downhill, on foot. Just follow the path opposite the bus stop, which leads through Victoria Park. Laureston Place and Castle Hill Road will bring you to Castle Street, at the end of which is the **Market Square**, built over the site of the ancient Roman harbor. From there take King and Bench streets to Marine Parade. Along the way you will pass Townwall Street, where the tourist office is located.

There are splendid views of the harbor from **Marine Parade** (5), but for an even better look you should walk out on the **Prince of Wales Pier** (6), which offers wonderful panoramas of the famous White Cliffs. From here you can watch the comings and goings of the speedy hovercrafts and leisurely ferries. No quick trip through the Channel Tunnel will ever match the experience of a genuine sea voyage to the Continent.

Return to Market Square and the:

WHITE CLIFFS EXPERIENCE and DOVER MUSEUM (7), ☎ (01304) 214-566, Internet: www.doveruk.com/tourism/wce. *Admissions Apr.–Oct., daily 10–5 (remains open until 6:30); Nov.–March, daily 10–3 (remains open until 4:30). Closed Christmas Day, Boxing Day, New Year's Day. Adults £5.75, seniors £4.60, students £4.60, children (4-14) £3.95. Tickets include admission to the adjacent Dover Museum. Café.* &.

This multimedia extravaganza, set amid actual archaeological digs, brings the area's turbulent history to life with the latest in theatrical technology. Two themes are followed: **Roman Encounters**, featuring a Roman street and quayside, the actual Roman ruins over which the Experience was built, life among the Roman soldiers, and more; and **Our Finest Hours**, where local everyday life during the horrors of World War II is re-created.

The adjacent **Dover Museum** is included in the same admission, so pop in for a look at what may be the world's oldest seagoing boat, a 3,500-year-old Bronze Age vessel unearthed in Dover in 1992. There's also a vast collection of artifacts spanning thousands of years of Dover's history.

Nearby, on New Street, is the **Roman Painted House** (8). Britain's answer to Pompeii, this excavated 2nd-century town house has lovely painted walls and an intact underfloor heating system. *Well preserved and beautifully presented, it is open from April through September, on Tuesdays through Sundays, from 10–5. Adults £2, seniors and students 80p.* ☎ *(01304) 203-279.*

Now follow Cannon Street and Biggin Street to the **Old Town Gaol** (9) in the historic Town Hall. Prison life in Victorian times is re-created in 14 dismal cells, where you can experience its awfulness before making your escape. There is also a genuine Victorian court room, where you can witness a "felon" being sent to the gallows. *Open June–Sept., Tues.–Sat. 10–4:30 and Sun. 2–4:30; rest of year Wed.–Sat. 10–4:30 and Sun. 2–4:30. Adult £3.50, seniors and children £2.10.* ☎ *(01304) 242-766.*

St. Edmund's Chapel (10) on Priory Road is on the way back to the train station. Dating from the 13th century, it ceased religious services in 1544 and was later used as a forge. In 1968 the tiny wayside chapel was re-consecrated and is thought to be the smallest in England in regular use.

Trip 15

Romney, Hythe & Dymchurch

A ride on the Romney, Hythe & Dymchurch Railway is a pure delight. There are no famous sights along its 14-mile length, just the exhilarating joy of being hauled across the Romney Marshes aboard a miniature steam train. This fun-filled daytrip is the perfect antidote to a steady diet of cathedrals, castles, and stately homes.

Opened in 1927, the railway is one of the most popular attractions in southern England. Its one-third-scale locomotives are faithful replicas of famous engines that once served on the main lines. Over 300,000 passengers, not all of them children by any means, are carried each year in the diminutive coaches. Join them in the fun and you'll be glad you did.

GETTING THERE:

Trains leave twice an hour from London's Charing Cross Station for Folkestone Central Station, with a journey time of about 90 minutes. Service is reduced on Sundays, and some trains split en route. Return trains run until mid-evening. From Folkestone you can travel the five miles by bus or taxi to Hythe, where the steam line begins.

By car, take the A20 and M20 roads to Newingreen/Stanford (Junction 11), then the A261 to Hythe. The total distance is 68 miles southeast of London.

PRACTICALITIES:

Good weather is necessary to really enjoy this trip. The Romney, Hythe & Dymchurch Railway operates daily from Easter to the end of September, and on weekends in March and October. Service is more frequent during the peak summer months. Fares vary according to the journey taken, but are quite reasonable. For more information about the steam railway contact their offices in New Romney, ☎ (01797) 362-353. The local **Tourist Information Centre** in Folkestone, ☎ (01303) 258-594, is near the harbor. Two Internet sites to check are: www.southeast england.uk.com, and www.kenttourism.co.uk. The entire trip is in the county of Kent.

FOOD AND DRINK:

Meals and snacks are available at the Dungeness and New Romney

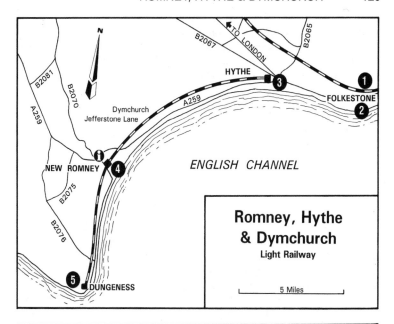

Romney, Hythe & Dymchurch Light Railway

5 Miles

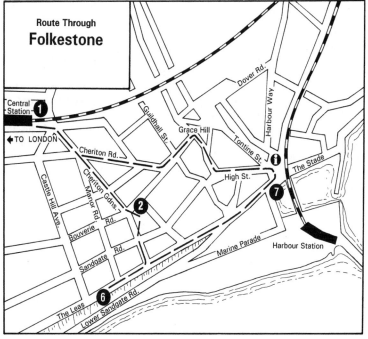

Route Through Folkestone

stations, and drinks are served on the miniature bar car attached to some of the trains. A few nearby restaurants and pubs are:

La Tavernetta (Leaside Court, Clifton Gardens, near Castle Hill Ave. and The Leas in Folkestone) Italian cuisine. ☎ (01303) 254-955. ££

Emilio's Portofino (124a Sandgate Rd., 3 blocks southwest of the bus station in Folkestone) Another Italian restaurant. ☎ (01303) 255-762. ££

Butt of Sherry (5 Theatre St., Hythe) A wine bar with traditional English fare. X: Sun., Mon. eve. £

The Pilot (on the beach at Dungeness) An unusual pub noted for fish and chips. ☎ (01797) 320-314. £

SUGGESTED TOUR:

Numbers in parentheses correspond to numbers on the map.

Those coming by train will begin their trip at **Folkestone Central Station** (1). From here follow the map to the **Folkestone Bus Station** (2), a few blocks away. Board a bus for Hythe and ask to be let off at the Light Railway Station. You could, of course, take a taxi directly from Folkestone Central to Hythe, a distance of about five miles.

The Romney, Hythe & Dymchurch Light Railway Station in **Hythe** (3) is next to the Royal Military Canal, which was built as a defense during the Napoleonic Wars. A short walk along its banks is a pleasant diversion if you have a wait before the next train departure. Take a careful look at the posted schedule and decide whether you want to go just to New Romney, or make a stop there and then continue on all the way to Dungeness. Note that a very few of the miniature trains are hauled by diesel traction, in which case you might want to wait for steam.

The ride from Hythe to New Romney takes about 35 minutes, stopping at Dymchurch and Jefferstone Lane along the way. **New Romney** (4) is the headquarters of the railway and has several interesting things to see, including yards, engine shops, and the fascinating **Toy and Model Museum.** Here you can relive childhood dreams with vintage toys and two working model railways, and do it free if you have a round-trip ticket from Hythe to Dungeness. There is also a buffet serving anything from drinks to full meals, and a gift shop.

Continuing on to **Dungeness** (5), the rails follow very close to the sea. This is a lovely and sparsely inhabited region, a perfect spot for the nuclear power plant at the end of the line. Getting off there, you may visit the lifeboat station and perhaps climb to the top of the **Old Lighthouse.** Built in 1901 to a height of 143 feet, it is open whenever the trains run.

Those traveling back to London via Folkestone will probably want to see a bit of that town before they leave. From the bus station it is an easy walk to **The Leas** (6), a promenade with magnificent maritime views. The **harbor** (7) is in the oldest part of town. Return via the quaint and narrow High Street, then head back to Central Station by bus, taxi, or on foot.

*Rye

A relic from the Middle Ages, the once-great seaport of Rye got stranded when its harbor silted up in the 16th century. Today, only small craft can sail the two miles up the River Rother to the town's quayside. In a way this is fortunate, as it left England with a well-preserved medieval port that still clings to its salty past. Rye is alive with the smell of the sea, and working fishermen still walk its ancient streets, side by side with their many visitors. For tourists, it easily ranks as one of the most enjoyable towns in Britain.

GETTING THERE:

Trains depart London's Charing Cross or Victoria stations frequently for either Ashford or Hastings, where you change to a local for Rye. The total journey takes less than two hours. Return trains run until mid-evening, with reduced service on Sundays and holidays.

By car, the shortest route is to take the A21 from London to Flimwell and change to the A268. Rye is 63 miles southeast of London.

PRACTICALITIES:

Rye may be savored on a fine day in any season. The local **Tourist Information Centre**, ☎ (01797) 226-696, is at The Quay in the Heritage Centre. They offer an audio walking tour of the town, available in English, French, or Japanese. Outdoor **markets** operate on Thursdays near the train station. The annual **Rye Festival**, held for two weeks in early September, offers music, literary events, films, visual arts, workshops, and children's events. Rye is in the county of East Sussex and has a population of about 4,500.

FOOD AND DRINK:

Rye has plenty of quaint old inns, tea shoppes, and pubs. Some choices are:

Flushing Inn (Market St., near the Town Hall) A 15th-century inn noted for its seafood. ☎ (01797) 223-292. X: Mon. eve., Tues., Jan. ££ and £££

Fletcher's House (Lion St., just north of St. Mary's Church) Enjoy meals in a historic medieval house. ☎ (01797) 223-101. X: weekdays. ££

Mermaid Inn (Mermaid St.) An old smugglers' haunt from the 15th century. ☎ (01797) 223-065. ££

Ypres Castle (Gun Garden, below Ypres Tower) A cozy pub with decent lunches and a great view. £

The Mariners (High St.) Light lunches in a tea shop. ☎ (01797) 223-480. £

SUGGESTED TOUR:

Numbers in parentheses correspond to numbers on the map.

Leaving the **train station** (1), walk straight ahead and turn left on Cinque Ports Street. In a few yards you will pass remnants of the original 14th-century town walls, just behind a parking lot. The **Land Gate** (2) is the only remaining town gate of the three that once protected Rye. It was probably constructed about 1340 and originally contained machinery for a drawbridge across the town ditch.

Walk uphill along Hilder's Cliff, enjoying marvelous views across the Romney Marsh. Much of this lowland was once an open ocean, but that was before the sea receded as the River Rother silted up and the tides washed countless pebbles onto the shore.

Make a right down Conduit Hill to the **Augustine Friary** (3), commonly known as The Monastery. Originally built in 1379, it served as a refuge for persecuted French Huguenots in the 16th century. Today it houses a pottery that's open to the public. Now return to High Street and follow it to the Old Grammar School, erected in 1636 and immortalized by Thackeray. Opposite this is the 400-year-old George Hotel.

A left onto Lion Street leads past Fletcher's House, once a vicarage and now a restaurant. The dramatist John Fletcher was born here in 1579. At the corner of Market Street stands the **Town Hall** (4), which contains some interesting artifacts, including the gruesome gibbet cage with the remains of a notorious 18th-century murderer who was executed in the town. *Open to the public by appointment only.*

In a few more steps you will come to *St. Mary's Church (5), first erected between 1150 and 1300. Facing the top of Lion Street is the *church clock, the oldest in England still functioning with its original works. Two figures above the clock face strike the quarter hours but not the hours. A plaque between them proclaims "For our time is a very shadow that passeth away." Climbing to the top of the *tower is well worth the effort. An extremely narrow staircase leads to the bell-ringing room where various combinations of "changes" are posted. In the same room is the venerable clock mechanism, complete with an 18-foot-long pendulum. A ladder goes to the bell room itself, and another to the roof, from which there's an unsurpassed **view** of the entire area. A visit to the church interior is also worthwhile. *Open daily, 10–dusk, weather permitting. Tower visit: adults £2, seniors and students £1.* ☎ *(01797) 222-430. Church interior is* ♿.

Across the churchyard stands a curious oval-shaped brick **water reservoir**, built in 1735 but no longer used. Bear right and stroll down to **Ypres Tower** (6). Pronounced *Wipers*, this is the oldest existing structure in town.

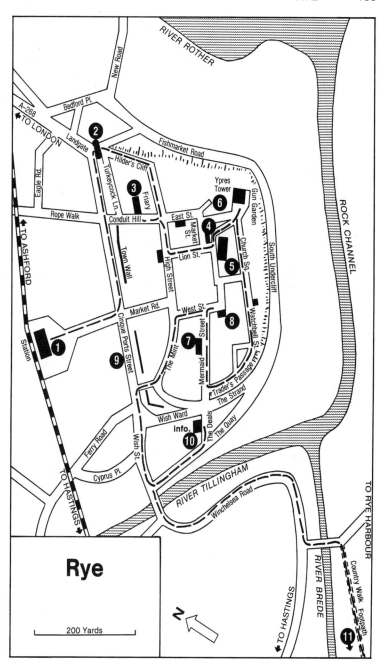

Rye

200 Yards

Largely unchanged since it was first constructed as a defensive fortification around 1249, it ceased to have any military value in later years and became home to one John de Ypres. The town bought it back in 1513 for use as a jail, a function it served until 1865. Now part of the **Rye Castle Museum**, the tower houses artifacts related to smuggling, law and order, and iron work. There is a good view from its terrace. Just below this is the **Gun Garden**, an emplacement for artillery pieces that once defended England's shores. The **rest of the museum** is located nearby, on East Street. Here you can see local pottery, Rye's old fire engine, fashions from the past, model ships, and much more from the town's illustrious past. *Open April–Oct., daily 10:30–5:30; Nov.–March, weekends only 10:30–4:30. Combined admission: adults £3, seniors £2, children (7–16) £1. Tower only: adults £2, seniors £1.50, children 75p.* ☎ *(01797) 226-728. Partially* &.

Walk down lovely, cobbled Church Square. This soon becomes Watchbell Street, whose name derives from the warning bell once housed there. Along the way you'll pass a Spanish-style Catholic church. At the end is the **lookout**, overseeing the harbor.

Traders Passage leads to ***Mermaid Street**, quite possibly the most picturesque thoroughfare in all England. Go uphill to the **Mermaid Inn** (7), a famous hiding place for smugglers and highwaymen, first built in the late 15th century and much altered over the years. It is now a hotel and restaurant, the perfect spot for a refreshment break. Walk through a passage into the courtyard for a look.

Continue up Mermaid Street and turn right on West Street. Here, where the street bends, is the **Lamb House** (8), formerly the residence of the Lamb family, which for a long time provided several of Rye's mayors. Henry James lived in this house from 1897 until 1916, writing several of his best-known novels here. *It is now owned by the National Trust and receives visitors on Wednesdays and Saturdays, April through October, from 2–6, last admission at 5:30. Adults £2.50, children £1.25.* ☎ *(01892) 890-651.*

Stroll back down West Street to High Street and turn left to The Mint, then make a right into **Needles Passage**. This narrow path takes you through a gap in the old town wall and down a few steps. To the right, at 20 Cinque Ports Street, is the **Rye Treasury of Mechanical Music** (9), a noisy but thoroughly enchanting exhibition of barrel organs, musical boxes, reed organs, dance organs, player pianos, and the like. Naturally, they all work, and will all be demonstrated during the hour-long tour. *Open March–Oct., daily 10–5; Nov.–Feb., Wed.–Mon. 11–4. Adults £3, seniors £2, children £1.50.* ☎ *(01797) 223-345.* &.

Follow the map down Wish Street and turn left just before the bridge, leading onto The Strand. Here you'll find an interesting group of 19th-century **warehouses** (10) bearing testament to the town's past as a trading port. One of these houses the **Heritage Centre and Tourist Office**, as well as the acclaimed **Story of Rye**, a highly entertaining sound-and-light show enveloping a three-dimensional model of the town. *Shown every half-*

hour, daily from 9–5:30 from mid-March through Oct., and on weekends from 10–3 the rest of the year. Adults £2, seniors £1.50, children £1. ☎ *(01797) 226-696.* ♿.

Before leaving Rye, you might want to take a delightful stroll in the countryside. From the bridge at the foot of Wish Street it is only about 1.5 miles to **Camber Castle** (11), built by Henry VIII in the 16th century. Just follow the map to the public footpath along the River Brede, a well-marked trail leading through pleasant sheep-grazing land. The walk is worthwhile even if the castle is closed. *Castle open July through Sept., Saturdays only, 2–5. Adults £2, children £1.* ♿.

Royal Tunbridge Wells

Y ou won't find any medieval or even Tudor buildings in Royal Tunbridge Wells, which remained a forest until the discovery of its mineral springs in 1606. Soon after that, however, the nobility from London began coming in droves. An elegant spa developed, attracting aristocrats down through the days of Queen Victoria. Like Bath, Royal Tunbridge Wells reached its peak under the guidance of that 18th-century dandy, Richard "Beau" Nash, who as Master of Ceremonies organized balls, concerts, and other entertainments for the smart set. Alas, fashion is fickle, and by the time of the Regency many of its patrons had switched their allegiance to upstart Bath.

Today's Tunbridge Wells (to use its more common name) is still a very lovely place, retaining much of the style that made it famous. The Pantiles, an elegant 18th-century promenade adjoining the spring, could very well be considered the most beautiful urban street in England. Though its days of greatness have faded, the town and its heritage center, A Day at the Wells, offers a fascinating glimpse into a gracious past.

This trip can easily be combined with the one to Battle, which is on the same rail line.

GETTING THERE:

Trains to Tunbridge Wells leave frequently from London's Charing Cross Station, with reduced service on Sundays and holidays. The trip takes just under one hour. Return trains run until mid-evening.

By car, Royal Tunbridge Wells is 36 miles southeast of London via the A21 road.

PRACTICALITIES:

This trip can be made at any time in good weather. The local **Tourist Information Centre**, ☎ (01892) 515-675, Internet: www.tunbridgewells.gov.uk/tourism, is in the Old Fish Market on the Pantiles. The town features several events, including the Georgian Festival in late July, the Sedan Chair Race in late August, the Festival of Food & Drink in September, and the Winter Street Festival in late December. Royal Tunbridge Wells is in the county of Kent and has a population of about 60,000.

FOOD AND DRINK:

Some choice places for lunch are:

Thackeray's House (85 London Rd., 5 blocks northwest of the train station) Located in the home of the author, William Makepeace Thackeray, and regarded as the best in town. ☎ (01892) 511-921. X: Mon. £££

Downstairs at Thackeray's (as above, with its own entrance) Imaginative gourmet cuisine at affordable prices, so it's very popular. Reserve. ☎ (01892) 537-559. X: Sun., Mon. ££

The Regency Restaurant (26 The Pantiles) Light meals in a traditional tearoom setting; outdoor tables on The Pantiles in season. £

Beau Nash Tavern (Mount Ephraim, opposite The Common) Tucked away in a mews, this pub serves light meals at lunch. £

SUGGESTED TOUR:

Numbers in parentheses correspond to numbers on the map.

Leaving **Tunbridge Wells Station** (1), turn right and follow High Street to Chapel Place. This leads to *The Pantiles (2), an 18th-century pedestrian walk that has scarcely changed since Regency days. Its name derives from the square clay tiles with which it was paved in 1700. The original iron-impregnated **Chalybeate Spring** (3) is under the porch of the Bath House at the northern end. From Easter until the end of September you can sample its faintly rusty-tasting water, served by the town's "dipper." There are many elegant shops in the area selling antiques, books, gifts and the like.

Strolling along, you'll soon come to the delightful Musick Gallery above a small shop, from which musicians once entertained the gentry. The **Corn Exchange** with its statue of Ceres, the goddess of agriculture, now houses a wonderful exhibition:

A DAY AT THE WELLS (4), ☎ (01892) 546-545. *Open daily throughout the year, 10–5, closing at 4 from Nov. through March. Adults £4.65, seniors, students and children £3.65*

Step into a long-vanished summer's day in 1740 as you amble through authentic scenes of elegant (and scandalous!) Royal Tunbridge Wells, peopled by figures in period costumes. Beau Nash is your guide, and there are sounds, smells, and music as along with the sights of a vanished age. Children will enjoy their special audio commentary.

Return to Chapel Place and visit the **Church of King Charles the Martyr** (5), whose name reflects the local Stuart sympathies. Built from 1676 to 1696, it is the oldest in town and has an outstanding ceiling of ornamental plasterwork. Lunchtime concerts are featured in July and August. *Open*

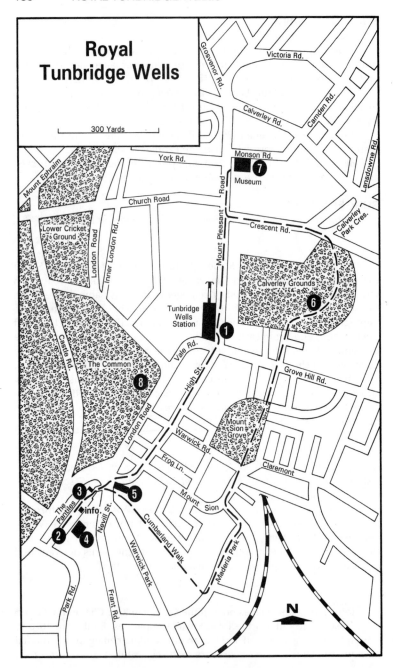

Royal Tunbridge Wells

300 Yards

Mon.–Sat. 11–3. Free, donations accepted. ☎ *(01892) 511-745.*

From here follow the map along a shady lane and local streets to **Calverley Grounds** (6), a beautiful town park. Calverley Park Crescent, just beyond, is somewhat reminiscent of Bath when seen from the garden side.

Walk over to the **Museum and Art Gallery** (7) on Mount Pleasant Road. Here you will see an excellent collection of Victoriana, local crafts, toys, costumes, and assorted bygones. *Open Mon.–Sat., 9:30–5. Closed Sun., bank holidays, Easter.* ☎ *(01892) 547-221. Free.* ♿.

A fine way to spend the remainder of your time is to take a stroll through **The Common** (8), a 250-acre park with unusual rock formations.

Trip 18

Battle

The Battle of Hastings was probably the most significant event in English history. It was fought on that fateful day in 1066, not at Hastings, but on a hill six miles inland where the attractive village of Battle now stands. Visitors may wander around the fields and, with the help of explanatory signs, re-create in their minds the conflict that signaled England's entry into European civilization. Also waiting to be explored are the ruins of the great abbey begun by William the Conqueror to commemorate the event.

The story of the Battle of Hastings is well documented by the famous Bayeux Tapestry, a replica of which is in the Battle Museum. Briefly, what happened is that the childless King Edward of England promised the throne to his cousin, Duke William of Normandy. He even sent Harold Godwinson, his brother-in-law, to France to confirm the pledge. Upon the death of King Edward, however, Harold took the crown himself. Feeling betrayed, William assembled a mighty army and invaded England. Meanwhile, Harold was successfully fighting off a third claimant to the throne, the King of Norway, at Stamford Bridge near York. On hearing of Duke William's invasion, he rushed his tired troops 200 miles south and engaged the Normans at Battle. The two armies were nearly matched in strength. Harold, occupying the higher ground, might have won except for a brilliant ruse on the part of William, who feigned defeat and trapped the English on the lower ground. By the end of that long, bloody day of October 14th, 1066, Harold lay dead and the sun set forever on Anglo-Saxon England.

It is possible to combine this daytrip with the one to Royal Tunbridge Wells.

GETTING THERE:

Trains to Battle depart London's Charing Cross station at half-hour intervals, with slightly reduced service on Sundays and holidays. The journey takes about 75 minutes, and return trains run until mid-evening.

By car, Battle is 57 miles southeast of London via the A21 and A210 roads.

PRACTICALITIES:

You can visit Battle at any time since the abbey and battlefield are open daily all year round. For further details, contact the **Tourist Information Centre** at 88 High Street, ☎ (01424) 773-721, Internet: www. battletown.co.uk. The annual **Battle Festival,** featuring a wide variety of events, is held from about mid-June to late June. Battle is in the county of East Sussex and has a population of about 6,000.

FOOD AND DRINK:

Battle has a good selection of restaurants and pubs, including:

Blacksmith's (43 High St., near The Almonry) English and Continental cuisine in a 16th-century building. ☎ (01424) 773-200. X: Mon. ££ and £££

Pilgrim's Rest (opposite the Abbey Gatehouse) Lunch in a 15th-century half-timbered house, or in the garden. ☎ (01424) 772-314. ££

1066 Inn (12 High St., just north of the Abbey Gatehouse) A friendly pub with home-cooked food. ☎ (01424) 773-224. £ and ££

Ye Olde King's Head (Mount St., just off High St.) This 15th-century pub offers home-cooked meals. ☎ (01424) 772-317. £

SUGGESTED TOUR:

Numbers in parentheses correspond to numbers on the map.

Leaving the **railway station** (1), a Victorian Gothic structure dating from 1853, turn right and follow Lower Lake and Upper Lake to The Green. On your left you will pass the abbey wall and come to the **Abbey Gatehouse** (2), built in 1338 and one of the finest in England. Pass through it into the:

*BATTLEFIELD AND ABBEY (2–4), ☎ (01424) 773-792. *Open April–Sept., daily 10–6; Oct., daily 10–5; Nov.–March, daily 10–4. Closed Dec. 24, 25, 26, New Year's Day. Adults £4, seniors £3, children £2. Last entry one hour before closing. Special events from Apr.–Oct.*

Enter the grounds and follow the sign for the one-mile country walk around the ***Battlefield** (3). This easy trail is lovely, but watch out for sheep droppings and be sure to close any gates that you've opened. All along the way there are relief models explaining the progress of the battle.

The origins of the ***Abbey** (4) date from a vow made by William the Conqueror on the day of the battle to build a church on the site if God led him to victory. This promise was kept, with the high altar erected on the very spot where Harold fell. The abbey continued to grow until being disbanded by Henry VIII in 1539 and given to his Master of the Horse, who destroyed most of the buildings. Only one structure remains fully intact today, and that is used as an independent co-ed school and cannot be visited. Of the ruins, the most interesting is the **Dorter,** or monks' dormitory. Walk out on the nearby terrace for a good overall view of the battlefield.

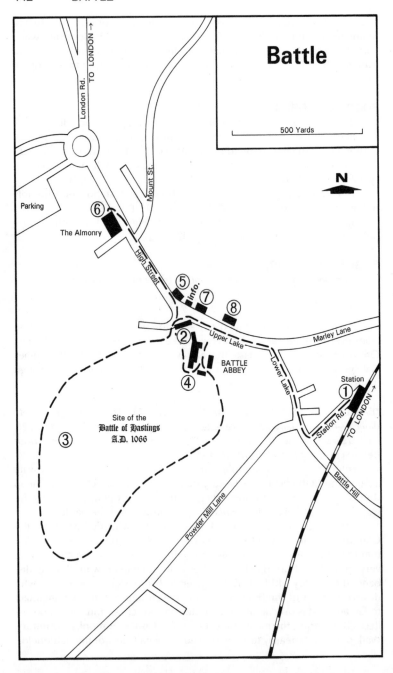

Across The Green is the **Battle Museum** (5), where models explain how the battle was fought. Also on display is a copy of the Bayeux Tapestry, a facsimile Domesday Book, coins, and other historical items. *Open April–Sept., Mon.–Sat. 10:30–4:30, Sun. 10–noon. Adults £1, accompanied children free, otherwise 20p.* ☎ *(01424) 773-116.*

Stroll up High Street past many old houses to **The Almonry** (6), a 15th-century building where you can watch the history of Battle unfold in a sound-and-light show at the Town Model. *Open Mon.–Sat. 10–4:30. Admission £1. Gift shop. coffee shop.* ☎ *(01424) 772-210.*

Heading back to the train station takes you past **Buckley's Yesterday's World** (7), a commercial re-creation of the century from 1850 to 1950. Shops, homes, and even Queen Victoria herself come to life with push-button animations, complete with sound and smells. *Open daily from 10–6. Times vary in Nov.–March. Last admission at 5. Adults £3.95, seniors £3.65, children (4–15) £2.85. Café.* ☎ *(01424) 775-378.*

A bit farther down the road stands **St. Mary's Church** (8) with its Norman nave, 14th-century wall paintings, and fine 15th-century tower. *Open Easter–Sept., daily; rest of year Wed., Thurs., Fri. 10–noon.* ☎ *(01424) 773-649.*

Hastings

An intriguing combination of past and present, Hastings has managed to maintain its heritage while prospering as a modern resort. In a sense it is really two towns split neatly down the middle.

With origins going back to the 7th century, Hastings became one of the Cinque Ports during the time of Edward the Confessor. It had a harbor then, which silted up during the 12th century, never to be successfully rebuilt. William the Conqueror invaded the town in 1066 after landing his Norman troops at nearby Pevensey Bay. The famous Battle of Hastings was fought a few days later on a hill six miles to the northwest, the site of today's village of Battle. During the Hundred Years War of the 14th century the town was repeatedly pillaged by the French. It survived as a fishing village, a role it still plays, and in the 19th century became the popular resort it is today.

This trip can easily be combined with one to either Rye, Battle, or Tunbridge Wells as there are excellent rail and road connections.

GETTING THERE:

Trains to Hastings leave from London's Charing Cross Station at frequent intervals. The journey takes about 90 minutes, and return service operates until mid-evening.

By car, Hastings is 63 miles southeast of London via the A21 highway.

PRACTICALITIES:

Being a seaside resort, Hastings is best visited during the summer, although the main attractions are open all year round. Good weather is essential to enjoy this trip fully.

The local **tourist office**, ☎ (01424) 781-111, Internet: www.hastings.gov.uk, is by the Town Hall on Queens Square. During the summer there is also a branch near the net shops.

FOOD AND DRINK:

You can find any kind of food in Hastings. Some choice establishments are:

Röser's (64 Eversfield Place, near Hastings Pier) Elegant dining, with luncheon specials. ☎ (01424) 712-218. X: Sat. lunch, Sun., Mon. ££ and £££

Judge's (51 High St., in the Old Town) A cozy place with traditional English fare. X: Sun., Mon. £

First In, Last Out (14 High St., in the Old Town) A pub with meals and a good selection of beers. X: Mon. lunch. £

SUGGESTED TOUR:

Numbers in parentheses correspond to numbers on the map.

Leaving the train station (1), follow Havelock Road and Castle Street to Marine Parade. Continue up George Street to the **West Hill Lift**, which will spare you a climb to the castle. *Operates April–Sept. daily 10–5:30; Oct.–March daily 11–4. Adults 80p, seniors & children 40p.* ☎ *(01424) 781-111.* From the top of the hill, bear left to the cliff overlooking the beach for a marvelous view and the:

1066 STORY in HASTINGS CASTLE (2), West Hill, ☎ (01424) 781-111. *Open Easter–Sept., daily 10–5; Oct. to Easter, daily 11–3:30. Adults £3, seniors and students £2.40, children £1.95.*

Hastings Castle was built by William the Conqueror shortly after the Battle of Hastings. Now little more than a romantic ruin, it is still very much worth exploring. Be sure to visit the **1066 Story**, where those dramatic events of long ago are brought to life with modern audiovisual technology—all inside a re- created medieval siege tent.

Stroll over to the:

SMUGGLERS ADVENTURE in ST. CLEMENT'S CAVES (3), West Hill, ☎ (01424) 422-964. *Open Easter–Sept., daily 10–5:30; rest of year, daily 11–4:30. Closed Dec. 25–26. Adults £4.50, seniors £3.75, children £2.95.*

St. Clement's Caves are an extensive and somewhat bizarre network of rambling subterranean passages, partly natural and partly man-made. They were used in centuries past by smugglers, a drama recalled today in the **Smugglers' Adventure** exhibition deep within the labyrinth. The adventure walk encounters over 50 life-size figures in re-created settings, complete with sound effects and a few surprises. There is also a museum and a video theater.

The most interesting part of Hastings is its **Old Town**, a picturesque fishermen's quarter of narrow streets and ancient buildings. Descend into it via Exmouth Place and turn left on Hill Street. **St. Clement's Church** (4) dates from the 14th century. Two cannon balls are lodged in the south wall of its tower, the one on the right being the result of a French bombardment in the late 17th century. The other one was put there just to balance things off. Inside, there are some fine stained-glass windows and two superb old brasses.

Walk down to High Street and turn left to the Old Town Hall, now the **Museum of Local History** (5). Life-size mannequins provide a touch of the past while other displays are concerned with the Battle of Hastings, the story of the Cinque Ports, and smuggling—once a major vocation in these parts. ☎ (01424) 781-155.

Continuing up High Street with its Tudor homes on the left, you will come to the Stables Theatre, which at one time housed horses for the 18th-century Old Hastings House at the top of the street.

Return by way of All Saints' Street. Destroyed by the French in 1377, All Saints' Church was rebuilt in the 15th century. Inside, there is a well-preserved mural from that time depicting the Last Judgement. Farther along, on the left, is the Piece of Cheese, a peculiar wedge-shaped house that resembles its name.

Probably the best-known sight in Hastings is of its **Net Shops** (6), an extraordinary group of tall black wooden sheds used by fishermen to store their nets. The unusual shape, unchanged since Elizabethan times, was dictated by high rents on the available ground between the sea and cliff. Next to this is the fish market, a place where local fishermen sell the day's catch right off the boat.

The **Fishermen's Museum** (7) on Rock-a-Nore Road houses the *Enterprise*, the last fishing vessel to be built in Hastings before the local shipyards closed in 1909. It is typical of the luggers, a style of wide boats with thick bottoms designed to be beached in these harborless waters. Like most of the Hastings luggers, she ferried men back from Dunkirk in that heroic rescue of 1940. There are other fascinating items in the museum as well. *Open April–Oct., daily 10–5, Nov.–March, daily 11–4. Free.* ☎ *(01424) 461-446.*

Just up the road a few yards is the **Shipwreck Heritage Centre**, where over 3,000 years of maritime history are illustrated with exhibitions of underwater treasures. There is a spectacular audiovisual show and working radar equipment allowing you to monitor shipping activity in the English Channel. *Open April–Oct., daily 10:30–5. Adults £2.20, seniors and students £1.50, children £1.25.* ☎ *(01424) 437-452.*

Nearly adjacent to this is the **Sea Life Aquarium Hastings**, one of those modern aquariums where you can walk below the sea without getting wet—and look up at the sharks. There's also a touch pool, a seabed, a sea lab, a film, and more. *Open daily 10–5. Adults £5.25, seniors and children £3.50. Restaurant, gift shop.* ☎ *(01424) 718-776.*

From here you can stroll back along the shore. The character quickly changes to that of a resort as you pass a small boating lake and amusement area. **Hastings Pier** (8) has the usual fun and games. Beyond it, to the west, lies the more elegant St. Leonards, which developed in the early 19th century.

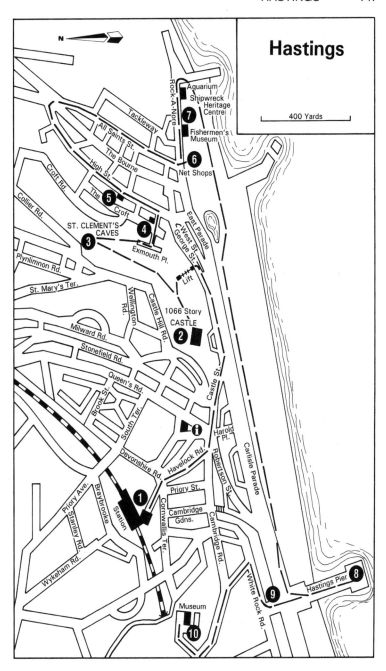

N

Hastings

400 Yards

Rock-A-Nore

Aquarium
Shipwreck
Heritage
Centre

7

Fishermen's
Museum

Tackleway

All Saints St.

The Bourne

High St.

6

Net Shops

Croft Rd.

The
Croft

5

Collier Rd.

East Parade

ST. CLEMENT'S
CAVES

4

3

West St.
George St.

Exmouth Pl.

Plynlimnon Rd.

St. Mary's Ter.

Lift

Wellington Rd.

Castle Hill Rd.

1066 Story
CASTLE

2

Milward Rd.

Stonefield Rd.

Queen's Rd.

Brook St.

South Ter.

Castle St.

Harold
Pl.

ℹ

Devonshire Rd.

Havelock Rd.

Robertson St.

Carlisle Parade

Priory Ave.

Braybrooke

Stanley Rd.

Wykeham Rd.

Station

1

Cornwallis Ter.

Priory St.

Cambridge
Gdns.

Cambridge Rd.

White Rock Rd.

Hastings Pier

8

9

Museum

10

The **White Rock Theatre** (9), opposite the Pier, displays the renowned 80-yard-long Hastings Embroidery, depicting events in British history from the Battle of Hastings to modern times. *You can see the embroidery on Tues.–Sun., 11–4:30. Adults £2, seniors, students, and children £1.* ☎ *(01424) 781-010.*

The **Museum and Art Gallery** (10), on the way back to the train station, is worth a stop. It has interesting collections of Sussex ironwork, local ceramics, and a fantastic pavilion from a 19th-century Indian Colonial palace. *It is open Mondays through Fridays from 10–5, Saturdays from 10–1 and 2–5, and Sundays from 3–5.*

From here it is only a short stroll back to the train station.

Bluebell

The glorious Age of Steam is alive and well on the Bluebell Railway! People who love old trains will rejoice in this delightful trip as they ride across unspoiled countryside in antique coaches hauled by locomotives that date as far back as 1872.

No mere amusement, the Bluebell was a working standard-gauge branch line from 1882 until 1958, when it closed for economic and political reasons. Preservation by a dedicated band of amateurs began the following year, and since 1960 the railway has become one of the most popular attractions in southeastern England. Being a non-profit organization, staffed largely by volunteers, has allowed it to devote much of its income to improvements. The Bluebell's growing collection of locomotives is equaled only by the National Railway Museum in York. Not only is the rolling stock collection growing, but so is the railway itself as it pushes north to East Grinstead where it will once again connect with British Rail. It now operates trains as far as Kingscote station, just a mile and a half from the ultimate goal, offering an 18-mile round trip. For a special treat, the Bluebell also features the Golden Arrow Pullman, a train of genuine Pullman cars dating from 1924, which must be booked in advance.

As an extra bonus, the National Trust's magnificent 18th-century Sheffield Park Garden is within easy walking distance of the Bluebell's southern terminus.

GETTING THERE:

Trains operated by Connex South Central depart London's Victoria Station for the 55-minute ride to East Grinstead. From there, the Bluebell Railway operates bus service 473 to and from Kingscote Station, connecting with Bluebell trains. A joint ticket from London is available.

By car, take the A23 and A22 south from London, going past East Grinstead, then the A275 to Sheffield Park Station and do the train trip in reverse. The total distance is about 45 miles. Going by car is preferred as it gives you more scheduling options.

PRACTICALITIES:

Open all year, the Bluebell Railway operates daily from May to September and during local school holidays; and on weekends throughout the year. Sheffield Park Station is open for viewing even when there are no trains running, daily 11 to 4, except Christmas Day. For current information, ☎ the Bluebell Railway at (01825) 722-370 (24-hour recording) or (01825) 723-777 (business hours), Internet: http://visitweb.com/bluebell. For Golden Arrow Pullman information or reservations, ☎ (01825) 722-008.

Adult fares vary from £1.60 to visit the station at Sheffield Park to £5.80 for a half-line round trip in third class to £10 for a full line round trip in first class. Children are half-price, and dogs as low as 30p. There is a bargain family rate, and a bargain combination fare that includes transport by rail and bus from London's Victoria Station. BritRail passes are not accepted on the steam line.

The Bluebell Railway is mostly ♿ accessible, although it is best to inquire in advance about specific needs.

FOOD AND DRINK:

Complete inexpensive meals and snacks are available in the restaurant (£) at Sheffield Park Station. The wonderful Victorian refreshment room (£) on platform 2 at Horsted Keynes Station serves draft beer and other beverages during pub hours, and has snacks and other refreshments at all times. With advance reservations, you can dine aboard the luxurious Golden Arrow Pullman (£££).

SUGGESTED TOUR:

Numbers in parentheses correspond to numbers on the map.

Those coming by train will begin at British Rail's **East Grinstead Station** (1). A Bluebell Railway bus leaves from the front of the station, connecting with Bluebell steam trains. This takes you two miles to **Kingscote Station** (2), built in the Victorian style in 1882, abandoned in 1958, and lovingly restored in 1993.

Board the train and enjoy the nine-mile *ride to Sheffield Park, the southern end of the line. Along the way you will pass the site of the former West Hoathly station before plunging into the half-mile-long **Sharpthorne Tunnel** (3). Next stop is **Horsted Keynes** (4), a former junction station where two lines met, and the northern terminus of the Bluebell from 1960 until 1992. There is often activity here as cars are shunted about. The carriage shed is usually busy with restoration projects on the large stock of vintage coaches. Other old cars are parked on sidings near the station; some of these may be inspected.

The journey continues to *Sheffield Park Station** (5), the headquarters of the railway. You may visit its locomotive sheds, which house a large collection of steam engines ranging in age from over 120 years old to some built as late as 1958. On the far platform is a **museum** of railway relics.

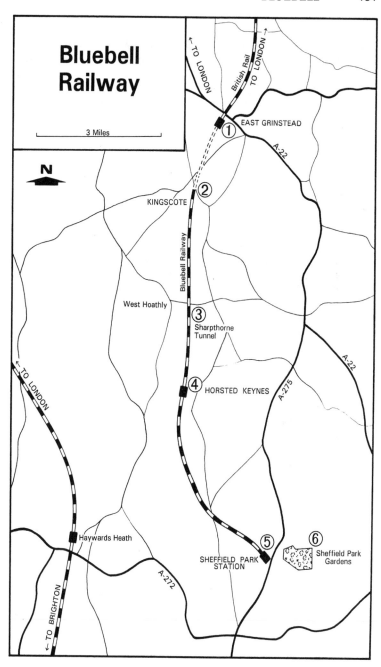

Bluebell Railway

3 Miles

N

TO LONDON
British Rail
TO LONDON
① EAST GRINSTEAD
A-22

② KINGSCOTE

Bluebell Railway

West Hoathly
③ Sharpthorne Tunnel

TO LONDON

④ HORSTED KEYNES
A-275
A-22

Haywards Heath

⑤ SHEFFIELD PARK STATION
⑥ Sheffield Park Gardens

TO BRIGHTON
A-272

Those coming by car will begin their trip here at Sheffield Park, doing it in reverse.

While here, you may be interested in taking a half-mile walk to the **Sheffield Park Garden** (6), a lovely place with rare trees and shrubs spaced among four lakes at different levels. It was laid out by the famous landscape architect Capability Brown during the 18th century and is especially noted for its rhododendrons and azaleas in May and June, as well as for its water lilies, daffodils, bluebells, gentians, and autumn colors. *Open April–Oct., Tues.–Sun. 10:30–6 or dusk; March, Nov.–Dec., Tues.–Sun. 10:30–4; Jan.–Feb. weekends 10:30–4 or dusk. Last admission an hour before closing. Adults £4.20, children £2.10.* ☎ *(01825) 790-0231.* ♿.

Brighton

Londoners have been tripping down to Brighton in search of amusement since the mid-18th century, when a local doctor first promoted his famous sea cure. What made the town fashionable, though, was the frequent presence of naughty George IV, then the pleasure-loving, womanizing Prince of Wales, who began construction on his Royal Pavilion in 1787. Brighton remained an aristocratic resort until the coming of the railway turned it into the immensely popular "London-by-the-Sea" that it is today.

The town itself is actually very old, dating from at least Roman times. It was mentioned in the famous *Domesday Book* of 1086 as *Brighthelmstone*, then a tiny fishing village. Traces of what Brighton looked like before becoming a resort can still be found in the area of The Lanes, a colorful district between the Pavilion and the sea.

Brighton, recently merged with adjacent Hove, has no equal as an easy and fun-filled daytrip from London. Here you will mix with every sort of Englishman, from aristocrats to cockneys, and visit elegant places as well as popular amusements.

GETTING THERE:

Trains operated by Connex leave London's Victoria Station at about half-hour intervals for Brighton, a ride of about one hour. Service is reduced on Sundays. There are also frequent trains operated by Thameslink from London's King's Cross Thameslink and Blackfriars stations, a 90-minute ride. Return service operates until late evening.

By car, Brighton is 54 miles south of London via the A-23, bypassing Gatwick on the M-23.

PRACTICALITIES:

Most of the major sights are open daily, but the art museum closes on Wednesdays and some major holidays. A bright, warm day will add to your enjoyment. The local **Tourist Information Centre**, ☎ (01273) 292-599 or 292-589, Internet: www.brighton.co.uk, is at 10 Bartholomew Square, opposite the Town Hall. You might ask them about local bicycle rentals or buses to nearby attractions.

A hop-on, hop-off open-top double-decker **bus service** connecting most of the tourist sights and providing commentary is operated by Guide

Friday from late March through October. Buses operate every 20 or 30 minutes. All day fares: Adults £6.50, seniors and students £5.50, children (5–12) £2.50. Single ride fares are also offered. Pay the driver, or buy a ticket at the Tourist Information Centre. ☎ (01273) 746-205, Internet: www.guidefriday.com.

Brighton and Hove has a rather comprehensive **local bus service**, with fares as low as 70p (35p for seniors and children) and a one-day saver ticket for unlimited rides for £2.40. Ask at the Tourist Information Centre for a map and schedule.

Brighton and Hove has a population of about 250,000 and is in the county of East Sussex.

FOOD AND DRINK:
From a huge selection, some great places for lunch are:
English's Oyster Bar (29 East St., in The Lanes) Considered to have the best seafood in town. ☎ (01273) 327-980. X: Sun. eve. £££

Terre à Terre (71 East St., in The Lanes) International vegetarian dining at the gourmet level. Reservations suggested. ☎ (01273) 729-051. X: Mon. lunch. ££

Brown's Café (3–4 Duke St., in The Lanes) An extremely popular place for traditional meat, fish, and vegetarian dishes, plus sandwiches, salads, pizza, and the like. ☎ (01273) 323-501. £ and ££

Donatello (3 Brighton Place, in The Lanes) Pizza and other Italian dishes. ☎ (01273) 775-477. £

Food for Friends (17–18 Prince Albert St., in The Lanes) Innovative vegetarian food in an informal setting. ☎ (01273) 202-310. £

SUGGESTED TOUR:
Numbers in parentheses correspond to numbers on the map.

Leaving the marvelously Victorian **train station** (1), follow the map to **Old Steine** (2), an easy stroll of about ten minutes. Along the way you'll pass the Royal Pavilion, a treat best saved for the end of the tour. Old Steine (pronounced *Steen*) is the center of activity in Brighton and is probably named after a stone on which fishermen dried their nets in those quiet centuries before the town became London's playground.

Continue straight ahead to the **Palace Pier** (3), a gaudy Victorian structure dating from 1899 that juts some 1,717 feet, nearly a third of a mile, into the English Channel. On it you will find a fantastic variety of fun houses, rides, shows, shops, bar, fish-and-chips, and people from all over Britain, with accents ranging from pure North Country to London Cockney. *Open daily, 10–midnight; 9–2 a.m. in summer. Free admission, free deck chairs. Partially &.*

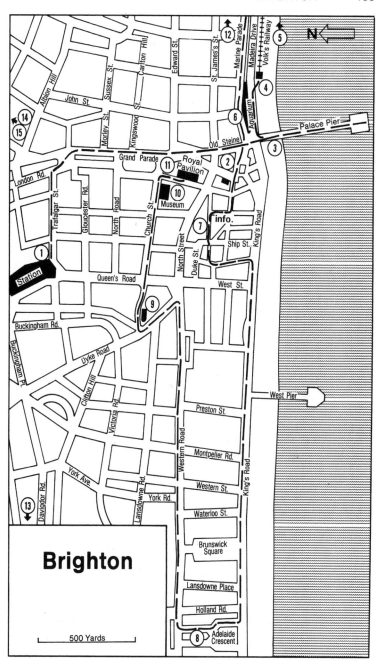

Brighton

The best way to explore the beach is to take a ride on **Volk's Railway** (4). This quaint, open train has been operating since 1883 and was the first in Britain to run on electricity. It follows right along the edge of the beach from near Palace Pier to the marina at Black Rock, a distance of about a mile. *Volk's Railway operates from Easter through mid-September, daily 11–5. Single fares: adults £1, children 50p.* ☎ *(01273) 292-718. Limited* ♿ *access.*

Brighton Marina (5, off the map) is the largest in Europe and can accommodate over 2,000 yachts. Just west of this is the "naturist" beach, where—as the tourist office so tactfully puts it—clothes need not be worn.

Return by walking along Marine Parade with its attractive 19th-century terraces, squares, and crescents. The distance is only a bit over a mile, but you could, of course, take a bus or Volk's Railway. At the end, near the Palace Pier, is the **Brighton Sea Life Centre** (6), a modern aquarium where you can observe strange marine life in re-created natural surroundings while strolling through England's longest underwater glass tunnel. Multi-sensor displays introduce you to over 60 marine species. *Open every day except Christmas, from 10–5 or later. Adults £5.50, seniors and students £4.25, children (4–14) £3.95.* ☎ *(01273) 604-234.* ♿.

Just beyond Old Steine lies the original Brighton, now known as **The Lanes** (7). No longer inhabited by fishermen, this warren of narrow traffic-free alleyways has become a fashionable center of boutiques, antique shops, pubs, and restaurants. The Lanes are a good place for aimless strolling, although you should not miss Brighton Square and Duke's Lane, the most attractive of the tiny byways. This is also a great place for lunch or a refreshment break.

Walk out onto **King's Road** and turn right along the beach. This is the main promenade of Brighton, a stretch of seaside lined with the traditional entertainments. Fish-and-chips shops, ice cream stands, the famous Brighton rock candy—it's all here. As you approach Hove the atmosphere changes to one of sedate elegance.

Make a right at **Adelaide Crescent** (8), a beautiful open area of green surrounded by Regency town houses from the early 19th century. From here you can either return along King's Road or take Western Road back to Brighton. Your next stop should be the **Church of St. Nicholas** (9) on Dyke Road. Originally built in 1380 and reconstructed in 1853, it has a remarkable 12th-century Norman font. The churchyard is a perfect spot to rest before pressing on.

A short stroll down Church Street leads to the:

BRIGHTON MUSEUM and ART GALLERY (10), Church St., ☎ (01273) 290-900. *Open Mon., Tues., Thurs., Fri. and Sat. 10–5, Sun. 2–5. Closed Wed., Good Fri., Dec. 25–26, New Year's Day. Free. Partially* ♿.

A very worthwhile stop, the museum's collection of Art Nouveau and Art Deco pieces is probably the best in Britain. In addition, there are several Old Masters, superb porcelains, silver, furniture, and a fascinating display of local history—along with a gallery of fashion history. Don't miss Salvador Dali's sofa, a sexy sculpture in the shape of Mae West's lips.

Brighton's stellar attraction is just around the corner:

*ROYAL PAVILION (11), ☎ (01273) 290-900. *Open daily 10–5, closing at 6 from June–Sept. Closed Dec. 25–26. Adults £4.50, seniors and students £3.25, children (under 16) £2.75. Partially* ♿.

King George IV, then known as "Prinny," began this hedonistic pleasure palace while still Prince of Wales. Over the years from 1787 to 1822 it evolved from a classical structure into the bizarre pseudo-Oriental fantasy that it is today. The final design, from 1815 on, was the work of John Nash, the greatest architect of the Regency period. Before entering the pavilion you should stroll around it as the best views face Pavilion Parade.

The *interior of the palace is every bit as extravagant as the outside. The king used the pavilion until 1827, and it was also used by his brother King William IV and, in turn, by Queen Victoria. Its end as a royal residence came in 1850 when Victoria, not amused by the theatricality of it all, sold the pavilion to the town for a fraction of its value. Another century passed before the palace was fully restored to its former splendor as the result of a permanent loan, made by Queen Elizabeth II, of original furnishings.

NEARBY SIGHTS:

Brighton has several other interesting attractions that may be reached by local bus, car, or rented bicycle. Ask for directions at the Tourist Information Centre. The best of these are:

Rottingdean Village (12), a picturesque spot four miles east of Brighton on a cliff overlooking the sea, once home to Rudyard Kipling.

British Engineerium (13), located in a former pumping station on the edge of Hove Park on Nevill Road, has a magnificent collection of stationary steam engines and mechanical inventions from the Victorian era. *Open daily 10–5. Live steam first Sun. in month. Adults £3.50, seniors and children £2.50.* ☎ *(01273) 559-583.* ♿.

Preston Manor (14), two miles from Old Steine on London Road, is an 18th-century Georgian mansion in a lovely setting. *Open Mon. 1–5, Tues.–Sat. 10–5, Sun. 2–5. Adults £3.10, seniors and students £2.60, children (under 16) £1.95.* ☎ *(01273) 2900-900.*

Stanmer Village (15) preserves a turn-of-the-century atmosphere of rural England and is located four miles north of Brighton along Lewes Road.

Trip 22

Arundel

L ike a vision from a fairy tale, the picture-book town of Arundel nestles snugly at the base of its massive castle. Both date from the time of the Norman Conquest, and possibly even earlier. Arundel was mentioned in the *Domesday Book* of 1086 as a port of some consequence, which it remained throughout the Middle Ages. There is still a good deal of boating activity on its river, the Arun, which flows into the sea at nearby Littlehampton. Delightful country walks can be made along its banks and to the Wildfowl & Wetlands Centre, or through peaceful Arundel Park. Those preferring more sedentary activities will find excellent antique and crafts shops, charming pubs, and a small museum. The main attraction remains, of course the castle—one of the finest in all England.

GETTING THERE:

Trains to Arundel leave hourly from London's Victoria Station. The journey takes about 80 minutes, with return services until mid-evening.

By car, Arundel is 56 miles south of London via the A24 and A29 roads.

PRACTICALITIES:

Avoid coming on a Saturday or between late October and the end of March, when the castle is closed. The local **Tourist Information Centre,** ☎ (01903) 882-268, is at 61 High Street, below the castle. Ask them about the marvelous **Arundel Festival** held in late August. Arundel is in the county of West Sussex, and has a population of about 3,000.

FOOD AND DRINK:

Among the many restaurants, pubs, and tea rooms are:

Norfolk Arms (22 High St.) Traditional English dishes in an old coaching inn. ☎ (01903) 882-101. ££

Castle View (63 High St., next to the tourist office) A French restaurant in the center of things. ☎ (01903) 883-029. ££

Belinda's (13 Tarrant St., just southwest of High St.) A 16th-century tea room with old-fashioned home-cooked lunches. ☎ (01903) 882-977. X: Mon. £ and ££

White Hart (12 Queen St., near the river) A pub and restaurant with real ale and homemade food. ☎ (01903) 882-374. £ and ££

SUGGESTED TOUR:
Numbers in parentheses correspond to numbers on the map.

Leaving the **train station** (1), turn left and follow The Causeway and Queen Street to the River Arun. Because the castle does not open until noon, you might want to begin with a short **country walk** of a bit over one mile.

To do this, cross the bridge and turn right on Mill Road, passing a parking lot. Continue on until you come to a recreation ground on the right. Just beyond this turn right on a well-defined track that leads to the river, then turn right and follow the embankment with its gorgeous views of town and castle. Back near the bridge are the ruins of the **Dominican Priory** (2), founded in the mid-13th century for preaching friars near the bridge and market place where townspeople came together.

Follow the map uphill to:

*ARUNDEL CASTLE (3), ☎ (01903) 883-136. *Open April–late Oct., Sun.–Fri. noon–5. Last admission at 4. Closed Sat. Adults £6.70, children £4.20. Restaurant. Gift shop.*

Arundel Castle is everything a great fortress should be. Built in the late 11th century, it was besieged by Henry I in 1102 and again by King Stephen in 1139. After severe damage caused by Parliamentary forces during the Civil War in 1643, it fell into a dilapidated state until restoration began in the 18th century. What you see today is mostly a romantic Victorian vision, a stately home with all the trappings of a medieval stronghold. Throughout most of its history, the castle has been the seat of the dukes of Norfolk and their ancestors, the Fitzalans. This family, among the highest nobility in England, has always remained Roman Catholic despite centuries of persecution, a fact that explains much of what you'll see in Arundel.

Enter the castle grounds and walk around to the **Barbican Tower** of 1295. Once inside, turn hard right and follow the marked route to the 11th-century keep, which was occupied only during a siege. A banner is flown from its top when the duke is in residence. Return and enter the living quarters by way of the **Stone Hall**. The immense ***Barons' Hall** features some interesting paintings, including a portrait by Van Dyck. The route leads past the **Dining Room** and the drawing room, which has an appealing lived-in quality and several fine portraits by Gainsborough, Reynolds, and Van Dyck. The elaborate bed in the **Victoria Room** was made for the queen's visit in 1846. From here you go through the handsome **Library** and several smaller rooms to an exit near the keep the shop and restaurant.

Before leaving the castle grounds, take a walk over to the 14th-century **Fitzalan Chapel** (4). Many of the earls of Arundel and dukes of Norfolk are buried here. A wrought-iron grill and glass wall separates this Catholic

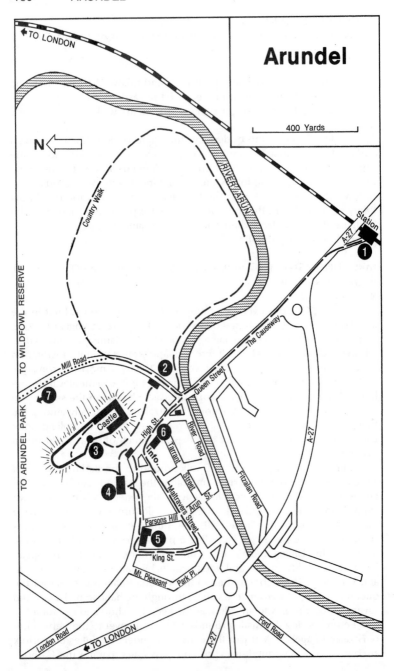

chapel from the Anglican parish church, another part of the same building.

Exit through the gate and stroll up London Road. On your right is the
Protestant part of the church, which makes an interesting contrast and
should be visited.

Just beyond this stands the Roman Catholic **Cathedral of Our Lady and
St. Philip Howard** (5), begun in a grandiose French Gothic style in 1869 as a
parish church. It became a cathedral only in 1965, when a new bishopric
was created for the region. Inside is the tomb of the 13th Earl of Arundel,
canonized in 1970 as Saint Philip, who died in the Tower of London in 1595
for the crime of praying for the success of the Spanish Armada. Other features of the cathedral include its attractive rose window above the west
door, and its fine stone carvings throughout. *Open daily 9–6, or dusk
when earlier. Free.* ☎ *(01903) 882-297.*

Follow the map to the **Arundel Museum and Heritage Centre** (6), in the
same building as the Tourist Information Centre. It features displays of
bygone times with models, tools, weapons, clothes, photographs and the
like. *Open late March through late Sept., Mon.–Sat. 10:30–5, Sun. 2–5.
Adults £1, seniors and children 50p.* ☎ *(01903) 882-344.*

Two other places in Arundel may interest you, both just off the map
but within easy walking distance along **Mill Road** (7). They are **Arundel
Park**, a gorgeous 1,100-acre spread of natural beauty beginning at
Swanbourne Lake, and the **Wildfowl & Wetlands Centre** where you can
observe a great variety of waterfowl from hidden vantage points. *The latter is open daily from 9:30–5:30, closing at 4:30 p.m. in winter. Last admission an hour before closing. Closed Christmas Day. Adults £4.75, children
£2.75. Restaurant. Gift shop. Picnic facilities.* ☎ *(01903) 883-355.* ♿.

Trip 23

Chichester and Bosham

Both history and natural beauty dominate the coastal region of West Sussex. Long a doorstep to the Continent, its strategic location on the English Channel made it a place where battles were fought and trade flourished. Three aspects of its character are explored on this delightful daytrip—the medieval town of Chichester, the Roman Ruins at Fishbourne, and the Saxon hamlet of Bosham.

Celts occupied the territory for hundreds of years, with one of their tribes ruled by a king named Cogidubnus. When the Romans invaded Britain in AD 43, Cogidubnus—no fool—submitted without a fight, became a Roman citizen, and retained his local power. The palace at Fishbourne was probably his reward. The invaders also built him a proper Roman capital, *Noviomagus*, later to become Chichester. Cogidubnus played a pivotal role in English history, for his defection allowed the legions of Claudius to conquer Britain so swiftly and easily.

With the departure of the Romans about AD 410, the region was overrun by barbaric Saxons. Their conversion to Christianity first occurred at Bosham in the 7th century. Bosham also figured in the Norman Conquest of 1066, its church being pictured on the famous Bayeux Tapestry.

William the Conqueror brought peace and unity to Britain, and Sussex prospered as a trading center. By medieval times, Chichester had become quite an important town. Many of its fine structures survive today, side by side with those of later eras. Bosham, now a yachting center, preserves the feeling of bygone days in a sublimely beautiful setting, the perfect place to end this day's outing.

GETTING THERE:

Trains leave London's Victoria Station hourly for Chichester, arriving there about 90 minutes later. Be careful to board the correct car, as some trains split en route. Return service operates until mid-evening.

By car, Chichester is 63 miles southwest of London. Take the A3 to Guildford and then switch to the A286.

PRACTICALITIES:

Good weather is essential for this largely outdoor trip. Most of the attractions are open daily, except that a few museums close on Sundays and Mondays, and during the depths of winter the Roman Palace at Fishbourne is open only on weekends. The local **Tourist Information Centre**, ☎ (01243) 775-888, is at 29A South Street, between the train station and the cathedral. The world-famous **Chichester Festivities** is held every July. Chichester is in the county of West Sussex, and has a population of about 26,000.

FOOD AND DRINK:

Being a festival town, Chichester has an unusually good selection of restaurants and pubs in every price category, including:

Comme Ça (67 Broyle Rd., north of the Festival Theatre) Your best choice for excellent French cuisine. ☎ (01243) 788-724. X: Sun. eve., Mon. ££ and £££

Hole in the Wall (1 St. Martin's St., near St. Mary's Hospital) A casual place with a loyal clientele. ££

Clinch's Salad House (14 Southgate, near the station) Healthy food, mostly vegetarian. ☎ (01243) 788-822. X: Sun., evenings. £

The Medieval Crypt (South St., near Canon Lane) Light lunches in an ancient crypt. X: Sun. eve. ☎ (01243) 537-033. £

Royal Arms (East St., by the Market Cross) A popular pub with good food. £

Nag's Head (St. Pancras St., at the end of East St., near the walls) A pub with decent meals. £

And in **Bosham**, you may want to try:

Millstream Restaurant (Bosham Lane) A lovely place for French and English cuisine. ☎ (01243) 573-234. ££ and £££

Berkeley Arms (near Bosham Lane) A friendly local pub with meals. ☎ (01243) 573-167. £

SUGGESTED TOUR:

Numbers in parentheses correspond to numbers on the map.

Leaving the **train station** (1), walk up Southgate and South Street to the **Market Cross** (2). This medieval shelter, the most elaborate in England, was erected in 1501 by a local bishop. The town's Roman origins become obvious at this point, with the four main streets meeting at right angles in the center.

Stroll down West Street and turn left at the cathedral's detached **Bell Tower**, the only one of its kind in the country, to:

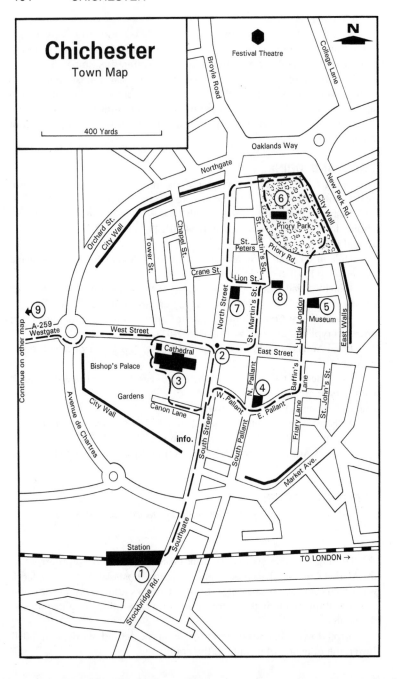

Chichester
Town Map

400 Yards

*CHICHESTER CATHEDRAL (3), ☎ (01243) 782-595. *Open daily, 7:30–7, closing at 5 in winter. Restricted visits during services and concerts. Guided tours Easter Mon.–Oct., Mon.–Sat., 11 and 2:15. Suggested donation £2. Café. Gift shop.* &.

Chichester Cathedral, predominantly Norman, was consecrated in 1108. Its 277-foot spire collapsed in 1861 and was rebuilt in 1866. Inside, it has a remarkably comfortable, almost cozy atmosphere. For nearly 900 years this has been the repository of a vast collection of art objects. The nave has two aisles, an unusual arrangement, separated from the choir by a carved stone screen from 1475. Note the modern pulpit, installed in 1966. The beautifully-carved **misericords** and Bishop's Throne in the choir are outstanding, but the best works here are the two ***Romanesque wall carvings** just opposite them in the south aisle. These depict the *Raising of Lazarus* and *Christ at the Gate of Bethany,* and are the finest of their kind in England.

A visually exciting point of focus is provided by the vivid tapestry of abstract design behind the contemporary **High Altar**. Roman floor **mosaics** from a much earlier structure on the same spot can be seen in the south aisle near the retro-choir. Not to be missed is the ***stained-glass window** by Marc Chagall, and the modern Graham Sutherland painting.

Leave by the main entrance and turn left into the **Cloisters**. Their irregular 15th-century walls enclose a garden known as the Paradise. From here follow St. Richard's Walk, a narrow and very charming passage, to Canon Lane. To the right, a 14th-century gateway leads to the Bishop's Palace and the public gardens. Return on quiet Canon Lane, lined with intriguing old houses, to South Street and turn left.

In a few yards make a right onto West Pallant. The **Pallants** are a miniature version of the town itself, reflecting a distinctly Roman layout. Once a special preserve of the bishop, these four streets are lined with outstanding 18th- and 19th-century buildings. The most notable of these is the **Pallant House** (4) of 1712 at the intersection with North Pallant, now faithfully restored with period furnishings and graced with two major collections of modern British art. There are also changing exhibitions and a period walled garden. *Open Tues.–Sat. 10–5, Sun. & bank holidays 12:30–5. Adults £2.80, seniors £2.20, students £1.70. Gift shop.* ☎ *(01243) 774-557.* &.

Continue along East Pallant and turn left at Baffin's Lane. Once across East Street this becomes Little London. If time permits, make a stop at the **District Museum** (5), housed in an 18th-century corn store at the corner of East Row. Its collections include artifacts of to local life and history, from prehistoric to modern times, and Roman armor. *Open Tues.–Sat. 10–5:30. Free.* ☎ *(01243) 784-683. Partially* &.

Now follow Little London into **Priory Park** (6). A shady footpath runs along the top of the medieval city walls, built on original Roman foundations. The 13th-century Greyfriars Church in the middle of the lawn houses the **Guildhall Museum**, featuring archaeological finds, which is usually open on Saturday afternoons in summer.

Walk down Priory Lane and turn left on North Street. A few blocks to the north lies the Festival Theatre, built in 1962 for the renowned Chichester Festival. Stop at the intersection of Lion Street and visit the elegant **Council House** (7) of 1731. On its outer wall is mounted a Roman stone, found nearby, that reads: *By the Authority of Tiberius Claudius, Cogidubnus, King Legate of Augustus in Britain.* In Latin, of course. Inside, there is a fine assembly room and council chamber, which may be inspected.

Lion Street leads to St. Martin's Square and **St. Mary's Hospital** (8), built in 1290. Since 1528 it has been an almshouse for the aged, a function it still serves. Its well-preserved medieval interior can be seen by appointment only. ☎ (01243) 779-554.

Follow the map past the Market Cross and along West Street to Westgate. From here it is about 1.5 miles to Fishbourne following the route shown on the area map. You can also get there by a number 700, 11, or 56 bus; or by hourly train from the station to Fishbourne Halt.

*FISHBOURNE ROMAN PALACE (9), Salthill Rd., Fishbourne, ☎ (01243) 785-859. *Open daily early Feb. to early Dec., 10–6, closing at 5 in March–July and Sept.–Oct., and at 4 in Feb., Nov.–Dec. Also open early Dec.–early Feb., Sun. only 10–4. Adults £4.20, seniors and students £3.50, children £2.20. Cafeteria. Gift shop. Special events. &.*

The Roman Palace at Fishbourne, the largest building of that era in Britain, was discovered in 1960 by workmen laying a water main. Those parts of it that survived the centuries of destruction and burial can only hint at the grandeur it must have had in the time of Cogidubnus. A museum and protective structure now covers a large part of the remains. To understand these, it is helpful to first watch the short film shown frequently in the museum's theater, and to study the scale model. Outside, a Roman garden has been planted with species from that era.

From here you can either return to Chichester or continue on to Bosham via bus 56 from near the intersection of Portsmouth Road (A27) and Salthill Road. Walking the two-mile distance, however, is more enticing. To do that, turn right on Portsmouth Road until you get to a restaurant called Casa Mama, then bear left on Old Park Lane. At the end of this you will find a public footpath going straight ahead, which follows a row of trees to the left. Walk along this until you cross a private road. Climb over

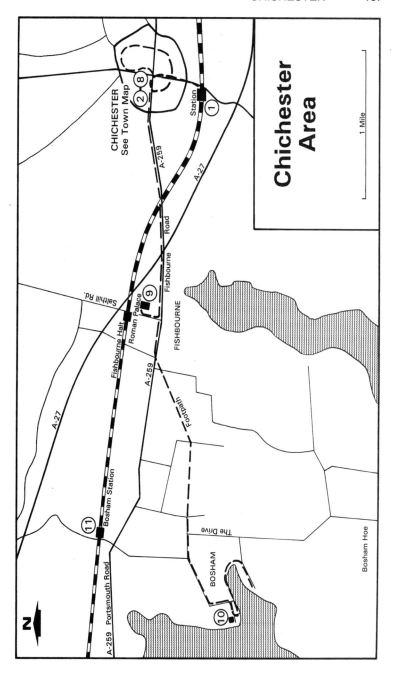

Chichester
Area

1 Mile

a stile and continue on the footpath, which soon turns into a paved road. Walk straight ahead, ignoring the sign to Bosham Hoe, and pass the Berkeley Arms Inn. The street now becomes Bosham Lane, which makes a left and leads to the harbor.

It was from ***Bosham** (pronounced *Boz-zum*) that Harold set sail in 1064 on that fateful journey that ended in the Norman Conquest. This delightfully dreamy village is actually much older than that, going back at least as far as the Romans. Turn right on High Street and follow it to **Bosham Church** (10). Begun around 1020, it incorporates parts of a Roman basilica of AD 350. The young daughter of King Canute, an 11th-century ruler of England and Denmark, is believed to be buried here.

Wander past the old mill, then return along the water's edge to Bosham Lane. A stroll along **The Trippet** to the opposite bank reveals the full nautical flavor of Bosham, while a visit to **Bosham Walk**, a local arts and crafts center, is a pleasant diversion. From here you can get bus 56 back to Chichester, running hourly Mondays to Saturdays, and every two hours on Sundays. The last bus is around 6 p.m. Ask locally for current schedules. If you prefer to take the train, just follow the map to the **station** (11), about a mile away. Trains to Chichester leave at least hourly from the platform on the far side of the tracks.

Guildford

Dating back at least a thousand years, Guildford is an unusually attractive old town with a rich architectural heritage. The Saxons named it *Gyldeford*—the ford of the golden flowers—after its strategic position on the River Wey. A Norman castle was built here, which remained a favorite royal residence for centuries. During medieval times Guildford became the county town of Surrey, a status it still holds. Throughout the Middle Ages the peaceful and prosperous town boasted a thriving woolen industry that died out in the 17th century, only to be replaced by another source of wealth, the shipping of goods by barge along its newly navigable river.

Guildford today is a remarkable blend of past and present. While it has done a good job of preserving the old, it also has some first-rate modern structures. The town is particularly rich in parks, gardens, and open spaces.

GETTING THERE:

Trains to Guildford leave London's Waterloo Station at least every half-hour, with a journey time of well under an hour. Return service operates until late evening.

By car, Guildford is 33 miles southwest of London via the A3 road.

PRACTICALITIES:

Guildford may be visited at any time, but note that the museums are closed on Sundays, and the castle is closed from October through March. The local **Tourist Information Centre**, ☎ (01483) 444-333, is at 14 Tunsgate, between the castle and the Guildhall. Some information is available on the Internet at: www.surreyweb.org.uk/surrey-tourism. Guildford is the county seat of Surrey, and has a population of about 62,000.

FOOD AND DRINK:

Some of the better restaurants and pubs are:

Café de Paris (35 Castle St., near the castle) Exceptional French cuisine in a combined bistro and restaurant. ☎ (01483) 534-896. X: Sun. ££

Number 1 Angel Gate (Angel Inn, High St., opposite Chapel St.) A 16th-century coaching inn with traditional English fare. ☎ (01483) 564-555. ££

The Gate (3 Milkhouse Gate, a block south of Guildford House)

Contemporary Mediterranean cuisine in a relaxed atmosphere. ☎ (01483) 576-300. X: Sat. lunch, Sun. eve. ££

Rumwong (16 London Rd., 2 blocks northeast of the Royal Grammar School) The tasty cuisine of Thailand in a colorful restaurant. ☎ (01483) 536-092. X: Mon. ££

Jolly Farmer (Millbrook, near the boathouse) A riverside pub with garden seating and homemade pub food. ☎ (01483) 538-779. £

Star (Quarry St. at High St.) Have lunch in a very old pub, alleged to be haunted. $

SUGGESTED TOUR:

Numbers in parentheses correspond to numbers on the map.

Leaving the **train station** (1), follow Park Street and Millmead to the River Wey, which was converted into a navigable waterway as early as 1653. Through a series of canals and locks it is joined with the Thames to the north, and a one time was open all the way to the south coast. Now owned by the National Trust, the Wey Navigation is very popular with pleasure boaters, who have replaced the commercial barges of old.

Cross the footbridge to Millmead Lock. From here you can stroll along the water past the **Guildford Boathouse** (2), which offers river cruises, boat rentals, and a cruising restaurant. To reach it, use the footbridge and return via Millbrook. *Cruises Easter through Oct., narrow boats all year. Daily, 9–6. Evening cruises to 10. Rates vary from £2.50 to £10 for adults, less for children, depending on length of cruise and food service. Row boat rentals.* ☎ *(01483) 504-494.*

The **Yvonne Arnaud Theatre** (3), delightfully located by Millmead Lock, is a modern circular structure that often previews productions before they open in London's West End. Its two restaurants and café overlook the river. ☎ *(01483) 440-000.* Just beyond is the town mill, built over a millrace and now used as a scenery workshop for the theater.

Cross Millbrook and follow Mill Lane to **St. Mary's Church** (4), the oldest building in Guildford. Its Saxon tower dates from about 1050, with the rest being completed by the 13th century.

Continuing along Quarry Street, take a look down Rosemary Alley, a steep medieval path to the river. Just beyond it is the **Guildford Museum** (5), which has exhibits of local archaeology and history as well as items connected with Lewis Carroll, author of *Alice in Wonderland,* who spent a great deal of his time in Guildford. *Open Mon.–Sat., 11–5. Free.* ☎ *(01483) 444-750.*

Pass through the adjacent Castle Arch, dating from 1265. To the right, on Castle Hill, is a private house called The Chestnuts that was leased by Lewis Carroll as a home for his six spinster sisters. This is where he died in 1898.

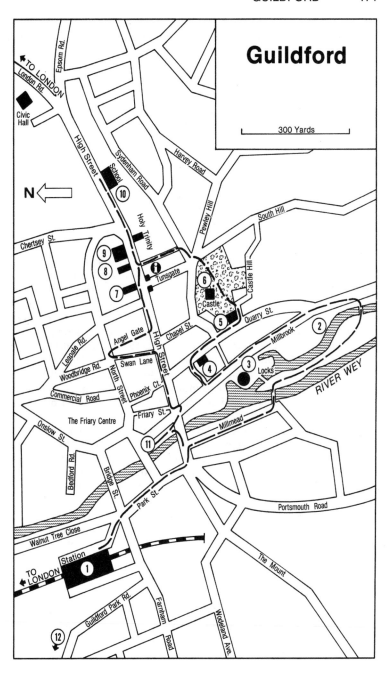

A path leads up to the **Castle Keep** (6). Built in 1170 on an earlier mound, it's all that remains of the great Norman castle that was once a favorite royal residence until it fell into neglect in the 15th century. Later used as a jail, the keep offers a marvelous **view** from the top. *Open daily from April–Sept., 10–6. Adults 85p, seniors and children 40p.* ☎ *(01483) 444-702.*

Leave the grounds and follow the map to Milk House Gate, a quaint narrow passageway just before the multi-story parking facility. This leads to High Street, across which to the left is the **Guildhall** (7) with its protruding clock, easily the most photographed sight in Guildford. Its dramatic façade was erected in 1683, but the main structure is Elizabethan. *Ask about the free guided tours on Tuesday and Thursday afternoons.* ☎ *(01483) 444-035.*

Head up High Street to the **Guildford House** (8) at number 155. Used for art exhibitions, it was built in 1660 and is noted for its beautifully molded plaster ceilings and carved wooden staircases. *Open Tues.–Sat. 10–4:45.* ☎ *(01483) 444-740.*

Just beyond stands **Abbot's Hospital** (9), or Hospital of the Blessed Trinity, an old almshouse with an interesting history. It was founded in 1619 by George Abbot, a poor local boy who was given a free education by the town. He rose to become the Archbishop of Canterbury and repaid the people of Guildford by building this home for their elderly poor, which is still used for that purpose. A guided tour of its splendid interior is available at stated times or by appointment. ☎ *(01483) 562-670.*

The **Royal Grammar School** (10) is a little farther up High Street. Its modern buildings are on the left side, but those on the right date from 1586. Enter the old courtyard and look around. Visitors are occasionally admitted to the library, which contains priceless old chained books. ☎ *(01483) 539-880.*

Return down High Street, passing Holy Trinity Church on the left. This Classical building was erected in 1763 on the site of the medieval church that collapsed in 1740. It was used as a cathedral from 1927 to 1961. Another classical structure, the **Tunsgate Arch**, directly opposite the Guildhall, fronted the former Corn Exchange when it was built in 1818. A road now passes beneath it.

Turn right on Angel Gate, a narrow lane by the side of the ancient Angel Inn. This leads to North Street, scene of a colorful farmers' market held on Fridays and Saturdays. Make a left and return by Swan Lane to High Street, which you follow to the river.

Use the underpass to reach the restored late-17th-century **Treadwheel Crane** (11) on the old town wharf, a relic of the former Wey Navigation. Up to ten men were needed to work it, unloading the barges that were the backbone of Guildford's prosperity. From here you can stroll back to the station via Friary Bridge or through the Friary Shopping Centre, a well-designed enclosed mall.

There is one more sight in Guildford that may interest you. It is the modern **Cathedral of the Holy Spirit** (12) on Stag Hill, reached via Guildford Park Road and Ridgemount, about one mile from the station. The first Anglican cathedral to be built on a new site in the south of England since the Reformation, it was begun in 1936 and consecrated in 1961. *Open daily 8:30–5:30. Donations accepted. Refectory restaurant for light meals.* ☎ *(01483) 565-287.* ♿.

Portsmouth

There is one very compelling reason to visit Portsmouth, and that is to go aboard H.M.S. *Victory*, Nelson's flagship at Trafalgar. Here you can relive one of the proudest moments in British history. Located on a naval base, the ship has been perfectly restored to the condition she was in on October 21, 1805, when she won the most decisive battle ever fought at sea,

Portsmouth, long known to sailors as "Pompey," has many other attractions as well, including the *Mary Rose*, a Tudor warship sunk in 1545, and H.M.S. *Warrior*, the sole survivor from the Royal Navy's ironclad era. There are also forts and fortifications, splendid harbor views, remembrances of D-Day, several museums, and a cathedral. Perhaps best of all, there's Old Portsmouth, which retains much of its nautical atmosphere despite heavy bombing during World War II.

The town was originally founded in 1194 by Richard the Lionheart but did not achieve real importance until 1495, when the first dry dock anywhere was established here by Henry VII. Since then, Portsmouth has grown to become one of the major naval bases in the world, a position it still holds.

GETTING THERE:

Trains to Portsmouth Harbour Station, the end of the line, leave frequently from London's Waterloo Station. The journey takes about 90 minutes, with returns operating until mid-evening.

By car, Portsmouth is 71 miles southwest of London via the A3 road. You may want to drive around the town instead of walking or taking buses.

PRACTICALITIES:

Portsmouth may be visited at any time except during the Christmas holidays. Most of the sights are open daily. The local **Tourist Information Centre**, ☎ (023) 92-826-722, Internet: www.portsmouthharbour.co.uk, is on The Hard, near the entrance to the Historic Dockyard. There are also branches on Clarence Esplanade near the Sealife Centre (summer only), and on Commercial Road, by the main shopping area. Portsmouth is in the county of Hampshire, and has a population of about 175,000.

FOOD AND DRINK:

Some good choices of pubs and restaurants are:

Lemon Sole (123 High St., Old Portsmouth, near the cathedral) Excellent seafood in the Old Town. ☎ (023) 92-811-303. ££

Barnaby's Bistro (56 Osbourne Rd., a few blocks north of Southsea Castle) Creative French, Italian, and English cuisine in smart surroundings. ☎ (023) 92-821-089. ££

The Ship & Castle (1–2 The Hard, by the Historic Dockyard) A colorful pub serving English and Indian fare. ☎ (023) 92-832-009. £ and ££

Sallyport Tearooms (35 Broad St. in Old Portsmouth) Teas and light lunches. ☎ (023) 92-816-265. X: Mon. £

Country Kitchen (59a Marmion Rd., a few blocks north of Southsea Castle) An attractive place for vegetarian dishes. ☎ (023) 92-811-425. X: Sun. £

Brown's Restaurant (9 Clarendon Rd., a few blocks northeast of Southsea Castle) Traditional English cuisine, friendly atmosphere. ☎ (023) 92-822-617. X: Sun. £

SUGGESTED TOUR:

Numbers in parentheses correspond to numbers on the map.

Leaving **Portsmouth Harbour Station** (1), turn left on The Hard and enter Flagship Portsmouth, the Historic Dockyard on the old naval base, where you can visit Britain's greatest historic ships as well as other attractions:

*FLAGSHIP PORTSMOUTH (2), H.M. Naval Base, ☎ (023) 92-861-512, Internet: www.compulink.co.uk/~flagship. *Open daily 10–5:30, closing at 5 in winter. Closed Christmas Day. An* **All Ships** *ticket, valid for two years, includes the 3 historic ships and the Naval Museum: Adults £11.90, seniors £10.40, children £8.90. A* Passport *ticket includes all of that plus a harbor water tour and more: Adults £14.90, seniors £12.90, children £10.90.* **Individual tickets** *to each of the ships are: Adults £5.95, seniors £5.20, children £4.45, with lower prices for the other attractions. NOTE that tickets for H.M.S. Victory are for tours at specific times; check yours carefully and be there when the tour starts. Restaurant. Gift shop. Partially.* ♿.

The attractions here are:

*H.M.S. Victory, shown by lively, timed guided tours. Each group is escorted through the entire vessel by a guide who is well versed in its history. Built in 1759, H.M.S. *Victory* has been in continuous commission since 1778. It was the flagship of Nelson's fleet during the Battle of Trafalgar in 1805, during which Nelson perished. His body was returned to England in a barrel of brandy aboard the ship. On Trafalgar Day (October

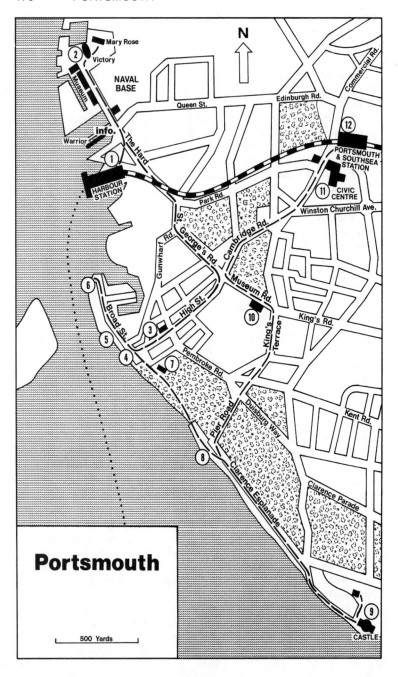

Portsmouth

21) each year, Nelson's famous signal "England expects that every man will do his duty" is flown from Victory's masts.

The **Royal Naval Museum**, occupying three old storehouses just a few steps away, is an interesting place to visit after the *Victory* tour. In addition to the expected material relating to Lord Nelson and the Battle of Trafalgar, there is material covering his personal life and galleries telling the story of the Royal Navy over the years. *Admission is included with the H.M.S. Victory tour, or with the combination tickets.*

The ***Mary Rose*** was the flower of Henry VIII's fleet, a revolutionary warship lost while defending Portsmouth in 1545. Long forgotten, its oaken hull lay preserved in the seabed mud for over four centuries. In 1979, a team led by Prince Charles began recovery work and in 1982 the remains of the ship were raised. These are now on display in a covered dry dock next to H.M.S. *Victory*. There is also a fascinating exhibition of *Mary Rose* artifacts in a boathouse close to the naval base entrance.

Just west of the entrance gate is **H.M.S. *Warrior***. This iron-hulled warship was built in 1860 as the world's fastest and best protected. She is the only remaining 19th-century capital ship in existence, the sole survivor of the Royal Navy's ironclad era. Completely renovated, *Warrior* offers an opportunity to imagine life as a Victorian sailor.

Two other attractions here are the **Warships by Water Tour**, taking you by boat past several naval ships, and the **Dockyards Apprentice Exhibition**, with its interesting glimpses of naval life.

Follow the map to High Street in Old Portsmouth. The **Cathedral of St. Thomas** (3) is a rather odd structure. It was begun in 1185 as a chapel, became a parish church in 1320, and a cathedral only in 1927. The old church now forms the choir and sanctuary, with a new, recently-finished nave that was started in 1935. Housed within the cathedral is the tomb of the Unknown Sailor, one of the crew of the Mary Rose who perished in 1545. Although not a great cathedral by any standard, it is certainly interesting and deserves a visit. *Open daily, 10–6.* ☎ *(023) 92- 823-300.*

At the end of High Street, next to the sea, is the 15th-century **Square Tower** (4), one of the first forts specially designed for cannon warfare. On its side is a gilded bust of Charles I that mysteriously survived the Civil War.

Turn right on Broad street and pass the **Sally Port**, the traditional point of embarkation for Britain's naval heroes. Just beyond this is the **Round Tower** (5). Begun in 1415, it was the first permanent defensive work to be built in Portsmouth. You can climb up on it for a good view. An iron chain ran across the harbor from here to prevent unfriendly ships from entering.

The Point (6) still retains some of the flavor of Old Portsmouth. Once known as Spice Island, this small peninsula fairly teemed with bawdy pubs and brothels. To this day it remains a colorful place for eating and drinking, and the perfect spot for a refreshment break.

Return on Broad Street and continue to the **Garrison Church** (7). Now in ruinous condition, it was founded in 1212 as a hospice but was disbanded in 1540. It then became an armory and later a residence for the military governors. Charles II was married here in 1622. The building was restored as a church in the 19th century and badly damaged during World War II.

Stroll down to **Clarence Pier** (8), a popular amusement area with the usual seaside amenities. From here you can walk or take a bus past the beautiful gardens of Southsea Common, passing the **Sealife Centre** along the way. This attraction uses the latest technology to create an illusion of strolling along the bottom of the sea, without actually getting wet. The sharks won't bite. *Open daily except Christmas, 10–7, closing at 5 in winter. Adults £5.50, seniors £4.25, students and children £4.* ☎ *(023) 92-734-461.* &.

Southsea Castle (9) was built in 1545 by Henry VIII, who watched his beloved *Mary Rose* sink from this site. Inside it is a museum of local military history and archaeology, and a time- tunnel experience on the castle's history. In summer, there are re-enactment days that bring the whole place back to life. *Open April–Oct., daily 10–5:30; Nov.–March, weekends only, 10–4:30. Closed Dec. 24–26. Adults £2, seniors, students and children £1.* ☎ *(023) 92-827-261. Partially* &.

Close by stands the **D-Day Museum**, featuring the 272-foot-long Overlord Embroidery, audio-visual shows, vehicles, weapons, and the like. This is the only museum in Britain devoted solely to the Normandy invasions. *Open April–Oct., daily 10–5:30; Nov.–March, Mon. 1–5, Tues.–Sun. 10–5. Last admission at 4. Closed Dec. 24–26. Adults £4.75, seniors £3.60, students and children £2.85.* ☎ *(023) 92-827-261.* &.

Return to Pier Road and follow it to Museum Road. You can also take a bus from the front of Southsea Castle if you're tired. The **City Museum** (10) displays decorative and fine arts from the 16th century to the present, as well as items relating to local history. *Open daily 10–5:30, last admission at 5. Closed Dec. 24–26. Free.* ☎ *(023) 92-827-261.* &.

At this point you could return directly to Portsmouth Harbour Station (1), or follow Cambridge Road to the **Civic Centre** (11). The Guildhall there is an outstanding Victorian structure flanked by modern glass buildings. To the north is the main shopping area along Commercial Road. This street leads, off the map, to the **Charles Dickens Birthplace Museum** at 393 Old Commercial Road. This is the actual house where the author's family lived while his father was a pay clerk in the dockyard, and has been furnished in a style appropriate to the year of his birth, 1812. *Open April–Oct., daily 10–5:30; Dec., daily 10–4:30. Adults £2, seniors £1.50, students and children £1.20.* ☎ *(023) 92-827-261. Limited* &.

The **Portsmouth and Southsea Station** (12) is a convenient place to get a train back to London.

Shanklin
(Isle of Wight)

J ust off the southern coast of England lies the Isle of Wight, a delightful island whose bracing air and spectacular scenery combine to form an unusual and very enjoyable daytrip destination. A favorite holiday retreat ever since the days of Queen Victoria, it remains relatively unknown to foreign travelers. Although the Isle of Wight shares a common heritage with the rest of England, its friendly people regard themselves as somehow different from the mainlanders. Here, British sophistication yields to simpler charms and London seems far away.

GETTING THERE:

Trains leave London's Waterloo Station hourly for Portsmouth Harbour Station, the ride taking about 1.5 hours. On arrival there, follow the crowds to the pier, a part of the station complex, and board the Wightlink ferry to Ryde. BritRail Passes are not accepted on the boat, so you may have to buy a ticket. Fifteen minutes later you will disembark at Ryde Pier Head. Get on the waiting train marked for Shanklin and take it as far as Sandown, a ride of 17 minutes. You will probably be returning from Shanklin, so be sure to get a round-trip ticket from London to there if you do not have a BritRail Pass. Combined tickets including the ferry are available. Check the return schedule on arrival to avoid missing the last evening connection back to London.

By car, follow the A3 from London to Portsmouth Harbour, a distance of 71 miles. Continue on by passenger ferry and rail or bus, as above. It is impractical to take a car to the Isle of Wight for only one day.

PRACTICALITIES:

The Isle of Wight is most attractive between mid-spring and early fall. Good weather is absolutely essential to enjoyment of this trip.

The **local tourist office** for Shanklin is at 67 High Street, near the Old Village, ☎ (01983) 862-942. For the island in general contact **Isle of Wight Tourism**, The Westridge Centre, Brading Road, Ryde, ☎ (01983) 813-800, Internet: www.isle-of-wight-tourism.gov.uk. Ferry schedules are available at www.wightlink.co.uk, ☎ (0990) 827-744.

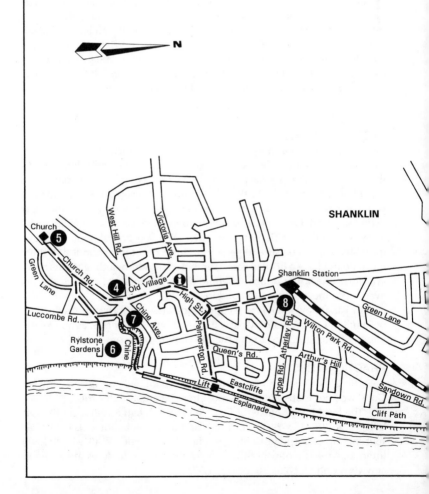

Shanklin
Isle of Wight

½ Mile

N

SHANKLIN

Church
5

West Hill Rd.

Victoria Ave.

Green Lane

Church Rd.

4 Old Village

i

Shanklin Station

Luccombe Rd.

Chine Ave.

High St.

Green Lane

7

8

Rylstone
Gardens 6

Chine

Palmerston Rd.

Queen's Rd.

Hope Rd.

Atherley Rd.

Wilton Park Rd.

Arthur's Hill

Sandown Rd.

Lift

Eastcliffe

Esplanade

Cliff Path

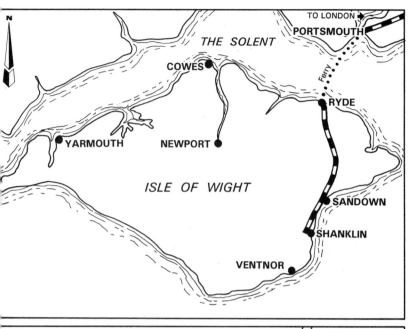

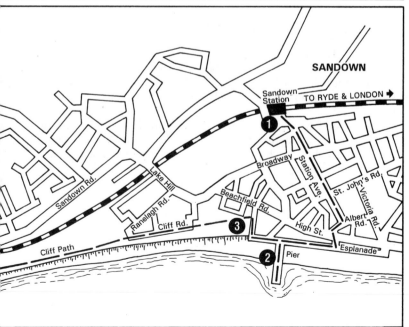

FOOD AND DRINK:

Being a popular tourist area, the Isle of Wight is well endowed with restaurants and pubs. Some choice establishments in the area covered by this daytrip are:

Biskra House Restaurant (17 St. Thomas' St., Ryde, near the ferry pier) Fine food in an old mansion with a view of the sea. ☎ (01983) 567-913. ££ and £££

The Hideaway (Cliff Path, Shanklin, 3 blocks north of Hope Rd.) A café and restaurant by day, a bistro by night. ☎ (01983) 864-145. ££

Room at the Top (23 High St., Shanklin) Traditional English fare in the center of town. ☎ (01983) 862-057. ££

Crab Inn (in the Old Village section of Shanklin) A quaint thatched-roof pub with meals. ☎ (01983) 862- 363. £ and ££

Queensmead (12 Queens Rd., Shanklin, 2 blocks inland from the pier) A small hotel with bar lunches and full dinners. X: January. ☎ (01983) 862-342. £ and ££

Bourne Hall (Luccombe Rd., near Rylstone Park) Light lunch and full dinners in a small hotel. ☎ (01983) 862-820. X: Dec., Jan. £ and ££

SUGGESTED TOUR:

Numbers in parentheses correspond to numbers on the map.

Leaving **Sandown station** (1), walk straight ahead down Station Avenue and make a right on Albert Road. This leads to The Esplanade, a road built atop a sea wall, which is crowded with vacationers during the season. The beach here is perhaps the best in England, with fine sand and a long, gradual slope. Ahead lies the **Pier** (2), an attractive modern structure; a stroll to its far end will reward you with a lovely panorama of sea, cliffs, and rolling hills.

Just beyond the pier turn right off The Esplanade and climb Ferncliff Crescent, which begins as steps. At the top make a left into **Battery Gardens** (3). Amble through this to Cliff Walk and follow the trail that leads to Shanklin. For the next 1.5 miles the pathway, sometimes becoming a road, clings to the upper edge of a steep precipice. Far below, tiny bathing huts make a tenuous hold on the narrow strip of sand between sea and cliff. Midway, you will pass the settlement of Lake. Shanklin now opens into view and beyond it lie the hills that define the southern end of Sandown Bay.

Below, turn right on Palmerston Road and follow it to the center of town. At High Street make a left, passing the tourist office, right out of the present century. The **Old Village** (4), oozing with quaintness, is just about everyone's vision of that imagined England of long ago. Thatched-roof cottages line the streets, many of them now restaurants, pubs, and gift shops. A more romantic place to stop for lunch could hardly be desired.

Continue straight ahead on Church Road to the **Old Parish Church** of St. Blasius (5), one of the most beautifully situated country churches you'll ever encounter. Architecturally undistinguished and of uncertain age—parts of it may date from the 14th century—it nevertheless works a strange charm on the visitor. Be sure to see its interior and graveyard.

Return on Church Road and turn right on Priory Road, then left on Popham Road to **Rylstone Public Park** (6). This lovely spot of sylvan splendor overlooking the sea is a delight to explore and the perfect place to sit down for a rest.

From here, Chine Hollow leads to the upper entrance of:

*SHANKLIN CHINE (7), ☎ (01983) 866-432. *Open mid-May to mid-Sept., daily 10–10; early April to mid-May and mid-Sept. through Oct., daily 10–5. Adults £2.50, seniors and students £1.50, children £1. Tea garden. Gift shop. Millennium exhibition featuring "A Century of Solent Sea and Sail." Limited ♿ access.*

Once notorious as the haunt of smugglers, Shanklin Chine descends into a deep and narrow ravine with plunging waterfalls. The word *chine* is peculiar to this area and derives from the Anglo-Saxon *cine*, meaning fissure. A path leads through the heavily wooded glen, passing a stone bridge, an aviary, a Heritage Centre, and a Victorian tea garden along the way. Following the right-hand trail after a fork near the lower end will reveal traces of Pluto, a secret pipeline built during World War II, which carried fuel from England down the chine and across the channel to the Normandy beachhead.

At the end, where the stream runs into the sea, turn left and climb up onto The Esplanade, a road along the beach. From here you can follow the map to **Shanklin Station** (8) and begin the return journey. The nearby lift will save an uphill climb. If you would rather walk some more, a particularly nice route to follow is along the beach to Sandown. There is a surfaced path going all the way.

Winchester

Winchester wears its history gracefully. The first "capital" of England, it was an important town from Roman times until the 12th century, when it lost out to rival London. Despite this decline, it remained a major religious and educational center, a role it still plays today. There are few places in England where the past has survived to delight the present quite so well.

Winchester's history goes back to the Iron Age, when the Belgae, a Celtic tribe, settled in the valley of the River Itchen. This became the Roman town of *Venta Belgarum*, the fifth- largest in Britain. Following the collapse of the Roman Empire, the Anglo-Saxons took over and, changing the name to *Wintanceaster*, made it the capital of their kingdom of Wessex. Threats from marauding Danes caused the rival kingdoms of England to unite behind Egbert, the king of Wessex, in the mid-9th century; an act that made Winchester the effective capital of all England. A few decades later, under Alfred the Great, the town reached its peak of importance, and afterwards became the seat of such kings as Canute, Edward the Confessor, and William the Conqueror. Winchester's time had passed, however, and during the Norman era the center of power was gradually transferred to London.

GETTING THERE:

Trains leave London's Waterloo Station at least twice an hour for the one-hour ride to Winchester, with returns until late evening.

By car, Winchester is 72 miles southwest of London via the M3 highway.

PRACTICALITIES:

This trip can be made at any time, although some sights are closed on Mondays, especially in the off-season. Open-air **markets** are held in the town center on Wednesdays, Fridays, and Saturdays. The local **Tourist Information Centre**, ☎ (01962) 840-500, Internet: www.winchester.gov.uk, is in the Guildhall on The Broadway. Winchester is the county seat of Hampshire, and has a population of about 37,000.

FOOD AND DRINK:

Winchester has a wide selection of restaurants and pubs in all price ranges, including:

Old Chesil Rectory (1 Chesil St., near the City Mill) Contemporary British cuisine served in Winchester's oldest house, circa 1450. ☎ (01962) 851-555. X: Sun., Mon. £££

The Elizabethan (18 Jewry St., near High St.) A 16th- century Tudor house with Anglo-French cuisine. ☎ (01962) 853-566. ££

Nine The Square (9 Great Minster St., near the City Museum) A wine bar for snacks and a restaurant for full meals. ☎ (01962) 864-004. X: Sun. ££

Wykeham Arms (75 Kingsgate St., near Winchester College) An 18th-century inn, now a pub with excellent meals. ☎ (01962) 853-834. X for food: Sun., Mon. eve. £

Royal Oak (Royal Oak Passage, just off High St.) Lunch in an ancient pub with plenty of atmosphere. X for food: Sun. ☎ (01962) 842-701. £

Cathedral Refectory (Inner Close, by the Cathedral) Light lunches made from fresh, local ingredients, as well as teas. ☎ (01962) 853-224. X: evenings. £

SUGGESTED TOUR:

Numbers in parentheses correspond to numbers on the map.

From the **train station** (1), follow Sussex Street to the **Westgate** (2), one of Winchester's two remaining medieval gatehouses. Built in the 12th century, its upper floors were added in 1380 and later served as a debtors' prison. It is now a small museum with an interesting collection of ancient armor and related objects. There's an excellent view from its roof. *Open April–Sept., Mon.–Fri. 10–5, Sat. 10–1 and 2–5, Sun. 2–5; Feb., March, and Oct., Tues.–Fri. 10–5, Sat. 10–1 and 2–5, Sun. 2–5. Closed Nov.–Jan. Brass rubbings. Adults 30p, seniors and children 20p. ☎ (01962) 848-269.*

Strolling down High Street, you will pass the **Old Guildhall** on the right. Its projecting clock and figure of Queen Anne were given to the town to commemorate the Treaty of Utrecht in 1713. On the roof is a wooden tower housing the curfew bell, still rung each evening at eight. The 16th-century **God Begot House**, opposite, occupies the site of a manor given by Ethelred the Unready to his Queen Emma in 1012.

A few more steps brings you to the **City Cross** (3). Also known as the Butter Cross, it was erected in the 15th century. Make a right through the small passageway leading to The Square. William the Conqueror's palace once stood here. The **City Museum** (4) has fascinating displays of local archaeological finds, including Celtic pottery, a Roman mosaic floor, and painted walls. *It is open during the same times as the Westgate, above. Free. ☎ (01962) 848-269. Limited &.*

Opposite this is the main attraction:

*WINCHESTER CATHEDRAL (5), ☎ (01962) 853-137. *Open daily, 7:15–6:30. Visitors Centre 9:30–5. Tours at 11 and 2, Mon.–Sat. Crypt tours at 10:30 and 2, Mon.–Sat. Evensong Mon.–Sat. 5:30, Sun. 3:30. Access limited during ser-*

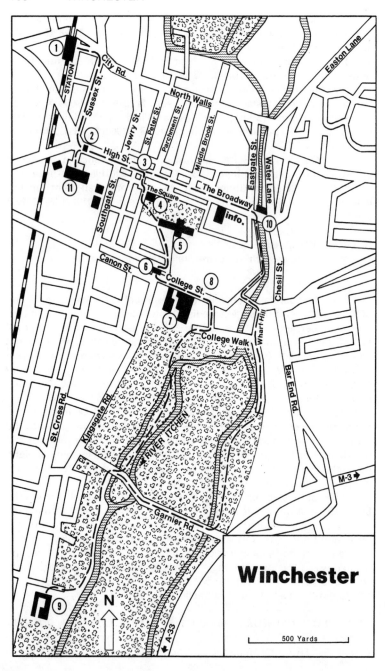

Winchester

500 Yards

vices. Café. Gift shop. Expected donation £2.50. &.

Winchester Cathedral, begun in 1079 on the site of earlier Saxon churches, is among the largest in Europe. During the 14th century the cathedral acquired a new Gothic nave, resulting in a mixture of styles ranging from robust Norman to graceful Perpendicular. Several of England's earliest kings are buried here, including Ethelwulf, Egbert, Canute, and William II Rufus, son of the Norman conqueror.

Enter the nave through the west doorway. The windows retain some of the original 14th-century glass, most of which was destroyed by Puritan zealots during the Civil War. About halfway down the nave, on the right, is the magnificent **Wykeham's Chantry**, dedicated to Bishop William of Wykeham, who was also the founder of Winchester College and New College at Oxford, as well as a noted statesman. Almost opposite this, on the north aisle, is an outstanding 12th-century **font**, carved with the story of St. Nicholas. The **tomb** of the authoress Jane Austen is nearby in the north aisle.

The massive transepts are almost unchanged since Norman times. Near the southeast corner is a chapel containing the tomb of Izaak Walton, author of *The Compleat Angler,* who died here in 1683. A doorway in the south wall leads to the **Library**, which has a 10th-century copy of the Venerable Bede's *Ecclesiastical History* as well as the rare 12th-century illuminated *Winchester Bible. Library open at variable times, Adults £1, children 50p.*

Continue up the south aisle and enter the **Presbytery**. Above the screens are six mortuary chests containing the bones of early English kings. Behind the **High Altar** is a magnificently carved 15th-century ornamental screen. Adjoining this is the **choir** with some outstanding early-14th-century stalls and misericords. The tomb of William II Rufus is under the tower. At the east end of the cathedral is the 12th-century **Chapel of the Guardian Angels**, and the modern **Shrine of St. Swithun**, the patron saint of British weather. If it rains on his day, July 15th, you're in for another 39 soggy days. Other sights include the crypt and the treasury.

Leave the cathedral and stroll through The Close, partially surrounded by the ancient monastery's walls. An arcade of the former Chapter House links the south transept with the Deanery. Dome Alley has some particularly fine 17th-century houses. Pass through the **Kingsgate** (6), the second of the two surviving medieval town gates. Above it is the tiny 13th-century **Church of St. Swithun-upon-Kingsgate**, which should definitely be visited.

Winchester College (7), the oldest "public" school in England, was founded in 1382 and is associated with New College at Oxford. *Open Mon.–Sat. 10–1 and 2–5, Sun. 2–5. Unbooked tours conducted April–Sept., 11, 2, and 3:15. Booked tours available by advance arrangement all year. Adults £2.50, seniors and children £2.* ☎ *(01962) 621-217.* &.

Continue down College Street to the ruins of **Wolvesey Castle** (8), begun in 1129 and destroyed in 1646 by Cromwell's forces during the Civil War. They are enclosed by part of the old city wall, but you can enter and take a look around. *Open April–Oct., daily, 10–6 or dusk. Adults £1.80. seniors £1.40, children 90p.* ☎ *(01962) 854-766.* ↻.

The adjacent Wolvesey Palace, thought to have been designed by Sir Christopher Wren, is now the bishop's residence.

From here there is a wonderfully picturesque **riverside walk**, said to be the inspiration for Keats' poem *Ode to Autumn.* It leads to the venerable Hospital of St. Cross, the oldest functioning almshouse in England. About a mile away, this medieval institution can also be reached by bus along St. Cross Road, but the delightful stroll along the stream is too lovely to miss. You can always ride back. To get there, just follow the map.

The ***Hospital of St. Cross** (9) has always had a tradition of providing a dole of bread and ale to weary wayfarers, which includes you. Ask and ye shall receive. Founded in 1136 by Bishop Henry de Blois, grandson of William the Conqueror, the institution cares for 25 brethren who live in 15th-century quarters and wear medieval gowns. There is a 12th-century Norman chapel and a 15th-century hall and kitchen that can be visited. Don't miss this. *Open in summer, Mon.–Sat. 9:30–5; winter, Mon.–Sat. 10:30–3:30. Closed Christmas Day. Adults £2, seniors and students £1.25, children 50p.* ☎ *(01962) 851-375.*

Those returning on foot can take the alternative route via Garnier Road. St. Catherine's Hill, across the river, has an Iron Age fort and the foundations of an early chapel at its summit, as well as an excellent view.

Back in Winchester, the footpath leads across the River Itchen alongside the medieval walls to the **City Mill** (10), part of which is now a youth hostel. There's been a mill here since Anglo-Saxon days. The present one, built in 1744, may be explored. *Open April–Oct., Wed.–Sun. and bank holiday Mon., 11–4:45; March, weekends only, 11–4:45. Adults £1, children 50p.* ☎ *(01962) 870-057.*

Turn left and follow **The Broadway** past the statue of King Alfred, who made Winchester a center of learning over a thousand years ago. The huge Victorian **Guildhall** of 1873 houses the tourist office. From here, High Street leads to The Castle, an administrative complex that includes the **Great Hall** (11), the sole remaining part of Winchester Castle. Dating from the early 13th century, the hall was the scene of many important events in English history. Go inside and take a look at the famous Roundtable, once associated with King Arthur but now known to be of 13th-century origin. *Open daily 10–5, closing at 4 on winter weekends. Free.* ☎ *(01962) 846-476.* ↻.

There are five military museums in the immediate vicinity that might interest you: the **Royal Green Jackets**, the **Light Infantry**, the **Gurkha**, the **Royal Hussars**, and the **Royal Hampshire Regiment**. From here it is only a short stroll back to the train station.

Southampton

G reat seaports are exciting places, having been touched by the world in ways that inland cities never experience. Through all of the changes in recent history, Southampton has maintained its cosmopolitan character and continues to thrive on international trade. There is a certain fascination to watching its ever-changing harbor scene and another to exploring its colorful past.

Southampton's recorded history begins with the Roman garrison of *Clausentum*. This was followed by the Saxon town of *Hamwih* where, in 1016, Canute was offered the crown of England. Large-scale trade with the Continent developed after the Norman Conquest, and in the 12th century the port became an embarkation point for many of Richard the Lionheart's Crusaders. During the Hundred Years War the town was often raided by the French, most notably in 1338. A serious decline, lasting 200 years, began in the 16th century. The Pilgrims departed from here in 1620, making a stop in Plymouth on their way to the New World. A few decades later, in 1665, Southampton was decimated by the plague.

Great places have a way of bouncing back. At its low point, Southampton discovered the spa business, becoming a fashionable seaside resort, a position it held until losing out to Brighton during the Regency. But there was still the harbor with its deep channels and four high tides a day. In the 1840s the railway came and vast docks were built. Southampton became England's gateway to the world. Millions of troops left from here during both world wars. The city was devastated by bombs in the early 1940s, and largely rebuilt in the decades that followed. Miraculously, most of its ancient treasures survived and are now part of the modern city.

GETTING THERE:

Trains operated by Southwest depart London's Waterloo Station at least twice an hour for Southampton. The trip takes 70 minutes or so, with returns until late evening.

By car, Southampton is 87 miles southwest of London via the M3 and A33 highways.

PRACTICALITIES:

Avoid coming on a Monday, when virtually all of the sights are closed.

The local **Tourist Information Centre**, ☎ (023) 80-221-106, Internet: www.southampton.gov.uk, is at 9 Civic Centre Road, opposite the Civic Centre and Art Gallery. Southampton is in the county of Hampshire, and has a population of about 207,000.

FOOD AND DRINK:

Some good places along the walking route are:

La Brasserie (33 Oxford St., 2 blocks north of the main gate to the docks) One of Southampton's best restaurants, French cuisine. ☎ (023) 80-635-043. X: Sat. lunch, Sun. ££

The Town House (59 Oxford St., 2 blocks north of the main gate to the docks) Homemade, healthy gourmet-level vegetarian cuisine. ☎ (023) 80-340-446. X: Sat. lunch, Sun., Mon. eve. ££

Golden Palace (17a Above Bar St., near the Bargate) An upstairs Chinese restaurant specializing in seafood and dim sum. ☎ (023) 80-226-636. £ and ££

The Star (26 High St., near Holy Rood Church) Bar lunches and full dinners in an 18th-century inn. ☎ (023) 80-339-939. £ and ££

The Red Lion (55 High St., near the Holy Rood Church) This partly 12th-century inn became the town's first pub in 1545. Bar and restaurant meals. ☎ (023) 80- 333-595. £ and ££

Duke of Wellington (Bugle St., near the Tudor House) Lunch in an ancient pub. £

SUGGESTED TOUR:

Numbers in parentheses correspond to numbers on the map.

Leaving the **train station** (1), follow Civic Centre Road past the tourist office to Above Bar Street and turn right. Continue on to **Bargate** (2), a particularly fine example of an early medieval fortification, once part of the ancient town walls. From here, Bargate Street leads along remnants of the walls to the Arundel Tower. The western section of the ramparts, originally dating from Norman times, is still in good condition and well endowed with explanatory signs. Climb to the walkway atop the walls and follow the map to Bugle Street.

The **Tudor House** (3) is a handsome, half-timbered 16th-century structure that now houses a museum of life in old Southampton. Be sure to see the 12th-century Norman merchant's house in its knot garden, adjoining the town wall. *Open Tues.–Fri. 10–noon and 1–5, Sat. 10–noon and 1–4, Sun. 2–5. Closed Mon. Free.* ☎ (023) 80-635-904. *Partially* &. On the other side of the square is St. Michael's Church, also dating from Norman times but heavily altered in the 19th century.

Follow Bugle Street to Westgate and turn right. You can climb the walls here for a view. The 14th-century West Gate opens onto Western

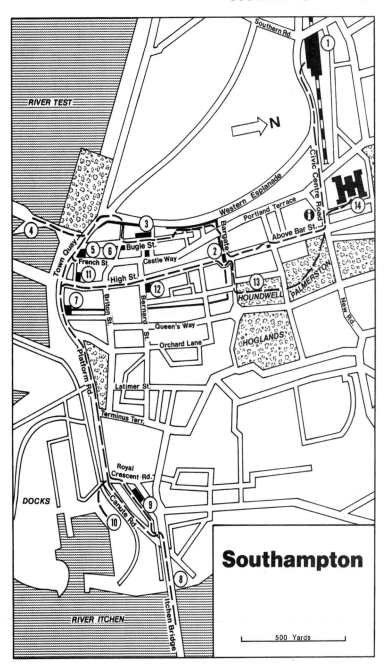

Southampton

Esplanade, once the quay from which the Pilgrims departed in 1620. Turn left and saunter down to the **Town Quay** (4), a new waterfront development that juts out into the harbor. From here you'll get great maritime vistas along with quite a variety of shops, cafés, and public activities.

Cross the street to the **Maritime Museum** (5) in the old 14th-century Wool House, once a warehouse and later a jail. Its attractions include a nautical history of Southampton, models of famous ships, and an interesting collection of seafaring artifacts. Of special interest is the **Titanic Exhibition** that brings back to life the terrible tragedy of the R.M.S. *Titanic,* which left Southampton on its maiden voyage in 1912, only to strike an iceberg and sink. First-hand accounts through the voices of survivors, and personal belongings of both passengers and crew are featured. *Open Tues.–Fri. 10–1 and 2–5, Sat. 10–1 and 2–4, Sun. 2–5. Closed Mon. Free.* ☎ *(023) 80-635-904. Partially* &.

Just a few steps up French Street is the:

MEDIEVAL MERCHANT'S HOUSE (6), ☎ (023) 80-221-503. *Open April–Oct., daily 10–6. Adults £2, seniors £1.50, children £1. Partial* &. *ground floor only.*

The Medieval Merchant's House was recently restored to its original 14th-century condition after centuries of neglect. A wine barrel hanging over its front attests to the owner's trade, and in fact local wine can still be purchased in the restored shop. You can explore the carefully re-created interiors at your own pace with the help of an audio device, absorbing the atmosphere and lifestyle of the 14th-century family that once lived there.

God's House Tower (7) on Platform Road is a 15th-century fortification that now houses a museum of archaeology. Step inside to see the fine displays of Roman, Saxon, and medieval finds from local digs around Southampton. *Open Tues.–Fri. 10–noon and 1–5, Sat. 10–noon and 1–4, Sun. 2–5. Closed Mon. Free.* ☎ *(023) 80-635-904.*

From here you can walk to the **Itchen Bridge** (8), a modern high-level span offering incomparable views of the entire harbor complex all the way out to the Isle of Wight. Along the way you will pass the main gate to the Ocean Dock, where the big liners call, just opposite Latimer Street.

Return and follow the map to the:

*HALL OF AVIATION (9), Albert Road South, ☎ (023) 80-635-830. *Open Tues.–Sat. 10–5, Sun. noon–5. Closed Mon. except school holidays. Adults £3, seniors and students £2, children (5–15) £1.50.* &.

The fascinating displays here include a World War II Spitfire and an actual Sandringham flying boat, once used for passenger service in the Pacific, that may be boarded. Ask for permission to climb up into the ***flight deck** and pretend to pilot the leviathan. The museum is a tribute to R.J. Mitchell, a local resident who developed the legendary Spitfire at his factory on the banks of the River Itchen.

The new waterfront development of **Ocean Village** (10) has something for everyone. Covering a 70-acre site, it offers a vast marina, a large waterside shopping mall with plenty of pubs and restaurants, a leisure center, and cruises around the harbor. Be sure to board the **S.S.** *Shieldhall*, Britain's last working coastal passenger and cargo steamer, which may be explored from stem to stern.

Continue on and make a right up High Street. The remains of a long Norman structure incorrectly known as "**Canute's Palace**" (11) are in Porter's Lane. High Street leads past the historic Red Lion Inn to the ruined **Holy Rood Church** (12) of the 14th century.

Now follow the route through **Houndwell** (13) and Palmerston Park to the **City Art Gallery** (14) in the massive Civic Centre. A fine museum, it specializes in British painting, especially that of the 20th century, and also has an excellent collection of Old Masters. *Open Tues.–Sat.10–5, Sun. 1–4. Closed Mon. Free.* ☎ *(023) 80-832-277. Café. Gift shop.* &.

From here it is only a short stroll back to the train station.

*Salisbury and Stonehenge

The cathedral city of Salisbury is a relative newcomer as English towns go. It was first settled in 1220 when the local bishop moved his cathedral down from the hilltop stronghold known as *Sarum.* Dating from prehistoric times, this earlier site was of great importance to the Romans, who called it *Sorviodunum.* Later becoming the Saxon settlement of *Searoburh,* it acquired a Norman castle and a cathedral during the 11th century. Frequent clashes between the clergy and the military, as well as harsh conditions imposed by a dry, windswept location, led to the establishment of a new town in the more hospitable meadows along the River Avon, just two miles to the south. After this, Old Sarum gradually died out. Its abandoned cathedral was demolished in 1331 and the stones reused for building a wall around the new town's cathedral close. By the 16th century the site was completely deserted although, as the rottenest of the Rotten Boroughs, it continued to send two members to Parliament until 1832.

The new town of Salisbury has always been a peaceful place that escaped the vicissitudes of history. Since its cathedral was one of the few to be based on a chapter of secular canons rather than a monastery, it quickly became a worldly center with all of the features of a thriving provincial capital. Salisbury today is an extraordinarily beautiful town made all the more fascinating by its proximity to the mysterious Stonehenge, one of England's most popular tourist attractions.

GETTING THERE:

Trains operated by SouthWest depart London's Waterloo Station at hourly intervals for the 1.5-hour ride to Salisbury, with return service operating until mid-evening. Schedules are reduced on Sundays and holidays. There is bus service for Stonehenge from Salisbury.

By car, Salisbury is 91 miles southwest of London via the M3 and A30 highways. To get to Stonehenge, take the A345 north to Amesbury, then the A303 and A344 west to the site. Stonehenge is about 10 miles from Salisbury. Old Sarum is along the way, about two miles north of Salisbury on the A345.

PRACTICALITIES:

Salisbury may be visited on any day, although some sights are closed on Sundays. The local **Tourist Information Centre**, ☎ (01722) 334-956, Internet: www.salisbury.gov.uk, is on Fish Row behind the Guildhall on Market Place. A colorful outdoor **market** is held there on Tuesdays and Saturdays until mid-afternoon. Salisbury is in the county of Wiltshire, and has a population of about 39,000.

FOOD AND DRINK:

The town is famous for its ancient pubs. Some of the best of these, and restaurants too, are:

Old Mill (Town Path, West Harnham) A delightful old mill by the River Nadder, with a great view and good food. ☎ (01722) 327-517. ££

Haunch of Venison (1 Minster St., near St. Thomas's Church) This famous pub restaurant dates from the 14th century. ☎ (01722) 322-024. ££

New Inn (41 New St., near North Gate) For non-smokers only, a fine pub serving good food in a 15th-century building. ☎ (01722) 327-679. ££

Harper's (6 Ox Row, by Butcher Row at the Market Place) Home-cooked English/Continental dishes in a friendly upstairs restaurant over-looking the Market Place. ☎ (01722) 333-118. X: Sun. lunch. £

Asia Restaurant (90 Fisherton St., between St. Thomas and the station) Good Indian fare at low prices. ☎ (01722) 327-628. £

Le Café Parisien (Oatmeal Row, Market Square) Light French café fare for lunch; sandwiches and the like. ☎ (01722) 412-356. £

Michael Snell (8 St. Thomas Sq., near St. Thomas's Church) Light meals in a coffee shop, with homemade sweets. ☎ (01722) 336-037. X: Sun. £

SUGGESTED TOUR:

Numbers in parentheses correspond to numbers on the map.

Depending on your arrival time, it is probably best to head out for Stonehenge immediately, getting there before the crowds get too thick. Buses leave from the train station (1) several times daily, and also from the bus station near the Market Place (11). Those driving their own cars should just follow the directions in "Getting There," above.

*STONEHENGE (2), near Amesbury, ☎ (01980) 624-715. *Open daily; late Oct. to mid-March, 9:30–4; mid-March through May, 9:30–6; June–Aug. 9–7; Sept. to mid-Oct. 9–6; mid-Oct. to late Oct. 9:30–5. Adults £4, seniors and students £3, children £2. Snack bar. Gift shop. Audio tour.* &.

Stonehenge is a massive circular group of standing stones, erected in several stages between the Late Neolithic and Middle Bronze ages. It seems to have been a temple of sorts, but anything beyond that is specu-

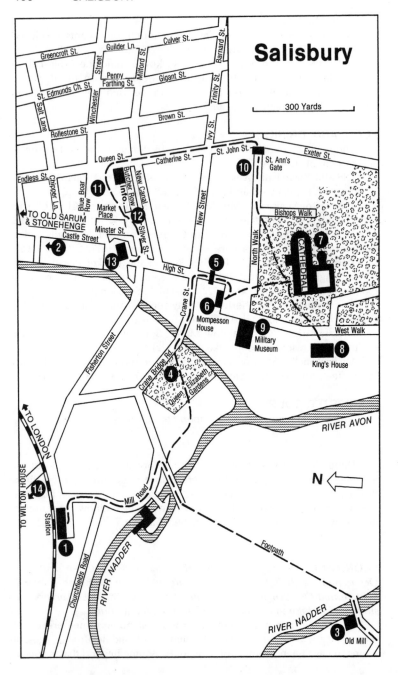

Salisbury

300 Yards

lation. What is truly marvelous about the place is that you can believe anything you want about it, no matter how outrageous, and no one can prove you wrong. Go right ahead and indulge your imagination. Perhaps Merlin really did build it by magic, or maybe it actually was an astronomical observatory, or even a temple of the Druids. Who knows? One thing is certain, however. What you get out of it is what you put in. To approach this site without preparation is to see a pile of rocks and little else. Pamphlets explaining some of the theories are sold near the entrance, although advance homework will make you visit more rewarding. Currently, there are plans afoot to move the A344 highway and the visitor center some distance from the site, restoring some of Stonehenge's mysterious natural setting.

On the way back you should try to make a stop at the ruins of **Old Sarum**, the original Salisbury, described in the introductory paragraph above. From there return to the train station and start exploring "new" Salisbury.

Leaving the **train station** (1), walk down to the River Nadder and cross it on a footbridge. A footpath from here leads through delightful countryside to the ancient **Harnham Mill** (3), parts of which may date from the 13th century. Now an inn, its bucolic setting is a scene right out of a Constable landscape. All along the way there are wonderful views of the cathedral.

Return to **Queen Elizabeth Gardens** (4) and follow the map across the 15th-century Crane Bridge. Turn right at High Street and stroll through **North Gate** (5), a 14th-century structure that once protected the bishops from rebellious citizens. The **Mompesson House** (6) on Choristers' Green, built in 1701, has an exquisite Queen Anne interior with notable plasterwork and an elegant carved oak staircase. There is also a delightful walled garden. Today, Mompesson House is owned by the National Trust. *Open late March through October, Sat.–Wed., noon to 5:30. Last admission at 5. Adults £3.40, children £1.70, garden only 80p.* ☎ *(01722) 335-659.*

From here it's only steps to:

*SALISBURY CATHEDRAL (7), The Close, ☎ (01722) 555-120, Internet: www.salisburycathedral.org.uk. *Open daily 8–6:30, remaining open until 8:15 from mid-May to mid-Sept. Donation: Adults £3.50, seniors and students £2.50, children £1.50. Tours. Cafeteria.* ♿.

Salisbury Cathedral was built over a very short time span, from 1220 to 1258, which accounts for its remarkable architectural unity. It is the purest example of the Early English style to be found anywhere in the kingdom. The graceful tower was added a century later and, at 404 feet, is the loftiest medieval spire on Earth.

At first glance, its interior seems somewhat disappointing for so majestic a structure. This is due to an overzealous spring housecleaning in the 18th century that stripped it of much of the medieval clutter that make other churches so fascinating. Yet, there are many interesting things to see, starting with the 14th-century **clock mechanism** at the west end of the north aisle. Still in operating condition, it is thought to be the oldest in England and perhaps in the world. The **West Window** contains some good 13th-century stained glass, as does the **Lady Chapel** at the east end.

Stroll out into the **Cloisters**, the largest in England, and visit the adjoining *Chapter House, whose treasures include one of the four existing original copies of the **Magna Carta**, as well as 13th-century sculptures illustrating scenes from the Old Testament. **Roof and tower tours**, offering great views, are held several times a day.

A stroll around Cathedral Close makes a pleasant break before continuing on. The Bishop's Palace, now occupied by the Cathedral School, and the Old Deanery are particularly fine 13th-century buildings within the precincts. Be sure to visit the **Salisbury and South Wiltshire Museum** (8) in the King's House along West Walk. Its displays include models and relics from Stonehenge and Old Sarum, along with items of local history, porcelains, 17th-century rooms, an old doctor's office, clothing, Turner watercolors, and the like. *Open Mon.–Sat. 10–5, and on Sun. in July and Aug., 2–5. Adults £3, seniors £2, children 75p. Restaurant.* ☎ *(01722) 332-151.* ♿.

You may also be interested in seeing **The Wardrobe** (9), a military museum of the Royal Gloucestershire, Berkshire and Wiltshire Regiment. Recalling life in a county regiment, it is located in another nearby historic house and features beautiful waterside gardens. *Open April–Oct., daily 10–4:30; Feb.–March and Nov.–Dec. Tues.–Sat. 10–4:30. Adults £2.20, seniors £1.90, children 50p. Tea room with light lunches.* ♿.

Follow North Walk to the **Malmesbury House** (10), an historic mansion that grew out of a 13th-century canonry. Now restored to its 18th-century splendor, it played a role in the Civil War and was home to a direct ancestor of the present queen. Charles II stayed here, as did the composer Handel, whose ghost (or perhaps someone else's) still haunts the premises. Visits, with or without apparitions, may be made by prior arrangement. ☎ *(01722) 327-027.*

Handel gave his first public concert in England in a room above the adjacent **St. Ann's Gate**. Pass under this and turn left on St. John's Street, following the map to the **Market Place** (11). Markets have been held here twice a week since 1361, a custom that continues today.

Cut through to Silver Street. The beautiful hexagonal **Poultry Cross** (12) was first mentioned in 1335 as the spot where poultry was sold. Around the corner, approached through alleyways, is **St. Thomas's Church** (13), one of the most interesting buildings in Salisbury. Founded in honor of Thomas à Becket about 1220, it was rebuilt in the 15th century and has a marvelous medieval fresco known as the *Doom Painting,* depicting the Last Judgement, above its chancel arch. This was whitewashed over during the Reformation and not rediscovered until the 19th century. The colorful area around the church is the perfect spot to wind up your tour.

If you decided not to go to Stonehenge, you might want instead to visit:

*WILTON HOUSE (14), Wilton, Salisbury, ☎ (01722) 746-720, Internet: www.wiltonhouse.com. *Located 2.5 miles west of Salisbury on the A30. Frequent bus service from central Salisbury on routes 60 or 61 (hourly on Sun.), or drive or take a taxi there. Open late March through Oct., daily 10:30–5:30, last admission at 4:30. Adults £6.75, seniors £5.75, children £4. Cafeteria.*

One of England's most attractive stately homes, Wilton is filled with outstanding art and has acres and acres of lovely gardens. Henry VIII gave the first Wilton House to William Herbert in 1541, who soon thereafter became the Earl of Pembroke. Destroyed by fire, it was rebuilt by the great architect Inigo Jones for the fifth earl. The present resident is the 17th Earl of Pembroke. Visits begin with a video, followed by a tour of the kitchen. Shakespeare dedicated the first folio of his plays to the third earl, so there's a statue of him in the hall. Wilton's most noted sight is the extravagant ***Double Cube Room** with its vast Van Dyke portrait of the Pembroke family. There is an American connection here as well, as this is where General Eisenhower planned much of the Normandy invasion of 1944. On the lighter side, check out the delightful display of some 200 costumed teddy bears in their own miniature house and stables. Don't miss the amazing ***Palladian Bridge**, spanning the River Nadder in the landscaped parkland.

Windsor and Eton

Windsor, like Stratford, Oxford, and the Tower of London, is one of England's greatest tourist attractions. It has just the right combination of elements to make an ideal daytrip destination for first-time visitors and seasoned travelers alike. To begin with, it is very close to the capital and easy to reach. Second, it contains within a small area much of what is considered to be typically English. There is the Royal Castle, still in use after 850 years, a picturesque riverside location on the Thames, a colorful Victorian town, and in Eton one of the great public schools that have molded British character since the Middle Ages. Add these together and you have a carefree and thoroughly delightful day ahead of you.

GETTING THERE:

Trains operated by Thames depart London's **Paddington Station** frequently for Slough, where you change to a shuttle train for Windsor & Eton Central. The total journey takes about 40 minutes, with returns until late evening. Service is reduced on Sundays and holidays. There is also direct service, operated by South West, from London's **Waterloo Station** to Windsor & Eton Riverside, taking about 50 minutes and running about twice an hour, less frequently on Sundays and holidays. Most travelers will find the route via Paddington to be more convenient.

By car, Windsor is 28 miles west of London via the M4 motorway. Get off at Junction 6.

PRACTICALITIES:

The Castle grounds and most attractions are open daily except for special events. If in doubt, check with the **Tourist Information Centre**, ☎ (01753) 743-900, 24 High Street, opposite the castle. An Internet site to try is: www.windsor-gb.co.uk.

Guide Friday operates a hop-on, hop-off open-top double-decker bus service from late March through October, running at frequent intervals on a continuous loop route through Windsor and Eton. All-day unlimited use fares are: Adults £6.50, seniors and students £5.50, children £2.50. Single fares are also available. A running commentary is provided. Buy tickets from the driver or the tourist centre. ☎ (01789) 294-466, Internet: www.guidefriday.com.

Windsor is in the county of Berkshire, and has a population of about 30,000.

FOOD AND DRINK:

Some good restaurants and pubs are:

IN WINDSOR:

The Orangerie (Thames St., near the bridge) English and French cuisine at an inn, once the home of Sir Christopher Wren. ☎ (01753) 861-354. X: Sat. lunch. £££

Good Measures (18a Thames St., by Boots' Passage) Quality English cuisine at reasonable prices. ☎ (01753) 854-812. ££

Punters Wine Bar (50 Thames St., near the bridge) Light lunches, dinners, and drinks, with outdoor tables beneath the castle. ☎ (01753) 865-565. ££

Sally Lunn's (11 Peascod St., near the castle) A Windsor branch of the Bath original, still following the 1680 recipe for those buns. Various savory creations and quintessential teas. ☎ (01753) 862-627. £ and ££

Carpenters Arms (Market St., behind the Guildhall) A comfortable pub with lunches. X for meals: Sun. ☎ (01753) 863-695. £

IN ETON:

Eton Wine Bar (82 High St., near the bridge) Healthy, imaginative cooking with a changing menu. ☎ (01753) 854-921. ££

The Cockpit (47 High St.) Enjoy Italian and other cuisines in this historic inn. X: Mon., Tues. lunch. ☎ (01753) 860-944. ££

SUGGESTED TOUR:

Numbers in parentheses correspond to numbers on the map.

Start your walk at the **Royal Windsor Information Centre** (1) at 24 High Street, opposite the castle and close to Central Station. Here you can check out the latest information and perhaps visit their small **Town & Crown Exhibition**, depicting the town's development and its relationship to the monarchy. *Open daily. Adults £1, children 50p.*

Cross the main street, passing the statue of Queen Victoria, and enter the grounds of:

*WINDSOR CASTLE** (2–4), ☎ (01753) 868-286, Internet: www.royal. gov.uk/palaces/windsor.htm. Open daily except certain days; check first. *Open March–Oct. 10–5:30 (last admission at 4); Nov.–Feb. 10–4 (last admission at 3). State Apartments closed much of June, parts of Oct., and parts of Nov. St. George's Chapel is closed on Sun. Adults £10, seniors over 60 £7.50, children under 17 £5. Reduced prices when parts of the castle are closed. Partial ♿, check in advance.*

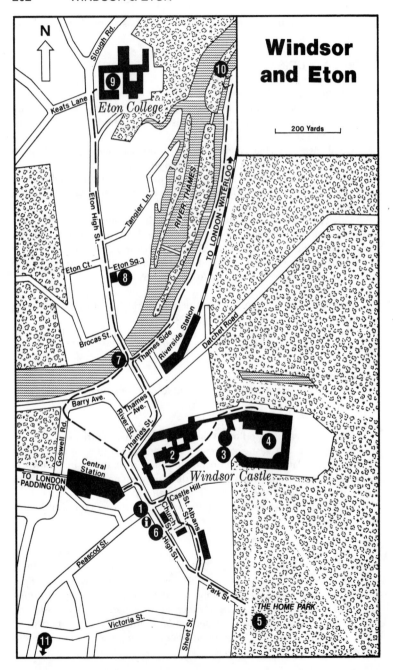

Windsor and Eton

200 Yards

Begun by William the Conqueror in the 11th century, **Windsor Castle** has been altered by nearly every succeeding monarch. It is the largest inhabited castle in the world and remains a chief residence for the sovereigns of England.

Enter through Henry VIII's Gateway and visit *St. George's Chapel (2), one of the most beautiful churches in England and home of its oldest order of chivalry, the Most Noble Order of the Garter, founded in 1348 by Edward III. Many of the country's kings and queens are buried here. Continue on past the massive **Round Tower** (3) and go out on the North Terrace, which has magnificent views up and down the River Thames. The entrance to the **State Apartments** (4) is nearby. Another appealing attraction is *Queen Mary's Dolls' House, a miniature 20th-century palace in exquisite detail, also entered from the North Terrace. The rest of your tour of the castle can be spent just poking about any area that is not off limits.

Leave the castle and stroll down Church Street, perhaps stopping at the Parish Church and Brass Rubbing Centre. Walk through the graveyard to St. Alban's Street. You might want to go down Park Street for a view of the **Long Walk** (5) in the Home Park.

The elegant **Guildhall** (6) on High Street was completed in 1689 by Sir Christopher Wren. Step onto its porch and note that the center columns do not quite reach the ceiling they allegedly support, a trick played by the architect to prove the soundness of his design. Continue down High Street and Thames Street, making a left at the footpath to the river. Along the way you'll pass a bowling green, tennis courts, and a lovely waterside park. **Boat trips** operated by French Brothers Ltd., some as short as 35 minutes, are available here. ☎ *(01753) 851-900, Internet: www.boat-trips.co.uk. Adults from £3.60, children from £1.80.*

The old **cast-iron bridge** (7) to Eton is reserved for pedestrians. Once across it follow High Street past numerous shops and pubs to the **Cock Pit** (8), a 15th-century timbered inn where cockfighting was once patronized by Charles II, the Merry Monarch. Outside it are the **town stocks** and an unusual Victorian mailbox.

Eton College (9) was founded in 1440 by Henry VI, himself a teenager at the time. It is the most famous of England's public (meaning very private) schools and has educated many of the nation's greatest leaders. As you walk around you will notice the peculiar traditional garb of the students, which makes them look a little like penguins. Parts of the school are open to visitors, including the schoolyard, cloisters, and the chapel. The Upper and Lower schools may also be seen, and guided tours are available. Be sure to visit the **Museum of Eton Life**, which re-creates life among the students in bygone times and is located in the cellars of the original 15th-century buildings. *Open late March to late April and early July to early Sept., 10:30–4:30; late April to early July and early Sept. to early Oct., 2–4:30.*

Guided tours at 2:15 and 3:15. The Chapel is closed on weekdays from 1–2, and on Sundays from 12:30–2. The entire college is closed on two days in June. Ordinary admission: Adults £2.60, children £2. Tours: Adults £3.80, children £3. ☎ *(01753) 671- 177, Internet: www.etoncollege.com.*

Return to the bridge. If you have any strength or time left you may want to take a pleasant walk along the Thames to the **Romney Lock** (10), or visit a pub before returning to London.

ADDITIONAL ATTRACTION:

If you have a kid in tow, or even if you're just a big kid yourself, and especially if you're staying overnight, consider a visit to nearby:

LEGOLAND WINDSOR (11), Windsor-Ascot Rd. (B3022), 2 miles south of Windsor, ☎ (0990) 040404, Internet: www.legoland.co.uk. Frequent bus service from near both train stations in Windsor. *Open mid-March through Oct., daily 10–6 or dusk if earlier, remaining open until 8 from mid-July to early Sept. Adults £16.50, seniors £10.50, children (3–15) £13.50. Restaurants. Picnic facilities. Shops.* &.

A British version of the Danish original, Legoland is a fun-packed theme park where children 2–12 can have a great time while learning all the while. There's a variety of rides for different age groups, challenging workshops, and a mini-Europe constructed from over 20 million Lego bricks.

*Bath

Legend has it that the hot mineral springs of Bath were discovered about 500 BC by Prince Bladud who, suffering from leprosy, was cured and became king as well as the father of Shakespeare's King Lear. Whatever truth lies behind this story, we do know that the Romans built a settlement here named *Aquae Sulis*, which served as their spa for nearly 400 years.

During the Middle Ages the waters of Bath were well known for their curative properties, but the splendor of the Romans went down the drain. Renovation began with Queen Anne's visit in 1702, and a "master of cere-monies" appointed to oversee the spa. This post remained after the queen's departure, being filled by a bizarre young gambler named Richard "Beau" Nash, who in the next 40 years virtually invented the resort busi-ness.

Nash began by persuading the local gentry into building a town of unmatched elegance, with design leadership falling to a visionary archi-tect named John Wood. Under his plan, individual houses were only com-ponents of a larger structure behind a common façade. Such thinking reached its height in that triumph of the Palladian style, the Royal Crescent, designed by Wood's son in 1767.

Today, Bath remains much the same as it was when Georgian aristo-crats made it their playground. The remains of the Roman era were uncov-ered and restored, adding to its attractions. Despite its stylish refinement, Bath makes a great daytrip destination largely because it is actually a *fun* place to visit. Many travelers, in fact, consider it to be nothing less than the most enjoyable town in England.

GETTING THERE:

Trains leave London's Paddington Station at least hourly for Bath Spa Station, a ride of about 80 minutes. Return service operates until late evening.

By car, take the M4 highway to Junction 18, then south on the A46. Bath is 119 miles west of London.

PRACTICALITIES:

Bath may be visited at any time. The local **Tourist Information Centre**,

☎ (01225) 477-101, Internet www.bathtourism.co.uk, is in the Abbey Chambers in Abbey Churchyard, by the Abbey. Another Internet site to try is: www.bathtap.co.uk.

The famous **Bath International Music Festival** fills the town with all manner of artistic activities from mid-May to early June. *☎ (01225) 463-362, Internet: http://Bathfestivals.com for information.*

Guide Friday operates hop-on, hop-off open-top double-decker buses on a circular route that goes by most of the attractions. Buy an all-day, unlimited use ticket, or a single fare ticket, from the driver. *☎ (01225) 444-102, Internet: www.guidefriday.com/bath. Runs every 15 min. from Easter to Oct., less frequently during the rest of the year. All-day tickets: Adults £8, seniors and students £6, children £3.*

Bath has a population of about 85,000.

FOOD AND DRINK:

Out of an enormous selection of restaurants and pubs, some good choices for daytrippers are:

Popjoys (Beau Nash House, Sawclose, adjacent to the Theatre Royal) An elegant Regency restaurant with inventive English cuisine. Reservations recommended, ☎ (01225) 460-494. X: Sun. ££ and £££

Café Retro (18 York St., near the Abbey) Inventive cuisine, BYOB. ☎ (01225) 339-347. ££ and £££

Pump Room (by the Roman Baths) Light lunches in the most genteel of settings, a real Bath experience. ☎ (01225) 444-477. ££

Woods Brasserie (9 Alfred St., near the Assembly Rooms) A popular-price offshoot of the adjacent Woods Restaurant, serving a similar quality of cuisine. ☎ (01225) 314-812. X: Sun. eve. ££

Number Five (5 Argyle St., near Pulteney Bridge) A popular bistro with inventive light dishes for every taste. ☎ (01225) 444-499. X: Sun., Mon. lunch. ££

Moon and Sixpence (6a Broad St., east of the Octagon) An upstairs/downstairs establishment with both buffet lunches and elaborate meals. ☎ (01225) 460-962. £ and ££

Sally Lunn's (9 N. Parade Passage, a block south of the Abbey) Bath buns form the basis for a vast variety of creative dishes in this historic house. ☎ (01225) 461-634. £ and ££

Demuth's Vegetarian Restaurant (2 N. Parade Passage, a block south of the Abbey) Fresh, imaginative vegetarian dishes in a colorful setting. ☎ (01225) 446-059. £

SUGGESTED TOUR:

Numbers in parentheses correspond to numbers on the map.

Leaving **Bath Spa Station** (1), walk straight ahead on Manvers Street past the bus station and turn left on North Parade. This soon becomes a colorful lane called North Parade Passage, a.k.a. **Old Lilliput Alley**, lined with some of the oldest houses in town. One of these is **Sally Lunn's House** (2), built in 1482 on Roman foundations, which as a coffee shop has been famous for its hot Bath buns since the late 17th century. They are still just as delicious, making this a favorite place for a break. You could also just pop in to see the original **kitchen** in the cellar, and the Roman walls. ☎ *(01225) 461-634. Open Mon.–Sat. 10–6, Sun. noon–6. Entry 30p.* At the end of the passage is **Abbey Green**, an especially attractive spot.

Turn right on Church Street and follow it two blocks to the **Abbey** (3). This splendid example of the Perpendicular style was begun in 1499, although it did not gain a roof until the 17th century. Earlier churches existed on the same spot for several hundred years before a cathedral was built in 1088, a Norman structure destroyed by fire in 1137. The present abbey is noted for its enormous clerestory windows that flood the interior with light, and for its vaulted ceiling, planned from the start but not added until 1864. ☎ *(01225) 422-462. Open Mon.–Sat. 9–6, Sun. noon–6; closing at 4:30 in winter. Requested donation £2.* ♿.

Walk across the Abbey Churchyard to the entrance of the:

*ROMAN BATHS and PUMP ROOM (4), ☎ (01225) 477-000, Internet: www.romanbaths.co.uk. *Open daily 9–6, closing at 5 in winter and on Sun. Adults £6.70, seniors £6, children £4. A joint ticket with the Museum of Costume is available. Gift shop. Partial* ♿.

The tour through this ancient complex includes a fascinating **Museum** of Roman and prehistoric relics, featuring the renowned gilt-bronze head of the goddess Minerva. An overflowing part of the original Roman reservoir is in this area, as is the **Great Bath**, a marvelously preserved pool that is today open to the sky. The original Roman lead plumbing is still in use, while the columns and statues above are Victorian additions. Another group of small baths and hypocaust rooms lie beyond, along with the King's Bath and the Circular Bath. A few of the ruins were discovered in the 18th century, but it was not until the 19th that the major finds were excavated. Above all of this is the famous **Pump Room**, an elegant Georgian assembly hall reflecting a gentility long vanished elsewhere. Be sure to see the wonderful equation clock of 1709, as well as the charming prints and 18th-century furniture. This is the perfect spot for a tea break or lunch, both served daily with live music by the Pump Room Trio.

Continue down Bath Street towards the Cross Bath and turn right into St. Michael's Place, then left through a narrow passage called Chandos Buildings to Westgate Buildings. Another right brings you to the **Theatre Royal** (5), first erected in 1720 but later rebuilt. It is adjacent to Beau Nash's last home, now a restaurant named after his mistress, Juliana

Bath

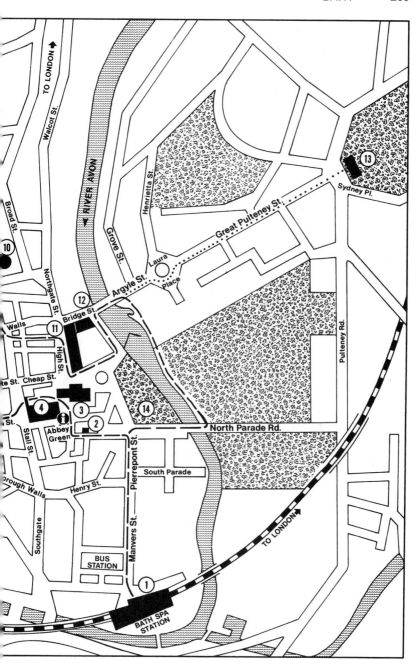

Popjoy. Follow the map by way of the narrow, cobbled **Queen Street** and continue through Queen Square, heading uphill through Royal Victoria Park. Along the way, to the right, is a marvelous little Georgian Garden of 1770, excavated in 1986 and recently restored by the town.

From the gravel walk you will have an excellent view of the ***Royal Crescent** (6), a magnificent sweep of 30 houses joined together in one continuous façade of 114 Ionic columns. Designed in 1767 by John Wood the Younger, this is regarded as the epitome of the Palladian style in England. Follow it around to **Number 1**, whose interior has been restored to its 18th-century splendor. This exquisite house is open to the public and is well worth a visit. *Open March–Oct.,Tues.–Sun., 10:30–5; and Nov. to mid-Dec., Tues.–Sun. 10:30–4. Adults £4, seniors, students, children £3.* ☎ *(01225) 428-126.*

Stroll down Brock Street to **The Circus** (7), a circular group of Georgian houses considered to be John Wood's finest work. It is arranged so that no street goes straight through, resulting in a view from every angle. Continue along Bennet Street, from which you can take an interesting little side trip by turning up Russell Street and making a right on Rivers Street to the **Bath Industrial Heritage Centre** (8), otherwise known as **Mr. Bowler's Business**. This Victorian engineering shop, brass foundry, and mineral-water plant is complete with all of its original machinery and related items. *Open Easter–Oct., daily 10–5; Nov.–Easter, weekends only, 10–5. Adults £3.50, seniors and children £2.50.* ☎ *(01225) 318-348.*

Now head for the **Assembly Rooms** (9). Also built by John Wood the Younger, this structure was the center of social activity in Bath, having witnessed many grand balls, banquets, receptions, and the like. The ***Museum of Costume** on its lower floor is the largest of its kind in the world. Clothes dating from as far back as the 16th century up to the present are very well displayed, many of them in period room settings. *Open Mon.–Sat. 10–5, Sun. 11–5. Adults £3.80, seniors £3.50, children £2.70. Joint ticket with the Roman Baths available.* ☎ *(01225) 477-752.* ♿.

The route leads down to Milsom Street, a major shopping thoroughfare, where the 18th-century **Octagon** (10) houses the **National Centre of Photography**. This intriguing museum has displays of both contemporary and early camera work, along with an outstanding collection of antique and modern photo equipment. It also serves as the headquarters of the Royal Photographic Society. *Open daily 9:30–5:30. Adults £2.50, seniors, students, children £1.75.* ☎ *(01225) 462-841. Shop. Café.*♿

Continue straight ahead past Upper Borough Walls and turn left through the charming Northumberland Place to High Street. The building on the other side is the **Guildhall** (11), whose banqueting room is one of the finest interiors in Bath. *This may be seen on Mondays through Fridays, from 9–5. Free.* ♿. Next to it is the **Covered Market**, which was founded in medieval times and remains very much alive in its 19th-century building.

Turning left around the Orange Grove brings you to Grand Parade. To the left, on Bridge Street, is the **Victoria Art Gallery**, a major venue for temporary exhibitions that also offers a fine permanent collection. *Open Tues.–Fri. 10–5:30, Sat. 10–5, Sun. 2–5. Free.* ☎ *(01225) 477-772. Partial ♿.*

The **Pulteney Bridge** (12) spanning the Avon is one of the few left in Europe to be lined with shops. Built in 1770 with obvious inspiration from the Ponte Vecchio in Florence, it makes a spectacular sight rising above the weir.

Once across it, you might want to make a **side trip** down Argyle Street and Great Pulteney Street to the **Holburne Museum** (13), which specializes in the arts of the Age of Elegance. Silver, porcelains, miniatures, and paintings by Gainsborough and others are among its attractions. *Open Easter to mid-Dec., Mon.–Sat. 11–5 and Sun. 2:30–5:30. Adults £3.50, seniors £3, children £1.50. Café.* ☎ *(01225) 466-669.*

Return almost to the bridge, then go down a flight of steps marked Riverside Walk to the River Avon and stroll past the weir. From the embankment on this side you can take a **boat ride** lasting about an hour. Check the tourist office for current schedules. When you get to the next bridge, climb the stairs and cross it. You are now on North Parade. The **Parade Gardens** (14) on the right are a good place to relax before returning to the station.

Trip 32

Wells

Completely dominated by its marvelous cathedral, England's smallest city has a timeless beauty that is rare, even in this lovely land. Other cathedral towns have grown and become worldly while Wells slept right through the turmoil of history. Its medieval ecclesiastical complex remains complete and untouched, the largest and best preserved in the country. A delight to explore on foot, Wells is the perfect place to become involved with the Middle Ages.

Just two miles away, reached by road or, better still, a tranquil woodland path, is the Wookey Hole, a great cave where early man lived over 2,000 years ago. A tour through its subterranean chambers combined with a visit to Wells makes this a very satisfying daytrip.

GETTING THERE:

Trains depart London's Paddington station at least hourly for the 80-minute ride to Bath Spa, where you change to a bus for Wells. This leaves from the Bath bus station, just one block away. Service to Wells operates hourly (every three hours on Sundays and holidays), taking about 80 minutes to cover the 20-mile distance through lovely villages and down country lanes. Be sure to check the return schedule.

By car, take the M4 to junction 18, then head south on the A46 to Bath. Change here to the A39 for Wells, which is 132 miles west of London.

PRACTICALITIES:

This trip may be made at any time, but note that transportation is reduced on Sundays and holidays. The Bishop's Palace and Gardens are open from Easter through October, Tuesdays through Fridays and Sundays; and daily in August. Good weather is essential if you intend to walk to the Wookey Hole. A colorful outdoor market is held in Wells on Wednesdays and Saturdays. Some shops close early on Wednesdays.

The local **tourist office**, ☎ (01749) 672-552, Internet: http://www.wells-somerset.com, is in the Town Hall on Market Place. Ask them about getting to the Wookey Hole.

FOOD AND DRINK:

There are many old inns and pubs in Wells, mostly in the Market Place and on High and Sadler streets. Out at the Wookey Hole there is a cafeteria, in addition to a nearby pub. Some good places to eat in Wells are:

The Swan (11 Sadler St., just west of the cathedral) Fine dining in a 15th-century building, now a small hotel. ☎ (01749) 678-877. ££

Crown (Market Place) A 15th-century inn associated with William Penn. ☎ (01749) 673-457. ££

Star (14 High St., just west of the Market Place) Bar lunches and full dinners in a 16th-century coaching inn. £ and ££

Market Place Hotel (Market Place) A 14th-century inn with bar snacks at lunch and full dinners in the evening. ☎ (01749) 672-616. £ and ££

The Good Earth (4 Priory Rd., south of the bus station) Vegetarian health food in a rustic environment. ☎ (01749) 678-600. X: Sun. £

The Cloisters (in the cathedral cloister) light lunches. ☎ (01749) 676-543. £

SUGGESTED TOUR:

Numbers in parentheses correspond to numbers on the map.

Leave the bus station (1) in Wells and follow the map to the **Market Place** (2), where an outdoor market is held on Wednesdays and Saturdays from 8:30 a.m. to 4 p.m. The tourist office is nearby.

Penniless Porch, where alms were once distributed, leads to:

*WELLS CATHEDRAL (3), ☎ (01749) 674-483. *Open daily 7–7, closing at 8:30 in July–Aug. and 6 in winter. Suggested donation: Adults £3, seniors £2, children £1. Tours. Gift shop. Restaurant.*

A church has stood here since AD 704, but the present structure was begun about 1180. Its astonishing ***west front** is from the mid-l3th century and is decorated with 297 medieval statues, all that remain of the original 400. At one time these were brightly colored, but weather has taken its toll over the centuries. It is still possibly the finest collection of sculpture from the Middle Ages in England.

Enter the nave and examine the remarkable **inverted arch** under the central tower. This was erected in the 14th century to support the newly completed tower, which was already collapsing. Unique in the world of Gothic design, it has done its job well. There is a marvelous ***clock** in the north transept that dates from 1392 and gives an animated performance as it strikes the hour. A spectacular stone staircase nearby leads to the **Chapter House**, one of the finest examples of its style in the country. Continue on through the choir to see the east window, which has some unusual old glass.

A stroll through the 15th-century **cloisters** will bring you to the grounds of the **Bishop's Palace** (4), one of the oldest inhabited houses in England. The strong walls and surrounding moat were added in the 14th century to protect the bishop from rioting townspeople. Be sure to cross the drawbridge, visit the palace, and then walk out to the gardens. **St. Andrew's Well** provides the setting for an almost magically serene ***view** of

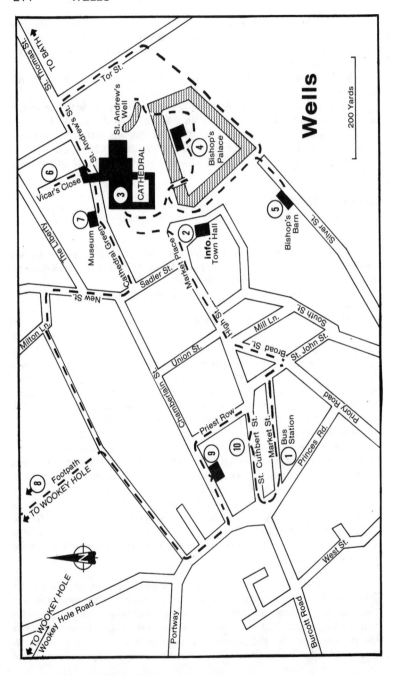

Wells

200 Yards

the cathedral. *The Bishop's Palace can be visited from Easter through Oct., Tues.–Fri. 10:30–6, and Sun. 2–6 p.m. During Aug. it is open daily. Combined admission for palace and gardens: Adults £3, seniors £2, students £1.50.* ☎ *(01749) 678-691.*

From the south corner of the moat make a right on Silver Street to the early-15th-century **Bishop's Barn** (5). Return along the moat and turn left on Tor Street. Another left at St. Andrew's Street leads to **Vicar's Close** (6), a 14th-century lane of immense charm—reputed to be the oldest inhabited medieval street in Europe—that is connected to the cathedral by a bridge over the Chain Gate.

Beyond the archway lies the **Wells Museum** (7) on Cathedral Green. Prehistoric artifacts from the Wookey Hole and other nearby caves are featured in its splendid collection, along with natural displays and local bygones. *Open April through Oct., daily from 10–5:30 (later in summer); and on Wed. and Sun. during the off-season. Adults £2, seniors and students £1.50, children £1.* ☎ *(01749) 673-477.*

At this point you may be interested in an invigorating hike to the Wookey Hole, two miles away. If your feet are not up to it but you would still like to go, you can take one of the hourly buses from the bus station (1), or a taxi. Those with cars should leave via Wookey Hole Road. On foot you could, of course, follow that same road, but there is a much better scenic route via a series of woodland paths. The map shows how to get out of town, and from there the route is well marked. Half of the distance is uphill, rewarding your efforts with glorious vistas. It may be wise to ask at the tourist office about trail conditions before setting out. The round trip from Wells, including seeing the caves, will take about three hours.

WOOKEY HOLE CAVES (8), Wookey Hole, Somerset, ☎ (01749) 672-243, Internet: www.wookey.co.uk. *Open daily except around Christmas, 10–5, closing at 4:30 in winter. Adults £7, children 4–16 £3.50. Cafeteria. Gift shops. Partial ♿, but not in caves.*

The Wookey Hole is more than a little commercialized. This is not a serious detraction from its splendors, and may actually make the visit more fun. You will be taken through the *caves by an experienced guide who is knowledgeable in their history and legends, especially that of the witch of the Dark Ages, who was turned to stone by a monk sent in to exorcize her spirit. Near the exit there is an **old paper mill** that is now a part of the complex. Demonstrations of hand paper-making are given almost continuously. Other parts of the mill are devoted to a fascinating collection of early **penny arcade amusements**, a **Magical Mirror Maze**, and a **Museum of the Caves**. There is also a working waterwheel.

Returning to Wells, there are two more places you may want to visit. The **Almshouses** (9) on Chamberlain Street date from the 15th century. **St. Cuthbert's** (10), one block away, is a parish church from the same era. It has quite an interesting interior and deserves to be seen.

Bristol

Bristol is a delightful city to visit, especially in summer. Few places combine the serious with the lighthearted quite so well. Where else can you see the sights from a vintage steam train or a tiny ferryboat? Or for that matter, explore the innards of an early-19th-century transatlantic steamship or peer into the cockpit of a Concorde jet? Not many English cities boast as many sidewalk cafés or outstanding restaurants. Culture is not overlooked, either. Bristol has its fair share of medieval buildings, superb museums, churches, two cathedrals, several arts centers, and a world-renowned theater.

A thriving port since Saxon times, Bristol's prosperity was founded on wool, wine, tobacco, and the slave trade. Its enterprising seamen sailed to the far corners of the known world, and in 1497 one of them, John Cabot, first braved the North Atlantic to discover Newfoundland. Its commerce with the New World expanded as did the size of its ships. Eventually the harbor became inadequate and a new one was built at nearby Avonmouth. Heavy bombing during World War II led to extensive reconstruction. Today, the old downtown harbor is used mostly for pleasure, an amenity that makes Bristol an attractive place to visit.

GETTING THERE:

Trains leave London's Paddington Station at least hourly for Bristol's Temple Meads Station, a journey of about 90 minutes. Return trains run until mid-evening. Be certain that the train you board is not just going to Bristol Parkway, which is out in the suburbs. Service is somewhat reduced on Sundays and holidays.

By car, Bristol is 121 miles west of London. Take the M4 to Junction 19, then the M32 into the center of Bristol.

PRACTICALITIES:

Bristol can be visited at any time in good weather. There is more activity, and more fun, on summer weekends. The Georgian House is open on Saturdays through Wednesdays, as is the Industrial Museum. The local **Tourist Information Centre**, ☎ (0117) 926-0767, Internet: http://tourism.bristol.gov.uk, is in historic St. Nicholas Church in the medieval heart of the city. Bristol has a population of about 400,000.

FOOD AND DRINK:

Out of a vast selection, some especially good choices for lunch are:

Harvey's (12 Denmark St., 2 blocks northeast of the cathedral) Located in the cellars of a famous wine shipper, Harvey's is renowned for its contemporary British cuisine. There is also a wine museum on the premises. ☎ (0117) 927-7665. X: Sat. lunch, Sun. £££

Riverstation (The Grove, just south of Queen Square) Right on the river, an upstairs/downstairs place with lower prices below. ☎ (0117) 914-4434. X: Sat. lunch. ££ and £££

Markwicks (43 Corn St., in the medieval heart of town) Quality dining in a former bank vault. ☎ (0117) 926- 2658. X: Sat. lunch, Sun., Mon. ££

The Glass Boat (Welsh Back, just east of Queen Square) Lunch, tea, or dinner aboard a floating barge in the Floating Harbour. ☎ (0117) 929-0704. ££

River Café (Redcliff Quay, 125 Redcliffe St., 2 blocks southeast of the tourist centre) On the river, with outdoor tables. ☎ (0117) 987-2270. X: Sun. eve. ££

Brown's Restaurant (38 Queen's Rd., near the City Museum) Large, fashionable, and very popular, this restaurant and bar features burgers, pasta, and all sorts of contemporary dishes. ☎ (0117) 930-4777. £ and ££

Arnolfini Café (Narrow Quay, at the south end of the quay) Casual meals in an arts center. ☎ (0117) 927-9330. £

Boston Tea Party (75 Park St., near the Georgian House) Fabulous sandwiches, vegetarian dishes, and the like. Very popular. ☎ (0117) 929-8601. £

SUGGESTED TOUR:

Numbers in parentheses correspond to numbers on the map.

Leaving **Temple Meads Station** (1), cross Temple Gate and follow Redcliffe Way to ***St. Mary Redcliffe** (2), the massive parish church that Queen Elizabeth I called "the fairest and goodliest" in all the land. Rebuilt in the 14th century, parts of it date from the 12th. If you have time for only one church during your visit, it should be this one. Americans will be interested in the prominent tomb of Admiral Sir William Penn (1621–70), whose son William founded Pennsylvania in 1682. Outside, in the churchyard, look for the gravestone of Tom, the church cat who kept the mice at bay from 1912 to 1927, and was given a grand funeral as a reward. *Open daily, 8–5. Free, donation appreciated.* ☎ *(0117) 929-1487.* ♿.

Continue across Redcliffe Bridge to Queen Square and turn right to King Street. One of the most colorful thoroughfares in town, this cobbled street is lined with old taverns as well as the Theatre Royal, home of the famous Bristol Old Vic repertory company.

Now follow the map to **Narrow Quay** (3), a lovely waterfront street where you'll find the Arnolfini Arts Centre. From here you can either walk to the next destination, or take one of the small open ferries that operate daily from April through September. However you get there, the **Industrial**

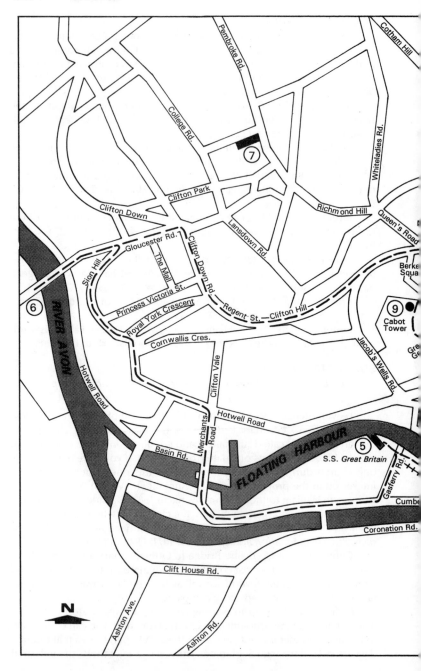

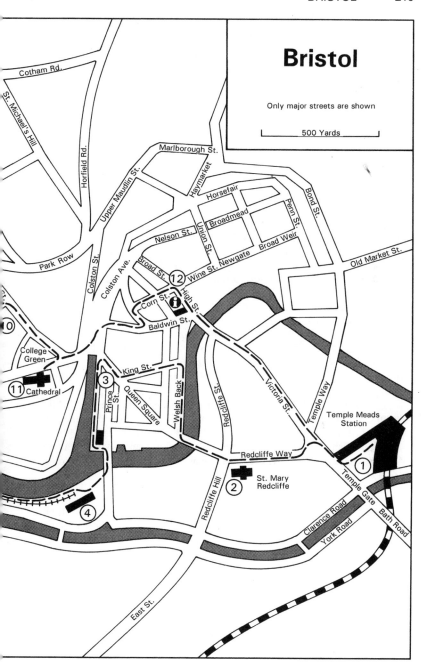

Bristol

Only major streets are shown

500 Yards

Cotham Rd.

St. Michael's Hill

Horfield Rd.

Marlborough St.

Upper Maudlin St.

Haymarket

Horsefair

Bond St.

Park Row

Colston St.

Colston Ave.

Nelson St.

Union St.

Broadmead

Penn St.

Broad Weir

Broad St.

Wine St. Newgate

Old Market St.

12

Corn St.

High St.

Baldwin St.

College Green

King St.

11 Cathedral

3

Prince St.

Queen Square

Welsh Back

Redcliffe St.

Victoria St.

Temple Way

Temple Meads Station

Redcliffe Way

1

St. Mary Redcliffe

2

Redcliffe Hill

4

Clarence Road

York Road

Temple Gate

Bath Road

East St.

Museum (4) is worth a stop. Its displays cover the full range of Bristol's industries, past and present, including carriages, sports cars, trucks, a steam crane, and a full-scale mock-up of the locally built Concorde. *Open April–Oct., Sat.–Wed. 10–5; Nov.–March, weekends only, 10–5. Closed Thurs. and Fri. Free.* ☎ *(0117) 925-1470.* ♿.

Continue on by ferry, on foot, or—when it's running—an ancient steam train, to the:

*S.S. *GREAT BRITAIN* and the *MATTHEW* (5), Gas Ferry Rd., ☎ (0117) 926-0680. *Open daily 10–5:30, closing at 4:30 in winter. Adults £4.50, seniors £3.50, children £3; admission may vary. Café. Gift shop. Museum. Partial ♿.*

Launched in 1843, the S.S. *Great Britain* was the first large steamer to be made of iron and the first to be driven by a screw propeller. Used for a while on the transatlantic run to New York, she proved unprofitable and was later put on the Australian service. Finally reduced to hauling coal to San Francisco, she was abandoned in the Falkland Islands after suffering damage during a hurricane in 1886. There she remained until 1937, when the hull was sunk off Port Stanley. In 1970 the S.S. **Great Britain** was refloated and towed all the way back to the very same dry dock in Bristol in which she was built.

This indomitable ship, along with other sights in Bristol such as Temple Meads Station and the Clifton Suspension Bridge, were all the work of the great 19th-century engineer, Isambard Kingdom Brunel, who also built the Great Western Railway. You traveled over this line if you came from London by train. Visitors may climb all over the ship, which is currently undergoing painstaking restoration to its original 1843 appearance.

Adjacent to the S.S. *Great Britain* is the **Matthew**, a replica of the 15th-century sailing ship used by John Cabot to discover Newfoundland in 1497, an historic journey that was re-enacted five centuries later in 1997.

While visiting these two famous ships, make a stop at the adjacent **Maritime Heritage Centre**, where the story of shipbuilding in Bristol is told. Meals and refreshments are available on the site.

From here you can take the ferry back to the town center and then board a bus to Clifton, or you can just walk there. The route shown on the map takes you past the locks of the Floating Harbour, a section of the River Avon in which boats are kept afloat during low tide. From there it is uphill, going by some elegant Georgian houses near the top.

The ***Clifton Suspension Bridge** (6), another creation of Brunel's, is among the most outstanding in Britain. Poised 245 feet above the Avon Gorge, it offers spectacular **views** to pedestrians who cross it. Return and climb the mound to the left for another superb vista, possibly stopping at the **Clifton Observatory, Camera Obscura and Cave**. England's only public camera obscura also has a tunnel running under the Downs to a natural cave that looks out on the bridge. *Open daily 10:30–5:30 in summer; 11–4 in winter. Adults £1, children 75p.* ☎ *(0117) 974-1242.* Don't miss the nearby **Clifton Suspension Bridge Visitor Centre** in Sion Place. Here you'll discover just how this fantastic bridge was built and maintained. *Open Mon.–Sat. 10–6, Sun. 10–4, shorter hours in winter. Nominal admission. Gift shop.* ☎ *(0117) 974-4664.*

There is bus service back to town from the corner of Gloucester Row and Clifton Down Road. You may be interested, however, in strolling over a few blocks to see the very contemporary **Clifton Cathedral** (7) on Pembroke Road. Consecrated in 1973, this Roman Catholic cathedral is a striking piece of modern architecture designed to meet the new forms of worship.

By bus or on foot, the next destination is the **City Museum and Art Gallery** (8) on Queen's Road. The collections include items of local archaeology, history, ceramics, and glass, as well as the fine and applied arts. With its unusual mixture of displays, this is really a fun place to visit. *Open daily 10–5. Free.* ☎ *(0117) 922-3571. Café. Gift shop.* ♿.

Just a short distance away is the **Cabot Tower** (9) on Brandon Hill, built in 1897 to commemorate the 400th anniversary of John Cabot's voyage to the New World. There are good views of the city and harbor from its 100-foot-high top. *Open 8–dusk. Free.*

Great George Street is a pleasant way to return to the town center. Along it is the **Georgian House** (10), an 18th-century merchant's home that's been lovingly restored to its original elegance by the City Museum. *Open April–Oct., Sat.–Wed. 10–5. Closed Thurs. and Fri. Free.* ☎ *(0117) 921-1362. Limited* ♿.

Park Street leads to College Green and the **Bristol Cathedral** (11). A mixture of many styles including Norman, Early English, Gothic, and Victorian, its construction spanned a period of over 700 years. The most interesting parts are the choir, which has wonderful misericords, the eastern Lady Chapel, and the Norman Chapter House, dating from 1160. *Open daily, 8–6. Suggested donation £1.50. Café. Gift shop.* ☎ *(0117) 926-4879.*

Continue up Baldwin Street and Corn Street to the intersection with Broad, Wine, and High streets. This was the old **medieval heart** (12) of the city. In front of the Corn Exchange of 1743 are four short pillars of bronze known as "nails," on which merchants completed their cash transactions. From these came the expression "paying on the nail." Make a right on High Street, cross Bristol Bridge, and follow Victoria Street back to Temple Meads Station.

ADDITIONAL ATTRACTION:

The Year 2000 marks the opening of **At Bristol**, an immense waterside complex located between the Cathedral and the Industrial Museum; a place where science, nature and art come together to stretch visitors' minds through discovery and participation. Learn more about it on the Internet at www.at-bristol.org.uk, or ask the tourist office.

Trip 34

Cardiff
(Caerdydd)

Here's a chance to sample some of the many charms of Wales on an easy daytrip from London. Only two hours by rail separates the metropolis from Cardiff, Europe's youngest capital city and one of its emerging tourist destinations. If you like what you see—and you probably will—you can always come back for more, perhaps making Cardiff your base.

New visitors are always surprised by this compact, friendly city, very different from what many expect. Well laid out with spacious streets and lovely parks, the Welsh capital features superb castles, a wonderful open-air museum that re-creates Welsh life from Celtic times to the present, and Techiquest—a major discovery center. Art lovers won't be disappointed either, at the National Museum of Wales; nor will anyone who samples the local cuisine.

Both the Romans and the Normans settled here, but the Cardiff of today is largely a creation of Victorian times. The Industrial Revolution and the opening of the Glamorganshire Canal in 1794 paved the way for the building of a vast harbor complex, at one time the world's leader in coal exports. This in turn meant great wealth for its leading citizens, including the Third Marquess of Bute, who just about owned the town in the late 19th century. An extravagant spender, he set an example of civic pride by financing much of Cardiff's beautifully planned expansion. Other tycoons followed his lead, making the city one of the most attractive in Britain.

GETTING THERE:

Trains to Cardiff leave London's Paddington Station at hourly intervals, making the journey in two hours. Return trains run until mid-evening. Service is reduced on Sundays and holidays.

By car, take the M4 all the way. Cardiff is 154 miles west of London.

PRACTICALITIES:

The National Museum of Wales is closed on Mondays (except Bank Holidays). The Welsh Folk Museum is closed on December 25 and 26, and on New Year's Day. Train service is slower on Sundays and holidays. Fine weather will greatly enhance this trip.

The local **tourist office**, ☎ (01222) 227-281, is on Wood Street, opposite the bus station and near Central Station. Ask them about the **Cardiff Card**, which could save you a few pounds, even on a one-day visit.

Cardiff has a population of about 280,000.

Sometime in mid-2000, Cardiff will get a **new telephone area code**. (029) replaces (01222), and the number 20 is added to the front of the existing number. Thus: (01222) 111-111 becomes (029) 20-111-111.

FOOD AND DRINK:

Cardiff has a wide variety of restaurants and pubs in all price ranges. The city is noted for its distinctive local beer, Brains. A few dining suggestions are:

IN THE CITY:

Benedicto's (4 Windsor Place, just off Queen St., near the Park Hotel) Exquisite cuisine with a strong French influence. ☎ (01222) 371-130. X: Sun. eve. £££

Gio's Ciao Ciao (38 The Hayes) Authentic Italian cuisine since 1983. ☎ (01222) 220-077. X: Sun. ££

La Brasserie (61 St. Mary St., city center) French dishes, with a good wine selection, ☎ (01222) 372-164. X: Sun. ££

Champers (61 St. Mary St., city center) A fun place for Spanish food, from steaks to fish, and tapas too. ☎ (01222) 373-363. ££

Crumbs (33 Morgan Arcade, off St. Mary St. in city center) A long-time favorite for vegetarian lunches. ☎ (01222) 393-007. X: evenings, Sun. £

Celebrity (in St. David's Hall, The Hayes) Good for lunch or meals before or after a concert. ☎ (01222) 878-463. X: Sun. lunch. £

Celtic Cauldron (Castle St., near the Castle) Traditional wholefoods in the Welsh manner, both meat and vegetarian dishes featured. ☎ (01222) 387-185. £

EDGE OF TOWN:

Blas ar Gymru *(A Taste of Wales)* (48 Crwys Road: bus 8 or 9 from Greyfriars Rd.) Traditional Welsh fare in a romantic medieval setting. ☎ (01222) 382-132. X: Sat. lunch, Sun. ££

SUGGESTED TOUR:

Numbers in parentheses correspond to numbers on the map.

Leave **Central Station** (1) and follow the map to the **Royal Arcade** (2), one of several charming Victorian ironwork-and-glass- covered walking streets for which Cardiff is noted. Passing a multitude of interesting shops, turn left into The Hayes. In a few steps you will come to St. David's Hall, a magnificent concert hall next to a modern shopping center. Bear left on the pedestrians-only Trinity Street, which leads past a huge enclosed food market. Just beyond this is **St. John's** (3), a 15th-century parish church noted for its tall tower and fine interior.

Follow Church Street to High Street and turn right. The entrance to Cardiff Castle is on Castle Street:

*CARDIFF CASTLE (4), ☎ (01222) 878-100, Internet: www.castle wales.com/cardiff.html. *Open May–Sept. daily 10–6, March–April and Oct. daily 10–5, Nov.–Feb. daily 10–4:30. Closed Dec. 25–26, Jan 1. Guided tours all year round, most frequently in summer. Tours including admission: Adults £5, seniors and children £3. Short tours at lower prices in the off-season. Admission to greens and keep only (no tour): Adults £2.50, seniors and children £1.50. Last entry an hour before closing. Tea room. Gift shop. & by arrangement.*

Originally a Roman fort dating from before AD 75, Cardiff Castle was later abandoned and rebuilt by the invading Normans during the 11th century. Their leader, Robert FitzHamon, had a circular moat dug within what remained of the Roman walls, in the center of which he threw up a mound of earth, called a *motte*, supporting a wooden tower. This was replaced by the present stone keep during the late 12th century. Further additions were made, including the large castle buildings outside the circular moat. The entire castle complex, having been continuously occupied from Norman times to the near present, has never suffered great damage, although it was captured on several occasions.

The real splendor of the castle as it now exists is, however, the result of a wildly romantic reconstruction begun in 1868 to satisfy the strange fantasies of the Third Marquess of Bute. To see this you will have to take a guided tour of the utterly extravagant, dreamlike interior. When the tour is over, visit the original keep in the northwest corner and note the Roman foundations, in lighter-colored stone, of portions of the outer wall.

Now follow Kingsway to the **City Hall** (5), focal point of the elegant Civic Centre, a handsome early-20th-century group of public buildings spaciously spread amid the gardens of Cathays Park. A short stroll behind the City Hall to the War Memorial reveals the careful planning that went into this complex.

Return via Museum Avenue to the **National Museum of Wales** (6). Exhibits here cover just about everything that could possibly pertain to that principality, and much more as well. Besides the exhibition on the Evolution of Wales, there are galleries devoted to archaeology, zoology, botany, and geology. Don't miss the fabulous ***art collection**, rich in treasures representing a diversity of European schools from medieval to contemporary. It is especially well endowed with works by Rodin, Renoir, Monet, Cézanne, Rubens, and that great 20th-century Welsh artist, Augustus John. *Open Tues.–Sun. (plus Bank Holiday Mon.), 10–5; closed*

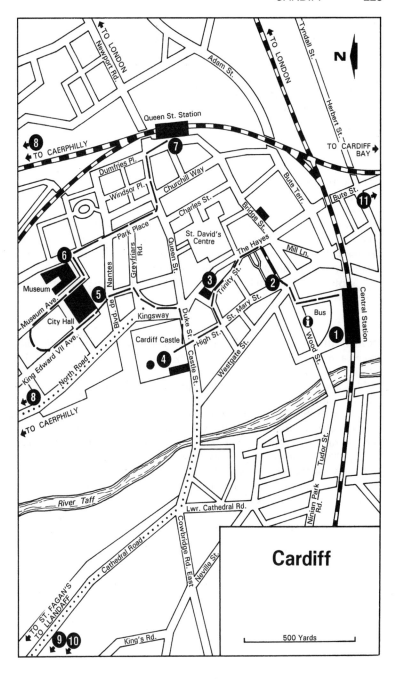

Cardiff

500 Yards

Mon., Dec 25, Jan 1. Adults £4.25, students and seniors £2.50, children 5–15 £2.50. Shops, restaurant. ☎ *(01222) 397-951, Internet: www.cf.ac. uk/nmgw/nmgc.* ♿. This is a must-see for all visitors to Cardiff.

At this point you will have to decide between going to **Caerphilly** to see its great castle, making a trip to **St. Fagan's** for the Museum of Welsh Life and possibly Llandaff for its cathedral, or exploring the recent developments at nearby **Cardiff Bay**. It is virtually impossible to include more than one in the same day, a good reason for either staying over or coming back another time.

CAERPHILLY:

If you chose Caerphilly, follow Park Place and Queen Street to the **Queen Street Station** (7) and board one of the frequent trains on the Rhymney Valley line for the 15-minute ride to Caerphilly. Those driving should follow North Road and Caerphilly Road (A469) direct to the castle. There is also an hourly bus service from the bus station in front of Central Station. Take bus number 26 for the 45-minute ride to Caerphilly.

Arriving at Caerphilly, leave the station and turn right on the main street. This goes straight for a few blocks, then bends right to:

*CAERPHILLY CASTLE (8), ☎ (01222) 883-143, Internet: www.castlewales. com/caerphil. *Open late March–late May, daily 9:30–5; late May–early Oct., daily 9:30–6; early Oct.–end Oct., daily 9:30–5; Nov.–late March, Mon.–Sat. 9:30–4 and Sun. 11–4. Closed Christmas and New Year's. Adults £2.50, seniors and children £2.*

Built in the 13th century, Caerphilly Castle is monstrously huge and was once armed to the teeth. It is the second-largest in Europe, exceeded in size only by Windsor. Whereas Cardiff Castle is strangely charming, Caerphilly intimidates and leaves you with a strong impression concerning the savageness of warfare.

As usual, the Romans were here first. Little, however, remains of their fort. The present structure was begun in 1268 by the Norman earl Gilbert de Clare, though it was partially destroyed two years later by the great Welsh patriot, Llywelyn the Last, the first Prince of Wales. Clare then recaptured his mighty fortress and went on building. In the end he had an impregnable stronghold, one that was to resist all further sieges. Strangely, it played no part in the conquest of Wales by Edward I, after which its military value declined. Even so, as late as the 17th century it still posed a potential threat, which Oliver Cromwell attempted to eradicate during the Civil War by blowing the place up. Fortunately for us, he did not reckon with the sturdiness of Clare's walls, and the net result of all that gunpowder was one **leaning tower**, which is still there, still leaning wildly out of perpendicular.

A printed guide for exploring the castle on your own is available at the entrance. Follow it and you will gain a good understanding of why this fortress was so difficult to attack. Those returning by rail should continue on to Cardiff Central Station (1), where they can change to an express for London.

ST. FAGAN'S AND LLANDAFF:

If you have decided on seeing St. Fagan's and maybe Llandaff instead of Caerphilly, you should return to the **bus station** in front of Central Station (1). From here you can take bus number 32, which leaves hourly for the four-mile, 25-minute ride to St. Fagan's. You can also drive there via Cathedral Road, following signs for the folk museum:

MUSEUM OF WELSH LIFE (9), St. Fagan's, ☎ (01222) 573-500, Internet: www.cf.ac.uk/nmgw/mwl.html. *Open daily 10–5, remaining open until 6 from July–Sept. Closed Dec. 24 and 25. Adults £5.50, seniors and students £3.90, children 5–15 £3.20, reduced admission from Nov.–Easter. Largely* ৬.

The Museum of Welsh Life at St. Fagan's re-creates rural life in Wales as it was in centuries past. Traditional buildings from all over the principality have been brought to this beautiful 100-acre estate and reassembled for posterity. Here you can watch skilled craftsmen practicing the old trades and visit the Elizabethan mansion, cottages, a watermill, a smithy, a saddlery, and many other attractions. There is also a modern exhibition hall housing centuries of bygones along with a restaurant. Be sure to buy a guide booklet so you won't miss anything—some of the best sites are very cleverly hidden.

Time permitting, you may want to continue on to the pretty village of Llandaff. To do this by bus you will first have to take bus number 32 from the folk museum, then transfer to a number 25, 33, or 62 bus en route. Ask the driver about this.

Llandaff Cathedral (10) dates from the 12th century. It was never a great cathedral, and was severely damaged during the Middle Ages, used as a beer hall by Cromwell's troops in the Civil War, and badly bombed during World War II. What makes it worth the trip is the incredible parabolic concrete organ loft bearing a 16-foot-high aluminum Jesus, Jacob Epstein's famous *Christ in Majesty* of 1960. Wander around the lovely grounds by the River Taff and then take bus number 33 or 62, running every 30 minutes Mondays through Saturdays and less often on Sundays, back to Central Station (1). You could also walk the 2.5-mile distance via Llandaff Fields and Cathedral Road.

CARDIFF BAY:

Cardiff's once-decaying **waterfront** (11) has come back to life as a major tourist destination featuring its own futuristic **Visitor Center**, ☎ (01222) 463-833 and a center for science discovery. To get there, head a mile or so south on Bute Street either by car, on foot, or on bus number 8 from Central Station. There is also a shuttle train from Cardiff's Queen Street Station.

The main attraction is **Techniquest**, Britain's leading hands-on science discovery center. A visit here will take several hours and is especially suitable for children, although most adults find it fascinating as well. *Open daily except for a Christmas break, Mon.–Fri. 9:30–4:30, weekends and Bank Holidays 10:30–5. Last admission 45 minutes before closing. Adults £5, seniors and children 5–16 £3.75. Extra charge for the Planetarium and Discovery Room.* ☎ *(01222) 475-475, Internet: www.tquest.org.uk. Gift shop. Cafeteria.* ⌖.

Exeter

Although it's a relatively long journey for a daytrip, Exeter has a number of attractions that make it all worthwhile. A few hours here will also give you a chance to sample the West Country, a part of England that you may very well want to return to for a longer stay.

Exeter began as a Celtic settlement, being taken over in AD 55 by the Romans, who called it *Isca Dumnoniorum* and used it as a frontier outpost. Portions of their stone walls, erected as early as the 3rd century, can still be seen. Continuously occupied ever since, it became the *Exanceaster* of the Saxons and was frequently plundered, right down to modern times, when much of it was wiped out by the bombs of World War II. Now a thriving modern city, Exeter still retains many of its medieval treasures as well as reminders that this was once an important seaport.

GETTING THERE:

Trains depart London's Paddington Station several times in the morning for the less-than-two-and-a-half-hour ride to Exeter's St. David's Station. Some require a change at Bristol Temple Meads. Those going on a Saturday in summer should make reservations. Return trains run until mid-evening. Service is poor on Sundays and holidays. There is also a slower route from London's Waterloo Station.

By car, Exeter is 172 miles southwest of London via the M3 followed by the A30 through Salisbury.

PRACTICALITIES:

A trip to Exeter requires good weather and an early start. Some of the sights are closed on Sundays and/or Mondays. The local **Tourist Information Centre**, ☎ (01392) 265-700, is in the Civic Centre on Paris Street. Exeter is the county town of Devon, and has a population of about 95,000.

FOOD AND DRINK:

Exeter has a number of historic inns and pubs, as well as several good restaurants. Some choices are:

Golsworthy's (St. Olaves Court Hotel, Mary Arches St., near St. Nicholas Priory) Exceptionally fine dining, in a Georgian house. ☎ (01392)

413-054. X: Sat. and Sun. lunch. ££

Ship Inn (Martin's Lane, just north of the cathedral) An historic inn favored by Sir Francis Drake and other sailors, with a pub and an upstairs restaurant. ☎ (01392) 270-891. X: Sun. £ and ££

White Hart (66 South St., between the cathedral and the Maritime Museum) An old inn, partly 14th century. Bar lunches and full meals. ☎ (01392) 250-159. £ and ££

Coolings Wine Bar (11 Gandy St., just southeast of the Royal Albert Museum) A casual and very popular place for traditional dishes and salads. ((01392) 434-184. X: Sun. £ and ££

Herbies (15 North St., near the Guildhall) A favorite for homemade vegetarian fare. ☎ (01392) 258-473, X: Sun. £

Hanson's (Cathedral Close) Traditional lunches or cream teas, right by the cathedral) ☎ (01392) 276-913. £

SUGGESTED TOUR:

Numbers in parentheses correspond to numbers on the map.

Leaving **St. David's Station** (1), you have a choice of walking or taking a bus or taxi to the cathedral, nearly a mile away. Those on foot should follow the route on the map.

*EXETER CATHEDRAL (2), ☎ (01392) 255-573. *Open Mon.–Fri. 7:30–6:30, Sat. 7:30–5, Sun. 8–7:30. Evensong service Mon.–Fri. at 5:39, Sat.–Sun. at 3. Guided tours Apr.–Oct., Mon.–Fri. at 11 and 2:30, Sat. at 11. Requested donation £2. &.*

Exeter's Cathedral is famous for its gorgeous interior and the unusual placement of its two Norman towers. Begun in the 12th century on the site of an earlier Saxon church, the cathedral was transformed during the 14th century into the lovely Gothic structure it is today. Its west front is heavily decorated with an amazing array of sculpted figures. "Great Peter," a six-ton bell in the north tower, still tolls the curfew each evening, as it has for nearly 500 years.

Enter the nave and look up at the richly colored roof **bosses**. The charming **Minstrels' Gallery**, midway down on the left, is used for Christmas carol recitals. In the north transept there is a superb 15th-century wall painting of the Resurrection and an **astronomical clock** from the same era that shows the Sun revolving around the Earth. The choir has a fabulous 14th-century ***Bishop's Throne** and interesting old misericords.

Complete your exploration of the cathedral and stroll out into the **close**. At the end of Martin's Lane is the small St. Martin's Church. Next to

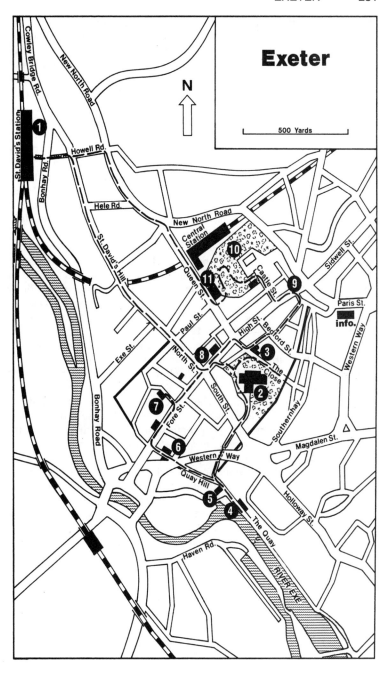

that is **Mol's Coffee Shop** (3), a 16th-century inn now used as a shop. You can enter it and ask to see the room where famous seamen such as Raleigh, Drake, and Hawkins once sipped their brew.

Now follow the map to The Quay and the **Quay House Visitor Centre** (4), a 17th-century structure now used for historic exhibitions and an audiovisual introduction to the city. *Open April through Oct., 10–5. Free.* ☎ *(01392) 265-213.* ♿.

While in the area, you might want to take a scenic stroll along The Quay and the River Exe to soak up some of the maritime atmosphere.

From here walk past the 17th-century **Customs House** (5), built on the site of an earlier quay. Continue on to West Street and the parish church of **St. Mary Steps** (6), which has a curious 17th-century clock in its bell tower as well as a Norman font. Opposite it, at number 24, is the **House that Moved**, a timber- framed structure dating from about 1500 that was moved on rollers in 1961 to make way for road construction. Take a look up Stepcote Hill, a steep medieval street that is little changed.

A right on Fore Street will take you past **Tucker's Hall**, a 15th-century guildhouse that is sometimes open. Turn left on The Mint and visit **St. Nicholas Priory** (7), once a Benedictine monastery founded in 1080 by William the Conqueror. Disbanded in 1536, it is now a **museum** featuring a fine Norman **undercroft**, a 15th-century **guest hall**, an ancient **kitchen**, and other rooms fitted with period furniture. *Open Easter through October, on Mon., Wed., and Sat., 3–4:30. Free.* ☎ *(01392) 265-858.* ♿.

Two other interesting churches in the area are **St. Olave's**, a strange building of the 14th century on Fore Street, and **St. Mary Arches** on Mary Arches Street, a 12th-century parish church with a Norman nave and Jacobean memorials.

Fore Street soon becomes High Street. On your left is the **Guildhall** (8), believed to be the oldest municipal building still in use in Britain. Built in 1330, it has an outstanding 16th-century façade projecting out over the sidewalk. *Visitors are welcome on Mon.–Sat., 10–5, subject to civic func-tions. Free.* ☎ *(01392) 265-500.* ♿.

Continue up High Street and turn right on Martin's Lane for one block, then left on Catherine Street past the ruins of a bombed-out 15th-century almshouse. Follow the map to the entrance of the **Underground Passages** (9). Guided tours are run through these medieval water tunnels that date from the 13th century and remained in use until about a hundred years ago. ***This trip is spooky and not for the claustrophobic.*** *They can be explored Mon.–Fri. from 1–5, and on Sat. 10–5. Admission: July and August, adults £3.50, children £2.50; September through June, adults £2.50, children £1.50. Includes exhibition and video.* ☎ *(01392) 265-887.* Nearby are remains of the ancient town walls, and the tourist office in the Civic Centre.

Return to High Street and make a right up Castle Street. To your left are scanty remains of a Norman gateway and, beyond, a Norman tower. Amble through the very pleasant **Rougemont Gardens** (10) and exit onto

Queen Street. A right brings you to the **Royal Albert Memorial Museum** (11), which has something for everyone. There are displays of art, ethnography, exploration, natural history, and many other subjects including the new World Cultures Gallery. *Open Mon.–Sat., 10–5. Closed Good Friday, Dec. 25, Jan. 1. Free. Gift shop. Café.* ☎ *(01392) 265-858.* &. This is a good place to spend your remaining time before returning to the train station.

Trip 36

Gloucester

Always an appealing place, the ancient river port of Gloucester is even more enticing since its decaying docks were transformed into a modern tourist attraction. Once-decrepit warehouses and quays now house the marvelous National Waterways Museum, while other Victorian industrial structures became museums, cafés, antique shops, and a shopping center. Equally attractive is the 11th-century cathedral with its delightfully cluttered interior, fan-vaulted cloisters, and Perpendicular tower. The surrounding neighborhood preserves a bygone charm that is among the most inviting in England.

Gloucester's Roman origins are obvious from its street layout. *Glevum*, as it was then called, was founded during the 1st century AD to protect the lowest practical crossing of the River Severn, and later used as a colony for retired Roman soldiers. During the Middle Ages it became an important place with frequent visits by royalty. Later a major industrial and shipping center, Gloucester is today being discovered by tourists looking for new sites to explore. Its name, incidentally, is pronounced "*Glo'ster.*"

GETTING THERE:

Trains depart London's Paddington Station several times in the morning for the under-two-hour ride to Gloucester. Some are direct express trains, but most require a change at Swindon. Service is reduced on Saturdays and poor on Sundays and holidays. Return trains operate until mid-evening. The route takes you through the scenic Cotswolds.

By car, Gloucester is 106 miles west of London. Take the M4 to Junction 15 at Swindon, then the A419 to Cirencester and the A417 into Gloucester.

PRACTICALITIES:

Gloucester's major attractions are open daily, but lesser ones close on either Sundays or Mondays. Boat trips around the harbor are offered from Easter to October. The local **Tourist Information Centre**, ☎ (01452) 421-188, is at 28 Southgate Street in the center of town. Gloucester is the county town of Gloucestershire, and has a population of 114,000.

FOOD AND DRINK:

There are several tourist restaurants and pubs near the cathedral and around the docks. Among your best choices are:

College Green (7–11 College St., by the cathedral) Traditional English cuisine with a view. ☎ (01452) 520-739. X: Sun. in winter. ££

Undercroft Restaurant (in the cathedral complex) Lunch in the Great Hall of a former monastery. £

Dick Whittington's (100 Westgate St., opposite the Folk Museum) A popular old pub with a good selection of lunch dishes. ☎ (01452) 502-039. £

Place on the Lock (in Gloucester Docks Antiques Centre) An atmospheric place for light lunches and teas. ☎ (01452) 330-253. £

SUGGESTED TOUR:

Numbers in parentheses correspond to numbers on the map.

Leave the **train station** (1) and follow the route on the map through a modern shopping district to **St. Michael's Tower** (2), a handsome 15th-century structure that was once part of a medieval church. It is located at The Cross, the meeting point of Gloucester's four main streets for nearly two millennia.

Stroll down Westgate Street and turn right into College Court. At its end is the **Beatrix Potter Centre** (3), a home chosen by the writer as the locale of her famous 1901 story *The Tailor of Gloucester*. Today it is both a shop and a delightful exhibition devoted to the World of Beatrix Potter. Among the displays are first editions of her books, a replica of the famous waistcoat, a working model of the mice busily sewing away, and even the "No more twist!" note. *Open Mon.–Sat., 9:30–5:30. Free. Gift shop.* ☎ *(01452) 422-856.*

Continue on to:

*GLOUCESTER CATHEDRAL (4), ☎ (01452) 528-095. *Open daily 8–6. Requested donation £3. Whispering Gallery £1. Guided tours Mon.–Sat. from 10:30–12:30. Evensong Mon., Tues., Wed., Fri. at 5:30, Sat. at 4, Sun. at 3. Book shop. Restaurant. Partially ♿.*

Gloucester Cathedral is a wonderful accumulation of styles evolved over the centuries, filled to the brim with interesting little details. Begun as a Norman abbey in 1089, it was the site of Henry III's coronation in 1216—the only time since the Conquest that an English monarch was crowned outside of Westminster. Its importance increased again in 1327 when the abbey accepted for burial the body of Edward II, which some other churches had refused. This made it a place of pilgrimage for supporters of the beleaguered, deposed, and murdered monarch. It also brought in considerable wealth, largely spent on rebuilding much of the abbey in the new, rather elegant, Perpendicular style of the 15th century. Barely a century later, in 1541, the abbey gained cathedral status after

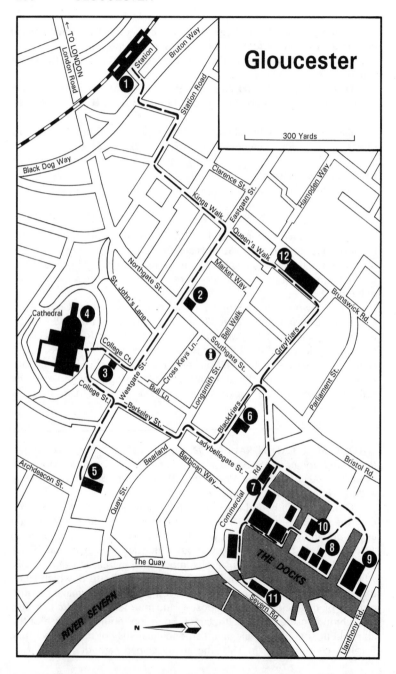

Gloucester

300 Yards

Henry VIII settled his dispute with the Pope by declaring England Protestant.

Inside, the **Nave** is still basically sturdy Norman although it sports an Early English ceiling of 1242. Americans might want to search along its north aisle for the memorial to John Stafford Smith (1750–1836), a minor English composer who wrote a tune that later became the *Star-Spangled Banner*. Exceptionally grandiose, the **Choir** was rebuilt by Edward III to honor his martyred father, whose lovely ***tomb** graces the north side of the adjacent presbytery. While there, take a look at the intricately-carved wooden choirstalls and misericords of 1350. Beyond, at the far east end, the late-15th-century ***Lady Chapel** represents the final development of the Perpendicular style in all its splendor.

For many visitors, however, the cathedral's chief glory is its ***Cloister**, reached via the north aisle. Dating from the mid- 14th century, its renowned fan vaulting is the earliest known example of this art in the nation.

Leave the cathedral precincts via College Street and turn right onto Westgate. The **Gloucester Folk Museum** (5), housed in half-timbered Tudor buildings, presents an engrossing introduction to Gloucester's past. Exhibits here include re-created workshops, artifacts of everyday life, a Victorian schoolroom, agricultural items, and the like. *Open Mon.–Sat. 10–5; and also summer Sun., July–Sept., 10–4. Free. Shop.* ☎ *(01452) 526- 467. Ground floor is* ♿.

Using the map as a guide, thread your way south toward the docks. Along the way you'll pass the **Blackfriars Priory** (6), founded in 1239 and disbanded in the mid-16th century after the Reformation. Later used as a house and workshop, parts of it eventually became a church and a school. The site, still the most complete Dominican friary in England, can only be seen from the outside, except on infrequent guided tours. *Tours June, July, Aug., Sun. and Bank Holiday Mon., at 3.*

Continue on to the **Soldiers of Gloucestershire Museum** (7), whose entrance faces the docks just south of Commercial Road. Fans of military museums will enjoy a visit to this recently-refurbished exhibition, which goes far beyond the usual old medals and moth-eaten uniforms. *Open Tues.–Sun., Bank Holiday Mon., and Mon. in June–Sept., 10–5. Adults £4, seniors £3, children £2. Gift shop.* ☎ *(01452) 522-682.* ♿.

You are now in the heart of the historic ***Gloucester Docks**, where restored sailing vessels and Victorian warehouses keep the city's maritime heritage very much alive. England's most inland port is located on the River Severn and is also connected directly with the sea by canal. Although shipping here dates from as early as Roman times, Gloucester really became an important port in 1580 when Queen Elizabeth I granted it permission to engage in foreign trade.

Amble along the waterfront to the **Mariners' Chapel** (8), built in 1849 to provide a place of worship for visiting sailors. Take a look inside, then stroll over to Gloucester's second great attraction, the:

*NATIONAL WATERWAYS MUSEUM (9), ☎ (01452) 318-054. *Open daily, 10–6, closing at 5 in winter. Last admission one hour before closing. Adults £4.50, children £3.50. Partial ♿.*

Occupying the largest warehouse of the docks, this thoroughly enjoyable museum brings two centuries of inland canal and river transportation to life once again with boats, working artifacts, interactive displays, and the like. Outside, you can board several of the vessels, take a short ***cruise**, watch demonstrations of bygone trades, ride a horse-drawn cart, or relax at a waterside café.

Another trip into the past is offered at the nearby **Robert Opie Collection of Advertising and Packaging** (10), which celebrates the consumer society from Victorian to recent times. With some 300,000 items of everyday life—and the advertising that sold them—this is the largest collection of its kind in the world. *Open March–Sept., daily 10–6; Oct.–Feb., Tues.–Sun. 10–5. Closed Dec. 24–26. Adults £2.95, children 95p. Tea room. Gift shop.* ☎ (01452) 302-309. ♿.

Cross the swing bridge and walk past the Merchant's Quay Shopping Centre, making your way across a lock gate to the **Antiques Centre** (11). Housed in a restored 19th-century warehouse, the center gathers together some 70 small antique dealers in an almost Dickensian atmosphere. *Open daily. Free entry. Restaurant.* ☎ (01452) 529-716.

The shortest route back to the train station takes you past the **City Museum and Art Gallery** (12), a venerable institution that tells the story of Gloucester from prehistoric to Victorian times. All kinds of things are displayed here, including dinosaur bones, a Roman archaeological site, medieval artifacts, period furniture, a living aquarium and beehive, and paintings. *Open July–Sept., Mon.–Sat. 10–5, Sun. 10–4; rest of year Mon.–Sat. 10–5. Adults £2, children £1.* ☎ (01452) 524-131.

*Oxford

There is practically nothing that you cannot learn at Oxford. Scores of independent schools compete with some 36 colleges that make up the 14,500-student university, each a closed world in itself, barricaded within its separate quadrangle. To this sheltered spot in the very center of England come thousands of visitors curious about English academic life and eager to see the countless treasures accumulated since medieval times.

The town of Oxford is older than the university, which itself dates from the 12th century. As far back as 912, *Oxenford*—the ford for oxen across the Thames—was mentioned in the Anglo-Saxon chronicles. In 1071 the conquering Normans built a castle and defensive walls. Oxford sided with the Royalists during the Civil War of the 17th century and to this day retains a little bit of that sense of privilege largely gone from the rest of Britain. Unlike Cambridge, with which it is inevitably compared, Oxford is also an industrial center, although you would hardly realize this from the old part of town.

There is far more to the town and its university than can possibly be seen in a single day. For this reason, the suggested tour has left out a great deal that is worthwhile and concentrated on a balanced blend of colleges, market-town atmosphere, parks, museums, and notable buildings. As a visitor, you may have to improvise somewhat as public accessibility to some of the places varies at the whim of individual colleges. This will present no problem, since if one quad is closed, another nearby will probably be open. It is always a good idea to ask the porter at each entrance about which specific points of interest are free to public inspection. Please remember that all of the colleges are private and that admission to them is a courtesy, not a right. The increasing crush of mass tourism has led some colleges to either restrict visits or to charge an admission fee.

GETTING THERE:

Trains operated by Thames Trains leave London's Paddington Station at least every half-hour for the one-hour trip to Oxford, with return service operating until late evening. Service is hourly in the late evening or early morning, and is reduced on Sundays and holidays. *For information* ☎ *(0345) 484-950, Internet: www.thamestrains.co.uk.*

Coaches (buses) are a low-cost alternative for this trip, making the run in about 90 minutes. Three different companies, **Oxford Tube**, ☎ *(01865) 772-250, Internet: www.stagecoach-oxford.co.uk;* **Oxford CityLink**, ☎ *(01865) 785-400, Internet: www.oxfordbus.co.uk;* and **National Express**, ☎ *(0990) 808-080, Internet: www.nationalexpress.com,* operate very frequent services from London's Victoria Coach Station to Oxford's bus station at Gloucester Green.

By car, Oxford is 57 miles northwest of London via the A40 and M40 highways. Parking is very difficult in the city. Use the **Park & Ride** car parks on the outskirts and take the frequent shuttle bus into Oxford.

PRACTICALITIES:

Oxford can be visited all year round, although it is less hectic and more accessible during the winter months between mid-October and March. The Ashmolean Museum is closed on Mondays and a few holidays, while some of the sights have shorter hours on Sundays. The local **Tourist Information Centre**, ☎ (01865) 726-871, Internet: www.oxford.gov. uk/tourism, is at The Old School on Gloucester Green, near the Ashmolean Museum. You might want to ask them about their special-interest guided walking tours. Another Internet site for tourist information is: www.oxfordcity.co.uk. The site for Oxford University is: www.ox.ac.uk.

Guide Friday offers one of their famous hop-on, hop-off open-top double-decker bus services, running frequently on a circular route that passes or comes close to nearly all of Oxford's attractions. The buses run daily all year round. One-day tickets for unlimited rides are: Adults £8, seniors and students £6.50, children 5–12 £2.50. Single fares between destinations are also available. Purchase tickets from the driver, the Guide Friday Tourism Centre at Oxford Railway Station, or the Tourist Information Centre. ☎ (01789) 294-466, Internet: www.guidefriday.com.

Oxford is the county town of Oxfordshire, and has a population of about 119,000.

FOOD AND DRINK:

A few choice pubs and restaurants are:

Elizabeth (84 St. Aldate's, near Christ Church) Excellent Continental cuisine, with an outstanding wine cellar. For reservations ☎ (01865) 242-230. £££

Bath Place (4 Bath Place, Holywell St., near New College) Outstanding French cuisine in a 17th-century cottage. Reserve, ☎ (01865) 791-812. X: Mon., Tues. lunch. ££ and £££

Brown's (9 Woodstock Rd., west of University Parks) A very popular place serving spaghetti, burgers, salads, and the like. ☎ (01865) 511-995. £ and ££

The Nosebag (9 St. Michael's St., near the Oxford Story) Healthy food, with vegetarian options, cafeteria-style. ☎ (01865) 721-033. £

Heroes (8 Ship St., a block south of the Oxford Story) Offers a wide variety of imaginative sandwiches at bargain prices. ☎ (01865) 723-459. £

Turf Tavern (4 Bath Pl., near the Bridge of Sighs) A pub in a 13th-century building on a small alleyway, with courtyard gardens. Good lunches. £

Bear Inn (Alfred St. at Bear Lane, by Christ Church) A traditional university pub in a 13th-century inn, with light meals. £

SUGGESTED TOUR:

Numbers in parentheses correspond to numbers on the map.

Leaving the **train station** (1), you have a choice of either walking or taking a bus or taxi to Carfax (2), a bit over a half-mile away. If you choose to walk, follow Park End Street past the **Oxford Canal**. This historic waterway was built in 1790 to provide transportation between London and Birmingham, using the River Thames from here to the capital. Until the development of the railways, it played a very important role in England's Industrial Revolution and is still navigable, being quite popular with pleasure boaters today. Look down it to the right to see the scanty remains of **Oxford Castle**, which dates from Norman times.

Continue on New Road and Queen Street to **Carfax** (2), whose name derives from the Latin *Quadri Furcus*, or four-forked. This crossing is the hub of Oxford. The **tower** in its northwest corner is all that remains of the 14th-century Church of St. Martin, and may be climbed for a magnificent ***view** of the famed "Dreaming Spires." *Open April–Oct., daily 10–5:30; Nov.–March, daily 10–3:30. Closed Dec. 25–Jan. 1. Adults £1.20, children 60p.*

Cross the intersection and walk down High Street, locally known as "The High," passing the 18th-century **Covered Market** with its colorful food stalls. When you get to Catte Street, turn left into Radcliffe Square and enter the **University Church of St. Mary the Virgin** (3). While the main body of the church dates from the 15th century, its **tower** is late 13th. A relatively easy climb to the top of this will allow you to see in advance the route of the walk to come. *Open daily 9–5, remaining open until 7 in July and Aug. Adults £1.50, children 75p.* ☎ *(01865) 243-806.*

Leaving the church, you are now facing the **Radcliffe Camera** (4), a massive domed building from 1737 that serves as a reading room for the Bodleian Library. To the left is Brasenose College, named after the 14th-century "brazen-nosed" doorknocker in its dining hall. Step into its quad for a look around.

At the far end of the square is the ***Bodleian Library** (5), the oldest in the world, originally founded in 1450 and entitled by law to a copy of every book published in the United Kingdom. It has millions of them scattered between this and a newer building on Broad Street. Visits may be made by

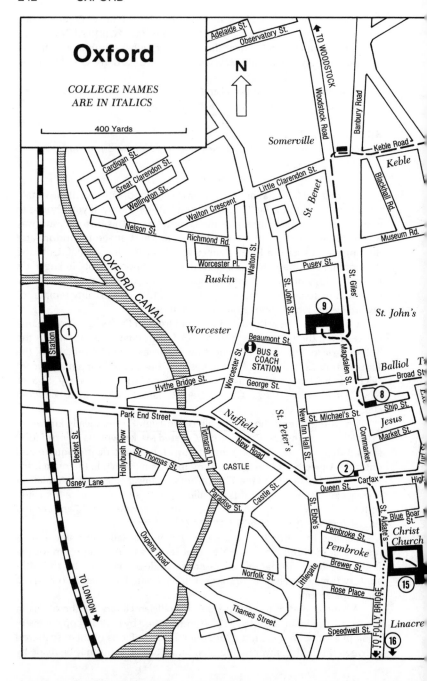

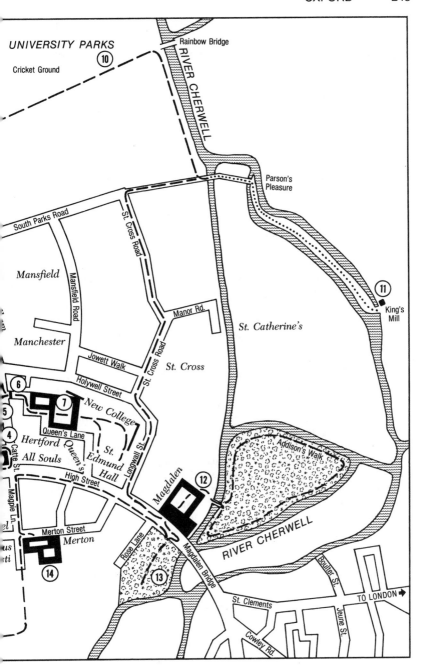

guided tour, which usually includes the Radcliffe Camera, above, and the Divinity School, below. *Tours at 10:30, 11:30, 2, and 3, daily, but in mornings only on Sat. No weekday morning tours in winter. Closed for special functions. Tours: £3.50, children under 14 not admitted.* ☎ *(01865) 277-188.* To one side of its courtyard is the 15th-century *Divinity School, which has one of the most beautiful stone-vaulted ceilings anywhere. *Open weekdays 9–5, Sat. 9–12:30.*

A doorway leads to the *Sheldonian Theatre, a magnificent auditorium designed by Sir Christopher Wren in 1669 to serve the secular ceremonial needs of the university. You can usually visit this, as well as climb up into its octagonal cupola for a nice view. *Open Mon.–Sat. 10–12:30 and 2–4:30, closing at 3:30 in winter. Adults £1.50, children £1.* ☎ *901865) 277-299.* Adjacent to this is the interesting **Museum of the History of Science**, which displays early scientific instruments and related objects, such as Einstein's blackboard. *Open Tues.–Sat. 10–4. Closed Bank Holidays, Christmas week. Free.* ☎ *(01865) 277-280, Internet: www.mhs.ox.ac.uk.*

Exit this complex of old buildings and stroll down New College Lane, with its famous **Bridge of Sighs** (6) linking two parts of Hertford College. Pass under it and amble into *New College (7), which is anything but new. Founded in the late 14th century by William of Wykeham, the bishop of Winchester, it has changed very little in the past 500 years. To the left of its unpretentious entrance are the cloisters, alive with a special feel of the Middle Ages. Just beyond are the **gardens**, one of the most delightful spots in Oxford. There you will find a well-preserved section of the old city walls that predate the college itself. While at New College, you should also try to see its remarkable **chapel**, noted for a strong modern statue of *Lazarus* by Jacob Epstein, a painting of *St. James* by El Greco, and some excellent 14th-century stained glass. *Open Easter–Sept., daily 11–5. Adults £1.50, seniors and children 50p. From Oct.–Easter hours are 2–4, entrance free, use Holywell St. gate.* ☎ *(01865) 279-555. Partial ⅛.*

Return to the Bridge of Sighs and walk down Broad Street. To your left is the Clarendon Building, which houses university administrative offices, and the Old Ashmolean Building. Blackwell's Bookshop, across the street, is world famous and makes an interesting stop. A bit farther along, to the left, is the **Oxford Story** (8). Visitors to this "experience" are seated at moving desks for a leisurely journey through the university's history, enjoying sights, sounds, and even smells from the past. *Open Apr.–Oct., daily 9:30–5, closing at 6 in July and Aug.; Nov.–March, daily 10–4:30. Adults £5, seniors and students £4.25, children £3.95.* ☎ *(01865) 790-055.*

Coming to Cornmarket, turn left for a look at **St. Michael's Church**, whose tower, dating from before 1050, was once part of the old city walls. This is Oxford's oldest building, and it may be climbed for some great views. *Open April–Oct., Mon.–Sat. 10–5, Sun. 12:30–5; Nov.–March, Mon.–Sat. 10–4, Sun. 12:30–4. Nominal admission.* ☎ *(01865) 240-940.*

Now follow Magdalen Street and make a left on Beaumont Street. Just a few steps down this is the renowned:

*ASHMOLEAN MUSEUM (9), ☎ (01865) 278-000, Internet: www.ashmol. ox.ac.uk. *Open Tues.–Sat. 10–5, remaining open until 6 on Wed. in May, June, July, Sun. 2–5, Bank Holidays 2–5. Closed Mon., Christmas, Easter, St. Giles' Fair in early Sept. Free, £2 donation requested. Café. Gift shop.* と.

This is the oldest public museum in Britain. In 1659 one Elias Ashmole received as a gift "twelve carts of curious things" from an incurable collector named Tradescant. To these he added his own similar collection and offered it all to the university on the condition that it erect a suitable building to house them. Since then, the acquisitions multiplied until they outgrew the Old Ashmolean and were moved in 1845 to the present structure. The collections are certainly eclectic enough. Along with the Leonardos, Raphaels, and Michelangelos are the French Impressionists, the Rubens and Rembrandts, plus the Hogarths and Constables. With these are displayed all sorts of archaeological and historical curios, including the lantern Guy Fawkes carried when he tried to blow up Parliament in 1605, several mummies, ancient coins, and musical instruments. You will need at least an hour to sample this treasure.

At this point you could cut the tour short by returning on Magdalen Street and following Cornmarket and High Street to Magdalen College (12). An enjoyable **two-mile walk** *through lovely parkland awaits those who continue on instead.*

Returning to the corner, make a left up St. Giles' until it becomes Woodstock Road. Cross the street and pass through the yard of the 13th-century St. Giles' Church, then cross Banbury Road and follow straight ahead on Keble Road. To your right is the supremely Victorian Keble College. Enter the **University Parks** (10) and follow the map past the Cricket Grounds where, if you're lucky, a match may be in progress. When you get to the Rainbow Bridge turn right and follow the banks of the River Cherwell. If the weather is fine, you may see students slowly punting along the water, stopping here and there in secluded spots to enjoy a picnic. A delightful side trip can be made by following the path to the ancient **King's Mill** (11). Return to town via St. Cross Road and Longwall Street, continuing on to the most beautiful college at Oxford.

*Magdalen College (12), pronounced *Maudlen,* was built during the 15th century and has long been among the best-endowed at Oxford. Its more than 100 acres include lawns, gardens, water walks, and a private deer park. There is a small admission for entry, which is made from High Street. The adjacent **bell tower** is perhaps the town's most famous landmark. Be sure to cross the small footbridge for a refreshing stroll along Addison's Walk. *Open daily 2–5, or dusk when earlier. Closed Dec 24–27 and June 27. Adults £2, seniors and children £1, free to all early Oct. to early April.* ☎ *(01865) 276-000, Internet: www.magd.ox.ac.uk. Teas and snacks in summer. Partially* と.

Back on High Street, turn left across Magdalen Bridge for a lovely view. If you would like to try your hand at **punting** (and are not afraid of getting wet), the boats may be rented by the hour at the foot of the bridge. The **Botanic Garden** (13), opposite, has been an inviting place to relax since 1621. With its rich collection of plants, trees, and with its tropical greenhouses, it now ranks as the most compact, most diverse collection of plants in the world. *Open daily 9–4:45. Closed Good Friday and Christmas Day. Admission April–August, adults £2, under 12 free. Admission is free during the rest of the year.* ☎ *(01865) 276-920.* ♿.

Return along High Street to Magpie Lane and turn left. At its end, to the left, is the entrance to ***Merton College** (14), generally considered to be the oldest at Oxford. Its picturesque Mob Quad of 1308, Treasury of 1274, and chapel of 1294 are the most interesting features. *Open Mon.–Fri. 2–4, weekends 10–4. Admission to library £1.* ☎ *(01865) 276-310.*

Now follow straight ahead to the cricket field and turn right to the entrance of Oxford's largest college, ***Christ Church** (15). Don't miss the **Dining Hall** with its portraits of notable alumni, including 14 prime ministers and William Penn. It is reached via a staircase. The **Cathedral of Oxford**, the smallest in England, is on the east side of the huge Tom Quad. Its age is uncertain, but it predates the entire university. Return to Tom Quad and take a look at **Tom Tower**. Every night at five past nine its bell tolls a curfew of 101 strokes, one for each of the original students. But why five past nine? Because Oxford lies 1° 15' west of the prime meridian, its time is uniquely its own. *Open Mon.–Sat. 9–6, Sun. 11:30–6. Closed Christmas Day. Adults £3, seniors, students, children £2.* ☎ *(01865) 276-492, Internet: www.chch.ox.ac.uk. Partially* ♿.

Enter onto St. Aldate's. From here you may want to make a little side trip to nearby **Folly Bridge** (16, off the map). Spanning the River Thames— called the *Isis* in Oxford—this bridge is the starting point for boat trips on the river, and is surrounded by attractive **pubs**, making it the perfect end to your walking tour.

Woodstock

Blenheim Palace is the attraction that brings thousands of visitors from all over the globe to the ancient town of Woodstock. One of the greatest of England's stately homes, it was built in the early 18th century as a fitting tribute to John Churchill, the first duke of Marlborough, who routed the French and Bavarians at the Battle of Blenheim in 1704. Before this, the vast property on which it sits was a royal hunting preserve. A manor house existed on the site since at least the time of Ethelred the Unready, everyone's favorite Saxon king. Henry I made great improvements, and his mansion remained a residence of royalty down through Tudor days. By the time Blenheim Palace was built, however, the old structure had almost fallen to ruin and all traces of it were demolished.

Woodstock itself originally grew up to service the royal manor. Several inns were established for this purpose, and today continue to provide hospitality to the many visitors who come to see Blenheim Palace. There is also a fine museum of rural life, an interesting church, and lovely old streets lined with picturesque buildings.

GETTING THERE:

Trains depart London's Paddington Station frequently hourly for the one-hour trip to Oxford, where you change to a local bus. There is also excellent bus (coach) service from London's Victoria Coach Station to Oxford, taking about 1.5 hours. **Local buses** leave from various points in Oxford. This service changes frequently, so check with the Oxford Tourist Centre (see page 240) for current details. The bus ride from Oxford to Woodstock takes less than 30 minutes.

By car, Woodstock is 64 miles northwest of London. Take the A40 and M40 to Oxford, then continue on the A44 to Woodstock.

PRACTICALITIES:

Blenheim Palace is open daily from mid-March through October. Fine weather will make this trip much more enjoyable. The local **Tourist Information Centre**, ☎ (01993) 813-276, is at the Oxfordshire Museum (6) on Park Street. Woodstock is in the county of Oxfordshire, and has a population of about 3,000.

FOOD AND DRINK:

The town of Woodstock has quite a few inns, pubs, and restaurants, including:

Feathers (Market St.) Elegant, dressy dining with French overtones in a small hotel. For reservations ☎ (01993) 812-291. £££

The Bear (Park St.) A coaching inn from the 16th century. ☎ (01993) 811-511. £££

Brothertons Brasserie (1 High St.) Light meals with a creative touch. ☎ (01993) 811-114. £ and ££

Black Prince (Manor Rd., just north along Oxford St.) A popular local pub with good food. ☎ (01993) 811-530. £

Blenheim Palace offers several places for a full meal or just a snack, including an inexpensive cafeteria.

SUGGESTED TOUR:

Numbers in parentheses correspond to numbers on the map.

Begin your visit at the **bus stop** (1) on Oxford Street opposite the Marlborough Arms Hotel and follow the map down Market and Park streets to the entrance of the Blenheim Palace grounds. The **Triumphal Arch** (2), designed in 1723 by Nicholas Hawksmoor as a monument to the first duke of Marlborough, is a fitting introduction to so grandiose a place. On your right is a lake created in 1764 by the renowned landscape architect Lancelot "Capability" Brown.

*BLENHEIM PALACE (3), ☎ (01993) 811-325. *Open mid-March through Oct., daily 10:30–5. Last admission at 4:45. Adults £8, seniors and students £6, children £4. Grounds only £1. Frequent events. Food service. Partial &.*

Blenheim Palace has been continuously occupied by the dukes of Marlborough since it was begun by Sir John Vanbrugh in the early 18th century as a gift from Queen Anne. Sir Winston Churchill, grandson of the seventh duke, was born here in 1874 and is buried nearby at Bladon Church. There is an exhibition of his personal belongings in the palace, which remains home to the present (11th) duke. To see its magnificent interior you can either take one of the frequent guided tours, lasting about an hour, or wander through on your own.

Be sure to explore at least part of the palace grounds after seeing the interior. **Boat rides** are available on the lake, or you can rent a rowboat on Queen Pool for some good exercise. The **Butterfly House**, where exotic tropical butterflies live in a virtually natural habitat, is another attraction included in the entrance fee. You can get to it by miniature railway or on foot. Close to this is the **Marlborough Maze** (4), the world's largest symbolic hedge maze, for which an extra charge is made.

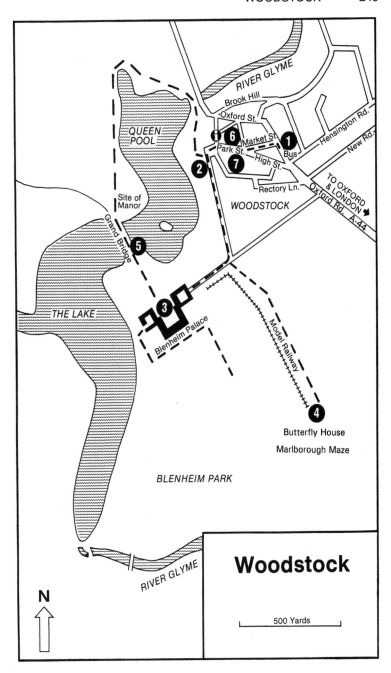

Woodstock

A pleasant way to return to Woodstock is to follow the route on the map. The **Grand Bridge** (5), an extravagant span over what was then only a creek, was part of Vanbrugh's original design. Most of it is now under water. The land just beyond it was the site of the old Woodstock Manor, for centuries a country residence for England's kings and queens.

Back in the village, stroll down Park Street and visit the small but interesting **Oxfordshire Museum** (6), which features displays of local life through the centuries along with temporary exhibitions. The local Tourist Information Centre is also here. *Open Tues.–Sat. 10–5, Sun. 2–5. Adults £1, seniors 50p, children under 18 free. Café. Gift shop.* ☎ *(01993) 811-456.* ♿.

The **town stocks**, outside the museum, have holes for five legs. Was this a joke or did Woodstock have an unusual number of one-legged culprits? The **Church** (7) is often overlooked but is actually a fascinating study in changing styles, ranging from Norman to Perpendicular. Beyond this, the village offers several interesting shops and some very appealing pubs in which to relax.

Warwick

Many visitors go to see the magnificent castle at Warwick but completely overlook the town itself. That's a pity, because this is surely one of the least spoiled places in England. Small and compact, it has a wonderful blend of Tudor and Georgian architecture, a splendid church, and several fine museums.

Warwick grew up around its castle, whose origins date back to a fortification built here in 914 by Ethelfleda, daughter of Alfred the Great, to protect her kingdom of Mercia. Nothing of this remains, but there are still traces of the motte built by William the Conqueror in 1068. The castle you see today is largely of 14th-century construction with great modifications made down through the years to convert the interior into a luxurious home. Sold to Madame Tussaud's in 1978, it is now a showcase combining medieval elements with those of a more recent stately home, and outfitted with the inevitable wax figures.

GETTING THERE:

Trains depart London's Marylebone (Chiltern Railway) and Paddington (Thames Trains) stations several times in the morning for Warwick. Both departure stations offer at least one convenient direct service taking about two hours. Return service operates until mid-evening. Service is reduced on Sundays and holidays. A combination rail and castle visit package is available from Chiltern Railways at Marylebone Station.

By car, Warwick is 96 miles northwest of London via the M40 to Junction 15, then the A429.

PRACTICALITIES:

The castle is open every day except Christmas Day, but some of the other sights are closed on Sundays or Mondays. The local **Tourist Information Centre**, ☎ (01926) 492-212, is in the Court House on Jury Street. Markets are held on Saturdays. Warwick is the county town of Warwickshire, and has a population of about 22,000.

FOOD AND DRINK:

Some choice places for lunch are:

Findons (7 Old Square, near St. Mary's Church) Contemporary English cuisine in a romantic setting. ☎ (01926) 411-755. X: Sun. ££

The Angry Cheese (St. Nicholas Church St., between St. John's House and the castle) Both a restaurant and a bistro, with two different menus. ☎ (01926) 400-411. X: Mon. £ and ££

Tudor House Hotel (92 West St., beyond Lord Leycester Hospital) Traditional, simple English dishes in a 15th-century inn. ☎ (01926) 495-447. £

Tilted Wig (11 Market Place, near the County Museum) A popular pub with a variety of English, International, and vegetarian dishes. ☎ (01926) 410-466. £

Charlotte's Tea Rooms (6 Jury St., east of the tourist office) Light home-cooked lunches, both indoors and out. ☎ (01926) 498-930. X: Mon. £

Pizza Piazza (33 Jury St., east of the tourist office) All manner of pizza and pasta. ☎ (01926) 491-641. £

There are also two cafeterias and a snack bar at the castle. Picnicking is permitted on the grounds.

SUGGESTED TOUR:

Numbers in parentheses correspond to numbers on the map.

Leave the **train station** (1) and follow the map to:

***WARWICK CASTLE** (2), ☎ (01926) 406-600, Internet: www.warwick-castle.co.uk. *Open daily except Christmas Day, 10–6, closing at 5 from Nov.–March. Last admission is half an hour before closing. Peak season (June–Aug.) admission: Adults £10.50, seniors £7.50, students £7.80, children 4-16 £6.25. Prices reduced Sept.–May. Special events. Gift shop. Restaurants. Café. Picnic area. Limited ♿, call ahead.*

Considered by many to be the finest medieval castle in England, it will easily take two or three hours to explore Warwick. Everything is well marked and explained. The main attractions include the **Barbican and Gatehouse**, a 14th-century complex featuring an exhibition on the life of Richard III; the **Armoury** with its superb collection of weapons; and the **Dungeon and Torture Chamber**, which has fascinating (if grisly) displays of medieval torture instruments. Beyond this, **Guy's Tower** may be climbed and the ramparts walked. The **Ghost Tower** is allegedly haunted by a 17th-century apparition. A major attraction—**"Kingmaker—A Preparation for Battle"**—brings to life the sights and sounds of 1471 as the Earl of Warwick readies his army for combat. More Victorian in character, the ***State Apartments** make a gorgeous show of baronial splendor. Next to them is the **Royal Weekend**, a re-creation of a turn-of-the-century house party enlivened with wax figures of famous nobility.

Beyond the castle are lovely **gardens** created by "Capability" Brown in

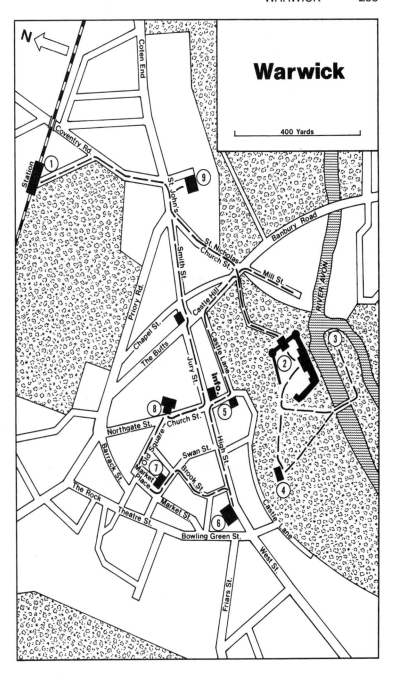

Warwick

400 Yards

the 18th century. Peacocks roam about the trees, some of which were planted by such luminaries as Queen Victoria and Prince Albert. Cross the bridge over the River Avon to an **island** (3) that has wonderful views of the south face. The **Conservatory** (4) is a fantasy recalling the spirit of Georgian times.

Leave the Castle and return to Castle Hill. A short walk down Mill Street will reward you with splendid views. Now follow the map to **Oken's House** (5), an Elizabethan dwelling that survived the devastating fire of 1694. It now houses an utterly delightful collection of antique and period dolls and toys. *Open Easter through Oct., Mon.–Sat. 10–5, Sun. 11–5; and Nov.–Easter, Sat. only, 10–dusk. Adults £1, children 75p.* ☎ *(01926) 495-546.*

Continue up Castle Street and make a left on High Street to the **Lord Leycester Hospital** (6), a group of picturesque 14th- century almshouses that have been used since the 16th century as a retirement home for old soldiers. One of these gentlemen will be happy to show you around, and then you can visit the restored 16th-century **Master's Garden**. *Open Tues. through Sun., 10–6, closing at 5 in winter. Adults £2.75, seniors £2, children £1.50. Garden open Easter–Sept., 10–4:30, with a nominal charge.* ☎ *(01926) 491-422.* Light lunches and teas are available at the Brethren's Kitchen here during the summer.

Walk down Brook Street to the **Warwickshire Museum** (7) in the Market Place. Displays here cover archaeology, natural history, and local bygones in addition to changing exhibitions. *Open Mon.–Sat. 10–5:30; and also Sun. from May–Sept., 2–5. Free.* ☎ *(01926) 410-410.*

St. Mary's Church (8), nearby, has parts dating from the 12th century, although it was largely rebuilt after the 1694 fire. Its 15th-century **Beauchamp Chapel* is incomparable, and its tower can be climbed for a nice view of Warwickshire. *Open daily 10–6, closing at 4 in winter. Free. Tower open daily in summer, weather permitting, nominal charge.* ☎ *(01926) 403-940.*

Jury Street leads past the **East Gate**, a relic of the old town wall, and as Smith Street to **St. John's House** (9). This beautiful 17th-century mansion is now a **museum** featuring period reconstructions of a parlor, a kitchen, and a Victorian classroom, along with costumes and musical instruments. There is a regimental military exhibition on the floor above. *Open Tues.–Sat. and Bank Holiday Mon., 10–5:30; and also on Sun. from May–Sept., 2:30–5. Free.* ☎ *(01926) 410-410.*

A short walk in the garden completes your tour before returning to the nearby train station.

*Stratford-upon-Avon

As someone once remarked, there's no business like show business. That, put simply, is what Stratford-upon-Avon is all about. The whole town is one vast theater, entertaining thousands of visitors a day. Despite this, it has miraculously managed to avoid the worst of tourism's trappings and still retains a quite genuine charm. Just about everyone who goes there enjoys the experience.

William Shakespeare was born in Stratford in 1564. This is also where he lived a great deal of his life and where he died in 1616. Many of the buildings associated with the Bard have been lovingly preserved and may be visited. The Royal Shakespeare Theatre, one of the greatest anywhere, is beautifully situated on the banks of the quiet Avon. There are several others attractions, some relating to Shakespeare and others not, but perhaps in the long run it is simply the atmosphere of this delightful old market town that is so memorable.

The best way to savor Stratford is to stay overnight and perhaps take in a performance at the theater. Those with cars will find that it makes an ideal base for exploring the midlands and the Cotswolds. If you can't do this, however, a daytrip from London is still very enjoyable.

GETTING THERE:

Trains operated by Thames Trains depart London's Paddington Station several times in the morning for Stratford-upon-Avon. One of these, leaving around 9 a.m., is a direct express taking a bit over two hours. Return trains operate until late evening. Service is greatly reduced on Sundays and some holidays.

Those staying over for a few days can take advantage of the **Shakespeare Country Explorer**, a three- or five-day combination deal that includes round-trip rail travel from London's Paddington or Marylebone stations to Leamington Spa, Warwick, or Stratford-upon-Avon plus unlimited travel on the Midland Red bus routes while there. Users also get special discounts to many attractions, festivals, restaurants, and shops. These tickets are sold at both Paddington and Marylebone stations in London.

Special Packages including rail and/or coach transportation, overnight accommodations, theater tickets, and dinner are available through travel agents in London and elsewhere.

By car, take the A40 and M40 to Junction 15, then the A46 to Stratford-upon-Avon, which is 96 miles northwest of London.

PRACTICALITIES:

The major sights in Stratford are open daily except on December 24, 25, and 26, with generally longer hours from March through October. A colorful **outdoor market** is held on Fridays at the square joining Greenhill and Wood streets. The local **Tourist Information Centre**, ☎ (01789) 293-127, accommodations (01789) 415-061, brochure requests (01789) 267-522, Internet: www.shakespeare-country.co.uk, is at Bridgefoot, between the canal and the bridge. You might ask them about renting a **bicycle** for a spin in the country.

Guide Friday operates a convenient hop-on, hop-off open-top double-decker bus service on a circular route connecting all of the tourist sights in and around Stratford-upon-Avon. These run very frequently, all year round. One day, unlimited use tickets: Adults £8, seniors £6.50, children £2.50. ☎ (01789) 294-466, Internet: www.guidefriday.com.

Stratford is in the county of Warwickshire, and has a population of about 22,000.

FOOD AND DRINK:

There are plenty of good restaurants and pubs in Stratford, including:

Box Tree (Waterside, in the theater) Classic food with a wonderful view of the Avon. Proper dress and reservations required, ☎ (01789) 293-226. X: when theater is closed. £££

The Boathouse (Swans Nest Lane, by Clapton Bridge) English and French cuisine overlooking the river. ☎ (01789) 297-733. X: Sun., Mon. lunch, Sat. lunch. ££ and £££

Raj Indian Cuisine (7 Greenhill St., between the station and the Birthplace) Indian Balti and Tandoori dishes. ☎ (01789) 267-067. ££

The Glory Hole (21 Sheep St., near New Place) Traditional English cuisine. ☎ (01789) 293-546. £ and ££

Dirty Duck (Waterside St., near the theater) Also known as the Black Swan, the actors' favorite pub and restaurant. ☎ (01789) 297-312. £ and ££

ASK Pizza & Pasta (Unit 10, Old Red Lion Court, Bridge St., a block west of the tourist office) A wide variety of simple Italian dishes. ☎ (01789) 262-440. £

River Terrace (Waterside, in the theater) Self-service cafeteria. ☎ (01789) 293-226. X: when theater is closed. £

SUGGESTED TOUR:

Numbers in parentheses correspond to numbers on the map.

Leave the **train station** (1) and follow the map to that most logical of beginnings:

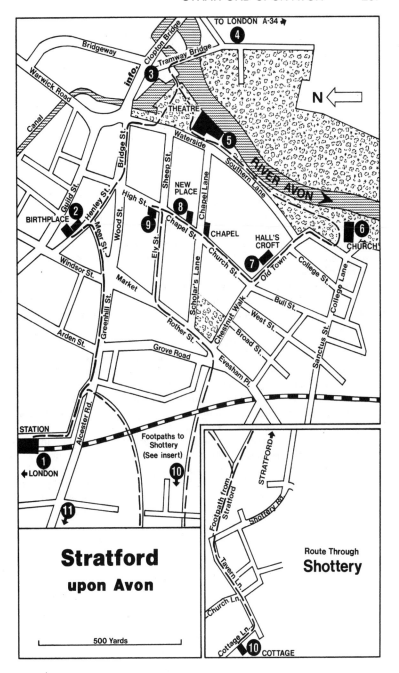

TO LONDON A-34

④

Bridgeway

Warwick Road

Clopton Bridge

Tramway Bridge

Info.

③

Canal

THEATRE

Waterside

⑤

Bridge St.

Sheep St.

Southern Lane

RIVER AVON

NEW PLACE

Chapel Lane

Guild St.

②

Henley St.

BIRTHPLACE

High St.

⑧

⑨

Chapel St.

CHAPEL

HALL'S CROFT

⑥

CHURCH

Meer St.

Wood St.

Ely St.

Scholar's Lane

Church St.

⑦

Old Town

College St.

College Lane

Windsor St.

Market

Greenhill St.

Rother St.

Chestnut Walk

West St.

Bull St.

Sanctus St.

Arden St.

Grove Road

Broad St.

Evesham Pl.

STATION

Alcester Rd.

Footpaths to Shottery (See insert)

① ◄ LONDON

⑩

⑪

Stratford
upon Avon

500 Yards

Footpath from Stratford

STRATFORD

Shottery Rd.

Route Through
Shottery

Tavern Ln.

Church Ln.

Cottage Ln.

⑩ COTTAGE

N ◄

*SHAKESPEARE'S BIRTHPLACE (2), ☎ (01789) 201-807, Internet: www.shake speare.org.uk. *Open late March to mid-Oct., Mon.–Sat. 9–5, and Sun. 9:30–5; rest of year Mon.–Sat. 9:30–4, Sun. 10–4. Closed Dec. 23–26. Adults £4.90, children £2.20. A **reduced price joint ticket** covering the three in-town "Shakespeare Properties" is available: Adults £7.50, seniors and students £6.50, children £3.70. Another combination covers these plus Anne Hathaway's Cottage and Mary Arden's House: Adults £11, students and seniors £10, children £5.50. All properties are partially ♿, but inquiries should be made first.*

Shakespeare's Birthplace is actually two houses joined together, the eastern half having been his father's shop and the western half the family residence. To the left of it is the modern **Shakespeare Centre**, which houses exhibitions, a library, and a study center. Enter this and wander through the delightful **garden**, complete with flowers, shrubs, and trees mentioned in his plays. The well-marked trail then takes you into the old house itself, where you will visit the bedroom in which Shakespeare was presumably born on or about April 23, 1564. The entire house is furnished as it might have been in his youth, including an interesting period kitchen and an oak-beamed living room.

Return on Henley Street, walk down Bridge Street, and turn right at Waterside. Stroll through **Bancroft Gardens**, going past the canal basin and locks. Overlooking this pleasant scene is the **Gower Memorial**, a life-size bronze statue of the Bard with figures of Hamlet, Lady Macbeth, Falstaff, and Prince Hal. The tourist office is nearby, as is **Cox's Yard** (3). This complex on the banks of the River Avon is complete with shops, a micro brewery, a pub, restaurants, and a new attraction, The **Stratford Tales**—a journey through time covering the characters, legends, and events that have shaped Stratford since the 16th century. *Yard open daily, 9:30 a.m. to 11 p.m., free. Stratford Tales open daily 10–5; adults £3.95, seniors £3.25, children under 16 £2.50.* ☎ *(01789) 404-600.* ♿.

Continue on and cross the footbridge over the Avon, a span formerly used by the horse-drawn tramway that once connected Stratford with Moreton-in-Marsh. From here you will have a beautiful view of the river and the modern Royal Shakespeare Theatre. Just beyond the bridge is the **Butterfly Farm** (4), where exotic flora and fauna exist in an indoor "natural" setting, the largest of its kind in Europe. *Open in summer, daily 10–6; in winter, daily 10–dusk. Adults £3.75, seniors £3.25, children £2.75.* ☎ *(01789) 299-288.* ♿. The 15th-century **Clopton Bridge** with its 14 arches, to the left, still carries heavy traffic.

Return and walk over to the **Royal Shakespeare Theatre** (5). Built in 1932 to replace a smaller 19th-century theater that burned down, its performances of Shakespearian plays are world-famous. Although tickets should be booked well in advance, they are frequently available on the day of performance. The attached **RSC Collection** has interesting mementoes of theatrical personalities and other Shakespeariana. You can ask here about **backstage tours** of the theater. *Box Office* ☎ *(01789) 295-623, tours (01789)*

412-602, *Internet: www.rsc.org.uk. Restaurants. Bars. Gift shops. Partial* &. Near this is the new **Swan Theatre**, especially designed to present plays by Shakespeare's contemporaries and playwrights influenced by him.

Thirsty travelers can refresh themselves at the famous **Dirty Duck Pub**, a.k.a. the Black Swan, closeby on Waterside. From here, a path leads along the river's edge, passing the **Brass Rubbing Centre** where you can make your own inexpensive souvenir of Stratford.

Continue on to ***Holy Trinity Church** (6), the scene of Shakespeare's baptism in 1564 and burial in 1616. Copies of the church registers showing both events are on display. His **tomb** is inscribed with the famous lines ending in *"and curst be he that moves my bones."* There are a few other interesting items in this 14th-century church, particularly the humorous **misericords** under the choir seats. *Open March–Oct., Mon.–Sat. 8:30–6, Sun. 2–5; Nov.–Feb., Mon.–Sat. 9–4, Sun. 2–5. Closed Good Friday and Christmas Day. Church free. Fee to view tomb: Adults 60p, seniors and students 40p.* ☎ *(01789) 266-316.* &.

Hall's Croft (7) on Old Town is the next stop. This splendid Tudor house was the home of Shakespeare's eldest daughter, Susanna, and her husband, Dr. John Hall. Its interior is well worth visiting for a glimpse of how a prosperous doctor's family lived in those days. Be sure to see the dispensary with its surgical instruments, herbs, and potions. A stroll through the **garden** in the rear is a delight. *Open late March to mid-Oct., Mon.–Sat. 9:30–5, Sun. 10–5; rest of year Mon.–Sat. 10–4, Sun. 10:30–4. Adults £3.30, children £1.60. See Shakespeare's Birthplace, above, for details on reduced-price combination tickets. Restaurant and tea room. Partial* &.

Turn right on Church Street and pass, on the right, the **King Edward VI Grammar School**, where the young Shakespeare learned his "small Latin and less Greek." Adjoining this is the 15th-century **Guild Chapel** with its noted fresco of the *Last Judgement* above the chancel arch. Just beyond, on Chapel Street, is the site of Shakespeare's own home, **New Place** (8), which he purchased in 1597 and in which he died in 1616. Its last owner, disturbed by tourists, demolished it in 1759; today only the foundations and **garden** remain. These can be reached by going through the **New Place Museum** in the former home of Thomas Nash, who was married to Shakespeare's granddaughter, Elizabeth Hall. *Open late March to mid-Oct., Mon.–Sat. 9:30–5, Sun. 10–5; rest of year Mon.–Sat. 10–4, Sun. 10:30–4. Adults £3.30, children £1.60. See Shakespeare's Birthplace, above, for details on reduced-price combination tickets. Partial* &.

Harvard House (9) has nothing to do with the Bard, but a lot to do with Harvard University. This outstanding example of a half-timbered Elizabethan structure was the home of the mother of John Harvard, whose donations helped found the famous institution in the U.S.A. Its richly decorated interior, filled with pewter from Roman times to the Victorian era, may be visited. *Open May–Oct., Tues.–Sat. and Bank Holiday Mon., 10–4:30. Free.*

Adjacent to this are two other buildings of similar style and age, one of them being the well-known **Garrick Inn**, named for the actor David Garrick who organized the first Shakespeare Festival here in 1769.

While in Stratford you will probably want to see:

*ANNE HATHAWAY'S COTTAGE (10), ☎ (01789) 204-016, Internet: www.shakespeare.org.uk. *Open late March to mid-Oct., Mon.–Sat. 9–5, Sun. 9:30–5; rest of year, Mon.–Sat. 9:30–4, Sun. 10–4. Adults £3.90, children £1.60. See Shakespeare's Birthplace, above, for details on reduced-price combination tickets. Partial &, inquire.*

This is certainly one of the prettiest (and most visited) sights in England. The home of Shakespeare's wife before their marriage, this 16th-century thatched-roof farmhouse is set in gorgeous surroundings. The furnishings are fairly authentic as the cottage remained in her family until late Victorian times. Located in the nearby hamlet of Shottery, about one mile from Stratford, it is easily reached by bus from Bridge Street or, better still, by rented bicycle, or on foot via a country path that begins at Evesham Place. The route is well marked and is shown on the map and its insert. Return by way of the other path to Alcester Road and the train station.

ADDITIONAL ATTRACTION:

Too far to walk to, but reachable by car, bus, bicycle, taxi, or Guide Friday bus, is the renowned:

MARY ARDEN'S HOUSE and THE SHAKESPEARE COUNTRYSIDE MUSEUM (11), Wilmcote, ☎ (01789) 204-016, Internet: www.shakespeare.org.uk. *Open late March to mid-Oct., Mon.–Sat. 9:30–5, Sun. 10–5; rest of year, Mon.–Sat. 10–4, Sun. 10:30–4. Adults £4.40, children £2.20. See Shakespeare's Birthplace, above, for information about reduced-price combination tickets. Café. Partial &.*

Mary Arden, Shakespeare's mother, is believed to have lived here before she married John Shakespeare and moved to Stratford-upon-Avon. Located some three miles northwest of Stratford, this Tudor farmstead continued farming operations into the 20th century and was purchased by the Shakespeare Birthplace Trust in 1930. The farm buildings making up the museum include a dovecote, barns, a second farmhouse, and a working blacksmith's forge. There are displays of rural life in the area from Shakespeare's time to the near-present, rare breeds of farm animals, falconry demonstrations, and a variety of events such as sheep shearing.

Coventry

Like the legendary phoenix, Coventry was reborn from the ashes of destruction. On the night of November 14, 1940 it suffered one of the most devastating air raids of World War II, leaving the city's center in rubble, its cathedral a smoldering ruin. Postwar construction followed a radically new plan based on the latest thinking. A stunning new cathedral in contemporary style rose alongside the shards of the old, which remain as mute testimony to the futility of war. Coventry today is a thoroughly modern city, and one that is well worth visiting.

Although its origins may date from a 7th-century convent, the history of Coventry really begins in 1043 with the foundation of a Benedictine abbey by Leofric, Earl of Mercia, and his wife Godgyfu. Known to the world as Lady Godiva, she is reputed to have ridden through the town naked, or at least stripped of her jewelry, to win tax relief for its citizens. By the 14th century Coventry was already an important mercantile center, expanding rapidly in the late 19th century with such new industries as sewing machines, bicycles, and the first English motorcar, a Daimler, in 1896. The city's contribution to the motor industry is beautifully told in its fascinating Museum of British Road Transport, which alone is worth the trip.

GETTING THERE:

Trains depart London's Euston Station at least twice an hour for the 75-minute journey to Coventry, with reduced services on weekends and holidays. Return trains operate until late evening.

By car, Coventry is about 100 miles northwest of London. Take the M1 to Junction 17, then the M45/A45 into town. You can avoid local traffic and parking problems by using the convenient Park & Ride facility on Kenilworth Road on the way into town and taking the frequent bus into city center. Parking there is free, and the round-trip bus fare is £1 for adults, 50p for children. Get off at the Broadgate stop, near the cathedral.

PRACTICALITIES:

Being a business city, Coventry is best visited on a working day when its pace is going full strength. All of the major sights are open daily except on December 24–26. The local **Tourist Information Centre**, ☎ (01203) 832-303, is in Bayley Lane, between the cathedral and the art museum. Two

Internet sites to check out are: www.coventry.gov.uk and www.coventry.org. Coventry is in the county of West Midlands, and has a population of about 300,000.

FOOD AND DRINK:

Restaurants in Coventry, with the exception of a multitude of fast-food outlets, are geared to the business trade. A few choices for lunch are:

Brittania Hotel (Cathedral Sq., just behind the cathedral) A large, modern hotel with several restaurants. ☎ (01203) 633-733. X: Sat. lunch. ££

Corks Wine Bar (4/5 Whitefriars St., 2 blocks southeast of the art museum) A contemporary menu, with an extensive wine list. ☎ (01203) 223-628. X: Sun. lunch. ££

Ostlers Eating House (166 Spon St., at the end of the walking tour) A cozy restaurant in a medieval house, with a variety of home-cooked dishes. ☎ (01203) 226- 603. X: Sun., Mon. lunch. ££

Brown's Café (Earl St., a block south of the cathedral) Meat, fish, vegetarian dishes, and salads. ☎ (01203) 221-100. £

Benedicts Coffee Shop (in the cathedral) A friendly place for lunch or light refreshments. ☎ (01203) 224-256. £

SUGGESTED TOUR:

Numbers in parentheses correspond to numbers on the map.

Leaving the **train station** (1), you have a choice of getting downtown by bus, taxi, or on foot. The very pleasant walk is a little under one mile and completely avoids traffic all the way. It is this separation of pedestrians from cars that makes Coventry such a special place. The path goes through parks, passes under and over busy thoroughfares, and winds up in a modern shopping center.

Broadgate (2), a large open square, is the heart of the city. Lady Godiva, or at least a statue of her, rides naked astride her horse in the center. The famous scene, complete with a naughty Peeping Tom, is reenacted hourly by animated figures under the clock on the south side.

Stroll over to the ruins of the **Old Cathedral** (3), all that remained following the terrible incendiary bombing of World War II. Miraculously, its 14th-century **tower** survived and may be climbed for a wonderful view of the city. At the far end is a crude altar with a cross made of two charred roof timbers. Behind this, a broken wall bears the touching inscription "Father Forgive." Few people can look at this without feeling a lump in the throat. Next to this stands the new:

*COVENTRY CATHEDRAL (4), ☎ (01203) 227-597, Internet: www.coventry cathedral.org. *Open daily, 9:30–6, closing at 5:30 in winter. Suggested dona-*

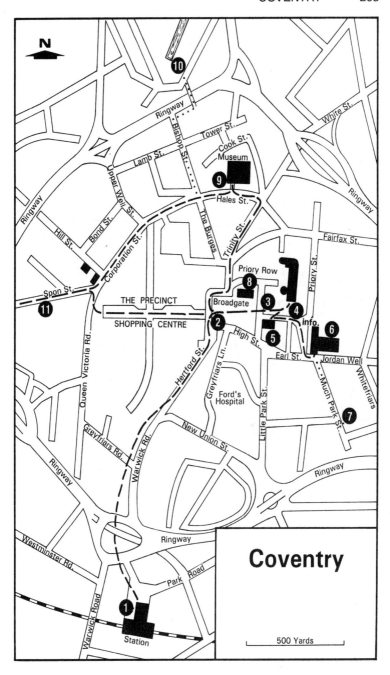

Coventry

500 Yards

tion £2. Visitor Centre open Easter through Oct., Mon.–Sat. 10–4; Nov.–Easter, Mon.–Sat. 11–3. Visitor Center admission: Adults £1.25, seniors and children 75p. Gift shop. Coffee shop. ♿.

The magnificent new cathedral, rising next to the shell of the old, was consecrated in 1962. A storm of controversy raged over the unorthodox design by Sir Basil Spence, but this has died down as its true splendor became apparent to all but the most die-hard of traditionalists.

Enter the nave and examine the **Baptistry** on the right. The stunning window of abstract stained glass is the largest made in this century. In front of it a three-ton boulder, taken from a hillside near Bethlehem, serves as a font. Beyond the original charred cross at the high altar hangs Graham Sutherland's **Christ in Glory* tapestry, the largest in the world. All around you are wonderful examples of modern design. The entire cathedral evokes a strong feeling of contemporary faith, more so perhaps than even the most splendid of Gothic structures. Its **Visitors Centre**, downstairs, presents an exciting audio-visual show dramatizing Coventry's history, along with three-dimensional holograms depicting the Stations of the Cross. Before leaving the cathedral, be sure to visit the **Chapel of Unity**, which is set aside for use by all Christian denominations. Outside, on the east wall near the entrance, there is a great bronze sculpture of **St. Michael and the Devil,* the last major work by Sir Jacob Epstein.

Exit through the Old Cathedral onto Bayley Lane. The **Guildhall of St. Mary** (5) is one of the few medieval buildings to have escaped destruction. Built in the 14th century and said to have once imprisoned Mary, Queen of Scots, it is still used for civic functions and is definitely worth a visit. *Usually open April–Oct., daily 10–4, but may be closed for special functions.*

The same narrow street leads past the tourist office to the **Herbert Art Gallery and Museum** (6), just a block away. In addition to an excellent collection of the visual and applied arts, the museum has interesting displays of local history, manufactures, bygones, and archaeology. *Open Mon.–Sat., 10–5:30, Sun. noon–5. Free. Gift shop. Tea room.* ☎ *(01203) 832-381.* ♿.

If you're interested, it's only a short stroll down Much Park Street to the **Coventry Toy Museum** (7), housed in the 14th-century Whitefriars Gatehouse. The house to which this led was visited by both Queen Elizabeth I and King James I, but has since fallen to ruin, while the gatehouse was put to a variety of uses including a second-hand clothes shop. It is now a museum of toys dating from 1740 to 1951. *Open daily, 2–4. Adults £1.50, seniors and children £1.* ☎ *(01203) 227-560.*

Return to Broadgate and make a stop at **Holy Trinity Church** (8), an attractive mixture of 13th- to 17th-century styles. It houses a rare medieval "Doom" wall painting. *Open daily.* ☎ *(01203) 220-418.* ♿.

Take a look down Priory Row and then follow the map past extensive redevelopment to the wonderful:

*MUSEUM OF BRITISH ROAD TRANSPORT (9), Hales St., ☎ (01203) 832-425, Internet: www.mbrt.co.uk. *Open daily 10–5. Closed Dec. 24–26. Free. Museum shop. Café.* ♿.

At one time Coventry had over one hundred automobile manufacturers, many of which are represented in the immense collection of cars dating from as far back as 1897. Begin your visit by strolling down ***Memory Lanes**, a display of vintage vehicles set in period street scenes, followed by **Royalty on the Road**—a collection of royal vehicles including the humble Mini Metro once owned by Princess Diana. Continue on through the ***Coventry Blitz Experience**, a virtual evocation of the World War II bombings featuring Montgomery's staff car. There is also a model world recalling the history of road transport in miniature, and a dramatic showing of the world's fastest land vehicle. Many more cars, trucks, buses, bicycles, motorcycles, and other wheeled vehicles complete the show.

At this point, ambitious walkers can make an interesting **side trip**, crossing the busy Ringway via a pedestrian footbridge. Just beyond this is the **Coventry Canal Basin** (10), opened to boat traffic in 1769 and still in use today by pleasure craft. The warehouses surrounding it date from as far back as 1787 to as recently as 1914. They are now used by artists, craftsmen, musicians, boat builders, and other creative types. Just beyond Bridge Number 1 is Drapers Fields, where in 1896 the Daimler Motor Company produced Britain's first automobile.

Before returning to the train station, you might want to head down Corporation Street to **Spon Street** (11), a colorful neighborhood of medieval buildings that somehow survived all the bombs. Now restored, they serve as restaurants, shops, art galleries, and the like. Nearby is a Tudor almshouse called Bond's Hospital, and the 14th-century St. John's Church. The latter was used as a prison for Royalists defeated by Cromwell and "sent to Coventry," as the phrase goes, by the Puritans.

Cross the main street and enter an enormous complex of shopping centers before returning to Broadgate and the train station.

Chester

Of all the ancient towns in England, Chester stands out as perhaps the best preserved. Its medieval walls remain intact, still surrounding the picturesque streets lined with half-timbered houses. The scene today, except for the traffic, is right out of an old engraving.

Originally known as *Deva,* Chester was founded about AD 60 as the headquarters camp of the Roman XX Legion, one of the three that guarded Britain. After their departure around AD 380, the town became an obscure settlement until the 10th century, when it was enlarged by Aethelflaeda, daughter of Alfred the Great. During the Norman Conquest of 1066 it held out against William the Conqueror longer than any other English town, but in 1070 the inevitable happened and Chester was made an earldom, granted by William to his nephew, Hugh of Avrances. The town prospered in its role as a port, with ships from all over Europe entering the harbor.

By the end of the Middle Ages, however, the gradual silting of the River Dee made shipping unprofitable. In the Civil War of the 17th century, Chester supported Charles I, but was badly defeated in 1645. The building of the Shropshire Union Canal in the late 18th century and the development of railways shortly afterwards brought back the prosperity that today makes Chester such a beautiful and thriving city.

GETTING THERE:

Trains leave London's Euston Station several times in the morning for the nearly three-hour journey to Chester. Some of these require a change at Crewe, and service is reduced on Sundays and holidays. Return trains operate until early evening.

By car, Chester is about 200 miles northwest of London. The fastest route is via the M1 to Rugby, then the M6 north to the M56. Head west on this and take the A56 into Chester.

PRACTICALITIES:

Chester can be visited any day of the week, although on Sunday some of the sights have reduced hours and rail service is not good.

The main tourist office is located in the Visitor Centre on Vicar's Lane by the Roman Amphitheatre. You can contact them at ☎ (01244) 402-111,

Internet: www.chestercc.gov.uk. There is a branch in the Town Hall on Northgate Street, near the cathedral.

Guide Friday operates a hop-on, hop-off open-top double-decker bus service on a circular route, with stops at most of the tourist attractions. The service operates daily from March through October, with buses every 15 minutes in June, July, and August, and every 20–30 minutes at other times. ☎ *(01244) 347-457, Internet: www.guidefriday.com.*

Chester is the county town of Cheshire, and has a population of about 80,000.

FOOD AND DRINK:

For a town its size, Chester is blessed with an exceptionally good range of restaurants and pubs. Some choices are:

The Arkle (in the Grosvenor Hotel, Eastgate St., near the Eastgate) Classic cuisine in opulent surroundings, with a wide selection of fine wines. Dress well and reserve, ☎ (01244) 324-024. X: Mon. lunch, Sun. eve. £££

Blue Bell (65 Northgate St., near the cathedral) Inspired English dishes in a 15th-century inn. ☎ (01244) 317-758. ££

The Garden House (1 Rufus Ct., off Northgate St. north of the cathedral) Meat, game and fish dishes along with vegetarian specialties, served both indoors and out. ☎ (01244) 320-004. X: Sun. ££

Katie's Tea Rooms (Watergate St., The Rows) Light lunches in two of Chester's oldest buildings. ☎ (01244) 400-322. £ and ££

Ye Olde King's Head (48 Lower Bridge St., near the Heritage Centre) An old half-timbered inn with a good restaurant. ☎ (01244) 324-855. £ and ££

Francs (14 Cuppin St., off Grosvenor St., near the Grosvenor Museum) Traditional French dishes at low prices; very popular. ☎ (01244) 317-952. £ and ££

What's Cooking? (Grosvenor St., near the Grosvenor Museum) A wide variety of American dishes, from burgers on. In business since 1978. ☎ (01244) 346-512. £ and ££

The Falcon (6 Lower Bridge St., near the Heritage Centre) A good choice for a pub lunch, with interesting selections. ☎ (01244) 314-555. £

Hattie's Tea Shop (5 Rufus Ct., off Northgate St., north of the cathedral) Light lunches, giant sandwiches, and desserts. ☎ (01244) 345-173. £

SUGGESTED TOUR:

Numbers in parentheses correspond to numbers on the map.

The **train station** (1) is a little over a half-mile from Eastgate, where the Old Town begins. You can cover this rather uninteresting distance by bus, taxi, or on foot. If you decide to walk, just follow the map.

Eastgate (2) is the main entrance to the city. The present structure was built in 1769, replacing medieval and Roman predecessors. Above the arch is an *ornamental clock tower commemorating Queen Victoria's Diamond jubilee. A climb up the steps will put you atop the ancient City Walls that still completely encircle the town. Follow the walkway to the right, passing the medieval cathedral and its modern detached bell tower. In a short while you will come to King Charles' Tower (3). According to legend, it was from here that Charles I witnessed the defeat of his Loyalist forces against Parliamentary troops in 1645.

At this point the walls follow the Shropshire Union Canal, built over the old town moat. Beyond Northgate there are excellent views of the Welsh hills in the distance. Soon you will cross a busy expressway on the modern St. Martin's Gate. Go down the steps on the far side to the canal locks (4) where, if your timing is right, you will see narrowboats passing through on their way to the basin below. This operation is fascinating to watch. Walk downhill past the locks and under the railway viaduct, then bear right and visit the canal basin where many of the water people tie up their boats. Retrace your steps past the locks and climb back to the city walls.

Continuing your circuit of the walls, you will pass the Goblin Tower and then Bonewaldesthorne's Tower. From here a spur wall leads to the Water Tower (5), built in 1322 and at one time surrounded by the River Dee. The walls now descend to street level at the Watergate (6), once the main gate leading to the port.

Turn left on Watergate Street, the *Via Principalis,* or main street, of Roman Deva. On the right is the Stanley Palace, a residence dating from 1591 that is now occupied by the English Speaking Union. It may be visited at set times. Beyond Nicholas Street you will pass Trinity Church on the left, and at Weaver Street encounter the first of the famous *Rows, an architectural feature unique to Chester. These consist of galleries that form a continuous protected walkway through the buildings of the main streets. One story above street level, they shield pedestrians from both weather and traffic. The origins of this strange but very practical building style are clouded in the mysteries of the Middle Ages. One particularly romantic theory has it that when the Rows were first built, probably in the 13th century, the streets were so cluttered with Roman ruins that passage at street level was difficult. Whatever their original purpose, they remain an attractive way to stroll about the town.

Climb the steps on the right side of Watergate Street and walk along the Row to number 51, Bishop Lloyd's House (7), the richest example of carved timberwork in Chester. A better view of it can be had from across the street. Other outstanding houses along this Row are the Leche House at number 21; the Crypt, now used for wine storage, at number 11; and God's Providence House at number 9, near the end. Some of these may be visited by entering the shops and asking permission to look around.

The intersection at Bridge Street is known as The Cross (8), after the stone High Cross that stands in front of St. Peter's Church. The Chester

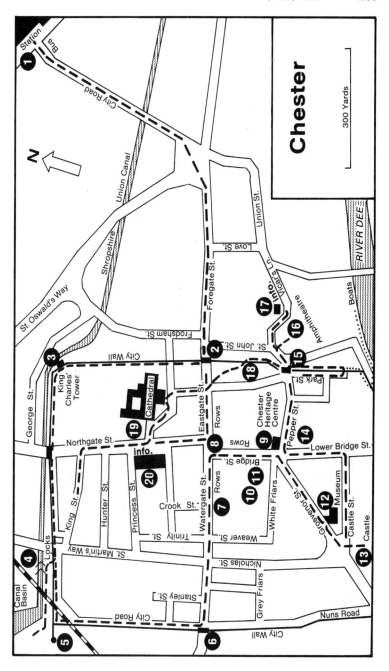

Chester

300 Yards

Town Crier shouts his proclamations here at 12 noon on Tuesdays through Saturdays, from May through August. Continue to the Row on the opposite side and follow Bridge Street to the right. There was once a Roman bath on this site, remains of which still exist in the crypts below. In two blocks you will reach the former St. Michael's Church, now the **Chester Heritage Centre** (9). Here, in addition to interesting artifacts, you can see an audiovisual presentation of the city's history. There is a well-stocked bookstall with local publications as well. *Open Sun., noon–5.*

Nearby, across Bridge Street and down Pierpoint Lane, is **The Dewa Roman Experience** (10), an archaeological site transformed into a theatrical show complete with the sights, sounds, and smells (!) of Roman Chester. *Open daily, 9–6; last admission at 5. Adults £3.80, seniors £3, children £1.90.* ☎ *(01244) 343-407.*

The **On The Air Museum** (11), practically next door on Lower Bridge Street, chronicles the story of British broadcasting from the days of crystal radios to satellite TV. The Golden Age of Wireless comes to life again with antique sets and recorded sounds; the Second World War is relived with period broadcasts. The workings of television are explained with working equipment, and there's a vintage sound shop where you can purchase restored classic radios, gramophones and the like. *Open Mon.–Sat. 10–5, Sun. 11–4:30. Closed Sun. and Mon. from Christmas to Easter. Admission to shop is free, with a charge for the museum.*

Stroll down Grosvenor Street to the **Grosvenor Museum** (12), which has an excellent exhibition of Roman life in Chester. Attached to it is an interesting 17th-century townhouse with room settings and costumes of bygone times. *Open Mon.–Sat. 10:30–5, Sun. 1–5. Free.* ☎ *(01244) 321-616.*

Chester Castle (13) is nearby. Construction on this began about 1070, but most of it was torn down during the 19th century to make way for government buildings. The only ancient structure still standing is the 13th-century Agricola Tower, which houses an old chapel. Close to it is the **Cheshire Military Museum**, which may be visited.

From here, Castle Street will take you to Lower Bridge Street, on which you make a left. You will soon pass the **Chester Toy and Doll Museum** (14), another nearby attraction. Over 5,000 toys from around the world and from different eras are on display, including the world's largest collection of Matchbox cars. *Open daily, 10–5. Adults £2; seniors, students, and children £1.* ☎ *(01244) 346-297, Internet: www.matchboxclub.com.*

At the corner of Pepper Street turn right and go through Newgate to the **Roman Gardens** (15), a collection of old ruins from other parts of town that have been relocated here. Continue on St. John's Street to the **Roman Amphitheatre** (16), of which only vestiges exist. Dating from about AD 100, this is the largest Roman structure of its type yet discovered in Britain.

Across the street is the **Chester Visitor & Craft Centre** (17) on Vicar's Lane. A tourist information office is located here, along with a variety of crafts shops and an audiovisual show of life in Chester's Rows. *Open May–Oct., Mon.–Sat. 9–7:30, Sun. 10–5; Nov.–April, Mon.–Sat. 9–5, Sun.*

10–4. Crafts shops. Café.

Return through Newgate and turn left on Park Street, passing an unusually attractive row of 17th-century timber-framed houses. At the end of the block climb the steps onto the **City Walls**. From here you can make a little side trip down to the River Dee, where boat trips are offered.

Back on the walls, continue over Newgate and the ancient Wolfe Gate to a modern pedestrian ramp on the left that leads to an indoor shopping center, the **Grosvenor Shopping Centre** (18). Here, in familiar surroundings, you can see the logical extension of the ideas incorporated in the medieval Rows adapted to contemporary use. Follow through the building and exit onto Eastgate Street.

St. Werburgh Street leads from here to:

*CHESTER CATHEDRAL (19), ☎ (01244) 324-756, Internet: www.chester cathedral.org.uk. *Open daily 7:30–6:30. Free, donations welcome. Gift shop. Café. Partial &.*

Begun as a Benedictine abbey in 1093 on the site of an earlier church, it was converted into a cathedral during the Reformation. Reflecting many centuries of change, its architectural styles range all the way from early Norman to late Perpendicular. Although not large, it is among the most interesting cathedrals in England. Be sure to see the **choir**, noted for its outstanding misericords, as well as the **cloister** and adjoining chapter house and refectory.

Leaving the cathedral, stroll up Northgate Street and walk a short distance down King Street for some pleasant views of Georgian houses. Returning on Northgate Street will bring you to the **Town Hall** (20), a Victorian Gothic structure that houses a branch of the tourist office. From here you can walk back to the train station.

Trip 43

St. Albans

The first Christian martyr in Britain was a Roman soldier named Alban, who lost his head around AD 209 for embracing the faith and sheltering a persecuted priest. The spot where this happened is now the town of St. Albans, overlooking the site of an important Roman city called *Verulamium*. An abbey in his memory was erected during the 8th century by King Offa II of Mercia. Following the Norman Conquest this was rebuilt and eventually became the great cathedral that it is today.

Verulamium itself died out after the fall of the empire, and slowly fell to ruin. Many of its stones were used to build the cathedral, but surprising amounts still remain in what is now parkland. There is a Roman theater, the only one of its kind in Britain, a well-preserved hypocaust, and large sections of the original walls. A splendid collection of archaeological finds is displayed in the Verulamium Museum. The town of St. Albans, on the other side of the River Ver, has a long and colorful history. Its medieval streets are lined with ancient structures which, added to the cathedral and remains of the Roman city, make this a satisfying destination for an easily accomplished daytrip.

GETTING THERE:

Trains leave London's King's Cross ThamesLink Station (connected by tunnel to the regular King's Cross Station) very frequently for the 25-minute run to St. Albans. They can be boarded earlier at London's Farringdon, City ThamesLink, Blackfriars, and London Bridge stations. Service is somewhat reduced on Sundays and holidays. Return trains run until late evening.

By car, St. Albans is 20 miles north of London via the M1 highway to Junction 6.

PRACTICALITIES:

Most of the sights are open daily throughout the year, with some closing or having reduced hours on Sundays and holidays. Open-air **markets** are held in St. Peter's Street on Wednesdays and Saturdays. There is also a Sunday Art Market from June through August. The local **Tourist Information Centre**, ☎ (01727) 864-511, Internet: www.stalbans.gov.uk, is in the Town Hall near the Market Place. St. Albans is in the county of Hertfordshire, and has a population of about 80,000.

FOOD AND DRINK:

There is no shortage of pubs and restaurants, of which some choices are:

Café des Amis (31 Market Place) An elegant place for excellent seafood and other Continental dishes. ☎ (01727) 853-569. X: Sun. £££

Upstairs, Downstairs (Waxhouse Gate, by the Clock Tower) English cuisine in a colorful setting. ☎ (01727) 854-843. ££ and £££

Chapter House Refectory (in the cathedral complex) Light lunches and refreshments. ☎ (01727) 864-208. X: Sun. lunch. £

Ye Olde Fighting Cocks (Abbey Mill Lane, by the river near Verulamium) A very ancient inn with substantial pub lunches. £

Kingsbury Mill Waffle House (St. Michael's St., in the Old Mill north of the Verulamium Museum) Belgian waffles with all kinds of healthy toppings, indoors or out. ☎ (01727) 853-502. X: Mon. £

SUGGESTED TOUR:

Numbers in parentheses correspond to numbers on the map.

Leave the train station (1) and follow Victoria Street to Chequer Street. This half-mile walk can be avoided by taking a bus. Once there, cut through a passageway to the **Market Place** and turn left. French Row retains much of its medieval appearance, including the 14th-century Fleur de Lys Inn where King John II of France was imprisoned following the Battle of Poitiers in 1356. Just beyond this is the **Clock Tower** (2), a flint-and-rubble structure of 1412, which is one of the few remaining curfew towers in the country. It may be climbed on weekends from Easter to October, from 10:30–5, for a good view.

Cross High Street and pass through the rebuilt Waxhouse Gateway, where pilgrims going to the shrine of St. Alban once bought their candles. From here a path leads to the west front of the:

*CATHEDRAL AND ABBEY CHURCH OF SAINT ALBAN (3), ☎ (01727) 860-780, Internet: www.stalbansdioc.org.uk/cathedral. *Open daily 9–5:45, closing at 1 on Christmas Day. Free, donation accepted. Audiovisual show: Adults £1.50, children £1. Guided tours at 11:30 and 2:30 on weekdays, 11:30 and 2 on Sat., and 2:30 on Sun. Gift shop. Restaurant. Mostly &.*

An abbey church dedicated to St. Alban stood here since Saxon times, but the present structure, one of the largest cathedrals in England, was begun in the 11th century by the Normans and incorporates many later additions. It did not become a cathedral until 1877, when a new diocese was created. The interior is rather plain but graceful. A good deal of the original **wall paintings**, once whitewashed by the Puritans, have been restored to their former splendor. Be sure to see ***St. Alban's Shrine** in the chapel behind the altar screen. Dating from the 14th century, this was later destroyed and rebuilt in 1872, when over 2,000 of its broken fragments were carefully pieced together. It was again restored in 1993, and re-consecrated.

The whole drama of the cathedral's history is brought to life with an audiovisual show in the south aisle, shown on weekdays from 11 to 4, on Saturdays from 11 to 3:30, and on Sundays from 2–5.

Leave the cathedral and stroll past the **Abbey Gateway** of 1361, at one time the town jail and now occupied by St. Albans School, founded in the 10th century. Abbey Mill Lane leads to the site of Roman Verulamium. The **Fighting Cocks Inn**, by the river, was a notorious center of cockfighting and claims to be one of the oldest pubs in England. It is also a fine place to stop for lunch or just a drink.

Cross the bridge and explore the remains of ancient **Verulamium**. The importance of this city is made obvious by the fact that it was the only town in Britain to be declared a *municipum*, a status that conferred Roman citizenship on its inhabitants. Founded shortly after the conquest of AD 43 and sacked by Boadicea in AD 61, it rose to become the third-largest city, after London and Colchester, in Roman Britain. The town flourished until about 410, when it fell into decay, and what was left after the stones were salvaged was slowly covered by earth.

Continue on past remains of the Roman walls to the **Hypocaust** (4), a preserved mosaic floor and heating system of a large house, now protected *in situ* by a modern structure. A path leads to the:

*VERULAMIUM MUSEUM (5), ☎ (01727) 866-100. *Open Mon.–Sat. 10–5:30, Sun. 2–5:30. Adults £3, seniors and children £1.70. Museum shop.* ᕒ.

Here the most modern techniques are used to display some of Roman Britain's greatest treasures. These include jewelry, household utensils, pottery, wall paintings, a bronze figure, and many other fascinating objects discovered during excavations. There are also re-created Roman rooms, some with the original wall plaster.

St. Michael's Church, near the museum entrance, was begun in 948 and still retains considerable traces of its original Saxon work. Inside, there is a monument to Sir Francis Bacon, who is buried here.

Walk across the street to the **Roman Theatre** (6), built to accommodate a crowd of 1,600 spectators. Semicircular in shape, it is the only one of its type in Britain. Although only the lower walls remain, visualizing what it must have looked like is not too difficult. *Open daily, 10–5, closing at 4 in winter. Adults £1.50, children 50p.* ☎ *(01727) 835-035.*

Return to St. Michael's Street and turn left. At the River Ver is the **Kingsbury Water Mill** (7), which operated until 1936. There was a mill on this site since Saxon times and the present one, restored in 1970, is now a delightful museum where you can climb around inside the old mechanisms. *Open Mon.–Sat. 11–6, Sun. noon–6. Adults £1.10, children 60p.* ☎

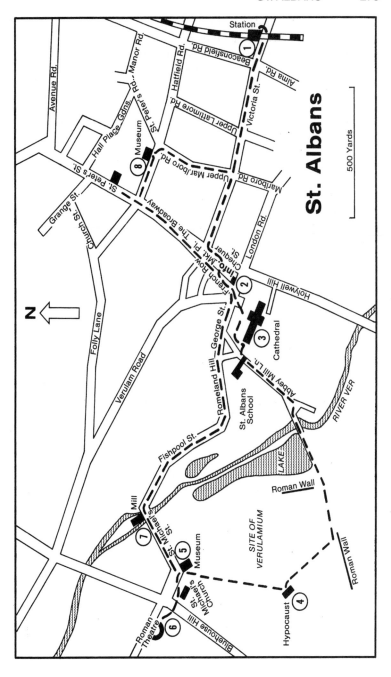

St. Albans

(01727) 853-502. The same structure also houses a charming waffle restaurant, which only adds to your pleasure.

Follow the map past wonderful old houses on Fishpool Street, Romeland Hill, and George Street. Turn left on French Row and continue up St. Peter's Street to St. Peter's Church. A right on Hatfield Road leads to the **Museum of St. Albans** (8), whose exhibits concentrate on local crafts and industries, bygones, natural history, and regional archaeology. *Open Mon.–Sat., 10–5, Sun. 2–5. Free. Gift shop.* ☎ *(01727) 819-340.* From here it's only a short walk back to the station.

Nottingham

Nottingham is a good introduction to the industrial Midlands, a part of England too often overlooked by visitors. This sprawling, vigorous, surprisingly attractive city has superb museums, excellent shopping facilities, and some of the most interesting pubs in the country.

Best known for the legendary Robin Hood, Nottingham dates back to the Anglo-Saxon village of *Snotingaham,* a site captured by Danes in AD 868. William the Conqueror built a massive castle here in 1068, which became a stronghold of bad King John in the 13th century. The Civil War began nearby when Charles I unfurled his banner in defiance of Parliament during the mid-17th century. It was the Industrial Revolution, however, that really molded the city's character and made it the thriving place it is today.

GETTING THERE:

Trains depart London's St. Pancras Station hourly for the less-than-two-hour ride to Nottingham. Service is reduced on Saturdays and poor on Sundays and holidays. Return service operates until early evening.

By car, Nottingham is 123 miles northwest of London via the M1.

PRACTICALITIES:

The best time to visit Nottingham is on a working day, when the city bustles with activity. Most of the museums are open daily. The local **Tourist Information Centre,** ☎ (0115) 915-53-30, is at 1 Smithy Row, just east of the Old Market Square. Nottingham is the county town of Nottinghamshire, and has a population of about 27,000.

FOOD AND DRINK:

Some choice places for lunch are:

Loch Fyne Oyster Bar (17 King St., 2 blocks northeast of Old Market Square) Seafood in the Scottish manner. ☎ (0115) 950-84-81. X: Sun. ££

Sonny's (3 Carlton St., 4 blocks east of the tourist office) Contemporary British cuisine in a smart setting. ☎ (0115) 947-30-41. ££

Merchants (29 High Pavement, near the Galleries of Justice) A popular local eatery and bar. ☎ (0115) 958-98-98. X: Sun. eve. ££

Ye Olde Trip to Jerusalem (Brewhouse Yard) An historic pub with origins in the 12th century. Traditional foods and daily specials. ☎ (0115) 947-31-71. £

Salutation Inn (Hounds Gate) A truly ancient historic pub with a large variety of tasty dishes. ☎ (0115) 950-46-27. £

SUGGESTED TOUR:
Numbers in parentheses correspond to numbers on the map.

Leaving the **train station** (1), turn right on Carrington Street and left on Canal Street. Follow the map to **Brewhouse Yard** (2), a group of 17th-century houses huddled against a cliff under the castle's ancient walls. Manmade caves lead from inside these to rooms carved from solid rock. The first building is the famous **Ye Olde Trip to Jerusalem**, which claims to be the oldest inn in England and one frequented by crusaders on their way to the Holy Land. It is alleged that Robin Hood himself quaffed a few beers here. The pub bears the date 1189, though this must refer to the underground portions only. In any case, it's a colorful place to stop for a drink.

The other houses now form the intriguing **Brewhouse Yard Museum of Nottingham Life**, which presents a realistic glimpse into everyday domestic and working life in Nottingham over the past three centuries, and is a treat not to be missed. Here you'll experience an old-time schoolroom, a Victorian home, a busy shopping day in the 1920s, caves used as air raid shelters, and much more. *Open daily 10–4, closed on Fri. from Nov.–Feb. Closed Dec. 24–Jan. 1. Admission free on Mon.–Fri. On weekends and Bank Holidays the charges are: Adults £2, seniors and children £1.* ☎ *(0115) 915-36-00. Gift shop. Partial* &.

Continue up Castle Road to the bronze **Statue of Robin Hood**, (3) where plaques depict scenes from the legend. Just beyond this, to the left, is the entrance to:

NOTTINGHAM CASTLE (4), ☎ (0115) 915-37-00. *Open daily, 10–5, closed Fri. from Nov.–Feb. Closed Dec. 24–Jan. 1. Admission free on weekdays. On weekends and Bank Holidays the charges are: Adults £2, seniors, students, and children £1. Cave tours on Mon.–Fri. at 2 and 3 (additional tours in summer), adults £2, children £1. Craft shop. Café.*

Once home to the evil Sheriff of Nottingham, the original Norman fortress was torn down in 1651 following the Civil War and replaced by a ducal palace, which became the city's major museum in 1878. It features a lively audio-visual presentation of the city's history along with artifacts, a collection of the fine and applied arts, archaeological finds, and the like. For many, the best attraction here is the somewhat strenuous *guided tour through subterranean passages, caves, and dungeons to the infamous *Mortimer's Hole. Lasting about 30 minutes, these are conducted at regular intervals in the afternoons, Mondays through Fridays.

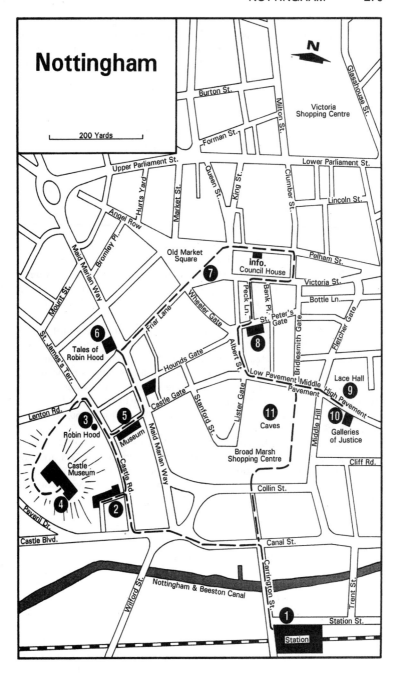

Nottingham

200 Yards

N

Burton St.
Victoria Shopping Centre
Forman St.
Upper Parliament St.
Lower Parliament St.
Hurts Yard
Market St.
Queen St.
King St.
Clumber St.
Lincoln St.
Angel Row
Bromley Pl.
Old Market Square
info. Council House
Pelham St.
Victoria St.
Maid Marian Way
Mount St.
Wheeler Gate
Friar Lane
Peck Ln.
Bank Pl.
St. Peter's Gate
Bridlesmith Gate
Bottle Ln.
Fletcher Gate
St. James's Terr.
6 Tales of Robin Hood
7
8
Albert St.
Lister Gate
Lace Hall
9
Hounds Gate
Low Pavement
Middle Pavement
High Pavement
Lenton Rd.
3
5
Castle Gate
Stanford St.
11 Caves
10 Galleries of Justice
Robin Hood
Museum
Maid Marian Way
Broad Marsh Shopping Centre
Middle Hill
Cliff Rd.
Castle Museum
Peveril Dr.
4
2
Castle Rd.
Collin St.
Castle Blvd.
Canal St.
Wilford St.
Carrington St.
Trent St.
Nottingham & Beeston Canal
1
Station St.
Station

Stroll over to Castle Gate and visit the **Museum of Costumes and Textiles** (5), which presents superb examples of the products for which Nottingham has long been noted. Costumes from 1790 to the mid-20th century are displayed in a series of authentically-furnished period room settings. *Open Wed.–Sun., 10–4. Closed Mon., Tues., Dec.24–Jan. 1. Free.* ☎ *(0115) 915-53-00.* Continue on to busy Maid Marian Way and turn left. The **Salutation Inn** at Hounds Gate is another famous medieval pub, and makes a very inviting pit stop.

You're now just a block away from the **Tales of Robin Hood** (6), an enjoyable commercial attraction where visitors take a dramatic ride through a re-created Sherwood Forest complete with figures, sounds, and smells. At the end, there's an exhibition and film on the "life" of the elusive outlaw, and a chance to try your hand at archery. *Open daily 10–6, last admission at 4:30. Closed Dec. 25–26. Adults £4.75, seniors and students £4.25, children £3.75.* ☎ *(0115) 948-32-84, Internet: http://members.aol.com/ trobinhood. Gift shop. Café.* &.

Now wander up Friar Lane to the **Old Market Square** (7), where a heavily-disguised Robin won the Sheriff's archery competition. Or so they say. Anyway, it's an impressive open area dominated by the massive **Council House**, home of the tourist office. At its far end turn right and stroll down to the 11th-century **St. Peter's Church** (8). Although modified in later years, its interior is still fascinating.

Low Pavement is reached via Albert Street. From here an interesting side trip could be made to the Lace Market district, beginning at High Pavement. If you're interested, the story of Nottingham lace is beautifully told at the **Museum of Nottingham Lace** (9). Demonstrations of both hand and machine lace making are given in the setting of an exquisite exhibition, and there's a shop with a fine selection of the finished product. *Open daily, 10–5. Closed Dec. 25–26, Jan. 1. Adults £2.95, seniors £2.50, children 5-16 £1.95.* ☎ *(0115) 989-73-65.*

Nearby, on the other side of the street, is the forbidding ***Galleries of Justice** (10), located in the old Shire Hall. Interactive displays and costumed interpreters take you from a simulated crime scene to an original 1905 police station that remained in use until 1985. There you'll be read your rights and fingerprinted. A trial follows, possibly sending you to hard labor in the prison laundry, or at least to Australia. The history of crime and punishment through the ages is well covered in two Victorian courtrooms, an 1800 prison, cave cells, and much, much more. In the end, you're free to leave, but be sure to allow plenty of time for the experience. *Open Tues.–Sun. and Bank Holidays, 10–5. Last admission at 4. Closed Dec. 24–26, Jan. 1. Adults £7.95, seniors £6.95, children 5-16 £4.95. Gift shop. Café.* ☎ *(0115) 952-05-58, Internet: www.galleryofjustice.org.uk. Mostly* &.

As you've no doubt discovered by now, Nottingham is riddled with man-made caves, some of which you may have encountered at Brewhouse Yard, the Castle, and at the Galleries of Justice. The best place to really explore them, however, is from the nearby **Broad Marsh Shopping Centre**

(11), conveniently on the way back to the train station. Here you'll find an attraction called the **Caves of Nottingham**, from which you can descend underground into a medieval tannery, a pub cellar, a Victorian slum, an air raid shelter, water wells, and more. *Open Mon.–Sat. 10–5, Sun. 11–5. Last admission at 4. Closed Dec. 24–26, Jan. 1. Adults £3.25, seniors, students, children £2.25.* ☎ *(0115) 924-1424.*

Stamford

One of the most beautiful towns in England, Stamford has changed little since its period of prosperity during Georgian times. Its narrow streets are lined with mellowed stone houses, and its many church spires look down on the peaceful River Welland. This is a delightful place to explore on foot, a tranquil town whose roots are planted firmly in the past. Nearby Burghley House is considered to be Britain's finest stately home of the Elizabethan era and is worth the trip in itself.

According to local legend, Stamford's history goes back to the time of King Bladud, centuries before the birth of Christ. What is more certain is that it was mentioned in a grant of about AD 600, and was the seat of an important college in the 14th century, although only traces of this remain today. During the Middle Ages it was home to several monasteries and nunneries, allegedly connected to each other by underground tunnels. In 1646, King Charles I spent one of his last nights here as a free man before being turned over to Cromwell's Parliament and beheaded.

A daytrip to Stamford is easily accomplished, and offers a wonderful chance to get away from the tourist hordes.

GETTING THERE:

Trains depart London's King's Cross Station frequently for Peterborough, where there is a connecting local to Stamford. The total journey takes about 90 minutes, with return trains until mid-evening. Service is reduced on Sundays and holidays.

By car, Stamford is 91 miles north of London via the A1 highway.

PRACTICALITIES:

Burghley House is open daily from Easter to early October, while the Stamford Museum is open on Mondays through Saturdays. The local **Tourist Information Centre**, ☎ (01780) 755-611, Internet: www.stamford.co.uk, is in the Arts Centre at 27 St. Mary's Street. Markets are held on Fridays and Saturdays. Stamford is in the county of Lincolnshire, and has a population of about 18,000.

FOOD AND DRINK:

Some choice places for lunch are:

The George of Stamford (71 St. Martin's High St., near the Town Bridge)

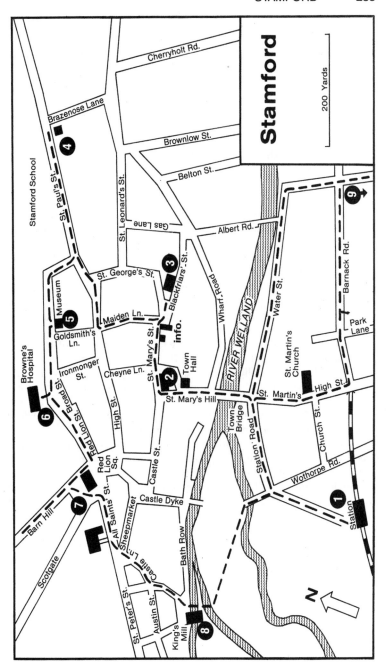

An historic 17th-century inn with an excellent restaurant. ☎ (01780) 750-750. ££

Lady Anne's Hotel (37 St. Martin's High St., near St. Martin's Church) Good food in a pleasant old country hotel. ☎ (01780) 481-184. ££

Raj of India (2 All Saint's St., just west of Red Lion Sq.) A favorite place for tasty Indian dishes. ☎ (01780) 753-556. ££

Green Man (29 Scotgate, near Red Lion Sq.) Lunch in a cozy pub. ☎ (01780) 753-598. X for food: Sun. £

SUGGESTED TOUR:

Numbers in parentheses correspond to numbers on the map.

Leave the **train station** (1) and follow the map across the Town Bridge to the Town Hall. Just beyond this is **St. Mary's Church** (2), built in the 13th century with an enormous spire added centuries later. Inside, there is a wonderful Corpus Christi chapel near the choir with a beautifully painted ceiling from about 1480.

Turn right on St. Mary's Street and pass the Old Theatre, opened in 1768. Around the corner is St. George's Square with its elegant Assembly Room of 1727. Both this and the theater have been restored and now house the **Arts Centre** and tourist office. **St. George's Church** (3) has some interesting medieval stained glass dating to a reconstruction of 1449.

Maiden Lane leads to High Street. The Public Library, a classical structure of 1804, was originally a meat market. Bear right and follow St. Paul's Street to the Stamford School, founded in 1532 with an earlier 12th-century chapel. Opposite this, incorporated in the school wall, is the ancient **gateway** (4) of Brasenose College, built for students who had fled Oxford in the 1330s, but demolished some 300 years later.

Retrace your steps and make a right up Star Lane. Broad Street has been a market since the earliest times. **Stamford Museum** (5) features a small but rather interesting collection of local history and archaeology. Be on the lookout for the life-size figure of one Daniel Lambert, a local man who weighed nearly 53 stone (739 pounds!) at the time of his death in 1809. He was the largest man in England. *Open Mon.–Sat., 10–5, and Sun. from April–Sept., 2–5. Admission free.* ☎ (01780) 766-317.

A little farther on is **Browne's Hospital** (6), one of England's most outstanding medieval almshouses. Founded in the 15th century, it has an attractive chapel and cloisters that may be visited, as well as a small museum of almshouse life. *Open May–Sept., Sat.–Sun., 11–4. Nominal admission.*

From here continue on to **Red Lion Square** (7). All Saints' Church dominates the scene with its towering spire; inside there are some fine old brasses. A stroll up Barn Hill will reward you with some particularly nice Queen Anne and Georgian houses. Stukeley House, at number 9, was the home of William Stukeley (1687–1765), the famous and rather eccentric archaeologist who first connected Stonehenge with the Druids. He was also the vicar of All Saints' Church.

A stroll down All Saints' Streets takes you past the Stamford Steam Brewery Museum, now closed for restoration. Hopefully this will reopen in the near future.

Follow the map down winding passageways to the ancient **King's Mill** (8) on the River Welland. Mentioned in the Domesday Book of 1086, it is now a home for retarded children. A path leads through a charming park to Station Road.

From here you can walk or drive to Burghley House, about a mile away:

*BURGHLEY HOUSE (9), ☎ (01780) 752-451, Internet: www.stamford.co.uk/ burghley. *Open April–early Oct., daily 11–4:30. Admission: Adults £6.10, seniors £5.85. Restaurant.*

Built in the 16th century, this is probably the finest Elizabethan mansion in all England. It is located in an enormous park designed in the 18th century by the famous landscape architect "Capability" Brown. The superb art collection must be the envy of many a major museum, with over 300 paintings including works by Brueghel and Gainsborough. These are displayed in rooms whose walls and ceilings are literally covered with depictions of frolicking gods and goddesses, especially in the Heaven Room and the Hell Staircase. Be sure to allow more than an hour to take it in before returning to the train station.

Trip 46

Lincoln

T here are really two Lincolns, one a hundred feet above the other. What is probably the finest cathedral in England dominates the countryside from its lofty perch in the upper town. It was here, on the site of a Celtic settlement, that the Romans built their fortress of *Lindum Colonia* in AD 47, one of the greatest colonies in Britain. As this grew, it descended the hill to the River Witham, and was taken over first by the Saxons and later by the Danes. William the Conqueror also knew a good location when he saw one. Parts of his castle, erected atop the hill in 1068, still stand among the later additions.

Lincoln is particularly rich in structures from Roman and early medieval times. Its wealth was based on the wool trade, which declined in the 14th century as business moved to larger ports on the seacoast. The plague of 1349 decimated its population and by the 18th century Lincoln was almost a ghost town. Revival started with the coming of the railways a hundred years later. Today it is the lower town that grows and prospers as a regional shopping center with high-tech industries, while the beautifully preserved ancient quarter on the hill attracts visitors by the thousands.

GETTING THERE:

Trains leave London's King's Cross Station several times in the morning for Newark Northgate, where they connect with locals (or buses) for Lincoln. The total journey takes about two hours, with return trains until mid-evening. Service is very poor on Sundays and holidays.

By car, Lincoln is 133 miles north of London. Take the A1 highway to Newark and then change to the A46.

PRACTICALITIES:

Lincoln may be visited just about any time, as most of the sights are open daily. Train service is almost non-existent on Sundays and holidays. The local **Tourist Information Centre**, ☎ (01522) 529-828, Internet: www.lin coln-info.org.uk, is at 9 Castle Hill, near the cathedral. Lincoln is the county town of Lincolnshire, and has a population of about 80,000.

During the tourist season, **Guide Friday** operates a hop-on, hop-off open-top double-decker bus service connecting the sights and the train station at either 30-minute or hourly intervals. Unlimited use fares for one day are: Adults £5.50, seniors and students £4, children £2. Single-ride fares are also available. Tickets are sold by the driver. ☎ (01522) 522-255, Internet: www.guidefriday.com.

FOOD AND DRINK:

There are a great many restaurants and pubs in all price ranges along most of the walking route. Some particularly fine choices are:

The Jew's House Restaurant (15 The Straight, just below Steep Hill) Imaginative food in the historic 12th-century Jew's House. ☎ (01522) 524-851. X: Sun., Mon., Sat. lunch. ££ and £££

Wig and Mitre (32 Steep Hill, below the cathedral) A traditional pub with tasty food served all day long. ☎ (01522) 535-190. £ and ££

Lion and Snake (79 Bailgate, near the cathedral) Lincoln's oldest pub offers both light and full restaurant meals, along with traditional hand-pulled beers. ☎ (01522) 523-770. £ and ££

Stoke's High Bridge Café (207 High St. at the river) Light lunches and afternoon teas in a 16th-century half-timbered house on the bridge. ☎ (01522) 513-825. X: Sun. £

Spinning Wheel (39 Steep Hill, below the cathedral) Light meals and pastries. ☎ (01522) 522-463. £

Brown's Pie Shop (33 Steep Hill) Lincolnshire meat pies and other delights. ☎ (01522) 527-330. £

Cloister Coffee Shop (in the cathedral) Inexpensive (but good) cafeteria fare right off the cloisters. £

SUGGESTED TOUR:

Numbers in parentheses correspond to numbers on the map.

Begin at **Central Station** (1) and turn right on High Street. At this point you will have to decide whether or not to make the climb on foot. The section between The Strait and the cathedral is very steep and closed to traffic, but includes some of the most picturesque sights in town. An alternative is to take a bus or taxi to the cathedral and alter the walk accordingly.

Those walking should continue on High Street to the **High Bridge** (2), originally built by the Normans in the 12th century. This is one of the few bridges in England to still carry a house, in this case a 16th-century half-timbered structure. Beyond this is the **Stonebow** (3), a 15th-century town gate on the site of an earlier Roman gateway. The **Guildhall**, built above the arch, may be visited. *Tours on Fri. and first Sat. of every month, 10:30 and 1:30. Free.* ☎ *(01522) 873-507.*

Pass under it and continue on High Street to The Strait, the heart of medieval Lincoln, where the real climb begins. The famous early-12th-century **Jew's House** (4), now a restaurant, is among the oldest domestic buildings in England. **Steep Hill**, an apt name, leads past several other ancient

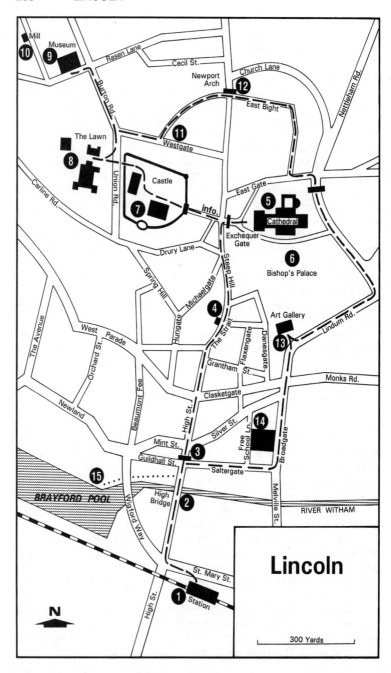

houses to Castle Hill. The tourist office is on the corner. Turn right and pass through the 14th-century Exchequer Gate to:

*LINCOLN CATHEDRAL (5), ☎ (01522) 544-544. *Open June–Aug., Mon.–Sat. 7:15 a.m.–8 p.m., Sun. 7:15–6; Sept.–May, Mon.–Sat. 7:15–6, Sun. 7:15–5. Evensong Mon.–Sat. at 5:15, Sun. 3:45. Suggested donation: Adults £3, seniors and children £1. Guided tours. Cafeteria. Gift shop. &.*

This considered by many to be the finest cathedral in England. Its fabric contains a mixture of every architectural style from early Norman to Victorian Gothic, but it is basically a product of the 12th and 13th centuries. The splendid **West Front**, facing you, incorporates parts of an earlier cathedral completed in 1092.

Enter the nave and stroll up to the south transept, which has a lovely rose window known as the ***Bishop's Eye**. Opposite this is the **Dean's Eye** in the north transept, a similar window of 13th-century stained glass. ***St. Hugh's Choir**, beyond the crossing, was begun in 1192 and is noted for its elaborately carved stalls, whose misericords are among the best in the country. Behind the High Altar is the renowned ***Angel Choir**, a supreme achievement in beauty. The famous carving of the **Lincoln Imp** can be seen atop the northeast column. At the rear of the cathedral is the great east window, the best of its period.

Walk out into the **Cloisters**, known for their carved wooden vaultings and bosses, and visit the **Library**, designed by Sir Christopher Wren in 1674. Close to this is the graceful 13th-century **Chapter House** where some of the first meetings of Parliament took place.

Leave the cathedral and stroll around its close, perhaps visiting the remains of the **Bishops' Old Palace** (6). In medieval times the bishops of Lincoln enjoyed power on a scale equal to the king's, and lived accordingly. All that came to an end during the Civil War, and the luxurious palace has since fallen to ruin. Strangely, the gardens here boast what is probably the most northerly vineyard in Europe. *Open April–Oct., daily, 10–6; Nov.–March, Sat.–Sun. 10–4. Adults £1.10, seniors and students 80p, children 60p. ☎ (01522) 527-468.*

Return to Castle Hill and enter:

LINCOLN CASTLE (7), ☎ (01522) 511-068. *Open Mon.–Sat. 9:30–5:30, Sun. 11–5:30, closing at 4 in winter. Adults £2.50, seniors £1.50, children £1. Restaurant. Gift shop. Limited &.*

Lincoln Castle was begun in 1068 by William the Conqueror himself. Little remains of the original structure besides portions of the wall, but there are attractions here that should not be missed. The castle was greatly modified over the centuries, used as a prison from 1787 to 1878, and currently houses courts, archives, and some interesting displays. To your left is the *Magna Carta Exhibition, where one of the four surviving original copies of the Magna Carta is on view. Signed by bad King John at Runnymede in 1215 and preserved in Lincoln ever since, this document is regarded as the foundation of civil liberties and the rule of law. Behind this is the former Old County Gaol (jail), where you can visit a very strange **chapel** with coffin-like pews, and experience a good old-fashioned "fire and brimstone" sermon being inflicted on the poor felons.

Outside the jail but still within the castle grounds, be sure to see the 13th-century **Cobb Hall** in the northeast corner, an eerie place of confinement and public execution until 1859. The **Observatory Tower** in the southeast corner can be climbed for an excellent view. The keep, or **Lucy Tower**, is probably of 12th-century origin and contains the graves of some criminals hanged in the 19th century.

Leave this powerfully evocative place via its West Gate and cross Union Road to **The Lawn** (8). Built in 1820 as a pioneering mental hospital, this impressive complex closed in the 1980s and has since been refurbished by the city as a mixture of attractions for both local citizens and visitors. Of particular interest is the **Archaeology Centre** where local digs are explained, the **Sir Joseph Banks Conservatory** where an extensive range of tropical plants is displayed in natural settings within a 5,000-square-foot greenhouse, and the **Charlesworth Suite** with its re-creation of life in the asylum that previously occupied this complex. There are also several shops, a restaurant, a tea room, and an information center.

Just north of The Lawn is the **Museum of Lincolnshire Life** (9), a vast and well-displayed collection of all sorts of bygones from the county's past. Among the items on display are traction engines and a tank, 19th-century room settings, and a noted collection of farming items. *Open May–Sept., daily 10–5:30; Oct.–April, Mon.–Sat. 10–5:30, Sun. 2–5:30. Closed Good Friday, Dec. 24–27. Adults £2, children 60p. Café. Gift shop. ☎ (01522) 528-448. Partially ♿.*

Almost around the corner from it stands the **Ellis Mill** (10), an 18th-century windmill that remained in service until 1940 and is now fully restored. *Open May–Sept., Sat.–Sun. 2–6; Oct.–April, Sun. 2–dusk. Adults 70p, children 30p. Gift shop. ☎ (01522) 523-870.*

Follow the map to the **Toy Museum** (11) on Westgate. As much for adults as it is for children, the vast collection of toys and amusements include working penny slot machines from seaside piers. Bags of the old pennies are available at the counter. Have fun! *Open Easter through Sept., Tues.–Sat. 11–5, Sun. and Bank Holidays noon–4; Oct.–Christmas Sat. and school holidays 11–5, Sun. noon–4. Closed Christmas to Easter. Adults £1.90, seniors £1.50, children 5–16 £1. Gift shop. ☎ (01522) 520-534. ♿.*

Continue on to **Newport Arch** (12). Dating from the 2nd century AD, this is the only remaining Roman gateway in Britain that still spans a road. Return on East Bight, passing the remains of a Roman wall and emerging at Eastgate.

Pottergate and Lindum Road lead to the **Usher Gallery** (13), a splendid collection of art, ancient relics, antique timepieces, porcelains, and other beautiful objects. *Open Mon.–Sat. 10–5:30, Sun. 2:30–5. Closed Good Friday, Dec. 24–26, Jan. 1. Adults £2, students and children 50p. Free on Fri. Café. Gift shop.* ☎ *(01522) 527-980.* ♿.

Just beyond, on Broadgate, is the **Greyfriars Exhibition Centre** (14), housing local archaeological finds, historical items, and the like in a 13th-century priory. *Open Wed.–Sat. 10–1 and 2–4. Closed Dec. 24–26, Jan 1. Free. Gift shop.* ☎ *(01522) 530-401. Limited* ♿.

From here you can head back to the train station via High Bridge, perhaps stopping at the adjacent **Brayford Pool** (15), a colorful old inland port that now serves as a marina. **Boat trips** aboard the MV *City of Lincoln,* lasting about one hour, are available here. *Operates daily from Easter to early Oct., departures at 11, noon, 1:30, 3, and 4. Adults £4, seniors and students £3.50, children £2.50. Snacks and bar.* ☎ *(01522) 546- 853.* ♿ *by prior arrangement.*

Trip 47

*York

Two hundred miles may seem like a long way to go for a daytrip, but York is really worth it. Incredibly, the train ride there takes less than two hours, zipping along at up to 140 mph! And if you're driving, why not stay overnight and explore the city at a more leisurely pace? Either way, York also makes a wonderful stopover en route to Scotland or the North of England.

The ancient Britons called it *Caer Ebrauc*, but York was really established in AD 71 by the Romans. Their fortress, known as *Eboracum*, became the headquarters of the Sixth Legion. The emperor Hadrian visited in AD 121, and Constantine the Great was proclaimed Emperor of Rome there in 306. After the fall of the empire and a dark era of destruction, York reemerged as the Saxon town of *Eoforwic*, playing a prominent part in the spread of Christianity and learning. In 867 it fell to the Vikings and acquired the named *Jorvik*, which lasted until 944 when it became part of the Anglo-Saxon kingdom of England.

William the Conqueror marched north to York following the Norman Conquest; putting down all revolts, scorching the earth around him, and building the inevitable castle. The city flourished as a religious center during the 13th century, but entered a period of decline in the 16th after Henry VIII put an end to the Church's power. Although little affected by the Industrial Revolution, York came back to life with the arrival of the railways in the 1830s, and has prospered ever since as a major communications center. For visitors, however, its chief attraction is its magnificently preserved past, those ancient stones that still bring to life the Roman, Viking, medieval, and later eras.

GETTING THERE:

Trains operated by GNER depart London's King's Cross Station at least hourly for the less-than-two-hour ride to York. Return trains operate until mid-evening; service is poor on Sundays and holidays. BritRail Pass holders will really get their money's worth on this trip.

By car, York is about 200 miles north of London. Take the M1 beyond Leeds, then the A64 into York. It is advisable to use the Park & Ride facility along the A64 at Askham Bar, taking the bus from there into the city. *Secure parking is free; the round-trip bus fare is £1.30.* ☎ *(01904) 431-388.*

PRACTICALITIES:

Most of the attractions in York are open daily throughout the year, but some close or have shorter hours on Sundays and/or holidays. The local **Tourist Information Centre**, ☎ (01904) 621-756, Internet: www.york.gov.uk, is in the DeGrey Rooms on Exhibition Square near Bootham Bar. There is also a handy branch in the train station. Either can help you find accommodations should you decide to stay overnight. Another Internet site to try is: www.york-tourism.co.uk.

Guide Friday operates a hop-on, hop-off open-top double-decker bus service connecting the various tourist sites at frequent intervals. One day tickets for unlimited rides cost: Adults £7.50, seniors and students £6, children £2.50. Pay the driver or purchase at the tourist office. ☎ (01904) 640-896, Internet: www.guidefriday.com.

York is in the county of North Yorkshire and has a population of 125,000.

FOOD AND DRINK:

York abounds in colorful, inexpensive restaurants and pubs. Some good choices for lunch are:

19 Grape Lane (19 Grape Lane, 2 blocks south of York Minster) Light, high-quality English lunches, both traditional and contemporary. ☎ (01904) 636-366. X: Sun. ££

Betty's (6 St. Helens Sq., 3 blocks southwest of York Minster) A traditional tea room with old-fashioned home cooking. ☎ (01904) 659-142. £

Plunket's (9 High Petergate, just south of York Minster) A friendly place for modern, light dishes. ☎ (01904) 637-722. £

St. William's Restaurant (College St. by St. William's College) Light lunches in a medieval courtyard. ☎ (01904) 634-830. £

Ye Olde Starre Inn (40 Stonegate, 2 blocks southwest of York Minster) Traditional pub food in a Victorian setting, with an outdoor beer garden. ☎ (01904) 623-063. £

The Rubicon (5 Little Stonegate, 2 blocks south of York Minster) A delightful place for vegetarian meals. BYOB. ☎ (01904) 676-076. X: Sun. lunch, Mon. lunch. £

Oscars Wine Bar & Bistro (8 Little Stonegate, 2 blocks south of York Minster) A wide variety of creative dishes, including vegetarian, served indoors or in a courtyard. ☎ (01904) 652-002. £

King's Arms (King's Staith, by the River Ouse) Lunch in a pub overlooking the river. £

SUGGESTED TOUR:

Numbers in parentheses correspond to numbers on the map.

Leaving the **train station** (1), you may prefer to begin with a nearby major attraction, or to save this treat for the end of the tour. Either way, don't miss the:

*NATIONAL RAILWAY MUSEUM (2), Leeman Rd., York, ☎ (01904) 621-261, Internet: www.nmsi.ac.uk/nrm/html. *Open daily 10–6. Closed Dec. 24–26.*

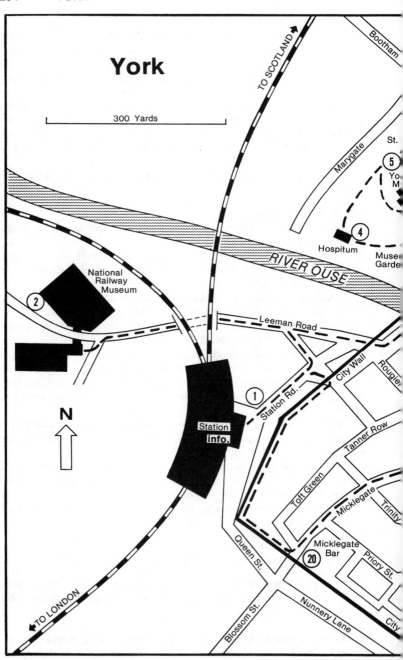

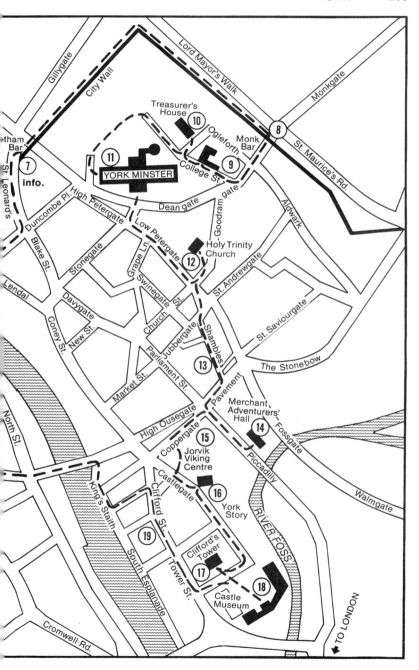

Adults £5.90, seniors £4.90, children 0–16 free. Restaurant. Café. Gift shop. &.

Located in refurbished railway buildings, this is the largest museum of its kind it Britain and probably the best in the world. Anyone who loves old trains will be absolutely mesmerized by the displays, ranging from a working replica of the 1829 *Rocket* to the Eurostar of today. Included are Queen Victoria's private cars, the world's fastest steam engine, and many, many others, exhibited both indoors and out in the yards. Allow plenty of time for this magnificent attraction.

Return via Leeman Road and, passing through the city walls, turn left on Station Road. Cross over the River Ouse on Lendal Bridge, then make a left into Museum Gardens, which you may want to visit. On your right is the **Multangular Tower** (3), a corner of the original Roman walls. Its lower 19 feet date from about AD 300, while the upper parts are medieval. A path to the left leads to the **Hospitum** (4), a 16th-century guest house of St. Mary's Abbey. Extensive archaeological collections are displayed on its two floors. Continuing along the path, you'll soon come to the ruins of the **Abbey** (5) itself, once the most important Benedictine monastery in the North of England. Next to this is the **Yorkshire Museum** (6), featuring splendid galleries of Anglo-Saxon and Viking life along with other ancient diggings. It's most important treasure is the famous *Middleham Jewel, a 15th-century gold pendant fitted with a whopper of a sapphire. There are also excellent special exhibitions. *Open April–Oct., daily 10–5; Nov.–March, Mon.–Sat. 10–5, Sun. 1–5. Adults £3.60, children £2.30.* ☎ *(01904) 629-745.*

Leave the gardens by the same gate and turn left on Museum Street. Another left at St. Leonard's takes you past the tourist office and the **City Art Gallery** on Exhibition Square, where you can see some six centuries of European paintings. *Open Mon.–Sat. 10–5, Sun. 2:30–5. Free. Museum shop.* ☎ *(01904) 551-861.* &.

Facing this is **Bootham Bar** (7), a defensive bastion dating from early Norman times. Cross the intersection and climb the steps to the top of the **City Walls.** From here the walk reveals wonderful glimpses of the Minster and its gardens. Descend at the next gate, medieval **Monk Bar** (8), and stroll down busy Goodramgate. The ending *-gate,* incidentally, is an old Viking word for street.

A right on College Street takes you past **St. William's College** (9), built in 1453 as a lodging for the Minster's chantry priests. It now serves as a general meeting place. Step through the doorway and enter the picturesque quadrangle, then continue on to the **Treasurer's House** (10). This 17th-century mansion, once the home of the Minster's treasurer, is well worth a visit for its gorgeous interior. *Open late March through Oct., Sat.-Thurs., 10:30–4:30. Closed Fri. Adults £3.50, children £1.75. Tea room. Art gallery.* ☎ *(01904) 624-247.*

A pathway leads through Dean's Park to the front entrance of:

*YORK MINSTER** (11), ☎ (01904) 624-426, Internet: www.yorkminster.org.

Open daily 7 a.m. to 8:30 p.m., closing at 5 in winter. Evensong Mon.–Fri. at 5, Sat.–Sun. at 4. Requested donation £2. Foundations and Treasury: Adults £1.80, children 70p. Chapter House: Adults 70p, children 30p. Crypt: Adults 60p, children 30p. Tower: Adults £2, children £1. The Foundations, Chapter House, and Tower are closed on Sun. mornings. Mostly &.

Both a cathedral and a minster, York Minster—the Cathedral Church of St. Peter—is the largest Gothic church in Britain. It stands on the site of the Roman military headquarters and of several earlier churches. The present structure was begun in 1220, requiring some 250 years to build. As you stroll around its spacious interior, be sure to see the ***Chapter House** just off the north transept, a wonder of medieval architecture whose conical roof spans a great distance without central support. Also in the north transept is the famous ***Five Sisters Window**—five giant lancets of 13th-century grisaille glass—and an astronomical clock of more recent date. Beyond the choir are several interesting chapels and the monumental **Great East Window** that celebrates the beginning and end of time in over 2,000 square feet of medieval stained glass.

While in the cathedral, you may want to climb 275 steps up the central tower for a bird's-eye view of the city. Another fascinating sight is the **Foundations and Treasury**, a spin-off of restoration work on the cathedral's foundations. Enter it by way of a staircase in the south transept. Here you can walk among the remains of the earlier churches and the Roman headquarters as well as see many of the Minster's treasures.

Leaving the Minster through the south doorway, make a left on Low Petergate, the *Via Principalis* of Roman York. At Goodramgate, turn left for a few yards and visit **Holy Trinity Church** (12), a small and extremely picturesque 14th-century church, now seldom used. Its box pews and Jacobean altar are quite interesting. Then cross King's Square and enter the ***Shambles** (13), one of the best-preserved medieval streets in Europe. Once the street of butchers, its overhanging, timbered buildings now house antique shops, booksellers, and similar enterprises.

At the end turn right onto Pavement, then make a left on Piccadilly, which leads to the **Merchant Adventurer's Hall** (14), built in the 14th century by the city's wealthiest trade guild. Visit the Great Hall and the Undercroft, where guild pensioners lived in cubicles as late as the 19th century. *Open April to mid-Nov., daily 8:30–5; rest of year Mon.–Sat. 8:30–3. Adults £1.90, children 60p.* ☎ *(01904) 654-818.*

Return on Piccadilly, turning left onto Coppergate, and visit the ***Jorvik Viking Centre** (15). Excavations here in recent years have unearthed the original Viking city of Jorvik, dating from the 10th century. Many of its buildings, now located beneath a modern shopping center, have been faithfully re-created. Together with Viking figures, sound effects, and even smells, these offer an opportunity to experience a glimpse of life in an age long past as you glide by in your magic timecar. At the end, you'll see an actual dig, visit a lab where artifacts are studied, and enter a gallery filled with the actual objects of a thousand years ago. *Open Jan.–Oct., daily 9–5:30, closing earlier in winter and spring; Nov.–Dec. daily 10–4:30. Closed Christmas Day. Adults £5.35, seniors and students £4.60, children £3.99. Gift shop.* ☎ *(01904) 643-2111, Internet: www.jorvik- viking-centre.co.uk.*

Stroll down to the **York Story** (16), an exhibition of the city's heritage housed in the former St. Mary's Church. Two thousand years of history are made clear by the clever use of models and audiovisual presentations. *Open Mon.–Sat. 10–5, Sun. 1–5. Adults £1.90, children £1.30.* ☎ *(01904) 628-632).*

Just beyond it stands the **Fairfax House**, described as one of the finest 18th-century townhouses in England. Its sumptuously restored interior is filled with period furniture and clocks, and is a treat for the connoisseur. *Open March–Dec., Mon.–Thurs. and Sat. 11–5, Sun. 1:30–5. Adults £3.75, children £1.50.* ☎ *(01904) 655-543.*

Continue on to **Clifford's Tower** (17), a defensive fortification built in the 13th century to replace an earlier one erected by William the Conqueror. In 1684 an explosion blew the roof off, and it remains in that condition today. You can climb to the top for a nice view. *Open April–June and Sept.–Oct., daily 10–6; July–Aug., daily 9:30–7; Nov.–March, daily 10–4. Adults £1.70, children 90p.* ☎ *(01904) 646-940.*

Just across the square is the:

*YORK CASTLE MUSEUM (18), ☎ (01904) 653-611. *Open Mon.–Sat. 9:30–5:30, Sun. 10–5:30. Adults £4.50, seniors, students, children £3.15.*

The York Castle Museum is among the most extraordinary folk museums in the world and a must for every visitor to York. Allow plenty of time to see it, even at the expense of skipping other sights. Housed in two former prisons, the museum displays a nearly endless succession of rooms, buildings, and even entire streets of bygone eras, each stuffed to overflowing with just about every item imaginable. A working outdoor watermill on the River Foss is part of it, as is the untouched condemned cell of the old prison. The route through the museum is very well laid out—just follow it and you won't miss a thing.

Beyond this, stroll north on Tower and Clifford streets past several commercial attractions, including the spine-chilling **York Dungeon** (19). Like its London counterpart, the Dungeon does its best to scare patrons with a the darker side of English history. Catch the plague! Follow a highwayman to the gallows! Meet up with ghosts of Roman legionnaires! *Open daily, 10–5:30, closing at 4 from Oct.–March. Adults £4.95, seniors £3.95, children £3.25.* ☎ *(01904) 632-599, Internet: www.yorkshirenet. co.uk/yorkdungeon.*

Cross the Ouse Bridge and follow Micklegate to **Micklegate Bar** (20), a Norman archway from which the heads of traitors were once displayed. A walk from here along the top of the city walls will return you to the train station, which also houses the entertaining **York Model Railway** should you have a wait for your real train.

*Cambridge

Cambridge, one of the most beautiful towns in Europe, has long been a favorite daytrip destination. For nearly 700 years its colleges vied with one another for architectural as well as academic excellence. Taking full advantage of its delightful riverside location, it developed an ambiance that sets it apart from any other college town in England. Inevitably, a comparison with Oxford must be made, but they are actually two very different places. Cambridge is serene, dreamy in character; while its older and larger rival is more intense, more worldly. Given the chance, you should really see both.

The site of Cambridge was important in ancient times, being the only practical place to cross the River Cam for miles around. In the centuries preceding the Roman conquest, a Celtic settlement was established just north of the river. This was taken over by the Romans and enlarged, spreading south after their departure. When the Normans came they built a castle, long vanished, on the site of the Roman camp. By the time of the Domesday Book, 1086, the town had some 400 houses and was already a trading center. From Cambridge northwards the River Cam, then called the Granta, was navigable all the way to the North Sea, a factor of vital importance in a time of poor land communications.

Scholars first gathered here around 1209 after being run out of Oxford by angry townspeople. Some of them stayed on and by 1284 the first proper college, Peterhouse, was founded. This was quickly followed by others, a university evolved, and the town flourished. New colleges are still being added, with a present total of 31 not including those independent of the university.

It is impossible to see all of Cambridge in a single day. The suggested tour was designed to include only the most notable highlights of the colleges, some of the town, a few museums, gardens, and the famous Backs along the river. Please remember that all of the colleges are private, and that admission to them is a courtesy, not a right.

GETTING THERE:

Trains from London depart frequently from both King's Cross and Liverpool Street stations, with better service from King's Cross. Most of these take less than one hour for the run to Cambridge, but some locals take 90 minutes. Return trains operate until late evening, and service is somewhat reduced on Sundays and holidays.

Coaches depart London's Victoria Coach Station for the two-hour ride to Cambridge about once an hour.

By car, Cambridge is 55 miles north of London via the M11.

PRACTICALITIES:

Cambridge may be visited in any season, although many of the colleges are closed to the public during student exams between mid-April and late June. Some museums are closed on Mondays. The local **Tourist Information Centre**, ☎ (01223) 322-640, Internet: www.cambridge.gov.uk, is on Wheeler Street just south of the Market Square. They offer daily guided **walking tours**, lasting about two hours. These depart at 1:30 all year round, plus at 11:30 most of the year, and also at 10:30 and 2:30 in peak seasons. Tours are limited at 20 persons; purchase your tickets as early as possible. Tickets are £6.50 per person, less when King's College is closed.

Guide Friday operates a hop-on, hop-off open-top double-decker bus service that goes by or near the attractions, and also the train station. All-day tickets for unlimited rides cost: Adults £8, seniors and students £6.50, children 5–12 £2.50. Single fares for local stops are available. Pay the driver, or purchase at the train station or tourist office. ☎ (01223) 362-444, Internet: www.guidefriday.com.

Cambridge is in the county of Cambridgeshire and has a population of about 100,000.

FOOD AND DRINK:

The town has a wide selection of restaurants and pubs, especially in the budget range. Some choices are:

Anchor Pub (Silver St., by the Mill Pond) An upstairs restaurant and a downstairs pub. ☎ (01223) 353-554. £ and ££

Browns (23 Trumpington St., opposite the Fitzwilliam Museum) Fresh, contemporary food from burgers to full meals, served in cheerful surroundings. ☎ (01223) 461-655. £ and ££

Hobb's Pavilion (Parker's Piece, 5 blocks southeast of the Market Square) Crêpes and other light meals. ☎ (01223) 367-480. X: Sun., Mon. £

The Little Tea Room (1 All Saints' Passage, opposite St. John's College) The perfect setting for light meals and teas, as cozy and old-fashioned as can be. ☎ (01223) 366-033. X: Sun. £

Rainbow Vegetarian Bistro (9A King's Parade, opposite King's College) A wide choice of vegetarian delights. ☎ (01223) 321-551. £

Fitzwilliam Museum Café (in the museum) An unusually good museum cafeteria. ☎ (01223) 332-900. X: Sun., Mon. £

SUGGESTED TOUR:

Numbers in parentheses correspond to numbers on the map.

Leaving the **train station** (1), you can either walk or take a bus or taxi to **Market Square** (2), a distance of about a mile. If you walk, just follow the map up Hills Road, Regent Street, and St. Andrew's Street, making a left on Petty Cury to the square. A colorful **outdoor market** is held here on Mondays through Saturdays.

Great St. Mary's Church, next to the square, is the University Church. You can enter it and climb to the top of its tower for an excellent view. *Tower open Mon.–Sat. 10–5, Sun. 12:30–5. Adults £1.50, children 50p.*

Make a left onto King's Parade and enter the Great Court of **King's College** (3). Founded by Henry VI in 1441, the school originally occupied a site directly to the north. Henry's ambitions grew, however, and what was then the center of medieval Cambridge was ruthlessly torn down to make way for a monumental college. At that point the War of the Roses intervened and Henry was deposed, leaving only part of the chapel finished and the rest an open field. It was another 280 years before any new buildings were erected. In the meantime, the chapel was completed during the reign of Henry VIII. This is, quite simply, the finest building in Cambridge and arguably the greatest Gothic structure in England.

Enter the *Chapel and look up at the miraculous fan vaulting on the ceiling, then at the dark wooden choir screen, and finally at the sheer expanse of glass. The total effect is breathtaking. Stroll through the choir and examine the *Adoration of the Magi* by Rubens that hangs behind the altar. An experience never to be forgotten is to return in the late afternoon for Evensong, a service held daily during terms. *Chapel open in terms, Mon.–Fri. 9:30–3:30, Sat. 9:30–3:15, Sun. 1:15–2:15 and 5–5:30; during vacation, Mon.–Sat. 9:30–4:30, Sun. 10–5. Adults £3, children £2.* ☎ *(01223) 331-212, Internet: www.kings.cam.ac.uk/tourism.*

Leaving the chapel, walk straight ahead past the Gibbs Building of 1724 and turn right into the *Backs*, those idyllic gardens and meadows along the River Cam that give Cambridge its special character. Cross the bridge for your first sight of this, then stroll back through the grounds of King's College to King's Parade, and turn left. Passing the Senate House and Gonville & Caius College, continue up Trinity Street to Trinity College.

With over 800 students, **Trinity** (4) is the largest college in Cambridge. It was founded by Henry VIII in 1546 and has long had connections with royalty. The Great Gate leads into the **Great Court**, so vast that the lack of symmetry along its sides is hardly noticeable. An extremely different atmosphere permeates the cloistered Nevile's Court, reached by passing through the hall at the west end. The magnificent *Wren Library*, built by Sir Christopher Wren in 1676, completes the west façade of the cloister. Containing such treasures as early editions of Shakespeare and the original manuscript of *Winnie-the-Pooh*, it is open to visitors except during exams. *Library open Mon.–Fri. noon–2 all year round, also on Sat. 10:30–12:30 during terms. Closed some major holidays and during exams. Admission £1.75. Internet: www.trin.cam.ac.uk/Tc/Wrenlib.*

Continue through a third court, turn right to the Backs, and cross a footbridge over the Cam.

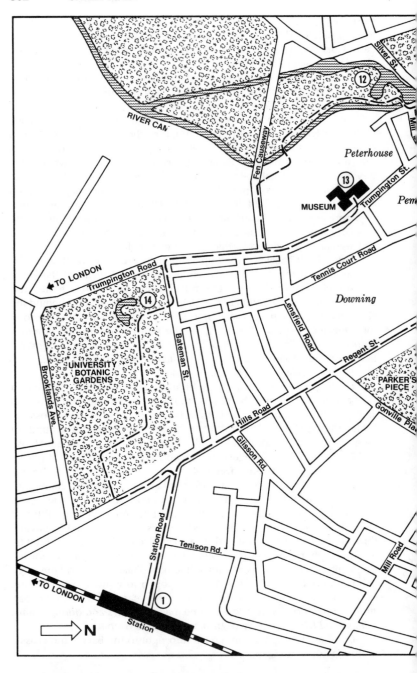

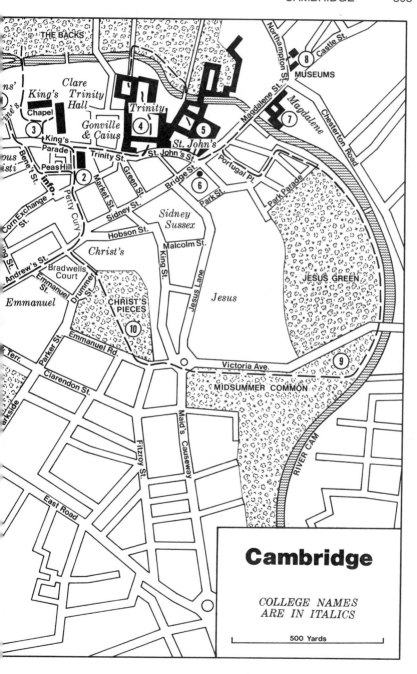

Cambridge

*COLLEGE NAMES
ARE IN ITALICS*

500 Yards

Follow the map and cross another bridge into **St. John's College** (5). To your left is the famous **Bridge of Sighs** that connects two halves of the college. Continue to the first courtyard and cross a bridge into New Court, a Victorian Gothic structure of 1826. Return and stroll through two more courts to the main entrance at the junction of Bridge Street and St. John's Street.

The fascinating **Round Church** (6) of 1130 was inspired by the Holy Sepulchre in Jerusalem. It is one of the very few medieval circular churches surviving in England. Restored during the 19th century, it still coveys the character of early Norman architecture.

Now follow Bridge Street to **Magdalene College** (7). Pronounced *Maudlen*, it was founded in 1428 and refounded in 1542, using the buildings of a former Benedictine monks' hostel. Samuel Pepys was a student here from 1650 to 1653 and left behind his collection of books, including an original manuscript of his immortal diary. These can be seen, kept in Pepys' unique bookshelves, in the library facing the second court. *Open Mon.–Sat. 11:30–12:30 and 2:30–3:30.*

Magdalene Street is lined with restored 16th- and 17th-century houses. Turn right and follow it to the **Folk Museum** (8), which features re-created room settings of bygone years as well as other memorabilia relating to Cambridge's past. *Open April–Sept., Mon.–Sat. 10:30–5 and Sun. 2–5; Oct.–March Tues.–Sat. 10:30–5 and Sun. 2–5. Admission £1.* ☎ *(01223) 355-159.* While there, you might want to stop in at the famous **Kettle's Yard**, an important collection of modern art in a nearby house on Northampton Street. *Open Tues.–Sun. 2–4. Free.* ☎ *(01223) 352-124, Internet: www.cam.ac.uk/CambArea/KettlesYard.*

At this point you can skip ahead to Queens' College (11) by following the map, or continue on for a lovely walk along the river and through a park. To do this, turn left into Portugal Place, make another left at New Park Street, and a right on Thompson's Lane.

Amble along the picturesque footpath by the river's edge. Once beyond Victoria Avenue turn right through **Midsummer Common** (9). Crossing the Four Lamps intersection, walk down Short Street and into a pleasant park called **Christ's Pieces** (10). Arriving at Drummer Street, continue on Bradwells' Court, then turn right to Petty Cury and return to Market Square (2). A left here leads down Peas Hill to Bene't Street. Make a right and then a left into Trumpington Street. In another block turn right and pass through St. Catherine's College.

Across Queens' Lane is the imposing entrance to ***Queens' College** (11), often regarded as the most charming in Cambridge. Little changed over the centuries, Queens' appears today much as it did in the 15th century when it was founded by two separate queens (thus the spelling). Enter the medieval Old Court, built in 1449, and pass through the Cloister Court of 1495. From here cross the so-called **Mathematical Bridge**, a curious wooden span over the Cam, first erected in 1749 without the use of nails or other fasteners. Unfortunately, someone took it apart to "discov-

er" its secret, and nobody has ever been able to put it back together cor-
rectly. The present bridge is a near copy, except that its builders cheated
by using bolts. *College open daily 1:45–4:30, and also 10:30–12:45 during
vacation. Closed during exams. Admission £1.* ☎ *(01223) 335-511.*

Turn right and stroll down along the river to the Grove, a garden with
lovely views. Returning to Cloister Court, walk through the Walnut Tree
Court and the Old Court, then exit onto Queens' Lane. If you've had
enough walking by now, you could go directly to the Fitzwilliam Museum
(13), or to Emmanuel Street and take a bus or taxi to the station.

If you choose to carry on, make a right on Silver Street and a left at
Laundress Lane. This leads to the **Mill Pond** (12), where punts (flat-bot-
tomed boats) may be rented for a cruise on the Cam. It looks easy, but
inexperienced punters often wind up in the drink, so be careful!

Now walk along the path, crossing a footbridge to the left, and turn
right to the Fen Causeway. Follow this to Trumpington Street. To the left is
the ***Fitzwilliam Museum** (13), one of the most important art museums in
England. Its collection ranges from ancient Egyptian to Impressionist art
and includes, besides paintings, drawings, and sculpture, a vast assort-
ment of armor, silver, porcelains, and manuscripts. You could easily spend
the better part of a day here, but a quick tour can be done in an hour or
so. *Open Tues.–Sat. 10–5, Sun. 2:15–5. Also open on Easter Mon. and Spring
and Summer Bank Holidays. Closed Mon., Good Friday, and Dec. 24–Jan. 1.
Free, but donation of £3 suggested. Café. Museum shop. Tours.* ☎ *(01223)
332-900, Internet: www.fitzmuseum.cam.ac.uk.*

Follow Trumpington Street to Bateman Street and turn left. To your
right is the entrance of the **University Botanic Gardens** (14), a delightfully
varied area devoted to research but also open to the public. *Open daily,
10–6, closing at 4 in winter. Greenhouses open 10–3:45. Closed Dec. 24–26.
Admission charge on weekdays from March–Oct., and on all weekends
and Bank Holidays: Adults £1.50, seniors and children under 18 £1, handicapped free.* ☎ *(01223) 336-265.* ♿.

Stroll through it and exit onto Hills Road, which is close to the train
station.

Trip 49

Ely

Ely's origins are shrouded in Anglo-Saxon folklore; fascinating to read but far too complex to go into here. At one time this was virtually an island, surrounded by the marshy Fens that for centuries had defied all attempts at drainage. Great quantities of eels lived in these swampy waters, accounting for the old name of *Elig*, or eel island, later corrupted to Ely.

In AD 673 an abbey for both monks and nuns was founded here by St. Etheldreda, which eventually led to the construction of Ely Cathedral. The town was sacked by the Danes in 870, and a hundred years later the King's School was established. Hereward the Wake, the "last of the English," defended the island against William the Conqueror until 1071, when the Anglo-Saxons finally succumbed to Norman supremacy. Ely remained an isolated place until the Fens were drained during the 17th century. Since then it has become a prosperous market town whose charming atmosphere, majestic cathedral, and lovely old buildings attract visitors from all over.

This trip can be combined in the same day with one to Ipswich, Bury St. Edmunds, or King's Lynn. Cambridge is temptingly close but really requires an entire day by itself.

GETTING THERE:

Trains depart London's King's Cross Station hourly for the 90-minute ride to Ely, with returns until late evening. Service is greatly reduced on Sundays and holidays, leaving from Liverpool Street Station instead.

By car, Ely is 71 miles north of London. Take the M11 to Cambridge, then change to the A10.

PRACTICALITIES:

Avoid coming on a Sunday, when much of the town is closed, the cathedral busy, and train service poor. There is a colorful outdoor market on Thursdays, and an antiques & crafts market on Saturdays. The local **Tourist Information Centre**, ☎ (01353) 662- 062, is in Oliver Cromwell's House at 29 St. Mary's Street. Ely is in the county of Cambridgeshire, and has a population of about 10,000.

FOOD AND DRINK:

Ely has a surprising number of good restaurants and pubs. A few choices for lunch are:

Old Fire Engine House (25 St. Mary's St., near the tourist office) English fare from mostly local ingredients, served in an 18th-century house and art gallery. Very popular, reserve, ☎ (01353) 662-582. X: Sun. eve. ££

Dominiques (8 St. Mary's St., near the cathedral) Imaginative French and English dishes in a friendly café. ☎ (01353) 665-011. X: Mon., Tues. £ and ££

Minster Tavern (Minster Place, by the cathedral) A traditional old pub with both regular and vegetarian dishes. ☎ (01353) 663-994. £

Steeplegate Tearoom (16/18 High St., near the cathedral) Light meals with a variety of teas. ☎ (01353) 664-731) X: Sun. £

Almonry (by the cathedral) Light lunches and teas in a 12th-century undercroft, or out in the garden. ☎ (01353) 666-360. £

The Maltings (Ship Lane at Riverside Walk) Pub meals in a converted 19th-century brewery. ☎ (01353) 662-633. £

SUGGESTED TOUR:

Numbers in parentheses correspond to numbers on the map.

Leaving the **train station** (1), turn left on Station Road and then right on Annesdale. This leads to a delightful walk along the River Great Ouse, complete with pleasure craft and a waterside pub. From here follow the map to St. Mary's Street. **Oliver Cromwell's House** (2) was the home of the great Puritan from 1636 until 1647, two years before he became England's only dictator. Refurbished as it was in his time, the house features an audiovisual presentation of his life, a Civil War exhibition, Cromwell's study, and even a haunted bedroom! Other displays chronicle the origins of the 14th-century half-timbered structure, which in the 19th century became a brewery and inn, and later a vicarage for the adjoining church. Today it shelters the Tourist Information Centre as well. *Open Apr.–Sept., daily 10–5:30; Oct.–March, Mon.–Sat. 10–5, Sun. 10:15–3. Closed Dec. 25–26, Jan. 1. Adults £2.70, seniors, students, children £2.20.* ☎ *(01353) 662-062.*

Stroll across Palace Green to the splendid west front of:

*ELY CATHEDRAL (3), ☎ (01353) 667-735. *Open in summer, daily 7–7; winter, 7:30–6, closing at 5 on Sun. Evensong, Mon.–Tues. and Thurs.–Sat. 5:30, Sun. 3:45. Access limited during services. Adults £3, seniors and students £2.20. Tours. Brass rubbing. Tea room. Gift shop.* ♿.

Ely Cathedral was begun in 1081 on the site of St. Etheldreda's 7th-century abbey. The castellated west tower rises to a height of 217 feet. To the right of this is an unusual southwest transept. This was once balanced on the left by another transept that collapsed in the 15th century and was never replaced.

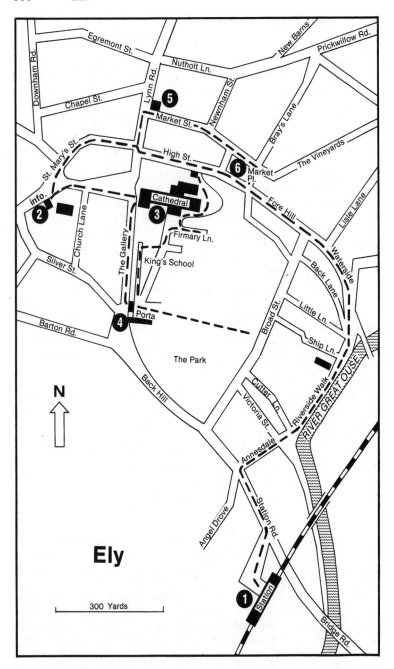

Ely

300 Yards

Enter the cathedral and look down the entire length of the nave, then up at the beautifully painted wooden ceiling. The central ***Octagon** under the crossing was a daring and ingenious solution to the problem of a heavy Norman tower that collapsed in 1322. Extending the full width of the nave, it is considered to be one of the highlights of English architecture. Beyond the screen are some nicely carved stalls. Walk over to the north transept and visit the huge and elaborately decorated 14th-century ***Lady Chapel**, which served as a parish church from Elizabethan times until 1938. Don't miss the very interesting ***Stained Glass Museum** with its well-lit collection of stained glass from medieval to modern times, rescued from redundant churches and secular buildings. *Museum open in summer, Mon.–Fri. 10:30–5, Sat. 10:30–5:30, Sun. noon–6; in winter, Mon.–Fri., 10:30–4:30, Sat. 10:30–5, Sun. noon–4:15. Adults £2.50, seniors, students, children £1.50.* ☎ *(01353) 660-347.* There is also a **Brass Rubbing Centre** where you can make your own souvenirs during the summer months.

Leave the cathedral and stroll down The Gallery to the **Ely Porta** (4), built in the 14th century as an entrance to the former monastery. It is now part of the King's School, one of the oldest public (meaning very private) schools in the country. Pass through it and examine the Monks' Granary to the right, now used as a dining hall by the school. The earthen mound just beyond this is all that remains of a 12th-century Norman castle.

Amble down the pathway for some wonderfully bucolic views of the cathedral, then return and make a right past more medieval buildings used by the school. Some of these, including the chapel, may be visited at certain times. Closer to the cathedral is Firmary Lane, a delightful little street.

Walk around the rear of the cathedral and come out on High Street. Continue on to Market Street and the **Ely Museum** (5), housed in the Old Town Gaol. Here you can see a fine collection of local bygones, toys, and artifacts, recalling local history from the Ice Age to modern times. *Open Tues.–Sun. and Bank Holidays, 10:30–4. Adults £1.80, seniors, students, children 6-15 £1.25.* ☎ *(01353) 666-655.* Complete your tour by meandering through some of the back streets to the **Market Place** (6), where an outdoor market is held on Thursdays.

Trip 50

King's Lynn

Steeped in atmosphere and haunted by its past, King's Lynn is neither quaint nor picturesque. What makes it appealing, though, is the sharply medieval aura of its narrow streets and ancient buildings. Once an outpost of the Hanseatic League, its older sections are more reminiscent of northern Germany or the Low Countries than of England. Like so many great places, Lynn reveals itself slowly and with reluctance. Much of it is mundane. Yet, to stroll its quays and half-forgotten alleyways is to awaken memories of a world long vanished.

The River Great Ouse brought early prosperity to Lynn. Connecting the seaport with the rich hinterlands of England, the Ouse provided a watery route for commerce to follow. And follow it did. By the end of the 12th century, Lynn was the fifth-largest port in England and the center of trade with the frozen north. Then known as Bishop's Lynn, the town expanded rapidly during the 11th century and began its Hanseatic association in the 13th. When exports declined in the 14th century, the port turned to coastal shipping and fishing. Henry VIII knew a good thing and made the place his own in 1537, changing the name to King's Lynn. Prosperity continued through the 18th century, when the coming of the railways rendered the inland waterways and coastal shipping obsolete, making Lynn the backwater port and market town that it is today.

GETTING THERE:

Trains depart London's King's cross Station hourly for the under-two-hour ride to King's Lynn, with returns until late evening. Service is reduced on Sundays and holidays.

By car, follow the M11 to Cambridge and switch to the A10. King's Lynn is 103 miles north of London.

PRACTICALITIES:

This trip can be taken in any season, but avoid coming by train on a Sunday. Colorful **outdoor markets** are held every Tuesday and Saturday. The local **Tourist Information Centre**, ☎ (01553) 763-044, is in the Custom House (5) on Purfleet Quay. King's Lynn is in the county of Norfolk, and has a population of about 40,000.

FOOD AND DRINK:

You'll find pubs and restaurants all along the walking route, including:

Rococo (11 Saturday Market Place) Creative, modern British cuisine in a smart setting. Reservations needed, ☎ (01553) 771-483. X: Sun., Mon. lunch. ££ and £££

Griffins (Duke's Head Hotel, Tuesday Market Place) Inventive International dishes in an historic country hotel. ☎ (01553) 774-996. ££

Riverside Rooms (in the Arts Centre) An atmospheric restaurant on the river's edge, with indoor and outdoor seating. ☎ (01553) 773-134. X: Sun. ££

Tudor Rose (St. Nicholas St., off Tuesdays Market Place) A 15th-century inn with a restaurant. ☎ (01553) 762-824. £ and ££

Giffords (Purfleet St., off King St.) A wine bar with good-value meals, including vegetarian. ☎ (01553) 769-177. X: Sun. eve. £

Hog's Head (High St., below Tuesday Market Place) A busy pub with good ales. ☎ (01553) 660-780. £

SUGGESTED TOUR:

Numbers in parentheses correspond to numbers on the map.

Leave the **train station** (1) and follow the map to the **Tuesday Market Place** (2), an attractive open square where a colorful outdoor market is held each Tuesday. At its far end turn right on St. Nicholas Street and stroll over to **St. Nicholas' Chapel**, founded in 1145 to handle the overflow from St. Margaret's Church, which by the 12th century was already too small for the growing population. The present structure dates from 1419 but is now closed. Behind it is **True's Yard** (3), all that's left of an old fishing community that was largely demolished during a slum clearance in the 1930s. Two adjoining cottages have been lovingly restored to tell the story of the hard, dangerous life the Northenders lived in the 1850s and 1920s. A guide will take you around, and perhaps let you into the old St. Nicholas' Chapel. *Open daily, 9:30–3:45. Nominal admission. Gift shop. ☎ (01553) 770-479. Largely ♿.*

Return to the Market Place, noticing the fine old houses on its north side, and make a left. At the far corner of Water Lane is the Corn Exchange, an exuberant Victorian building of 1854, now converted into a theater. Turn right on Ferry Street and walk out to the quay for some good views of the old harbor. There is a tiny ferry from here to West Lynn.

The **King's Lynn Arts Centre** (4) is a complex fronting on King Street. It occupies the former ***Guildhall of St. George***, the oldest and largest medieval merchants' guild building in England. Built around 1410, this may be the only building still standing in England in which Shakespeare probably performed in one of his own plays. Again used as a theater, it is the center of the annual King's Lynn Festival held in late July. *Open to visitors Mon.–Fri. 10–4, Sat. 10–1 and 2–3:30; except when it's in use. Free. ☎ (01553)*

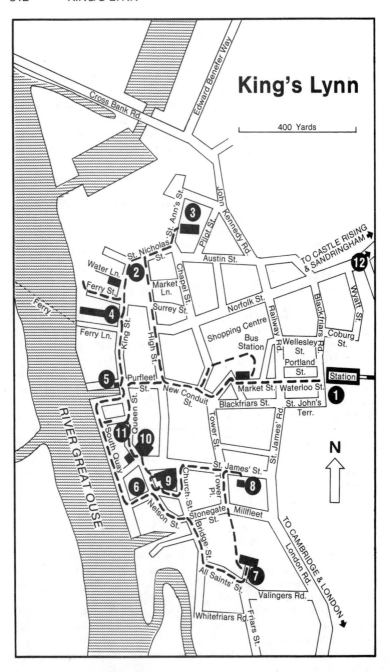

King's Lynn

400 Yards

773-578. The adjoining structures, all beautifully restored, now house an art gallery and restaurant.

King Street has hardly changed through the centuries. Wealthy merchants once lived in the homes along its west side, behind which stand ancient warehouses and private wharfs. Here and there, narrow alleyways lead to the river. The same pattern of residences and adjoining warehouses repeats itself on Queen Street and other streets parallel to the Ouse. At the corner of Purfleet Street, once a *fleet*, or creek, is located the most notable structure in Lynn, the *Custom House (5). Built in 1683 as a merchants' exchange, it was designed in the Palladian style by the town's mayor, Henry Bell, who was also an accomplished architect. The niche over its entrance contains a statue of Charles II. This elegant structure now houses the Tourist Information Centre.

Turn right into King Staithe Square. A *staithe* is a waterside depot equipped for loading boats. The Bank House on its south side has historic significance as it was from here that the explorer Samuel Cresswell successfully set out in 1850 to discover a northwest passage to India. Note the statue of Charles I above the doorway.

Turn left and follow South Quay. King Staithe Lane, to the left, is a delightful remnant of the past. Continue along the quay and make a left into St. Margaret's Lane. The **Hanseatic Warehouses** (6), now restored and used as offices, were built in 1428 by the Hansa merchants as their local depot. Next door to them is Hampton Court, a great block of merchants' homes, countinghouses, warehouses, and apprentices' quarters, begun before 1200 but considerably altered later.

Turn right on Nelson Street, which has some very attractive old façades. Follow Bridge Street to All Saints' Street. Along the way you will pass the timber-framed Greenland Fishery of 1605. In the 18th century it became a pub frequented by whalers, hence its name. It is now used for offices. Making a left up Church Lane, stop at **All Saints' Church** (7), built in the 14th century over Norman foundations. The painted rood screen is about 600 years old. Continue through the churchyard to Tower Place and turn right down St. James' Street to the **Greyfriars Tower** (8). Dating from the 15th century, this is all that remains of the old Greyfriars monastery that was disbanded by Henry VIII.

Return to St. James' Street and turn left, then make another left on Church Street. A right on Priory Lane leads to the Priory Cottages. In the courtyard, reached through an archway, stand some magnificently preserved old houses, once part of a Benedictine priory established about 1100. Go around the corner and visit **St. Margaret's Church** (9), one of the few parish churches to have two towers. A mixture of styles ranging from Norman to Victorian, the huge church was founded about 1100 and is noted for its two great Flemish brasses, each nearly ten feet long. Don't miss the flood marks by the entrance; the latest, and highest, being dated 1978. They tell a lot about the hazards of living in Lynn.

Cross the Saturday Market Place to the 15th-century **Guildhall of the**

Holy Trinity (10), incorporating parts of the present Town Hall and the Old Gaol. Inside this lurks a scary exhibition called **Tales of the Old Gaol House**, recalling stories of local witches, murderers, robbers, and highwaymen set in the original 18th- and 19th-century cells. The tour begins in King's Lynn's 1930s police station and ends as the culprits meet their doom. Included in the visit is an astonishing collection of regalia, including the famous so-called "King John Cup," probably of 16th-century origin but having nothing to do with the tyrant who, however, did grant the royal charter of 1204. Among the borough archives is the Red Register of 1300, one of the oldest paper books in the world. *Open Easter through Oct., daily 10–5; Nov. to Easter, Fri.–Tues. 10–5. Last admission at 4:15. Adults £2.20, seniors and children £1.60. Gift shop.* ☎ *(01553) 774-297.* ♿.

Thoresby College, opposite the Guildhall on Queen Street, was built about 1500 and is now a youth hostel. Farther along, at number 46 Queen Street, you will come to the **Town House Museum of Lynn Life** (11). This superb attraction re-creates ordinary life in Lynn throughout the ages, with all manner of artifacts on display. *Open in summer, Mon.–Sat. 10–5, Sun. 2–5; in winter Mon.–Sat. 10–4. Closed Bank Holidays. Gift shop. Nominal admission.* ☎ *(01553) 773-450. Limited* ♿.

Turn right on Purfleet Street and follow the map through a modern shopping center. From the **bus station** there you can get a ride to nearby Castle Rising or Sandringham before ambling back to the train station.

NEARBY SIGHTS:

Castle Rising (12), built in 1138, is one of the best Norman castles still standing in England. It can be reached by taking the bus marked for Hunstanton, which runs every half-hour. Ask the driver to let you off at the right place and be sure to inquire about the return schedule before leaving Lynn. The ride takes only 20 minutes. *Castle open April–Oct., daily 10–6; Nov.–March, Wed.–Sun. 10–4. Adults £2.30, seniors and students £1.70, children £1.20.* ☎ *(01553) 631-330.*

Sandringham, a home of the Royal Family, lies just beyond this on the same bus route. Purchased by Queen Victoria in 1862, its 600-acre spread of landscaped beauty was the favorite residence of George V. *Open April–Sept., daily 11–4:45. Closed when the Royal Family is in residence, usually mid-July to early Aug. Ask at the tourist office. Adults £4.50, seniors £3.50, children £2.50; less for just the grounds and museum.* ☎ *(01553) 772-675.* Those with cars should follow the A149 north in the direction of Hunstanton.

Bury St. Edmunds

Bury St. Edmunds has been called the nicest town in the world. An exaggeration perhaps, but this is really a delightful place to explore. The ruins of its great abbey are wonderfully picturesque, and Bury itself, spared the effects of industry, is an elegant reminder of what prosperous country towns were once like.

Its history began during the late 9th century when Edmund, the last king of East Anglia, was defeated by marauding Danes, shot full of arrows, and beheaded. Later made a saint, the martyr was honored with a shrine at *Beodricesworth*, today's Bury St. Edmunds. An abbey was founded there in 945 and rebuilt by King Canute in 1021. For centuries this remained a place of holy pilgrimage. It was there that the English barons met in 1214 to demand that King John ratify the Magna Carta. In 1539 the great abbey was disbanded by Henry VIII and gradually became the romantic ruin that it is today.

Bury offers other attractions as well, including a cathedral, the marvelous Manor House Museum, and one of the most enjoyable folk museums in England. By rushing a bit, it is possible to combine this trip with one to either Ely or Ipswich.

GETTING THERE:

Trains operated by Anglia Railways depart London's Liverpool Street Station several times in the morning for Ipswich, where you change to a local for Bury St. Edmunds. The total journey time takes under two hours, with returns operating until mid-evening. Alternatively, you can depart from London's King's Cross Station and change trains at Cambridge instead, a slightly longer route. Service is greatly reduced on Sundays and holidays.

By car, Bury is 75 miles northeast of London. Take the M11 and A11 to Newmarket, then the A14 into Bury.

PRACTICALITIES:

Bury may be visited at any time, and is especially interesting on Wednesdays and Saturdays, when **outdoor markets** are held. The local **Tourist Information Centre**, ☎ (01284) 764-667, Internet: www.stedmunds.co.uk, is at 6 Angel Hill, near the Abbey Gate. Bury is in the county of Suffolk, and has a population of about 34,000.

FOOD AND DRINK:

Bury is noted for its Greene King ales, especially their Abbot Ale. These are served, among other places, at **The Nutshell** on The Traverse, which claims to be England's smallest pub. Some good places to eat are:

The Vaults (in the Angel Hotel by the Abbey Gate) Imaginative dishes served in the vaults beneath an ancient inn. ☎ (01284) 753-926. ££

Maison Bleue (at Mortimer's, 31 Churchgate St., 2 blocks west of the cathedral) Noted for its excellent seafood. ☎ (01284) 760-623. X: Sat. lunch, Sun. ££

Scandinavia Coffee Shop (30 Abbeygate St., opposite the Abbey Gate) A convenient place for light lunches, sandwiches, coffees and teas. £

Masons Arms (Whiting St., near the Guildhall) An old favorite pub with meals. ☎ (01284) 753-955. £

Cathedral Refectory (at the cathedral) Light lunches and afternoon teas in an extension of the cathedral. ☎ (01284) 754-933. £

SUGGESTED TOUR:

Numbers in parentheses correspond to numbers on the map.

Leave the **train station** (1) and follow the map down Northgate Street to the **Abbey Gate** (2), erected in 1327 following an uprising of the towns-people. Stroll through the lovely Abbey Gardens to the 13th-century **Abbot's Bridge**, then walk along the River Lark to the ruins of the **Abbey** (3). A plaque marks the location of the high altar where in 1214 the assembled barons of England swore they would compel the despised King John to grant them their rights by signing the Magna Carta, which he finally did a year later at Runnymede. The largest surviving part of the 11th-century abbey is its **West Front**, whose Samson's Tower now houses the **Abbey Visitor Centre**. Here you can find out more about the Abbey, the legend of St. Edmund, and the historical significance of the town. Walk over to the ruined **Charnel House**, whose crypt is filled with ancient bones, then leave the abbey grounds. *Gardens open Mon.–Sat. 7:30 to a half-hour before dusk, Sun. and Bank Holidays 9 to a half-hour before dusk. Free. Tea room in summer. Gift shop.* ☎ *(01284) 763-110. Mostly &.*

St. **Edmundsbury Cathedral** (4) dates from 1503, but did not become the seat of a bishop until 1914. Since then, major modifications have been made in the Gothic style, giving it a highly attractive interior that repays a visit. The 12th-century **Norman Tower**, opposite, serves as its bell tower. *Cathedral open June–Aug., daily 8:30–8; Sept.–May, daily 8:30–6. Suggested donation £2.* ☎ *(01284) 754-933. &.*

Turn left on Crown street and visit St. **Mary's Church** (5), one of the finest in the region. Built in the 15th century, it houses the tomb of Mary Tudor, sister of Henry VIII. The church is famous for its magnificently carved wooden ceiling.

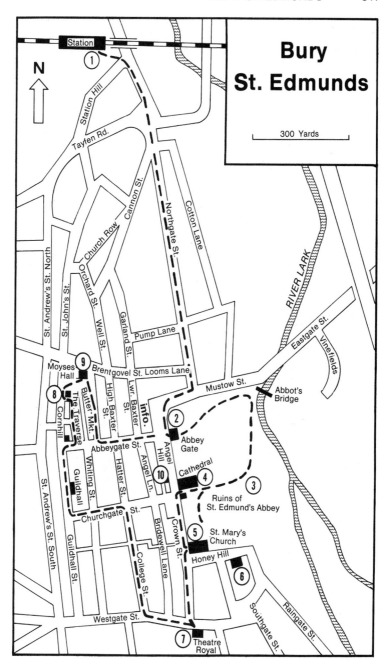

Bury
St. Edmunds

300 Yards

N

Station

Station Hill

Tayfen Rd.

Church Row

Cannon St.

Orchard St.

Well St.

St. Andrew's St. North

St. John's St.

Garland St.

Northgate St.

Cotton Lane

Pump Lane

RIVER LARK

Eastgate St.

Vinefields

Brentgovel St.   Looms Lane

Moyses
Hall

Lwr. Baxter St.

High Baxter St.

Info.

Mustow St.

Abbot's
Bridge

The Traverse

Butter Mkt.

Cornhill

Abbey
Gate

Abbeygate St.

Angel Hill

Guildhall

Whiting St.

Hatter St.

Angel Ln.

Cathedral

Ruins of
St. Edmund's Abbey

St. Andrew's St. South

Churchgate   St.

Crown St.

St. Mary's
Church

Honey Hill

Guildhall St.

Bridewell Lane

College St.

Westgate St.

Southgate St.

Raingate St.

Theatre
Royal

Just a few steps down Honey Hill stands the marvelous:

*MANOR HOUSE MUSEUM (6), ☎ *(01284) 757-076. Open Tues.–Sun. 10–5, and Bank Holiday Mon. Adults £2.70, seniors, students, children £1.75. Tea room. Gift shop.* &.

Bury's major museum is an elegant display of the fine and applied arts housed in an 18th-century mansion. There's a lot to admire here, from paintings and prints to furniture and costumes, but the star of the show is the incredible ***Gershom Parkington Collection of Clocks and Watches**. Unobtrusive interactive terminals allow visitors to discreetly explore the history of any item on display, while retaining the atmosphere of a private house rather than a museum littered with explanatory signs.

Continue down Crown Street to the **Theatre Royal** (7), a Regency structure from 1819 that was thoroughly restored by the National Trust. Its delightful interior may usually be visited. *Open Mon.–Sat. 10–8, except during rehearsals and performances. Closed Bank Holiday Mon. Free.* ☎ *(01284) 769-505.* The **Greene King Brewery**, across the street, has apparently been there since 1799 and offers tours. Ask at the tourist information centre about this.

Follow the map past the medieval **Guildhall** on Guildhall Street, and the Victorian Corn Exchange on Cornhill. The Traverse is a colorful lane featuring the smallest pub in England, The Nutshell, and a fine 17th-century inn, the Cupola House.

The **Market Cross Art Gallery** (8), housed in Robert Adam's only public building in East Anglia, specializes in changing exhibitions. *Open Tues.–Sat. 10:30–5.* ☎ *(01284) 762-081.* Cross the open square to the 12th-century **Moyse's Hall** (9), one of the oldest domestic buildings in England. Previously used as a house, an inn, and a jail, it was converted into a museum in 1899. All manner of fascinating junk is on display, including items of historical interest, bygones, and archaeological finds. Among its treasures is a lock of Mary Tudor's hair, and a book covered with the skin of a convicted murderer. *Open Mon.–Sat. 10–5, Sun. 2–5. Adults £1.50, seniors, students, children 95p.* ☎ *(01284) 757-488. Gift shop. Limited* &.

Return via Butter Market and Abbeygate Street to Angel Hill. On your right is the **Athenaeum** (10), a Regency social center where Charles Dickens once gave readings. Its Adam-style ballroom may be seen when not in use. Dickens also immortalized the nearby Angel Hotel in his *Pickwick Papers*. From here you can head back to the train station.

Colchester

N o other town in England has a recorded history quite as old as Colchester's. Beginning as a small settlement in the Bronze Age, it became an important place by the 1st century AD when Cunobelin, Shakespeare's "Cymbeline," made it his capital. This was captured by the Romans in AD 44 and became their first colony in Britain, *Colonia Camulodunum*. After the fall of the empire the Anglo-Saxons took over, calling it *Colneceaster*. William the Conqueror built a mighty castle here, and all through the Middle Ages the town thrived on its cloth trade.

Colchester remains a flourishing place, and a very attractive one at that. Its handsome streets are lined with an absorbing mixture of the old and the new, including Roman walls, a surprisingly well-preserved Norman castle keep, many medieval houses, and structures of every age since. There is enough here to keep you busy all day, but those in a hurry may want to combine their visit with one to nearby Ipswich, easily reached by train or car.

GETTING THERE:

Trains operated by Anglia Railways leave frequently from London's Liverpool Street Station for the 50-minute trip to Colchester, with returns until late evening. Service is greatly reduced on Sundays and holidays.

By car, Colchester is 56 miles northeast of London via the A12.

PRACTICALITIES:

Several of the attractions are closed on Sundays, while the colorful **outdoor market** is held on Fridays and Saturdays. The local **Visitor Information Centre**, ☎ (01206) 282-828, Internet: www.colchester. town.co.uk, is at 1 Queen Street, opposite the Hollytrees Museum. From June through September they conduct guided walking tours departing daily at 11 a.m. and lasting nearly two hours. Adults £2, seniors £1.50, children £1. Colchester is in the county of Essex, and has a population of about 157,000.

FOOD AND DRINK:

Colchester has been noted for its oysters since Roman times. Some good places for lunch are:

Rose and Crown (East Hill, beyond the river) A 15th-century inn with a fine restaurant. ☎ (01206) 866-677. X: Sun. eve. £££

George Hotel (116 High St., near the castle) A renovated medieval inn with a restaurant and grill. ☎ (01206) 578-494. ££

Warehouse Brasserie (12 Chapel St. North, 3 blocks southwest of Holy Trinity Church) Imaginative cuisine, vegetarian options, and modest prices, all set in an old warehouse, ☎ (01206) 765-656. X: Sun. eve. £ and ££

North Hill Exchange (19 North Hill, at Nunn's Rd.) A brasseries with good, standard food. ☎ (01206) 769-988. X: Mon. £ and ££

Poppy's Tea Room (17 Trinity St., south of Holy Trinity Church) Light lunches and snacks in delightful surroundings. ☎ (01206) 765-805. X: Sun. £

Toto's (5–7 Museum St., near the Hollytrees Museum) Pizza, pasta, and the like. ☎ (01206) 573-235. £

SUGGESTED TOUR:

Numbers in parentheses correspond to numbers on the map.

The **train station** (1) is nearly a mile from High Street, where the sights begin. You can cover this partly uphill distance by bus, taxi, or on foot. Once there, turn left past the wonderfully Victorian Town Hall and left once again on West Stockwell Street.

This quiet and charming old area is known as the **Dutch Quarter**, where refugee Flemish weavers settled in the 17th and 18th centuries. **St. Martin's Church** (2) has an interesting 12th-century tower. Turn right through the churchyard and follow East Stockwell Street and St. Helen's Lane, passing several fine old houses, to the 13th-century St. Helen's Chapel. A left on Maidenburgh Street leads to remains of the ancient **Roman walls**. Stroll along these, then make a right to the castle.

*COLCHESTER CASTLE MUSEUM (3), ☎ (01206) 282-931. *Open March–Nov., Mon.–Sat. 10–5 and Sun. 2–5; Dec.–Feb., Mon.–Sat. 10–5. Last admission at 4:30. Adults £3.60, seniors and children 5-15 £2.30. Guided tours additional: Adults £1, children 60p. Partial ♿.*

The only part of Colchester Castle that survives today is its enormous keep, the largest in England. Built by the Normans about 1085 on the foundations of a Roman temple, it now houses the fabulous **Colchester Castle Museum** of late Celtic and Roman antiquities. Here you can see how Queen Boadicea of the Iceni tribe mowed down the Romans with her sword-studded chariot in AD 60, listen in as a witch confesses, feel the weight of Roman armor, smell the aromas of a 17th-century apothecary shop, and experience much more. The excellent guided tours, held several times a day, take you into hidden corners of the castle that are otherwise closed.

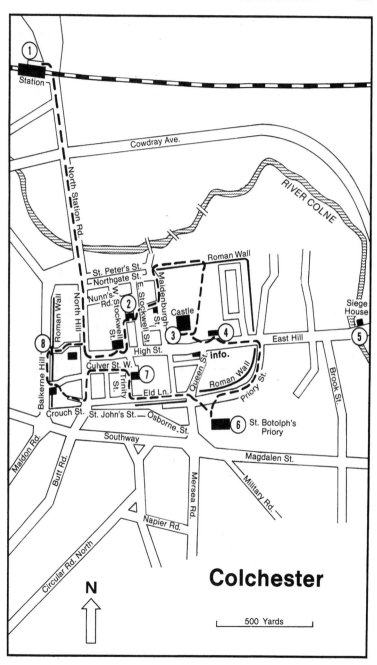

Colchester

Walk over to the **Hollytrees** (4), a Georgian mansion dating from 1718. This is occupied by a splendid museum of 18th- and 19th-century bygones, costumes, toys, and curios. *Open Tues.–Sat. 10–noon and 1–5. Free.* Another nearby museums is the **Natural History**, housed in the former All Saints' Church. *Open Tues.–Sat. 10–1 and 2–5. Free.* Also close by is the **Minories Art Gallery**, which features changing exhibitions and a café serving light lunches. *Open May–Sept., Mon.–Sat. 10–5; and Oct.–Apr., Mon.–Sat. 10–4. Free.* ☎ *(01206) 577-067.*

Continue down High Street to the 15th-century St. James's Church near the corner of Priory Street. From here you can make a side trip down East Hill to the half-timbered **Siege House** (5) on the River Colne, which still bears bullet marks from the 17th-century Civil War and is now a restaurant.

A stroll down Priory Street takes you past a fine section of the Roman wall. Turn left into the very romantic ruins of **St. Botolph's Priory** (6), a 12th-century Augustinian foundation destroyed during the siege of 1648. From here follow the map along Eld Lane, passing some inviting pubs, and turn right on Trinity Street.

Holy Trinity Church (7) has a Saxon tower made of Roman bricks. Nearby, on Trinity Street, is **Tymperley's Clock Museum**, a restored 15th-century timber-framed home filled with locally-made clocks from the 18th and 19th centuries. *Open April–Oct. only, Tues.–Sat. 10–1 and 2–5. Free.*

Make a left on Culver Street West and follow the map to the **Balkerne Gate** (8), originally built in the late 1st century AD by the Romans. Turn right and stroll down a passageway past the modern Mercury Theatre and the fantastic Victorian water tower, known locally as "Jumbo." From High Street you can either walk or take a bus back to the station.

Ipswich

S tep out of the train station at Ipswich and you might at first wonder what brought you here. Initial impressions, however, can be misleading as this ancient town does have plenty of character and a peculiar charm that slowly takes hold as you stroll its venerable streets. A visit to Ipswich will be appreciated by those who value living atmosphere above preserved quaintness.

Located ten miles inland at the navigable head of the Orwell estuary, Ipswich was first settled in prehistoric times. It became the important Anglo-Saxon port of *Gipeswic* as early as the 7th century. Trade expanded under Norman rule, and the town was granted a charter by King John in 1199. Ipswich flourished through the 16th century, when a decline set in that was not reversed until Victorian days. Since then, it has continued to grow as a prosperous seaport and regional center.

This trip may easily be combined in the same day with one to Woodbridge or Colchester, or less easily with Bury St. Edmunds.

GETTING THERE:

Trains operated by Anglia Railways depart London's Liverpool Street Station frequently for the 70-minute ride to Ipswich, with returns until late evening. Service is greatly reduced on Sundays and holidays.

By car, Ipswich is 74 miles northeast of London via the A12.

PRACTICALITIES:

Ipswich should really be seen on a Saturday or weekday, when its streets are alive with activity. The Ipswich Museum is closed on Sundays, and both that and the Christchurch Mansion are closed on Mondays. The local **Tourist Information Centre**, ☎ (01473) 258-070, Internet: www.ipswich.gov.uk/tourism, is in St. Stephen's Church on St. Stephen's Lane, adjacent to the Buttermarket Shopping Centre. Ask them about tours of the historic Tolly Cobbold Brewery, which is located within walking distance of the last stop on the suggested tour. Ipswich is in the county of Suffolk, and has a population of about 130,000.

FOOD AND DRINK:

Noted for its Tolly Cobbold ales, Ipswich enjoys a number of colorful pubs, and some good restaurants as well. A few choices are:

The Galley (25 St. Nicholas St., a block east of the Unitarian Meeting House) Excellent International cuisine, including game, seafood and lobster. ☎ (01473) 281-131. X: Sun., Bank Holidays. £££

Dhaka (6 Orwell Pl., 3 blocks north of the Old Custom House) Noted for its fine Indian cuisine. ☎ (01473) 251-397. ££

Mortimers on the Quay (Wherry Quay, near the Old Custom House) Specializes in fresh fish and seafood dishes. ☎ (01473) 230-225. X: Sat. lunch, Sun. £ and ££

Great White Horse (Tavern St., near the Town Hall) A 16th-century inn associated with Charles Dickens; pub lunches and a restaurant. ☎ (01473) 256-558. £ and ££

SUGGESTED TOUR:

Numbers in parentheses correspond to numbers on the map.

Leaving the **train station** (1), cross the River Orwell and follow Princes Street to Franciscan Way. Use the underground passage to cross this busy intersection, then turn right to the **Willis Corroon Building** of 1975, a highly successful curved curtain wall of tinted reflective glass that represents the best in modern British architecture. Adjacent to this, and in complete contrast but blending well with it, is the **Unitarian Meeting House** (2) of 1699, one of the earliest nonconformist chapels in England. If the door facing Friars Street is open, you might want to take a look at the lovely interior with its fine pulpit attributed to Grinling Gibbons, its box pews, and its 17th-century Dutch chandelier.

Follow the map to Westgate Street. A short side trip can be made up High Street to the **Ipswich Museum** (3), which features collections of local archaeology, geology, and natural history—all refreshingly displayed in a rather old-fashioned manner. Its noted **Roman Villa Gallery** of costumed figures in authentic Roman room settings is highly worthwhile. *Open Tues.–Sat., 10–5. Closed Good Friday, Dec. 24–26, Jan. 1. Free. Gift shop.* &.

The pedestrians-only Westgate Street leads to **Corn Hill** (4). Mostly Victorian in character, this large open square is dominated on the south by the imposing **Town Hall** of 1867, and by the ornate Post Office of 1880.

Stroll down Tavern Street and turn left on Tower Street. The civic church of **St. Mary-le-Tower** (5) has an unusually tall spire and some good carved woodwork inside. Continue on to **St. Margaret's Church** (6), a richly detailed 15th-century flint structure considered to be the finest church in town.

A path leads into one of the best public parks in England, and to what is undoubtedly the most notable attraction of Ipswich, ***Christchurch Mansion** (7). This elegant country house, begun in 1548, was twice visited by Queen Elizabeth I. Its many period rooms are filled with antiques dating from Tudor to Victorian times, and with painting by such local Suffolk

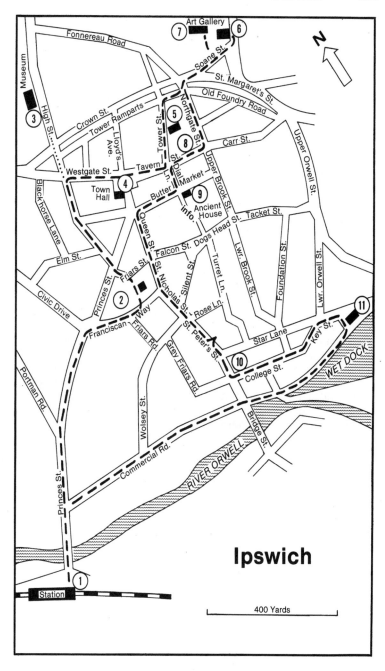

Ipswich

artists as Gainsborough and Constable. Don't miss the interesting kitchen and laundry. *Open Tues.–Sat. 10–5.* ☎ *(01473) 253-246.*

The route now takes you down Soane and Northgate streets to the **Great White Horse Hotel** (8), whose basic structure dates as far back as the 16th century. Charles Dickens stayed here and described it in his *Pickwick Papers,* while other guests have included King George II, Louis XVIII of France, and Lord Nelson.

Another famous sight in Ipswich is the *Ancient House (9) on Butter Market, reached by following the map. Also known as *Sparrowe's House* and just about as picturesque as a house can be, this magnificent example of a 16th-century timber-framed building is profusely decorated with extraordinary carvings in high relief. Its interior, now a bookstore, may be visited.

Just around the corner is the new Arras Square, named after the city in northern France. The **Tourist Information Centre** is located here in the medieval St. Stephen's Church, while around it stands the very modern Buttermarket Shopping Centre. Cross through this and follow the map towards the river, passing some beautiful old houses en route. The passageway between numbers 9 and 13 on St. Peter's Street is particularly interesting. Turn left on College Street and examine **Wolsey's Gate** (10), all that remains of a college begun in 1528 by Cardinal Wolsey, a local butcher's son who rose to the very top, only to fall again when Henry VIII tired of his manipulations.

Continue on to the **Old Custom House** (11) on the quay. Always a busy scene, the colorful waterfront is a fascinating place to explore before returning to the station. Lovers of fine ale are within walking distance of the **Tolly Cobbold Brewery**, where equipment dating from as far back as 1723 is still in use. You can take a tour, sample the result, and enjoy some good pub food at the same time; but be sure to check the current opening times with the tourist office first.

Woodbridge

Beautifully situated at the head of a tidal estuary, the little market town of Woodbridge still clings to its Elizabethan past. Unpretentious, unspoiled, and well off the beaten path, it has long been a favorite retreat for artists and poets.

Woodbridge was first mentioned by name in King Edgar's charter of 970, and is described in the Domesday Book of 1086. The name is probably a corruption of the Anglo-Saxon *Udebryge*, most likely meaning Woden's Town, after their pagan deity. A priory was established in the 12th century near the site of the present parish church. Soon afterwards the town acquired status as a market place. When the plague subsided in 1349, Woodbridge began to prosper through its wool trade.

During the 17th century the town became an important shipping and shipbuilding center, but this declined as the ever-increasing draft of larger boats made the harbor obsolete. Today, its docks are limited to small pleasure craft, sparing it the industry of larger ports.

This trip can easily be combined in the same day with one to nearby Ipswich.

GETTING THERE:

Trains operated by Anglia Railways leave London's Liverpool Street Station frequently for Ipswich, where you change to a local for Woodbridge that runs at two-hour intervals. The total journey takes about 90 minutes with good connections, and returns run until mid-evening. Service is reduced on Sundays and holidays.

By car, Woodbridge is 81 miles northeast of London via the A12.

PRACTICALITIES:

Good weather is necessary to enjoy this trip. The Tide Mill is open daily from May to early September, and on weekends in October. An outdoor **market** is held on Thursdays on Market Hill. The local **Tourist Information Centre**, ☎ (01394) 382-240, is located at the train station. A useful Internet site to check is: www.barringer.co.uk. Woodbridge is in the county of Suffolk, and has a population of about 11,000.

FOOD AND DRINK:

Woodbridge has several pleasant country pubs and restaurants, including:

Spice (17 The Thoroughfare, in the town center) Tasty, creative dishes with Southeast Asian and Mediterranean influences, in a relaxed atmosphere. ☎ (01394) 382-557. X: Sun. ££

Crown Inn (Thoroughfare, in the town center) Pub lunches and full dinners. ☎ (01394) 384-242. £ and ££

Bull Hotel (Market Hill, by the Shire Hall) A simple country inn with meals. ☎ (01394) 382-089. £

Olde Bell and Steelyard (New St. near Market Hill) A 15th-century pub with bar lunches. £

SUGGESTED TOUR:

Numbers in parentheses correspond to numbers on the map.

Leaving the **train station** (1), turn right on Quayside and follow it until you come to a sign pointing the way to the Tide Mill. Make a right, crossing the tracks, and walk out to the wonderfully picturesque **Tide Mill* (2), the last remaining example of its kind in England. A water mill has existed on this spot since the 12th century, while the present structure was erected in 1793 and continued operations until 1957. Tide mills were commonly situated at the heads of estuaries leading from the sea. Completely restored to working order in 1982, the Woodbridge mill offers **demonstrations* when the tides are right. *Open May–early Sept., daily 11–5, and on weekends only in Oct., 11–5. Adults £1, children 50p. Gift shop.* ☎ *(01473) 626-618.*

During the summer season, short **boat trips** on the river are available from the quayside. *Operates May–Sept., daily 2–5. £2.* ☎ *(01473) 382-318.*

From here you can take a beautiful **country walk** of about 2.5 miles by following the route below. Otherwise, head directly to Market Hill (6) and carry on from there.

Begin the country walk by strolling past the **docks** (3), which once made Woodbridge a thriving commercial port, and continue along the river wall. This attractive promenade has long been a favorite with artists. In a short while, the trail turns inland and enters the woods at **Kyson Hill** (4). Passing a cross-path, you will come to a junction. Take the macadam path to the right, climbing through the National Trust parkland and crossing the railway on a bridge. By now the trail has become a road that soon turns sharply to the left. Just before the turn you will see a house called Cross Trees on the right. Take the woodland path to the right between the house and the bend in the road. When this emerges on Lane Road make a right and then another immediate right at the intersection.

A few yards beyond, climb a flight of concrete steps on the left side

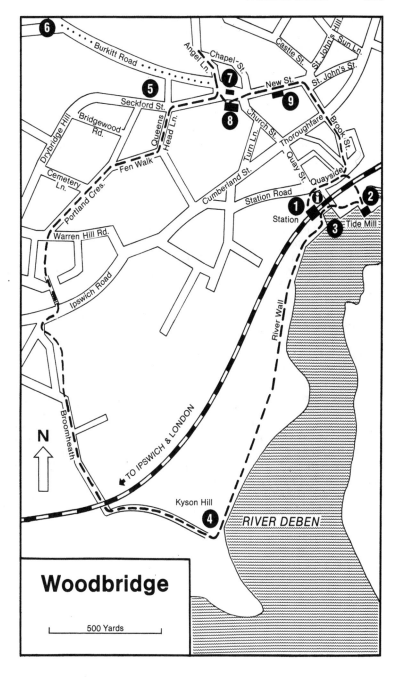

Woodbridge

500 Yards

of the road. This leads to a macadam path between backyards of houses. When you come to a fork, keep right. Continue on to Portland Crescent. Follow straight ahead past a cemetery, beyond which Fen Walk keeps to the right of a row of poles. Turn left when you come to a junction and climb the steps to Seckford Street. To your left is the **Seckford Hospital and Almshouses** (5), built around 1840. Turn right and follow Seckford Street to Market Hill.

At this point, ambitious hikers can turn left and walk out Theatre Street, soon becoming Burkitt Road, to **Buttrum's Mill** (6). Built in 1836, this is one of England's finest windmills. Although it ceased commercial operations in 1928, it is still maintained and open to the public. *Open May–Sept., Sat., Sun., and Bank Holidays, 2–6.* ☎ *(01473) 583-352.*

The ancient core of the community, **Market Hill** (7) is the site of the present open-air market held on Thursdays. There are several attractive old buildings, including a few pubs, on this square. Dominating all of them is the **Shire Hall**, erected in 1575 and now used on the ground floor by the town council. Above this is the **Suffolk Horse Museum**, devoted to the Suffolk Punch breed of heavy working horses. Developed in the 15th century around Woodbridge, the breed nearly became extinct in the 1960s, but has now been saved. Climb the steps and learn all about these remarkable animals, and also about rare cattle, sheep, and pigs. *Open Easter Mon. through Sept., daily 2–5. Adults £1.50, seniors and children 80p.* ☎ *(01394) 380-643.*

Stroll down charming Angel Lane, which is lined with 17th- and 18th-century cottages.

Returning to Market Hill, visit the **Parish Church of St. Mary** (8), built in the Perpendicular style during the early part of the 15th century. It's an unusually interesting old church, worth an exploration. Close by, at 5A Market Hill, is the small, friendly **Woodbridge Museum**, where you can trace the history of Woodbridge and its townspeople, as well as enjoy an exhibition concerning the famed Anglo-Saxon sites at nearby Sutton Hoo and Burrow Hill. *Open mid-July through Aug., Mon.–Tues. and Thurs.–Sat., 10–4, Sun. 2:30–4:30; April to mid-July and Sept.–Oct., Thurs.–Sat. 10–4 and Sun. 2:30–4:30. Adults £1, children 30p. Gift shop.* ☎ *(01394) 380-502.*

New Street leads down to the quay, passing **Ye Olde Bell and Steelyard Inn** (9), one of the oldest pubs in England, along the way. Overhanging the road from this is a 17th-century steelyard—a balance scale once used to weigh wagon loads coming to and from the market for toll-collection purposes. It was last used in the 1880s, a rare survival from the turnpike era.

After a sharp turn, New Street intersects with Thoroughfare, the main shopping street of Woodbridge. Continue straight ahead on Brook Street and turn right at Quayside, returning you to the station.

*Norwich

Norwich lives in a curious time warp where the past keeps bumping into the present. Essentially a medieval city of great distinction, its twisting, cobbled lanes are charged with the vitality of modern living. It has all the expected features of an English country town; a massive castle, a splendid cathedral, and more ancient churches than anyone would care to count. Its narrow streets run every which way and make about as much sense as the meanderings of a drunken cow. Yet somehow it all seems to work, for Norwich is truly alive and ready to step into the future.

Located in a loop of the River Wensum some 20 miles from the sea, Norwich began as an Anglo-Saxon settlement that by the 9th century was already trading with the Continent. Destroyed by the Danes in 1004, it was soon rebuilt by the Normans and has prospered ever since. When its wool industry declined it took to other pursuits such as brewing, metalworking, food processing, shoe-making, and insurance. Norwich has always adapted to changing times, and in the process has never lost sight of its heritage.

GETTING THERE:

Trains operated by Anglia Railways depart London's Liverpool Street Station hourly for the under-two-hour ride to Norwich, with return trains operating until mid-evening. Service is reduced on Sundays and holidays.

By car, Norwich is 109 miles northeast of London. Take the M11 to Great Chesterford, then the A11.

PRACTICALITIES:

Norwich may be visited at any time of the year, but avoid coming on a Sunday, when some of the sights are closed. The local **Tourist Information Centre**, ☎ (01603) 666-071, Internet: www.norwich.gov.uk, is in the Guildhall on Market Place. Norwich is in the county of Norfolk, and has a population of about 171,000.

FOOD AND DRINK:

There are numerous pubs and restaurants along nearly all of the walking route. A few choices are:

Maid's Head Hotel (Tombland, near the cathedral) In business for over 700 years on the same site, this old hotel has two fine restaurants. ☎ (01603) 209-955. ££ and £££

Marco's (17 Pottergate, near the Market Place) Superb Italian cuisine with homemade pasta. ☎ (01603) 624-044. X: Sun., Mon. ££ and £££

Pinocchio's (11 St. Benedict's St., 2 blocks north of City Hall) A busy Italian brasserie with a large menu. ☎ (01603) 613-318. X: Sun., Mon. lunch. ££

Ribs of Beef (24 Wensum St., near the river, northwest of the cathedral) An Edwardian pub with river views and lunches. ☎ (01603) 619-517. £ and ££

Pizza One and Pancakes Too (24 Tombland, just west of the cathedral) A casual, friendly, and crowded place for pizza, crêpes, pastas, and the like. ☎ (01603) 621-583. £

Adam and Eve Pub (Bishopgate, northwest of the cathedral) Pub grub at Norwich's oldest drinking establishment, reportedly established in 1249. ☎ (01603) 667-423. £

Britons Arms Coffee House (9 Elm Hill, between the cathedral and St. Peter Hungate) Light lunches in the quaintest of cottages. ☎ (01603) 623-367. X: Sun. £

The Treehouse (14 Dove St., 2 blocks north of Market Place) Healthy vegetarian food above a health food store, or outdoors in summer. ☎ (01603) 763-258. X: Sun. £

Assembly House (Theatre St., south of the Market Place) Inexpensive cafeteria meals in an elegant Georgian structure. ☎ (01603) 626-402. X: Sun. £

SUGGESTED TOUR:

Numbers in parentheses correspond to numbers on the map.

Leave the **train station** (1) and follow the map to Tombland, a delightful open square. Pass through the Erpingham Gate of 1420 and visit:

*NORWICH CATHEDRAL (2), ☎ (01603) 764-385. *Open daily 7:30 a.m. to 7 p.m., closing at 6 from mid-Sept. to mid-May. Evensong Mon.–Fri. at 5:15, Sat. and Sun. at 3:30. Suggested donation £2. Café. Gift shop. Tours.* ♿.

Begun in 1096, this is, with the exception of Durham, the most completely Norman cathedral in England. Its spire towers to a lofty 315 feet, exceeded in height only by that of Salisbury. The most magnificent view is of its east end, which is supported by majestic flying buttresses.

Enter the exceptionally long **nave** and look up at the marvelous ***roof bosses**. These tell the story of both Testaments, but make it clear only to those with eagle eyes or binoculars as they are 70 feet above your head.

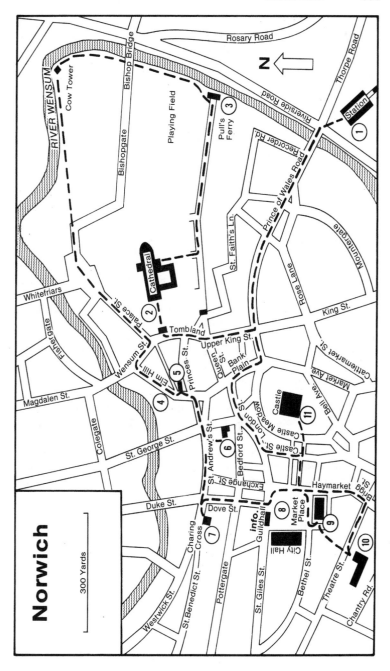

Norwich

300 Yards

The **choir** has some extremely good wood carvings, especially on the *mis-ericords. The ancient **Bishop's Throne**, behind the high altar, is older than the cathedral itself and probably dates from the 8th century. Stroll past the rounded apse, paying attention to the lovely St. Luke's Chapel, and then go out into the **cloisters**. These contain some wonderfully sculpted *bosses, even better than those in the nave.

Leave the cathedral via the south transept and follow the map through its lovely close to **Pull's Ferry** (3). Built in the 15th century, this was once a water gate from which a canal ran to the cathedral. Stroll along the riverside walk past the playing field. There is a beautiful view of the cathedral from here and, with luck, perhaps a cricket match in progress. Continue on past the 13th-century **Bishop Bridge**, one of the oldest spans in England still in use. Cow Tower, just as ancient, guards a bend in the river. The path ends at the Adam and Eve pub, which claims to have been here since 1249. Walk down Palace Street and return to Tombland.

Elm Hill (4) is the most delightful street in Norwich. The quaint medieval houses lining this cobbled lane have all been restored and are now used as antique shops, art galleries, restaurants, and the like. Be sure to stroll down the alleyways that lead between the buildings. Probably the oldest structure here is the Britons Arms, a 15th-century timbered building with a thatched roof.

St. Peter Hungate (5), at the intersection of Princes Street, is now a museum of church art with fascinating displays of manuscripts, vestments, alabaster carvings, icons, and related treasures. Perhaps the most interesting of these is a 14th-century coffin complete with skeleton. If you'd like to try your hand at brass rubbing, this is the place. *Open April–Sept., Mon.–Sat., 10–5. Free. Charge for brass rubbing.* ☎ *(01603) 667-231. Partial* ♿.

Take a look down Princes Street, then turn right and stroll over to the **Bridewell Museum** (6). Housed in a 16th-century merchant's home later used as a prison for tramps and beggars, the museum features intriguing displays of local crafts and industries. *Open April–Sept., Tues.–Sat., 10–5. Adults £1.30, children 60p.* ☎ *(01603) 667-228. Partial* ♿.

Close to this, at 3 Bridewell Alley, is the unusual **Coleman's Mustard Shop & Museum**, celebrating the long history of one of Norwich's most famous products. *Open Mon.–Sat., 9:30–5. Free.*

Return to St. Andrew's Street and turn left to the *Strangers' Hall **Museum** (7), a complex, rambling structure that dates in part from 1320 and was also once a merchant's house. Since 1922 this has been the city's museum of domestic life, with exhibits covering a range of decor and furnishings from early Tudor to late Victorian times. The building itself is well worth the visit, and the displays within are absolutely first rate. *Presently under renovation and open by appointment only, check the tourist office* *for details of reopening.*

Walk over to the **Market Place** (8), bounded on the north by the 15th-century Guildhall, home of the tourist office, and to the west by the overpowering City Hall of 1938. A colorful **outdoor market** has been held here since the Middle Ages, a tradition that continues every day except Sundays. If you visit only one other church besides the cathedral, be sure to make it **St. Peter Mancroft** (9), the most outstanding in Norwich. Located just south of the market, this splendid 15th-century parish church is noted for its fine hammerbeam ceiling and the medieval stained glass in its east window.

It is only a short stroll to the **Assembly House** (10), a graceful Georgian structure whose interior preserves the flavor of the 19th century. Now used for civic and cultural functions, it may be visited and is also a good place for inexpensive meals or elegant teas.

Follow the map to:

NORWICH CASTLE (11), ☎ *(01603) 223-624. Open Mon.–Sat. 10–5, Sun. 2–5. Admission price varies by season: Adults £3.40 in July–Sept., £2.50 in April–June and Oct.–Dec., £2.40 in Jan.–March. Seniors and children's rates follow the same pattern. All prices include entry to the Regimental Museum. Tours of the Battlements and dungeons are extra: Adults £2, seniors £1.50, children £1. Café. Gift shop. Mostly &.*

Norwich Castle was begun by Henry I about 1130 on a lofty mound overlooking the city. Heavily altered, it was used as a prison until 1887 and is now a museum of major importance. The superb collections range from art, particularly that of the Norwich School, to local archaeology, natural history, and social history. Don't miss taking one of the spine-chilling ***Dungeon Tours**, which depart from the balcony of the keep. These include a steep climb to the battlements followed by a descent into the hellish prison dungeons, where you can examine death masks of hanged convicts, and other grim artifacts. Allow plenty of time to see the castle. Exit through an old prison tunnel that becomes a World War I trench, complete with sound effects, as it ends in the Regimental Museum. From here it's an easy walk back to the station.

Section IV

HISTORICAL PERSPECTIVES

This brief chronological outline of England's history and the reigns of its rulers should help place events in context with each other.

c. 5000 BC	Thawing of the last Ice Age separates the British Isles from Europe.
c. 3500 BC	Neolithic culture flourishes.
c. 2800–1500 BC	Construction of Stonehenge during the Bronze Age.
c. 600 BC	Settlement of Britain by Celts from Europe.
54 BC	Romans under Julius Caesar probe Britain.
AD 43	Roman conquest of England.
AD 61	Queen Boadicea sacks Roman London.
313	Introduction of Christianity in Roman Britain.
350–597	Invasion by Angles, Saxons, and Jutes.
410–442	Roman legions abandon Britain.
597	St. Augustine re-establishes Christianity.
731	The Venerable Bede writes his *Ecclesiastical History*.

ANGLO-SAXON PERIOD

802–839	King Egbert
839–856	King Ethelwulf
856–860	King Ethelbald
860–866	King Ethelbert
866–871	King Ethelred I
871–899	King Alfred the Great
871–899	Alfred the Great defeats the Danes, unites England.
899–924	King Edward the Elder
924–940	King Athelstan
940–946	King Edmund the Elder
946–955	King Edred
955–959	King Edwy the Fair

959–975	King Edgar
975–978	King Edward the Martyr
978–1016	King Ethelred the Unready
1016	King Edmund Ironside
1016–1035	King Canute the Great
1037–1040	King Harold I Harefoot
1040–1042	King Hardicanute
1042–1066	King Edward the Confessor (Saint)
1066	King Harold II
1066	Battle of Hastings, the Norman Conquest.

NORMAN ERA

1066–1087	King William I (The Conqueror)
1086	The *Domesday Book* completed, allowing effective government.
1087–1100	King William II Rufus
1100–1135	King Henry I Beauclerc
1135–1154	King Stephen

PLANTAGENET ERA

1154–1189	King Henry II
1170	Assassination of Thomas à Becket at Canterbury.
1189–1199	King Richard I Lionheart
1199–1216	King John
1215	King John signs the Magna Carta.
1216–1272	King Henry III
1272–1307	King Edward I Longshanks
1295	Parliament begins.
1307–1327	King Edward II
1327–1377	King Edward III
1337	The Hundred Years War with France begins.
1348–1349	The Black Death (bubonic plague) strikes.
1377–1399	King Richard II

HOUSE OF LANCASTER

1399–1413	King Henry IV
1413–1422	King Henry V
1422–1461	King Henry VI
1455–1485	Wars of the Roses between the houses of Lancaster and York.

HOUSE OF YORK

1461–1483	King Edward IV
1483	King Edward V
1483–1485	King Richard III

HOUSE OF TUDOR

1485–1509	King Henry VII
1509–1547	King Henry VIII
1534	King Henry VIII breaks with the Pope in Rome, becomes head of the Protestant Church of England.
1547–1553	King Edward VI
1553–1558	Queen Mary I
1554	Catholicism restored.
1558–1603	Queen Elizabeth I
1559	Protestantism re-established.
1568	Mary, Queen of Scots, beheaded.

HOUSE OF STUART

1603–1625	King James I
1605	The Gunpowder Plot — Guy Fawkes leads a Catholic conspiracy to blow up Parliament.
1611	King James Bible published.
1625–1649	King Charles I
1642–1649	The Civil War pits Parliament against the monarchy.
1649	King Charles I beheaded by Parliament, royalty renounced, the Commonwealth established.
1649–1660	The Commonwealth.
1653–1658	The Protectorate, England ruled by Oliver Cromwell.
1660	Restoration of the monarchy.
1660–1685	King Charles II
1666	The Great Fire of London.
1685–1688	King James II
1689–1694	King William III and Queen Mary II (joint sovereigns)
1694–1702	King William III
1702–1714	Queen Anne
1707	Union of England and Scotland as Great Britain.

HOUSE OF HANOVER

1714–1727	King George I
1727–1760	King George II
1756–1763	The Seven Years War (French & Indian War) establishes British supremacy in North America.
1760–1820	King George III
1775–1783	War of American Independence.
1795–1815	Napoleonic Wars with France.
1800	Great Britain and Ireland form the United Kingdom.
1811–1820	The Regency period.
1820–1830	King George IV
1825	First railway service begins.
1830–1837	King William IV
1837–1901	Queen Victoria

1854–1856	The Crimean War with Turkey.
1899–1902	The Boer War in South Africa.

HOUSE OF SAXE-COBURG GOTHA

1901–1910	King Edward VII

HOUSE OF WINDSOR

1910–1936	King George V
1914–1919	The First World War.
1919	Ireland declares independence.
1936	King Edward VIII
1936–1952	King George VI
1939–1945	The Second World War.
1952–	Queen Elizabeth II

Index

Special interest attractions are also listed under their category headings.

Accommodations 12–13
Air travel 10-11
ART MUSEUMS:
  Ashmolean Museum, Oxford 245
  Brighton Museum & Art Gallery
    156
  City Art Gallery, York 296
  Fitzwilliam Museum, Cambridge
    305
  Herbert Art Gallery, Coventry
    264
  Holburne Museum, Bath 211
  Kettle's Yard, Cambridge 304
  Manor House Museum, Bury St.
    Edmunds 318
  National Art Gallery, London 48
  National Museum of Wales,
    Cardiff 224
  Pallant House, Chichester 165
  Royal Academy of Arts, London
    65
  Southampton Art Gallery 193
  Tate Gallery, London 46
  Usher Gallery, Lincoln 291
  Victoria & Albert Museum,
    London 55-56
  Victoria Art Gallery, Bath 210
  Wallace Collection, London 64
Arundel 158-161

Bath 205-211
Battle 140-143
Bluebell Railway 149-152
BOAT TRIPS:
  Bath 211
  Bristol 217, 220
  Cambridge 305
  Gloucester 238
  Greenwich 75, 79
  Guildford 170
  Hampton Court 96
  Isle of Wight 179

Lincoln 291
Ocean Village, Southampton 193
Oxford 246
Portsmouth 177
Richmond 90
River Thames, London 22
Rochester 112
Westminster Pier, London 22-23
Windsor 203
Woodbridge 328
Woodstock 248
Bosham 162, 168
Brighton 153-157
Bristol 216-221
British Rail 21-22, 102-106
Bury St. Edmunds 315-318

Cambridge 299-305
Canterbury 117-122
Cardiff 222-228
CASTLES:
  Arundel 160
  Camber, Rye 135
  Cardiff 224
  Caerphilly, Wales 226
  Castle Rising 314
  Clifford's Tower, York 298
  Colchester 320
  Dover 124-126
  Guildford 172
  Hastings 145
  Norwich 335
  Nottingham 278
  Lincoln 289-290
  Rochester 111
  Southsea, Portsmouth 178
  Tower of London 33-35
  Warwick, 251, 252
  Windsor 201-203
  Wolvesey Castle, Winchester 188
CATHEDRALS:
  Arundel 161

Bristol 221
Bury St. Edmunds 316
Canterbury 120
Chester 271
Chichester 165
Clifton 221
Coventry 262-264
Ely 307-309
Exeter 230
Gloucester 235, 237
Guildford 170
Llandaff, Wales 227
Lincoln 289
Norwich 332
Portsmouth 177
Oxford 246
Rochester 111
St. Albans 273
St. Pauls, London 30–32
Salisbury 197-198
Southwark, London 71
Wells 213
Westminster, London 46
Winchester 185-187
York Minster 296-297
Chester 266-271
Chichester 162-168
City of London 20, 25–37
Colchester 319-322
COUNTRY WALKS:
Arundel 161
Battle 141
Chichester 166
Hampstead Heath, London 88
Oxford 245
Rye 135
Stratford-upon-Avon 260
Winchester 188
Woodbridge 328-330
Coventry 261-265

Dover 123-127

Ely 306-309
Eton 200, 203–204
Exeter 229-233

Faversham 113-116
Folkestone 130
Food and Drink 13

GARDENS:
Botanic Garden, Oxford 246
Chelsea Physic Garden, London 51
Hampton Court, London 96, 100
Kensington Gardens, London 55
Kew Gardens, London 91-94
Museum of Garden History, London 72
Ranelagh Gardens, London 51
St. James's Park, London 47
Sheffield Park Garden 152
Stamford 285
University Botanic Gardens, Cambridge 305
Warwick 254
Gloucester 234-238
Greenwich 79-84
Guildford 169-173

Hastings 144-148
Historical Perspectives 337-340
HISTORIC HOUSES:
Anne Hathaway's Cottage, Stratford-upon-Avon 260
Carlyle's House, London 54
Dr. Johnson's House, London 27
Fenton House, London 86-88
Georgian House, Bristol 221
Harvard House, Stratford-upon-Avon 259
Keats' House, London 88-89
Lamb House, Rye 134
Medieval Merchant's House, Southampton 192
Mompesson House, Salisbury 197
Number 1 Royal Crescent, Bath 210
Oliver Cromwell's House, Ely 307
Shakespeare's Birthplace, Stratford-upon-Avon 258
Treasurer's House, York 296
Tudor House, Southampton 190
HISTORIC PUBS:
Fighting Cocks Inn, St. Albans 274
Prospect of Whitby, London 78
Ye Olde Bell & Steelyard Inn, Woodbridge 330

Ye Olde Cheshire Cheese, London 30
Ye Olde Trip to Jerusalem, Nottingham 278

HISTORY MUSEUMS:
Battle Museum 143
Brewhouse Yard Museum of Nottingham Life 278
Bridewell Museum, Norwich 334
British Museum, London 62-63
Cabinet War Rooms, London 42
Canterbury Heritage Museum 122
Castle Museum, York 298
City Museum, Bristol 217, 220
City Museum, Gloucester 238
City Museum, Winchester 185
D-Day Museum, Portsmouth 178
District Museum, Chichester 165
Dover Museum 126
Ely Museum 309
Fleur de Lis Heritage Centre, Faversham 114
Folk Museum, Cambridge 304
Gloucester Folk Museum 237
Guildford Museum 170
Guildhall Museum, Rochester 109-111
Hastings Museum of Local History 146
Ipswich Museum 324
Imperial War Museum, London 42, 73
Moyse's Hall, Bury St. Edmunds 318
Museum of Lincolnshire Life, Lincoln 290
Museum of London 37
Museum of Richmond 94
Museum of St. Albans 276
Museum of Welsh Life, St. Fagan's 227
National Maritime Museum, Greenwich 82-83
Nottingham Castle Museum 278
Oxfordshire Museum, Woodstock 250
Royal Naval Museum, Portsmouth 177
Rye Castle Museum 134
St. John's House, Warwick 254

Salisbury & South Wiltshire Museum 198
Stamford Museum 284
Strangers' Hall Museum, Norwich 334
Stratford Tales, Stratford-upon-Avon 258
Town House Museum, King's Lynn 314
Tudor House, Southampton 190
Warwickshire Museum, Warwick 254
Wells Museum 215
Holidays 15

Ipswich 323-326
Isle of Wight 179-183

King's Lynn 310-314
Lincoln 286-291

LITERARY INTEREST:
Bloomsbury, London 63
Carlyle's House, London 54
Charles Dickens Birthplace, Portsmouth 178
Charles Dickens Centre, Rochester 109
Dr. Johnson's House, London 27
Guildford 170
Keats' House, London 88-89
Lamb House, Rye 134
Shakespeare's Globe Exhibition, London 72
Sherlock Holmes Museum, London 64
Stratford-upon-Avon 255-260
London 12-13, 19–100

LONDON ATTRACTIONS:
All Hallows-by-the-Tower Church 33
Bank of England 36
Banqueting House 41
Barbican, The 37
BBC Experience 63
Big Ben 42
British Museum 62-63
Buckingham Palace 47
Cabinet War Rooms 42
Canary Wharf 76
Carlyle's House 54
Chelsea 49-54

Covent Garden 59
Design Museum 70
Docklands 74-78
Dr. Johnson's House 27-28
Fenton House 86-88
Globe Theatre 72
Greenwich 79-84
Guildhall, The 36
Hampstead 85-89
Hampton Court 96-100
Harrods 56
H.M.S. Belfast 70
Houses of Parliament 45-46
Imperial War Museum 73
Jewel Tower 46
Keats House 88-89
Kensington 49, 54-56
Kensington Gardens 55
Kensington Palace 41, 54-55
Kenwood House 88
Kew Bridge Steam Museum 91
Kew Gardens — see Royal
   Botanic Gardens
Lincoln's Inn 62
London Bridge 32
London Dungeon 71
London Transport Museum 59
Madame Tussaud's Waxworks 64
Millennium Dome 84
Monument, The 32
Museum of Garden History 72
Museum of London 37
National Army Museum 51
National Gallery 48
National Maritime Museum 82-83
National Portrait Gallery 48
Natural History Museum 55
Number 10 Downing Street 41
Old Bailey, The 37
Piccadilly Circus 58, 65
Prince Henry's Room 27
Richmond 90-95
Royal Botanic Gardens 91-94
Royal Hospital 51
Royal Mews, The 47
St. Bride's Church 30
St. Clement Danes Church 26
St. Helen Bishopgate Church 36
St. James's Park 47
St. Katherine Docks 78
St. Magnus the Martyr Church 32

St. Martin-in-the-Fields Church
   41, 48
St. Olave's Church 36
St. Paul's Cathedral 30–32
St. Thomas's Operating Theatre
   71
Science Museum 55
Shakespeare's Globe Exhibition
   72
Sherlock Holmes Museum 64
Sir John Soane's Museum 62
South Bank Arts Centre 72
Southwark 66-72
Southwark Cathedral 71
Tate Gallery 46
Temple, The 27
Thames Barrier 84
Theatre Museum 59
Tower Bridge 70
Tower of London 33-35
Trafalgar Square 39-41, 48
Victoria & Albert Museum 55-56
Wallace Collection 64
West End, The 56-65
Westminster 38-48
Westminster Abbey 42-45
Westminster Bridge 42
Westminster Cathedral 46
Whitehall 41
Ye Olde Cheshire Cheese Pub 30

MARITIME INTEREST:
Cutty Sark, Greenwich, London
   82
Flagship Portsmouth 175
Gloucester Docks 237-238
Golden Hinde, London 71
H.M.S. Belfast, London 70
H.M.S. Victory, Portsmouth 175
Maritime Museum, Southampton
   192
National Maritime Museum,
   Greenwich, London 82-83
Shipwreck Heritage Centre,
Hastings 146
S.S. Great Britain, Bristol 220
Money Matters 16

Norwich 331-335
Nottingham 277-281

Oxford 239-246

Palaces — see Stately Homes
Portsmouth 174-178
Public transportation in London
20–23

RAILFAN INTEREST:
   Bluebell Railway 149-152
   National Railway Museum, York
      293-296
   Romney, Hythe & Dymchurch
      Railway 128-130
   Volk's Railway, Brighton 156
Railpasses 104-106
Rail travel 21-22, 102-106
Restaurants and pubs 13–14
Rochester 108-112
ROMAN RELICS:
   Bath 207
   Chester 270
   Colchester 319, 320
   Lincoln 291
   London 33, 35
   Pharos, Dover 126
   Roman Museum, Canterbury 121
   Roman Painted House, Dover 127
   Roman Palace at Fishbourne 166
   St. Albans 272, 274
   York 292. 296
Romney, Hythe & Dymchurch
   Railway 128-130
Royal Tunbridge Wells 136-139
Rye 131-135

St. Albans 272-276
Salisbury 194-199
SCIENCE MUSEUMS:
   Museum of the History of
      Science, Oxford 244
   Natural History Museum, London
      55
   Science Museum, London 55
   Techniquest, Cardiff 228
Shanklin 179-183
Southampton 189-193
Stamford 282-285
STATELY HOMES & PALACES:
   Arundel Castle 160
   Blenheim Palace, Woodstock 248
   Buckingham Palace 47

Burghley House, Stamford 285
Christchurch Mansion, Ipswich
   324
Hampton Court 96-100
Kensington Palace 54
Kenwood House, London 88
Kew Palace 93
Mompesson House, Salisbury
   197
Royal Pavilion, Brighton 157
Sandringham, King's Lynn 314
Warwick Castle 251, 252
Wilton House, Salisbury 199
Windsor Castle 201-203
Stonehenge 195-197
Stratford-upon-Avon 255-260

Telephone 16
Theatre 15
THEME EXHIBITIONS:
   At Bristol 221
   BBC Experience, London 63
   Buckley's Yesterday's World,
      Battle 143
   Cabinet War Rooms, London 42
   Canterbury Tales, Canterbury
      118
   Charles Dickens Centre,
      Rochester 109
   Day at the Wells, A, Royal
      Tunbridge Wells 137
   D-Day Museum, Portsmouth 178
   Dewa Roman Experience,
      Chester 270
   Dungeon Tours, Norwich 335
   Galleries of Justice, Nottingham
      280
   H.M.S. Victory, Portsmouth 175
   Jorvik Viking Centre, York
      297-298
   Kingmaker — A Preparation for
      Battle, Warwick 252
   Legoland Windsor 204
   London Dungeon 71
   Madame Tussaud's Rock Circus,
      London 65
   Madame Tussaud's Waxworks,
      London 64
   Mary Rose Exhibition,
      Portsmouth 175
   Oxford Story 244

Royal Weekend, Warwick 252

Sea Life Aquarium, Hastings 146

Sea Life Centre, Brighton 156

Sea Life Center, Portsmouth 178

Shakespeare's Globe Exhibition, London 72

Sherlock Holmes Museum, London 64

Smugglers' Adventure, Hastings 145

Tales of Robin Hood, Nottingham 280

Techniquest, Cardiff 228

1066 Story, Hastings 145

Tower Bridge Experience, London 70

White Cliffs Experience, Dover 126

Wookey Hole Caves, Wells 215

World of Espionage, Dover 126

Tourist information 18, 23-24

TRANSPORT MUSEUMS:

Bluebell Railway 149-152

Hall of Aviation, Southampton 192

London Transport Museum 59

Museum of British Road Transport, Coventry 265

National Maritime Museum, Greenwich, London 82

National Railway Museum, York 293-296

National Waterways Museum, Gloucester 238

Romney, Hythe & Dymchurch Railway 128-130

S.S. Great Britain, Bristol 220

Volk's Railway, Brighton 156

Tunbridge Wells — see Royal Tunbridge Wells

Train travel 21-22, 102-106

UNUSUAL MUSEUMS:

Bank of England Museum, London 36

BBC Experience, London 63

Bramah Tea & Coffee Museum, London 70

Britain at War Museum, London 71

British Engineerium, Brighton 157

British Museum, London 62-63

Chester Toy & Doll Museum 270

Clink Prison Museum, London 72

Coleman's Mustard Museum, Norwich 334

Coventry Toy Museum 264

D-Day Museum, Portsmouth 178

Design Museum, London 70

Draper's Museum of Bygones, Rochester 111

Fan Museum, Greenwich, London 84

Fishermen's Museum, Hastings 146

Guildhall Clock Museum, London 37

Imperial War Museum, London 73

Industrial Museum, Bristol 217, 220

Kew Bridge Steam Museum, London 91

Kingsbury Water Mill, St. Albans 274

Museum of Costume, Bath 210

Museum of Costumes & Textiles, Nottingham 280

Museum of Eton Life 203

Museum of Garden History 72

Museum of Nottingham Lace 280

Museum of Welsh Life, St. Fagan's 227

National Army Museum, London 51

National Centre of Photography, Bath 210

National Portrait Gallery, London 48

Oken's House (toys), Warwick 254

Old Royal Observatory, Greenwich, London 82

On The Air Museum, Chester 270

Robert Opie Collection of Advertising & Packaging, Gloucester 238

Rye Treasury of Mechanical

Music 134
Sherlock Holmes Museum,
    London 64
Sir John Soane's Museum,
    London 62
Soldiers of Gloucestershire
    Museum, Gloucester 237
Suffolk Horse Museum,
    Woodbridge 330
Theatre Museum, London 59
Toy Museum, Lincoln 290
Tymperley's Clock Museum,
    Colchester 322

Wales 222-228
Warwick 251-254
Wells 212-215
Winchester 184-188
Westminster 38-48
Windsor 200-204
Woodbridge 327-330
Woodstock 247-250

York 292-298

Daytrips

• OTHER EUROPEAN TITLES •

Daytrips GERMANY

By Earl Steinbicker. 60 of Germany's most enticing destinations can be savored on daytrips from Munich, Frankfurt, Hamburg, and Berlin. Walking tours of the big cities are included. Expanded 5th edition, 352 pages, 67 maps. ISBN: 0-8038-9428-7.

Daytrips SWITZERLAND

By Norman P.T. Renouf. 45 one-day adventures in and from convenient bases including Zurich and Geneva, with forays into nearby Germany, Austria, and Italy. 320 pages, 38 maps. ISBN: 0-8038-9417-7.

Daytrips SPAIN & PORTUGAL

By Norman P.T. Renouf. Fifty one-day adventures by rail, bus, or car — including many walking tours, as well as side trips to Gibraltar and Morocco. All the major tourist sights are covered, plus several excursions to little-known, off-the-beaten-track destinations. 368 pages, 18 full-color photos, 28 B&W photos, 51 maps. ISBN: 0-8038-9389-2.

Daytrips IRELAND

By Patricia Tunison Preston. Covers the entire Emerald Isle with 50 one-day self-guided tours both within and from the major tourist areas. 400 pages, 58 maps. ISBN: 0-8038-9385-X.

Daytrips FRANCE

By Earl Steinbicker. Describes 45 daytrips — including 5 walking tours of Paris, 23 excursions from the city, 5 in Provence, and 12 along the Riviera. 4th edition, 336 pages, 55 maps, 89 B&W photos. ISBN: 0-8038-9366-3.

Daytrips ITALY

By Earl Steinbicker. Features 40 one-day adventures in and around Rome, Florence, Milan, Venice, and Naples. 3rd edition, 304 pages, 45 maps, 69 B&W photos. ISBN: 0-8038-9372-8.

Daytrips HOLLAND, BELGIUM & LUXEMBOURG

By Earl Steinbicker. Many unusual places are covered on these 40 daytrips, along with all the favorites plus the 3 major cities. 2nd edition, 288 pages, 45 maps, 69 B&W photos. ISBN: 0-8038-9368-X.

Daytrips ISRAEL

By Earl Steinbicker. 25 one-day adventures by bus or car to the Holy Land's most interesting sites. Includes Jerusalem walking tours. 2nd edition, 206 pages, 40 maps, 40 B&W photos. ISBN: 0-8038-9374-4.

Daytrips

• AMERICAN TITLES •

Daytrips WASHINGTON, D.C.

By Earl Steinbicker. Fifty one-day adventures in the Nation's Capital, and to nearby Virginia, Maryland, Delaware, and Pennsylvania. Both walking and driving tours are featured. 368 pages, 60 maps. Revised 2nd edition. ISBN: 0-8038-9429-5.

Daytrips PENNSYLVANIA DUTCH COUNTRY & PHILADELPHIA

By Earl Steinbicker. Completely covers the City of Brotherly Love, then goes on to probe southeastern Pennsylvania, southern New Jersey, and Delaware before moving west to Lancaster, the "Dutch" country, and Gettysburg. There are 50 daytrips in all. 288 pages, 54 maps. ISBN: 0-8038-9394-9.

Daytrips SAN FRANCISCO & NORTHERN CALIFORNIA

By David Cheever. Fifty enjoyable one-day adventures from the sea to the mountains; from north of the wine country to south of Monterey. Includes 16 self-guided discovery tours of San Francisco itself. 336 pages, 64 maps. ISBN: 0-8038-9441-4.

Daytrips HAWAII

By David Cheever. Thoroughly explores all the major islands — by car, by bus, on foot, and by bicycle, boat, and air. Includes many off-beat discoveries you won't find elsewhere, plus all the big attractions in detail. 288 pages, 55 maps. ISBN: 0-8038-9401-5.

Daytrips NEW ENGLAND

By Earl Steinbicker. Discover the 50 most delightful excursions within a day's drive of Boston or Central New England, from Maine to Connecticut. Includes Boston walking tours. 336 pages, 60 maps, 48 B&W photos. ISBN: 0-8038-9379-5.

Daytrips NEW YORK

Edited by Earl Steinbicker. 107 easy excursions by car throughout southern New York State, New Jersey, eastern Pennsylvania, Connecticut, and southern Massachusetts. 7th edition, 336 pages, 44 maps, 46 B&W photos. ISBN: 0-8038-9371-X.

Daytrips FLORIDA

By Blair Howard. Fifty one-day adventures from bases in Miami, Orlando, St. Petersburg, Jacksonville, and Pensacola. From little-known discoveries to bustling theme parks; from America's oldest city to isolated getaways — this guide covers it all. 320 pages, 47 maps, 28 B&W photos. ISBN: 0-8038-9380-9.

HASTINGS HOUSE
Book Publishers

9 Mott St., Norwalk, CT 06850
☎ (203) 838-4083, Fax (203) 838-4084.
☎ orders toll-free (800) 206-7822
Internet: www.daytripsbooks.com

ABOUT THE AUTHOR:

EARL STEINBICKER is a born tourist who believes that travel should be a joy, not an endurance test. For over 35 years he has been refining his carefree style of daytripping while working in New York, London, Paris, and other cities; first as head of a firm specializing in promotional photography and later as a professional writer. Whether by public transportation or private car, he has thoroughly probed the most delightful aspects of countries around the world — while always returning to the comforts of city life at night. A strong desire to share these experiences has led him to develop the "Daytrips" series of guides, which he continues to expand and revise. Recently, he has been assisting other authors in developing additional "Daytrips" books, further expanding the series. He presently lives in the Philadelphia suburbs.